Applied Triple Helix (University–Government–Industry) Models for AI Innovation

Mohieddine Rahmouni
King Faisal University, South Africa

Mossab Saud Alholiby
https://orcid.org/0000-0002-8899-8770
King Faisal University, Saudi Arabia

Ben Othman Soufiane
King Faisal University, Saudi Arabia

IGI Global Scientific Publishing
Publishing Tomorrow's Research Today

Vice President of Editorial	Melissa Wagner
Director of Acquisitions	Mikaela Felty
Director of Book Development	Jocelynn Hessler
Production Manager	Mike Brehm
Cover Design	Jose Rosado

Published in the United States of America by
IGI Global Scientific Publishing
701 East Chocolate Avenue
Hershey, PA, 17033, USA
Tel: 717-533-8845 | Fax: 717-533-7115
Website: https://www.igi-global.com E-mail: cust@igi-global.com

Library of Congress Cataloging-in-Publication Data

No LCCN (CIP Data Pending)
ISBN13: 9798337396903
Isbn13Softcover: 9798337396910
EISBN13: 9798337396927

British Cataloguing in Publication Data
A Cataloguing in Publication record for this book is available from the British Library.

Table of Contents

Detailed Table of Contents

collaborative ecosystems capable of generating socio-economic value through integrated knowledge flows. A pivotal step in this process is the identification of quantifiable variables to evaluate systemic impacts and relationships, thereby facilitating the monitoring of innovation investments. This study addresses this gap by proposing a methodological framework for a prototype designed to advance sustainable, data-driven innovation.

Modern universities have shifted from basic teaching and research to becoming drivers of economic development and AI innovation. However, resource-constrained universities (RCUs) face a "vicious cycle" where limited funding, aging infrastructure, and a lack of specialized expertise prevent them from keeping pace with rapid technological shifts. Traditional academic structures are often too slow and rigid for the AI era, leaving many institutions marginalized in global innovation networks. To address this, the text proposes a "university-nested" ecosystem to operationalize the Triple Helix (university-industry-government) model through three mechanisms (1) Industry-co-designed micro-credentials for agile skills training, (2) Interdisciplinary Research Groups for collaborative problem-solving, and (3) Centres of Excellence to scale these partnerships sustainably. This roadmap enables RCUs to transform from passive degree-providers into proactive co-architects of technological innovation.

This chapter describes how fuzzy multi-criteria decision-making (MCDM) might enhance collaboration between government, business, and academic institutions. It demonstrates why cooperation in AI development entails ambiguity and conflicting

The translation of academic Artificial Intelligence (AI) research into scalable industrial solutions requires coordinated pathways that link scientific discovery with commercialization. This chapter examines how universities, industries, and government agencies collaborate across technology transfer mechanisms, joint research programs, incubators, and innovation pipelines to transform AI prototypes into market-ready systems. Case studies from healthcare and smart manufacturing illustrate how access to real-world data, engineering expertise, regulatory engagement, and controlled testing environments accelerate successful deployment. The chapter also highlights key challenges, including intellectual property issues, regulatory uncertainty, data limitations, and ethical risks, and emphasizes the need for responsible governance, interdisciplinary collaboration, and ecosystem-level support. A strategic roadmap is proposed to guide institutions toward sustainable AI innovation that balances technical rigor, societal values, and market readiness.

This chapter advances a theoretical framework positioning hybrid project management as an operational enabler of Triple Helix collaborations in AI-driven transportation infrastructure. While existing literature emphasizes strategic university-government-industry partnerships, insufficient attention addresses procedural mechanisms facilitating effective knowledge transfer across institutional boundaries. Drawing from project management theory, innovation systems research, and organizational behavior scholarship, this chapter demonstrates how hybrid models—integrating predictive lifecycle structures with adaptive Agile practices—address critical friction points: knowledge translation gaps between research and implementation, regulatory-innovation tensions in government projects, and interdisciplinary coordination challenges. The Triple Helix Process Integration Model maps project management practices to knowledge exchange mechanisms, offering theoretical advancement and practical guidance for stakeholders navigating AI partnerships in regulated environments.

Preface

ABOUT THIS BOOK

Artificial Intelligence has moved decisively from the margins of research laboratories into the core of economic strategy, public governance, and societal transformation. As AI systems increasingly shape productivity, public services, sustainability agendas, and everyday life, innovation can no longer be understood as the output of isolated institutions. Instead, it emerges from structured collaboration among universities, governments, and industry—an interaction most powerfully conceptualized through the Triple Helix model. *Applied Triple Helix (University–Government–Industry) Models for AI Innovation* responds to this reality by offering applied, data-driven, and policy-relevant perspectives on how collaborative innovation ecosystems can be designed, governed, and sustained in the age of AI.

This volume brings together theoretical advances, methodological frameworks, and real-world applications that demonstrate how the Triple Helix operates across diverse institutional contexts and sectors. From mature national innovation mechanisms such as Knowledge Transfer Partnerships to emerging models tailored for resource-constrained universities, the chapters show how structured collaboration can accelerate research translation, strengthen workforce readiness, and align AI development with national and regional priorities. Several contributions extend the analytical lens by incorporating decision-science tools, sustainability accounting, and computational modeling, enabling stakeholders to navigate uncertainty, evaluate impact, and make transparent, multi-criteria decisions in complex innovation environments.

A distinctive feature of this book is its emphasis on *operationalization*. Rather than treating the Triple Helix as a purely conceptual framework, the chapters illustrate concrete pathways for implementation, through micro-credentials, research groups, centers of excellence, hybrid project management approaches, and industry-facing innovation pipelines. Case studies spanning healthcare, transportation, agriculture, manufacturing, and smart farming demonstrate how AI solutions move from laboratory prototypes to scalable, socially responsible deployments when institutional roles are clearly defined and effectively coordinated. These applied insights highlight the importance of governance mechanisms, regulatory engagement, ethical oversight, and shared data infrastructures in enabling trustworthy AI innovation.

At the same time, the volume recognizes that AI innovation must be evaluated not only by technical performance or economic return, but also by its social and environmental consequences. By integrating ESG principles, sustainability accounting, and extended helix models, this book positions the Triple Helix as a foundation for long-term public value creation. It offers policymakers, academic leaders, industry practitioners, and researchers a comprehensive roadmap for designing AI ecosystems that are inclusive, resilient, and aligned with societal goals.

Applied Triple Helix (University–Government–Industry) Models for AI Innovation is intended as both a scholarly reference and a practical guide. It invites readers to rethink innovation governance in an AI-driven world and to engage collaboratively in shaping technologies that serve economies, institutions, and society at large.

Acknowledgement

Funding: This work was supported by the Deanship of Scientific Research, Vice Presidency for Graduate Studies and Scientific Research, King Faisal University, Saudi Arabia [Grant No. KFU260685].

Chapter 1

Knowledge Transfer Partnerships (KTP) as a Catalyst for University–Government–Industry Collaboration:

Strengthening Innovation and Graduate Employability

Panchalingam Suntharalingam
https://orcid.org/0000-0002-0125-9634
Birmingham City University, UK

ABSTRACT

This chapter explores Knowledge Transfer Partnerships (KTPs) in the United Kingdom as a leading model of university–government–industry collaboration that simultaneously drives innovation and enhances graduate employability. KTPs provide a structured mechanism through which academic expertise, public funding, and industry needs converge. The chapter analyses how the KTP framework embeds graduates known as Associates within organisations to deliver innovation projects supported by academic supervision and government oversight. Drawing on the principles of the Triple Helix (Government, Business, University), it evaluates the impact of KTPs on organisational competitiveness, research translation, regional development, and skills formation. The chapter positions KTPs as a scalable and internationally relevant model for strengthening innovation and preparing graduates

DOI: 10.4018/979-8-3373-9690-3.ch001

for future labour-market demands. It argues that KTPs represent one of the most effective and mature frameworks for aligning national innovation objectives with university missions and industry talent needs.

1.0 INTRODUCTION

In contemporary knowledge economies, innovation and skills development have become central drivers of national competitiveness and sustainable economic growth. Universities, governments, and industry organisations each play essential but distinct roles in generating new knowledge, translating research into practice, and developing a highly skilled workforce. Yet the increasing complexity of global challenges from digital transformation and climate adaptation to productivity stagnation and labour-market volatility requires deeper forms of collaboration between these sectors. As a result, models of structured partnership that can synchronise their capacities have become critically important. Within this context, Knowledge Transfer Partnerships (KTPs) in the United Kingdom represent a uniquely mature and impactful mechanism for fostering university–government–industry collaboration while simultaneously supporting innovation and graduate employability.

The theoretical foundation for such collaborations is often articulated through the Triple Helix model, which conceptualises innovation as an interactive, co-evolving process among universities, industry, and government (Etzkowitz & Leydesdorff, 2000). Rather than functioning as isolated consultants operating within fixed institutional boundaries, each helix (Figure 1) influences and overlaps with the others, creating hybrid spaces where research, policy, and commercial application intersect. This model highlights the importance of "entrepreneurial universities" capable of contributing to economic development, companies that exploit scientific knowledge for competitive advantage, and governments that enable innovation through strategic policy and funding. While the Triple Helix offers a compelling theoretical perspective, its effectiveness in practice depends on concrete mechanisms that operationalise collaboration. KTPs provide such a mechanism, enabling structured, project-based partnerships that integrate academic expertise with industry needs under the strategic oversight of government innovation agencies.

Figure 1. The Triple Helix Model: Strategic Interactions vs Triadic Structure

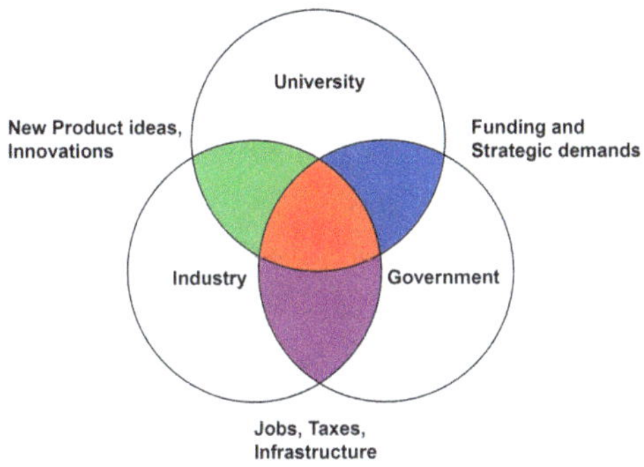

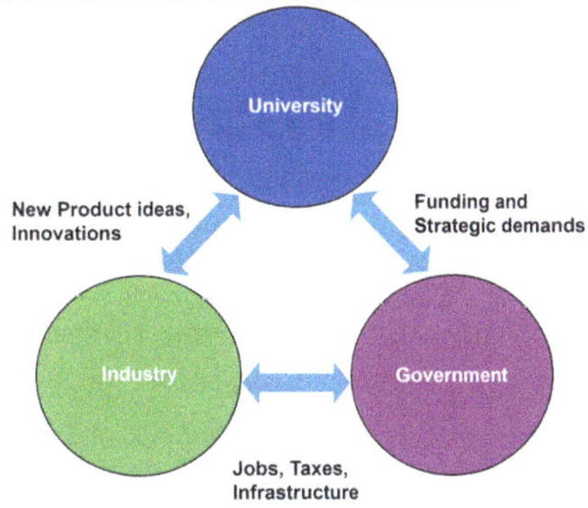

Figure 1, the Triple Helix model of innovation emphasises the dynamic interaction between universities, industry, and government as the key drivers of economic and technological progress. It conceptualises these three spheres as overlapping and interdependent, where knowledge and innovation flow through collaborative networks. In contrast, the triadic structure of KTPs refers more specifically to the practical framework of the partnership, which involves a university, a business (company), and an individual KTP associate. While the Triple Helix highlights the broader systemic collaboration between three institutional spheres, the KTP triadic structure focuses on the real-world operationalisation of this model, where the associate acts as the knowledge bridge between the academic and business entities, facilitating direct knowledge transfer and innovation. The KTP model, therefore, is a tangible manifestation of the Triple Helix concept, translating high-level collaboration into actionable partnerships at the individual project level.

The origins of KTPs can be traced to early UK initiatives in the 1970s with the first KTP in 1975 aimed at improving industrial productivity through the diffusion of academic knowledge into companies (Pates, 2023). Over time, the model has evolved into a mature policy instrument characterised by a triadic structure: an academic team, an industry partner, and a graduate known as the KTP Associate, who is embedded within the company to deliver an innovation project. This structure addresses well documented challenges in university–industry interaction, such as differences in organisational culture, misaligned timescales, and limited absorptive capacity in small and medium-sized enterprises (Perkmann et al., 2011). By establishing a jointly supervised role situated within the company but supported by academic expertise, KTPs facilitate continuous knowledge flow and capability building.

From an innovation perspective, KTPs provide a critical role in enabling companies particularly Small and Medium Enterprises (SMEs) to access research expertise that may otherwise be unattainable due to resource constraints or lack of in-house R&D

capacity. Numerous studies demonstrate that companies engaging in partnerships with universities are more likely to introduce new products, processes, or services (Bascavusoglu-Moreau et al., 2013)

KTPs enhance this effect by providing dedicated project management through the Associate and by requiring the development of long-term strategic plans for knowledge embedding. The result is a form of innovation that is not only technically robust but also organisationally sustainable. Increasingly, KTPs strengthen the broader innovation cycle by helping universities generate impact case studies, deepening civic and industrial engagement, and supporting government objectives around productivity and regional growth (Abreu et al., 2009).

Graduate employability has become a key priority for higher education institutions and policymakers. Labour-market conditions increasingly demand graduates who possess hybrid skillsets that combine disciplinary expertise with practical problem-solving, digital literacy, leadership, and adaptability (Tomlinson, 2017). Traditional degree programmes, while valuable, often struggle to fully equip graduates with these applied capabilities. KTPs directly address this gap by placing Associates in a unique position where they act simultaneously as researchers, project managers, and change agents. They lead high-impact innovation projects, interface with senior organisational stakeholders, and apply academic rigour to real-world challenges a combination that significantly accelerates their professional development.

The evidence suggests that KTP Associates realise strong long-term career outcomes, with many securing permanent roles within the partner organisation or moving into advanced positions across industry sectors (Wilson, 2012). Their experience positions them as "boundary-spanning professionals" capable of navigating the interface between technical domains and organisational strategy an increasingly valued competency in modern workplaces. KTPs offer a structured learning environment enhanced by formal training and development programmes, reinforcing graduates' employability beyond the immediate context of the project.

Despite these advantages, university–government–industry collaboration is not without challenges. Differences in institutional priorities, funding uncertainties, intellectual property negotiations, and varying expectations about project outcomes can create friction (Bruneel et al., 2010). KTPs mitigate many of these barriers through clear governance structures, predefined roles, and coordinated support from innovation agencies. Ensuring mutual benefit requires careful alignment of project objectives, effective communication, and sustained commitment from all partners. The complexity of innovation also means that impacts may vary across sectors and regions, highlighting the need for adaptable and context-sensitive partnership models.

The strategic relevance of KTPs extends beyond their immediate outcomes. As countries worldwide seek to strengthen innovation capacity and address skills shortages, KTP-style programmes offer replicable lessons for designing policy instruments that combine talent development with enterprise growth. The growing emphasis on "innovation-ready graduates" and the expanding role of universities as civic and economic actors provide an opportunity for the adoption of such models internationally. Emerging trends such as digitalisation, artificial intelligence, and transitions to net-zero economies underscore the need for partnership frameworks capable of accelerating knowledge diffusion and fostering interdisciplinary expertise.

1.1 Reconfiguring Institutional Roles: Beyond the Triad

The theoretical foundations of KTPs, particularly in relation to the Triple Helix model (Figure 1) and its extensions, deserve closer scrutiny. It is important to deepen the theoretical analysis by examining how KTPs not only adhere to the traditional Triple Helix framework but also contribute to the hybridisation of roles, reflexive adaptation, and boundary-spanning within the innovation process. How KTPs align with the Quadruple and Quintuple Helix extensions, which incorporate civil society and the environment into the innovation process will have a bearing on the project's tangible benefits. Through this analysis how KTPs reconfigure institutional roles and contribute to broader societal and environmental goals is demonstrated.

The Triple Helix model traditionally highlights the relationship between universities, industry, and government as the three central pillars in driving innovation. However, KTPs go beyond this basic triadic structure by reshaping the roles and functions of these institutions, promoting sustainability, net zero, hybridisation of roles and reflexive adaptation.

Hybridisation of Roles: Universities and Companies as Co-creators

In the KTP model, universities are not merely suppliers of knowledge, they are actively involved in co-creating new knowledge with companies. The involvement of KTP Associates, universities contribute not only theoretical insights but also practical expertise in solving real-world industrial problems. This collaboration goes beyond traditional academic roles, where universities are seen as passive knowledge providers. The embedded Associate bridges the academic and industrial worlds, ensuring that university knowledge is applied directly to organisational challenges. At the same time, companies are not just passive recipients but engage in research processes, contributing industry-specific insights that shape academic inquiry.

This way, KTPs blur the boundaries between universities and companies, creating a hybrid model of collaboration that supports both scientific inquiry and commercial application. This hybridisation fosters a deeper connection between the two sectors, pushing universities to align their research agendas with industry needs, while companies become more research-driven, expanding their capabilities to innovate.

Government as an Enabler and Facilitator

The role of government in KTPs extends beyond a regulatory or funding function. Governments actively shape the process by setting the innovation agenda and providing financial support, but they also engage in a facilitator role by encouraging long-term relationships between academia and industry. By offering grants and fostering partnerships, government agencies create the conditions for innovation to thrive across sectors. In KTPs, the UK government does not merely fund projects but engages as a strategic partner, ensuring that innovation is aligned with national priorities such as economic growth, sustainability, and regional development.

The hybridisation of roles in KTPs is a dynamic process that redefines traditional institutional functions. The university becomes an entrepreneurial institution, the company becomes more research-oriented, and the government facilitates innovation across both public and private sectors.

1.2 Reflexive Adaptation and Boundary-Spanning

A key feature of successful KTPs is the boundary-spanning role delivered by the KTP Associates. These professionals act as bridges between academia and industry, translating research insights into practical solutions and ensuring that both sectors learn from each another. This boundary-spanning role exemplifies the reflexive adaptation seen in KTPs, where partners continuously adjust their strategies in response to shifting demands and new challenges.

Boundary-Spanning Roles in Knowledge Transfer

KTP Associates are uniquely positioned to navigate between two practices, that of academic research and industrial practice. This boundary-spanning role enables them to absorb knowledge from both sides, facilitating the integration of cutting-edge research with practical business applications. The Associate's role extends beyond mere project management, it involves innovation leadership, where Associates drive the application of research in ways that address immediate industrial needs while ensuring that academic rigour is maintained.

KTPs foster reflexive adaptation an iterative process of knowledge exchange, where both universities and companies adjust their strategies and practices in response to insights gained through collaboration. This ongoing learning process enables KTPs to remain flexible and responsive to the changing needs of industry and society, ensuring that both academic and commercial objectives are met.

1.3 Aligning With the Quadruple and Quintuple Helix Extensions

While the traditional Triple Helix model remains central to understanding KTPs, recent developments in innovation theory suggest that the inclusion of additional societal and environmental dimensions such as civil society and the environment can provide a more holistic view of innovation systems. The Quadruple and Quintuple Helix models extend the Triple Helix by integrating these dimensions, highlighting the broader societal and environmental impact of innovation.

Environmental Sustainability: The Quintuple Helix and the Role of KTPs

The Quintuple Helix model further extends the innovation process by adding environmental sustainability as a key consideration. In this model, innovation is not only driven by technological, economic, and academic factors but also by the need to address global environmental challenges. KTPs are well-positioned to support this environmental dimension, particularly in sectors such as green technology, sustainability, and energy.

Many KTPs focus on developing products or processes that reduce environmental impact, such as sustainable manufacturing, energy-efficient technologies, and circular economy models. By incorporating environmental concerns into the innovation process, KTPs help companies align their commercial interests with societal and environmental needs, fostering more sustainable practices in industry.

Civil Society: Engaging Stakeholders Beyond the Triad

The Quadruple Helix model introduces civil society as a fourth dimension, recognising the role of public engagement in driving innovation. KTPs, by their nature, are often concerned with solving real-world problems that have societal implications. For example, KTP projects in the healthcare sector often involve collaborations with public institutions or focus on improving public services. In these cases, KTPs contribute not only to industrial growth but also to social welfare, health outcomes, and public policy development.

By engaging civil society in these innovation processes, KTPs help to ensure that innovation outcomes are socially responsible and aligned with public values. This engagement also enriches the knowledge transfer process by incorporating diverse perspectives, which helps companies and universities develop more inclusive, user-centred innovations.

This chapter situates Knowledge Transfer Partnerships within the broader discourse on innovation systems, graduate employability, and collaborative governance. It argues that KTPs exemplify an effective, scalable model that bridges institutional boundaries while delivering tangible benefits across all three helices. Through an examination of their structure, outcomes, and policy implications, the chapter contributes to a deeper understanding of how structured partnership models can strengthen both economic performance and workforce capability in knowledge-driven societies. KTPs demonstrate that when universities, industry, and government collaborate through clearly defined mechanisms, they can generate outcomes that exceed the capacity of any single sector acting alone.

Limitations and Sources

The analysis presented in this chapter is subject to several methodological limitations that may affect the comprehensiveness and objectivity of the findings. These limitations stem primarily from the sources used, the absence of primary data, and the narrow scope of the literature reviewed. A critical understanding of these limitations is essential for interpreting the conclusions drawn and for framing potential areas for further research.

Reliance on Official Evaluations and Case Reports: This chapter relies heavily on Birmingham City University's KTP evaluations and case reports provided by funding bodies such as Innovate UK and the Knowledge Transfer Partnerships (KTP) programme itself. While these documents provide useful and authoritative insights into the workings of KTPs, they are often inherently biased towards highlighting success stories and positive outcomes. This bias can:

- Overstate the effectiveness of KTPs by focusing on examples where the programme's goals (e.g., innovation, commercialisation, job creation) were successfully achieved, while underreporting instances where challenges, failures, or limitations arose.
- Mask structural issues, such as inequities in participation or difficulties in matching academic research with business needs, which are less likely to be showcased in official case reports and evaluations.

Although these sources are reliable, they offer an incomplete picture of the diverse experiences and nuanced challenges faced by KTP participants, particularly those who encounter difficulties in the implementation of their projects.

Absence of Primary Data (Interviews, Surveys): The chapter does not incorporate primary data from the key stakeholders involved in KTPs, including associates, companies, and academic partners. Interviews and surveys from these participants would have provided rich, qualitative insights into the lived experiences of individuals directly involved in the programme. The absence of such data limits the study in several ways:

- Missing perspectives on challenges: Without input from associates, companies, and academics, the analysis overlooks the specific difficulties and barriers encountered in the day-to-day operations of KTPs, including issues of workload, cultural differences, and the practicalities of collaboration.
- Limited understanding of impact: By not collecting feedback on the long-term impact of KTPs from participants themselves, the report lacks verifiable information on how the partnerships have affected career trajectories, business performance, or academic advancement.
- Lack of representative sample: Official reports and case studies typically represent the successful and well-documented partnerships. Primary data would have allowed for a more representative sample, including less publicised projects, and offered a broader understanding of the full range of experiences within the programme.

Limited Engagement with Critical Scholarly Literature on Knowledge Transfer

The analysis does not extensively engage with the critical scholarly literature on knowledge transfer (KT), which offers important theoretical frameworks, critiques, and alternative models. While the report discusses the practical aspects of KTPs, it does not sufficiently consider:

- Theoretical debates on the effectiveness of knowledge transfer, particularly in the context of unequal power dynamics between academic and industry partners, and the limitations of linear models of innovation.
- Critical perspectives on the concept of open innovation, which may be relevant given the growing emphasis on collaboration across sectors. Scholarly literature often highlights tensions between open access to knowledge and the protection of intellectual property, a concern that is not deeply addressed in this report.
- Alternative approaches to knowledge transfer, including more democratic or inclusive models that prioritise the involvement of underrepresented groups in innovation process (e.g., small businesses, women, ethnic minorities), an area where KTPs may need improvement.

Engaging with this literature could have enriched the chapter by providing a more critical view on KTPs, challenging some of the assumptions about their universal success and efficiency. While the findings in this chapter are based on reliable secondary data, the methodological limitations noted above suggest the need for a more holistic approach that includes primary data collection and a deeper engagement with critical scholarly literature on knowledge transfer.

Future research that incorporates these elements would provide a more comprehensive and balanced understanding of KTPs, addressing both their strengths and their limitations especially with the advent of AI. By expanding the scope of inquiry and integrating diverse perspectives, researchers can better assess how knowledge transfer partnerships function in practice and how they can be improved to address contemporary challenges in innovation.

2.0 UNDERSTANDING KTPS: ORIGINS, GOALS, AND DESIGN

The Knowledge Transfer Partnership (KTP) scheme is one of the longest-running and most established models of structured collaboration between universities, industry, and government. Its purpose is to facilitate the transfer of academic knowledge into organisational practice while simultaneously providing graduates with opportunities to lead innovation projects. This section traces the historical development of the KTP programme, explains its funding structures and partner roles, outlines the mechanisms through which knowledge exchange occurs, and compares KTPs with other forms of university–industry collaboration such as internships, cooperative education, and contract research.

2.1 History and Evolution of the KTP Scheme

The origins of the modern KTP scheme lie in the Teaching Company Scheme (TCS), launched in the United Kingdom in 1975. The TCS was created in response to concerns about the UK's declining industrial performance and growing gap between academic research and the needs of manufacturing companies (Pates, 2023) Inspired by earlier programmes designed to embed scientific knowledge within industry, the TCS aimed to create a conduit through which academic expertise could flow more effectively into organisations struggling with technological change.

The early rationale for TCS was twofold. First, policymakers recognised that although universities were generating knowledge at an accelerating pace, companies lacked the absorptive capacity and skilled personnel needed to translate that knowledge into innovation (Dodgson, 1991). Second, there was an urgent need to provide graduates with opportunities for applied learning and industry exposure.

By employing graduates directly within companies but under academic supervision the TCS sought to align knowledge creation with industrial innovation objectives.

Throughout the 1980s and 1990s, the scheme matured and expanded, receiving support from various government bodies including the Department of Trade and Industry and the Engineering and Physical Sciences Research Council. Evaluations consistently showed positive impacts on company performance, university collaboration, and graduate career trajectories (Senker & Senker, 1994). This credibility created the conditions for a major redesign in the early 2000s.

In 2003, the Teaching Company Scheme was rebranded and broadened as the Knowledge Transfer Partnership (KTP) programme. The shift signalled an expanded vision beyond manufacturing and engineering to include services, creative industries, digital technology, public-sector organisations, and non-profits (Bertoletti & Johnes, 2021). The modern KTP was designed to support a wider range of organisational challenges including strategic transformation, digitalisation, operations management, sustainability, and broader social innovation.

Since the creation of UK Research and Innovation (UKRI) and the strengthening of Innovate UK's role in national innovation strategy, KTPs have become a flagship instrument of the UK's knowledge exchange process. They are now internationally recognised as a best-practice model of sustained, government-supported university–industry collaboration (Perkmann et al., 2011). Although the programme remains UK-based, similar schemes have been adopted in countries such as Ireland, South Africa, Australia, and Malaysia, reflecting global interest in structured approaches to knowledge transfer and graduate development (Rasmussen & Wright, 2015).

2.2 Funding Model and Partner Roles

A defining characteristic of KTPs is their triadic partnership structure (Figure 1), which brings together:

- A company or host organisation (industry, public sector, or non-profit),
- A university or research institution, and
- A KTP Associate, typically a recent graduate or postgraduate researcher.

These projects are supported financially and administratively by government innovation agencies, primarily Innovate UK.

Funding Structure

KTPs operate on a co-funded model. Government typically contributes between 50% and 67% of total project costs, depending on the size and type of the host organisation. Small and Medium Enterprises (SMEs) receive a higher proportion of government support, recognising that they often lack the resources to independently fund Research and Development (R&D) or innovation projects (Howells, 2006). The remainder is contributed by the business partner. Funds cover:

- The Associate's full-time salary
- University academic supervision
- Travel and training allowances
- Project consumables
- Administrative support through the KTP Management Office

The cost-sharing model creates shared ownership of project outcomes while ensuring that the company remains sufficiently invested in the success of the collaboration.

KTP Roles and Responsibilities

The Company Partner

The company partner identifies a strategic challenge requiring new knowledge or capability. It provides the workplace environment for the Associate and ensures that senior management is engaged in project governance. Companies benefit not only from the innovation outcomes but also from enhanced absorptive capacity and talent development.

The University Partner

Universities supply academic expertise relevant to the project's aims. A named academic team usually comprising a lead academic, a supervisor and one or more supporting academics provides technical guidance, ensures research quality, and supports the Associate's professional development. For universities, KTPs offer opportunities for impact generation, applied research, and stronger industry relationships.

The KTP Associate

Associates are full-time project leaders, responsible for delivering the innovation objectives within the company environment. They act as "boundary spanners" who translate academic knowledge into practice while providing insights to the academic team (Lam, 2010). KTP Associates receive structured training from the funding agency, company and university that equips them with management, technical, and research skills, thereby enhancing their employability.

Government and Funding Bodies

Government agencies provide funding, monitoring, and evaluation. Innovate UK, for example, ensures that projects align with national innovation priorities and deliver measurable economic and societal impacts.

2.3 Mechanisms for Knowledge Exchange and Capability Building

The effectiveness of KTPs lies in their structured mechanisms for facilitating knowledge exchange, understood as the reciprocal flow of ideas, expertise, and learning between organisations. KTP structures deliberately address common barriers to university–industry collaboration, such as cultural differences, misaligned incentives, and communication gaps (Bruneel et al., 2010).

Embedded Expertise

By employing a graduate full-time within the host organisation, KTPs create a continuous, embedded presence of research-informed capability. This embeddedness helps companies overcome the "knowledge transfer" problem, knowledge that is difficult to transfer because it is context-dependent or tacit (Szulanski, 1996).

Academic Supervision and Project Governance

Academic teams maintain regular involvement through:

- Technical meetings
- Project and workplan reviews
- Joint problem-solving sessions
- Knowledge dissemination workshops

This sustained engagement supports absorptive capacity development by helping companies internalise new knowledge and capabilities (Cohen & Levinthal, 1990).

Training and Professional Development

Associates benefit from structured training in areas such as project management, innovation methods, leadership, and technical skills. This structured learning helps build individual and organisational capability. Associates often introduce new tools such as advanced analytics, design for manufacturing and assembly (DfMA), digital workflows, or scientific methodologies, helping companies modernise processes.

Two-Way Knowledge Flows

KTPs create reciprocal flows of knowledge. Companies gain university expertise; academics gain real-world insights that enhance teaching and research. Many academics report that KTPs generate new research questions or opportunities for publications, while companies often build long-term relationships leading to follow-on projects (Hughes & Kitson, 2012).

Organisational Learning and Sustainability

A core requirement of KTPs is the development of a post-project sustainability plan, ensuring that new capabilities are embedded beyond the project's conclusion. This might include new job roles, revised processes, or additional collaborations. The emphasis on sustainability distinguishes KTPs from more transactional modes of collaboration.

2.4 Comparison With Other Partnership Models

University–industry collaboration can take many forms. KTPs differ from other partnership models in terms of structure, depth of engagement, duration, and intended outcomes.

- Internships and Work Placements: Internships typically involve short-term student placements aimed at providing practical experience. While valuable for student employability, internships rarely include structured academic supervision or strategic organisational transformation. They are primarily learning experiences for students rather than innovation mechanisms for companies. KTPs, in contrast, place a graduate in a project leadership role, supported by academic expertise, with the aim of delivering measurable innovation outcomes (Tomlinson, 2017).
- Cooperative Education (Co-op) Programmes: Co-op programmes integrate work placements with academic study. They enhance student learning but are not designed to embed new capabilities within host organisations. Unlike KTPs, co-op students do not lead long-term innovation projects, nor do they operate under a formalised triadic partnership model.
- Contract Research: Contract research involves a company commissioning a university to conduct research on its behalf. While it offers technical expertise, it is typically transactional, short-term, and driven by deliverables rather than capability building (Perkmann & Walsh, 2007). Contract research does not usually involve graduate employment or structured knowledge exchange

mechanisms. KTPs differ by embedding a graduate in the company, providing academic supervision, and ensuring long-term organisational learning.

- Consultancy Services: Academic consultancy is typically advisory, offering insights without ongoing implementation support. It lacks the co-funded, immersive, and long-term structure of KTPs. Consultancy rarely contributes to graduate development or sustained capability building within the company.
- Collaborative Research Centres or Innovation Labs: These initiatives involve deep collaborations but are usually large-scale, multi-year, and resource-intensive. They are more suitable for major corporations or sectoral clusters. KTPs provide a more accessible and flexible model for small and medium-sized enterprises.

2.5 KTPs as the Triple Helix in Action

Knowledge Transfer Partnerships (KTPs) offer a concrete, operational expression of the Triple Helix model of innovation, which conceptualises economic and social development as emerging from dynamic interactions between universities, industry, and government. Rather than treating these spheres (Figure 1) as separate or sequential, KTPs embody their co-evolution, making them a particularly powerful mechanism for applied innovation. The three concepts are especially useful for understanding KTPs through a Triple Helix structure: hybridisation, boundary-spanning, and recursive learning.

Hybridisation: Blurring Institutional Roles

A defining feature of KTPs is the hybridisation of roles and identities across the university–industry–government link.

- Universities move beyond knowledge production into active roles in commercialisation, organisational change, and public value creation.
- Companies become sites of applied research, experimentation, and skills development rather than purely production or market-facing entities.
- Government, through Innovate UK and associated bodies, acts not only as a funder but as a system architect, shaping incentives, governance structures, and accountability mechanisms.

The KTP Associate is the most visible embodiment of this hybridisation. Positioned simultaneously as a researcher, employee, innovator, and change agent, the Associate operates at the intersection of academic rigour, industrial pragmatism, and policy objectives. This hybrid role challenges traditional career and organisational boundaries but is central to the effectiveness of the model.

Hybridisation also occurs at the organisational level: companies adopt academic practices (e.g. evidence-based decision-making, simulation, experimentation), while universities internalise industry logics (e.g. speed, commercial viability, regulatory compliance). The result is not a simple transfer of knowledge, but the co-production of new organisational capabilities.

Boundary-Spanning: Connecting Knowledge, Practice, and Policy

KTPs are explicitly designed as boundary-spanning mechanisms, bridging gaps between different epistemic, cultural, and institutional domains.

- Cognitive boundaries: Translating abstract research into actionable industrial solutions (and vice versa).
- Organisational boundaries: Aligning academic timelines and incentives with business delivery pressures.
- Sectoral boundaries: Enabling collaboration across private, public, and third-sector contexts.
- Policy–practice boundaries: Embedding public policy goals (e.g. net zero, health resilience, levelling up) into company-level innovation activities.

Boundary-spanning is not incidental but structurally embedded in the KTP model. Joint supervision arrangements, steering committees, and formalised reporting requirements create regular points of interaction where assumptions are challenged and knowledge is reinterpreted. These "boundary spaces" are where much of the value of KTPs are generated.

Importantly, boundary-spanning in KTPs is bidirectional. Knowledge does not flow only from universities to companies; industrial constraints, user needs, and regulatory realities feed back into academic research agendas, teaching curricula, and methodological approaches.

Recursive Learning: Iteration, Feedback, and Systemic Adaptation

KTPs exemplify recursive learning, a process in which learning is continuous, iterative, and embedded across multiple levels of the innovation process.

- At the project level, designs, models, or processes are iteratively refined through cycles of simulation, testing, implementation, and evaluation.

- At the organisational level, companies and universities adapt their internal practices as new capabilities are developed (e.g. digital workflows, R&D governance, interdisciplinary collaboration).
- At the system level, lessons from individual KTPs feed back into programme design, funding criteria, and policy priorities.

This recursive dynamic distinguishes KTPs from linear models of knowledge transfer. Rather than a one-off movement of expertise, KTPs create feedback loops in which learning reshapes future behaviour and institutional arrangements. Over time, this contributes to the evolution of regional innovation opportunities and national innovation policy.

Recursive learning also has a human dimension: Associates, supervisors, and managers develop new professional identities and competencies that persist beyond the life of a single project, reinforcing the long-term impact of the Triple Helix interaction.

KTPs as a Living Triple Helix Infrastructure

Taken together, hybridisation, boundary-spanning, and recursive learning position KTPs as more than a funding mechanism or skills programme. They function as a form of innovation infrastructure a repeatable, scalable way of operationalising the Triple Helix in practice.

By aligning academic knowledge production, industrial problem-solving, and public policy objectives within a single collaborative framework, KTPs demonstrate how the Triple Helix can move from theory to action. This reveals both the potential and the tensions of contemporary innovation systems: the need to manage hybridity, navigate boundaries, and sustain learning across institutional divides.

Defined by complex, systemic challenges climate change, health resilience, and digital transformation using AI, KTPs show how the Triple Helix collaboration can generate not only technological solutions, but also adaptive capacity within organisations and innovation systems themselves.

3.0 INNOVATION AND OUTCOMES THROUGH KTPS

As a formalised, structured partnership model, the KTP scheme is designed not only to transfer knowledge from academia to industry but to embed long-term capability within participating organisations. This section analyses the innovation outcomes generated through KTPs across company, university, and government perspectives, examining the mechanisms by which KTPs support product development, digital transformation, research impact, and regional productivity. Drawing on studies of university–industry collaboration and knowledge transfer systems, the discussion positions KTPs as an exemplary model of innovation-driven partnership activity.

Figure 2. Innovation, Employability, Policy and Strategic Implications

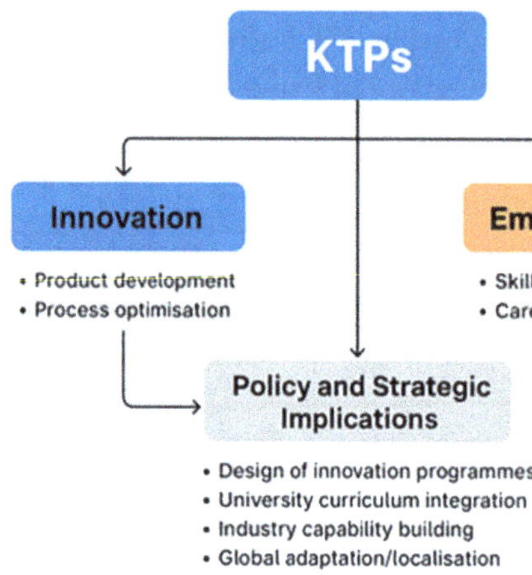

Figure 2, illustrates the interconnectedness of innovation with broader societal and economic outcomes. It highlights how innovation-driven projects, like KTPs, not only foster technological advancement but also enhance employability by equipping KTP associates with valuable, real-world skills. The figure underscores the policy implications, showing how such initiatives align with national priorities like skills development, economic growth, and regional levelling up. It draws attention to the strategic implications for businesses and academic institutions, demonstrating how KTPs support long-term sustainability, improve industry-academia collaboration, and contributes to the innovation process. Through these linkages, KTPs are positioned as key drivers of both individual career development and national policy objectives.

3.1 How KTPs Drive Company-Level Innovation

At their core, KTPs are designed to support organisations particularly small and medium-sized enterprises (SMEs) in overcoming innovation barriers such as limited R&D capacity, shortages of technical expertise, and constraints in organisational capability (Bascavusoglu-Moreau et al., 2013); Abreu et al., 2009). By embedding a KTP Associate within the company for 12 to 36 months, supported by academic leads and supervisors from a university, the scheme offers a unique combination of specialist expertise, project management structure, and knowledge-intensive resources. This design provides companies with capabilities they would often be unable to access independently, including advanced scientific knowledge, data analytics skills, digital technologies, and strategic management insights.

Empirical studies of university–industry interaction emphasise that companies benefit most when knowledge transfer is "relational" rather than transactional that is, when long-term trust, joint problem-solving, and reciprocal learning underpin collaborations (Perkmann & Walsh, 2007); Bruneel et al., 2010). KTPs operationalise these features through regular project meetings, formal governance structures, and dedicated roles that bridge organisational cultures. The Associate acts as a boundary-spanning figure, translating academic expertise into commercially meaningful applications while communicating industrial constraints and market realities back to the university environment (Pates, 2023); Abreu et al., 2009).

Case evaluations conducted by Innovate UK (the administering body) indicate that companies frequently experience tangible innovation outcomes from KTPs. For example, projects have supported the development of new products, significantly improved manufacturing efficiency, and enabled data-led transformation, particularly in sectors such as engineering, health technologies, sustainable energy, agricultural technology, and the creative industries. These company-level outcomes align with wider research on the benefits of collaborative R&D partnerships, which demonstrate positive effects on technological learning, absorptive capacity, and long-term strategic positioning (Durmusoglu, 2004; Etzkowitz & Leydesdorff, 2000).

KTPs also help companies develop internal capability beyond the lifespan of the funded project. This is consistent with the argument that the most sustainable innovation results from capability development rather than one-off knowledge acquisition (Bascavusoglu-Moreau et al., 2013). Companies involved in KTPs often recruit the Associate into a permanent role, retaining advanced competencies acquired through the partnership. As a result, KTPs have been shown to produce durable organisational changes, such as new data governance structures, improved quality management systems, and enhanced R&D cultures.

Synthesis of KTP Contributions to Innovation and Employability

The KTP model offers a multi-layered value proposition that benefits all participating stakeholders. For companies, particularly small and medium-sized enterprises (SMEs), KTPs provide access to specialised expertise, practical research applications, and structured project management support. By embedding a graduate Associate within the organisation, companies gain the capacity to undertake innovation projects that may have been beyond their internal capabilities. These projects frequently lead to tangible outcomes, such as the development of new products, improvements in process efficiency, adoption of digital technologies, and enhanced strategic decision-making. Beyond these immediate outputs, KTPs also build long-term organisational capability by transferring knowledge, creating skills within the workforce, and embedding innovation-oriented practices that persist beyond the funded project.

Universities also benefit significantly from KTP engagement. The programme provides opportunities to translate academic research into real-world applications, creating measurable impact while enriching the teaching and learning environment. Academics gain insight into industrial challenges, which can inform future research agendas, support the development of relevant curricula, and strengthen university–industry partnerships. The presence of Associates working at the interface of academia and industry supports knowledge co-creation, enhancing the relevance of research and creating a pool of highly skilled graduates ready to enter the workforce.

For graduates, KTPs serve as a powerful platform for developing employability and career readiness. Associates occupy hybrid roles that blend technical expertise, managerial responsibility, and innovation leadership. They gain hands-on experience in applying research to real-world problems, managing complex projects, and navigating organisational dynamics. These experiences equip them with a rare combination of technical, strategic, and interpersonal skills that significantly enhance their long-term career prospects. Many Associates go on to occupy leadership positions within industry or academia, reflecting the programme's ability to cultivate future-ready talent.

Governments derive substantial benefits from KTPs. By supporting innovation at the company level, the programme contributes to economic growth, productivity gains, and regional development. It also fosters the diffusion of research and development capabilities across sectors, strengthening national innovation systems. The KTP model aligns funding incentives with strategic outcomes, ensuring that public investment generates measurable returns in both economic and human capital terms. Collectively, the contributions of KTPs illustrate a holistic approach to fostering innovation, workforce development, and economic resilience.

The Role of KTPs in Strengthening Resilient, Knowledge-Driven Economies

KTPs exemplify how structured collaboration frameworks can contribute to the creation of resilient, knowledge-driven economies. In a rapidly changing global environment, where technological advancement, digital transformation, and knowledge-intensive industries are key drivers of competitiveness, KTPs provide a mechanism for aligning human, technological, and organisational resources.

One of the defining characteristics of KTPs is their ability to enhance the absorptive capacity of companies. By integrating new knowledge and skills into organisational processes, companies become better equipped to adapt to evolving market conditions and technological change. This capacity for continuous learning and innovation is crucial for economic resilience, as it enables companies to respond to disruptions, seize emerging opportunities, and maintain competitiveness over time.

KTPs promote regional and sectoral innovation by facilitating the flow of knowledge across university–industry–government networks. By connecting academic expertise with local companies, the programme helps to address disparities in innovation capacity and supports the development of innovation clusters in diverse regions. This distributed model strengthens regional economies, fosters inclusive growth, and contributes to broader national productivity objectives. At the sectoral level, KTPs support the adoption of advanced technologies, digital transformation, and process optimisation, enhancing the competitiveness of both traditional and emerging industries.

The programme also enables a strategic role in shaping workforce capabilities. By embedding highly skilled Associates into companies, KTPs develop a talent pipeline capable of driving innovation and leading organisational transformation. These graduates become catalysts for cultural change, promoting knowledge-sharing, continuous learning, and innovation-focused capabilities within companies as demonstrated in the Evac+Chair case study below. Over time, this creates a self-reinforcing cycle in which human capital development and innovation capabilities mutually strengthen each other, contributing to the resilience of the economy as a whole.

The triadic structure of KTPs linking universities, industry, and government supports systemic innovation. This model encourages coordination across multiple stakeholders, aligns incentives, and fosters a culture of collaboration. KTPs help to build processes where knowledge flows efficiently, innovation is embedded in organisational routines, and economic and social benefits are maximised as shown in the case study below.

3.2 Case Study: Knowledge Transfer Partnership (KTP) Between Birmingham City University, UK and Evac+Chair International, Birmingham, UK

Company Name: Paraid (a division of Evac+Chair International Ltd). Paraid, based in Birmingham, UK, is a recognised leader in the design and manufacture of innovative ambulance transfer equipment that saves lives and enhances dignity in critical situations. The company specialises in solutions for medical emergencies and for individuals facing access challenges when travelling by air, sea, or rail. Its products are trusted worldwide for their safety, reliability, and user-focused design.

Among its most significant innovations are advanced critical care transfer trolleys, specifically engineered for the road transport of neonates. These highly specialised devices support ambulance services and hospitals by enabling the safe movement of premature and critically ill infants, ensuring stability for both the patient and the life-support equipment they require.

The Strategic Challenge

The company designs and manufactures a range of bespoke incubator trolleys for both emergency and elective neonatal ambulance transport. These trolleys are engineered to carry incubators alongside critical life-support equipment such as respirators, ensuring that premature and sick infants receive continuous care during transfer. Each year in the UK alone, approximately 16,000 neonatal transfers take place. However, ambulance transport carries inherent risks, and incidents including crashes have previously resulted in significant danger to both patients and medical staff.

The Knowledge Transfer Partnership (KTP) project addressed this challenge by developing an innovative shock absorption device designed to integrate with standard UK and European ambulance trolleys. The system enables the secure attachment of the most widely used neonatal products, including oxygen supplies and other essential medical lines. In the absence of such a device, a 40mph collision can generate forces up to 30 times gravity (294 m/s^2). Any unsecured equipment in these conditions becomes a high-velocity projectile, presenting serious risk of injury to both the neonate and ambulance crew. Research from the United States highlights this risk, showing that 29% of fatalities in ambulance crashes occur among crew and patients in the rear compartment.

Beyond safety in crashes, the device significantly reduces g-forces transmitted to the neonate during heavy vehicle acceleration or deceleration common in emergency ambulance responses. Excessive g-forces are linked to brain bleeds, which can contribute to long-term conditions such as cerebral palsy. This innovation is anticipated to become one of the first products to exceed forthcoming EU legislation for ambulance safety.

The key technical challenge lay in designing and manufacturing an interface device that accommodates all life-support requirements while being universally compatible with both competitor and Paraid products. Crucially, the system ensured that all equipment remains securely attached during impact, eliminating the risk of equipment moving and setting a new standard in neonatal transport safety.

The KTP Application Process

KTPs are written and evaluated through a structured process administered by Innovate UK, the government body responsible for funding innovation. The business (Evac+Chair) and the academic partner (Birmingham City University) collaboratively detailed a 2-Year project proposal, outlining the innovation challenge, objectives, expected outcomes, and the role of the KTP Associate. The proposal had to demonstrate the potential for economic impact, technological advancement, and knowledge transfer. Evaluation of the KTP at the end of the project was done by Innovate UK based on criteria such as the quality of the partnership, the relevance of the research, the market need, tangible benefits, and the sustainability of the solution post-project. Innovate UK assessors review the alignment with national priorities, such as industry growth or regional development, and the capacity of the team to deliver the project successfully. The proposal met those criteria, and the project was funded, with ongoing monitoring by Innovate UK and reporting by the partners to ensure successful execution. Birmingham City University achieved an "Outstanding" Innovate UK award for the outcomes of this KTP and was short listed by Innovate UK for the "Best of the Best" KTPs in England, UK.

Impact and Beneficiaries

The Knowledge Transfer Partnership with Paraid (a division of Evac+Chair International) has delivered transformational results for the company, Birmingham City University, and the associate embedding new capabilities and creating measurable impact.

For the company (Paraid):

- Established a digital database of technical drawings and a 3D parts library, giving staff instant access to accurate product information, design files, and costings.
- Streamlined design-to-manufacture, reducing errors and accelerating bespoke trolley development.
- New lean design for manufacture and assembly (DfMA) techniques.
- Achieved 20% efficiency gains per design (measured against pre-KTP practice), worth an estimated £60,000 annually.
- Created three new high salary graduate jobs directly linked to the KTP.
- Delivered innovative, bespoke neonatal transport ambulance trolleys with greater speed and precision.
- Secured repeat customer orders worth over £20,000 for each ambulance trolley, strengthening Par-Aid's market leadership.

For company staff development & business growth:

- Dedicated training days and structured development plans upskilled 10 company staff members, including two who gained specialist digital expertise.

- Improved client collaboration and efficiency through accurate, accessible product data.

For the knowledge base (Birmingham City University):

- Research evidence confirmed that reducing g-forces in neonatal transport can prevent long-term injuries such as cerebral palsy (costing the NHS over £1 million per case).
- Published two academic papers that highlighted how Paraid's device addressed this urgent healthcare challenge.
- The KTP's success secured two further Innovate UK KTP grants for the university.
- Supported full-time employment of two Knowledge Base (KB) postgraduate students within Paraid's R&D division.

For the KTP associate:

- Transitioned to full-time employment with an enhanced salary.
- Achieved a first-class distinction in the company's new design and simulation software and qualified as a certified trainer.
- Presented internationally at the European Society of Paediatric and Neonatal Intensive Care (ESPNIC) in Austria, amplifying project visibility and impact.

Broader benefits:

Economic growth, strengthened UK healthcare innovation, and improved neonatal safety outcomes. This collaboration exemplified knowledge transfer at its best: delivering operational, academic, and societal benefits with a lasting legacy.

The Innovation and "Wow" Factor

Transporting neonates is one of the most critical and sensitive challenges in emergency medicine. Newborns, especially preterm infants, are extraordinarily vulnerable to vibration, shocks, and sudden movements during ambulance transfer. Traditional trolleys, designed for general patients, fail to meet these specific needs. A dedicated shock absorption system for neonatal transport is special because it transforms this high-risk process into a safer, more controlled journey, protecting fragile bodies and giving clinical teams confidence that care is not compromised during transportation.

The innovation goes far beyond technical refinement: it directly addresses a global healthcare gap. Every day, thousands of newborns require urgent transfer between hospitals, neonatal intensive care units, or from rural to specialised centres. A system that can significantly reduce harmful vibration is not just a medical upgrade, it is a lifesaving intervention. Its exploitation potential is vast. It can be integrated into ambulance fleets worldwide, adapted to different healthcare settings, and extended to other patient groups such as those with spinal injuries or severe trauma. Its scalability ensures that the impact is not confined to well-resourced regions but can also transform neonatal survival in developing countries, where road conditions are often challenging.

Theoretical Propositions

The Knowledge Transfer Partnership (KTP) between Birmingham City University (BCU) and Paraid, a division of Evac+Chair International, offers an insightful real-world example of the application of several theoretical propositions in innovation and knowledge transfer, including boundary-spanning and absorptive capacity.

- Boundary-Spanning: The KTP successfully illustrates the concept of boundary-spanning, which involves the collaboration between different sectors and knowledge bases. In this case, there was the interaction between academic research at BCU and practical, market-driven needs at Paraid. The collaboration transcended organisational boundaries, enabling the flow of critical knowledge from the academic world into the design and manufacturing of cutting-edge neonatal transport systems. The KTP also allowed Paraid to incorporate the latest research on g-forces and neonatal health, which would have been difficult to achieve without such academic-industry collaboration.
- Absorptive Capacity: Absorptive capacity refers to an organisation's ability to recognise the value of new information, assimilate it, and apply it to commercial objectives. Paraid demonstrated significant absorptive capacity by integrating new knowledge into their R&D processes, leading to innovations such as the shock absorption device for neonatal transport. The company not only absorbed the technical knowledge from BCU but also used it to enhance internal systems, streamline design-to-manufacture processes, and create new products tailored to real-world healthcare needs.

Generalisable Lessons for Policy/Program Design

Several key lessons can be extracted from this KTP (Evac+Chair) for broader policy and program design:

- Public-Private Partnerships: The success of this KTP highlights the value of public-private partnerships (PPPs) in advancing innovation. In this case, the collaboration between a public university and a private company facilitated the exchange of both knowledge and practical application, resulting in a product that addresses a clear societal need (neonatal transport safety). Policymakers should consider incentivising more PPPs, especially in sectors with direct public health benefits, like healthcare, where both research and practical innovation are often needed.
- Sector-Specific Innovations: This KTP underscores the importance of developing sector-specific innovations tailored to distinct needs, such as neonatal transport. Policy programs should encourage targeted innovations for highly specialised markets, rather than adopting a one-size-fits-all approach, especially in critical sectors like healthcare, where the stakes are higher, and the potential for impact is more significant.
- Support for Small and Medium-Sized Enterprises (SMEs): Paraid, as a smaller company within a larger corporate structure, was able to use the KTP to scale up its capabilities. Policymakers should aim to create more accessible innovation programs for SMEs, as they often face challenges in conducting high-risk, high-reward R&D on their own. The KTP has shown that when SMEs are provided with the right support, they can drive meaningful, impactful innovations.

Tensions or Adaptations in Real-World Implementation

While the KTP between BCU and Paraid was largely successful, the real-world implementation of such projects often comes with tensions or adaptations:

- Balancing Innovation with Practical Constraints: One of the primary challenges for the team was ensuring that the shock absorption device could integrate with existing ambulance equipment, which is often highly standardised across the UK and Europe. The need for universal compatibility required significant technical adaptation, highlighting a common tension in the design of innovative products: balancing cutting-edge solutions with the practical constraints of adapting existing ambulance trolley and complying with varying safety regulations.
- Sector-Specific Regulatory Challenges: The innovation in the KTP was particularly focused on meeting new EU legislation for ambulance safety. This regulatory shift created a challenge in aligning product development with anticipated legal requirements. Adapting to evolving regulations while maintaining product safety and functionality is a key tension faced by compa-

nies in the medical device industry and highlights the importance of keeping abreast of sector-specific regulations during innovation application.

- Interdisciplinary Communication: The collaboration between academia and industry requires effective communication across disciplines. The KTP involved complex technical knowledge from the university, which had to be translated into actionable, product-specific insights for Paraid. Such interdisciplinary translation is often fraught with challenges, from technical jargon to differences in work culture. The success of this KTP can be attributed to a clear mutual understanding between both parties, but it still underscores the importance of fostering strong communication channels when designing such programs.

Mini-Cases Across Sectors

To illustrate the variation in how knowledge transfer partnerships (KTPs) can span different sectors, here are three mini-cases:

- Digital Sector – Cloud Technology for Healthcare Data Management

A KTP between a leading UK university and a tech startup in the digital health sector enabled the development of a cloud-based platform for secure healthcare data management. The collaboration allowed the startup to integrate advanced encryption techniques researched by the university, while the university gained real-world insights into the challenges of data privacy regulations in healthcare. This partnership showcased how KTPs can facilitate the adoption of cutting-edge digital innovations in highly regulated sectors, albeit with tensions around data security and compliance with evolving regulations.

- Creative Sector – Digital Art Preservation

In the creative sector, a KTP involving a design university and a gallery focused on preserving digital art explored the use of blockchain technology to authenticate and track digital artwork. This collaboration helped the gallery navigate the growing demand for digital art preservation while also addressing challenges of authenticity and ownership in the digital realm. This case emphasises the tension between preserving artistic integrity and adapting new technologies to traditional art forms.

- Public Sector – Smart City Infrastructure

A public sector KTP between a local government and an engineering company led to the development of a smart traffic management system using AI and big data analytics. The partnership aimed to reduce urban congestion and optimise public transport routes. The tension here was in balancing the desire for high-tech solutions with the city's existing infrastructure, which was often outdated and not easily adaptable to new technologies. The lessons here emphasise the need for careful integration of new innovations into public services, ensuring that they complement and enhance rather than disrupt existing systems.

The KTP between Birmingham City University and Paraid exemplifies how boundary-spanning and absorptive capacity can be effectively integrated to drive innovation. The case study also underscores the need for tailored, sector-specific solutions and robust support for SMEs in policy design. Real-world implementation, however, involves addressing challenges such as regulatory adaptation, technological compatibility, and interdisciplinary communication. The mini-cases from other sectors, including digital, creative, and public sectors, further illustrate the variations and challenges in applying KTP models across diverse domains, offering key insights for future policy and program design in innovation and knowledge transfer.

3.3 Impact on Product Development, Process Optimisation, Digital Transformation, and Strategic Growth

The diverse impacts of Knowledge Transfer Partnerships (KTPs) extend across the full spectrum of organisational innovation, shaping how companies design products, refine processes, adopt digital technologies, and pursue long-term strategic growth. At their core, KTPs embed academic expertise and a dedicated Associate within the company, enabling companies to find solutions to technical or managerial challenges that they may lack the internal capacity to resolve. This structured collaboration supports rapid and evidence-based product development by introducing new research insights, prototyping methods, and design capabilities. At the same time, companies benefit from systematic process optimisation through improved operational workflows, enhanced quality management, and greater efficiency supported by analytical and data-driven approaches. As digital transformation becomes increasingly critical to competitiveness, KTPs help organisations modernise through the adoption of automation, data analytics, and digital infrastructure that might otherwise be inaccessible. Beyond immediate operational gains, these improvements contribute to wider strategic outcomes, including the expansion of market offerings, the strengthening of competitive positioning, and the development of long-term innovation capabilities. Through this integrated model, KTPs provide companies with both short-term performance improvements and lasting strategic advantages as demonstrated below.

Use of AI in the Evac+Chair KTP: Simulating Crash Tests, Material Strength, and Parametric Design

The Knowledge Transfer Partnership (KTP) between Birmingham City University and Paraid (a division of Evac+Chair International) used bespoke advanced artificial intelligence (AI) technologies to simulate crash tests, analyse material strength, and optimise the design of modular components for the neonatal ambulance trolleys. AI contributed a pivotal role in enhancing the development process, enabling virtual testing and parametric design that reduced the need for costly and time-consuming physical prototypes and testing. Here's a detailed look at how AI was used in these critical areas:

Simulating Crash Tests with AI: Simulating crash scenarios before conducting real-world tests is crucial in developing safe and reliable medical equipment like the neonatal transport trolleys. AI-driven finite element analysis (FEA) and computer-aided engineering (CAE) tools were employed to model and predict the performance of the trolleys during high-impact events, such as ambulance crashes or heavy acceleration/deceleration.

- Virtual Crash Simulations: By using BCU's custom AI-powered FEA software, the KTP team was able to simulate crash scenarios, including impacts at various speeds (e.g., 40mph collisions). The simulations modelled the forces acting on the trolley, equipment, and neonatal patients during an accident. The AI algorithms helped to predict how the trolley and shock absorption device would behave under extreme conditions, including the stresses placed on the trolley's structure, the g-forces transmitted to the neonatal patient, and the potential for injury.
- Optimising Safety Features: AI simulations allowed for the rapid iteration of different design parameters, ensuring that the shock absorption system could handle extreme forces without compromising safety. This reduced the risk of human error or inconsistencies in physical testing, providing accurate data on potential crash performance long before the physical prototype was crash tested. By identifying weak points in the design early on, the team was able to adjust parameters, strengthening the overall system.

Material Strength Analysis: The KTP also utilised AI to evaluate the strength of materials used in the construction of the neonatal transport trolleys. Machine learning algorithms were applied to analyse the behaviour of various materials under stress and simulate their performance in real-world conditions.

- Material Selection and Optimisation: Using AI, the team was able to model different material compositions for the trolley and shock absorption device. The machine learning algorithm was able to predict the optimal material properties required for the specific needs of neonatal transport such as flexibility, durability, and the ability to absorb shock without compromising structural integrity. This ensured that the materials selected would be robust enough to handle the forces of ambulance crashes while keeping the weight of the trolley manageable for ease of use.
- Strength-to-Weight Ratio: AI-driven simulations helped determine the ideal balance between strength and weight, critical for neonatal transport. By analysing the material strength under varying forces, AI enabled the academic team to identify materials that would perform reliably without adding unnecessary bulk to the trolley. This was especially important in ensuring the safety of the patient while maintaining manoeuvrability and ease of transport for medical staff.

Parametric Design for Modular Components: AI was also employed in creating parametric designs for the modular components of the ambulance trolley. Parametric design, which involves creating models that can be adjusted and adapted based on a set of parameters, was key in developing a system that could be easily modified to fit different ambulance configurations and meet varying healthcare needs.

- Modular Design Flexibility: AI allowed for the creation of modular pieces that could be customised based on specific needs, whether for different ambulance designs or specialised medical equipment. The parametric AI models could adjust dimensions, shapes, and components based on predefined constraints, ensuring that each part would integrate seamlessly with existing ambulance equipment and meet local safety standards.
- Optimising Component Compatibility: The AI models also accounted for the compatibility of different modular pieces, enabling the integration of the shock absorption system with both Paraid's existing trolleys and competitor products. This modular approach ensured that the system could be universally compatible, which was crucial given the wide variety of ambulance configurations in use across Europe and beyond.
- Accelerating Development: By automating the design process with AI, the KTP team was able to quickly test a wide range of variations in the modular components. This significantly reduced the time it would take to develop new prototypes and conduct costly physical crash tests, as the parametric designs were already optimised before being physically constructed. The result was a

more efficient development process and a faster route to market for the new neonatal transport trolleys.

Integration with Real-World Testing: AI simulations and virtual testing did not replace real-world crash testing but rather complemented it. The data generated through AI simulations were used to refine the physical prototypes before any actual physical crash tests were conducted. By ensuring that the trolley designs had already undergone rigorous virtual testing, the team could focus their physical testing efforts on fine-tuning the product rather than on basic design flaws.

- Minimising Physical Testing Risks: AI-driven simulations reduced the need for extensive physical testing, which could have potentially damaged the prototypes or result in costly revisions. The virtual tests provided a high degree of certainty regarding the design's performance, making the actual crash tests more focused and efficient.

The use of AI in the KTP between Birmingham City University and Paraid was a game-changer in the development of the neonatal ambulance trolley, offering a number of benefits such as cost savings, time efficiency, and enhanced safety. AI-powered simulations of crash tests, material strength, and modular design allowed the team to quickly iterate on designs, test safety features virtually, and ensure the final product met both technical specifications and real-world healthcare needs. This integration of AI technology significantly accelerated the development process, reduced risks, and resulted in a product that met the highest standards of safety and functionality, with the potential for widespread impact in both developed and developing regions.

Product Development

Many KTPs focus explicitly on product innovation, particularly in technology-intensive sectors. Through access to academic expertise in design, materials science, software engineering, or biotechnology, companies can accelerate product development cycles and reduce risks associated with experimentation. Research on collaborative innovation shows that access to academic labs, modelling tools, and analytical techniques enhances companies' ability to prototype, test, and commercialise new solutions (Durmusoglu, 2004). In KTP contexts, this often results in the creation of new product lines or the enhancement of existing ones.

An example frequently cited in Innovate UK summaries involves manufacturers using KTP support to integrate advanced materials or automation technologies into existing products, significantly improving reliability, sustainability, or cost competitiveness. Such outcomes echo the broader logic of open innovation: companies expand their cognitive and technological horizons by exploiting external research (Durmusoglu, 2004).

Process Optimisation

Beyond product development, KTPs play a vital role in process innovation, helping companies refine operational systems, supply chains, and production workflows. SMEs in particular often lack the analytical tools required to diagnose inefficiencies or redesign processes. With academic support, KTP Associates introduce methods such as Lean Six Sigma, modelling and simulation, machine learning for optimisation, or advanced data analytics (Abreu et al., 2009).

Evaluations of KTPs show that companies frequently achieve:

- reduced waste and improved resource efficiency
- higher throughput and better production scheduling
- improved quality assurance systems
- redesigned workflows that enhance staff productivity

These outcomes not only reduce operational costs but also strengthen organisational resilience and responsiveness, both critical features of innovation-driven competitiveness.

Digital Transformation

In recent years, a growing proportion of KTPs has focused on digital transformation, reflecting national priorities around Industry, artificial intelligence, cybersecurity, digital twins, and data-driven decision-making. Through the embedded Associate model, companies gain access to technical expertise that allows them to deploy digital tools they would otherwise be unable to implement effectively.

Examples of digital transformation outcomes include:

- implementation of predictive analytics for maintenance
- automation of manual processes using robotics or software tools
- data integration across legacy systems
- adoption of cloud-based infrastructure
- enhanced cyber-resilience strategies

The literature on digital innovation highlights that successful transformation requires not only technological upgrades but organisational learning and cultural change (Perkmann et al., 2011). KTPs facilitate this by embedding digital skills within companies through sustained interaction rather than short-term consultancy.

How AI and Advanced Digital Tools Are Reshaping KTPs

The introduction of artificial intelligence (AI), data science, and advanced digital tools has had a transformative effect on Knowledge Transfer Partnerships (KTPs), enabling more efficient, scalable, and innovative collaborations between academia and industry. As the scope of AI-driven projects continues to expand, KTPs are evolving to meet the unique demands and opportunities posed by these emerging technologies. In particular, AI is reshaping the ways KTPs operate, the skills required by participants, and how collaborations are structured. Here's a closer look at how AI and digital tools are reshaping KTPs, including new supervision models, skill sets, and the potential for virtual and distributed collaboration.

KTPs in the Age of AI: The rise of AI, machine learning (ML), and data science is significantly altering the landscape of KTPs. These innovations not only provide novel approaches to solving complex industry challenges but also necessitate new ways of designing and executing KTPs.

AI-Driven Innovation in KTPs: Data Science and Machine Learning Projects:

- KTPs have traditionally focused on transferring knowledge from academia to industry through collaboration, but the integration of AI technologies adds a layer of complexity and opportunity that pushes these collaborations to new frontiers. AI-driven innovations, such as machine learning algorithms and predictive analytics, can be applied across a wide range of industries from healthcare and manufacturing to transportation and creative sectors enhancing the potential outcomes of KTPs.
- Data Science Integration: AI-powered data science tools enable KTPs to address large-scale, complex datasets that were previously difficult to manage or analyse. For instance, a KTP focusing on healthcare innovation may utilise AI to analyse patient data for predictive analytics, improving medical decision-making and treatment plans. This not only drives innovation but also creates actionable insights for industry partners. As industries increasingly rely on big data and AI to improve operational efficiency, KTPs are adapting to include more data-driven projects, facilitating the development of models that can predict outcomes, optimise processes, and reduce risks.
- Machine Learning and Automation: In sectors like manufacturing, AI-powered machine learning tools are used to optimise production lines, predict maintenance needs, and reduce downtime. KTPs can utilise these technologies to help companies streamline operations and enhance product design.

In this context, AI helps to automate routine tasks, leaving human experts to focus on high-level strategy and innovation. For example, in the Evac+Chair KTP aimed at creating smart manufacturing solutions, AI was used to simulate production scenarios and recommend design adjustments based on real-time data, improving assembly time and quality.

New Skills and Supervision Models for AI-Driven KTPs

As AI becomes central to KTPs, the skill sets required by both academic and industry partners are evolving. Traditional KTPs relied heavily on domain expertise, but AI and digital tools introduce a need for new technical capabilities and a rethinking of supervision models.

- Data Science and AI Expertise: KTP associates now require advanced training in data science, machine learning, and AI development. Rather than just understanding the practical application of theories, KTP associates need to have hands-on experience with coding, algorithm development, and statistical modelling. Universities involved in KTPs are increasingly providing specialised courses in AI to ensure students and researchers have the technical skills necessary to contribute to these cutting-edge projects.
- Cross-Disciplinary Collaboration: AI projects often require interdisciplinary knowledge, merging fields such as engineering, computer science, and domain-specific expertise (e.g., healthcare, automotive). KTPs now demand a broader range of technical and non-technical skills to facilitate seamless collaboration. Professionals involved in KTPs must also have a grasp of AI concepts like deep learning, natural language processing (NLP), and data visualisation.
- Supervision Models: The role of mentorship and supervision is evolving in AI-driven KTPs. Traditional supervision focused on technical expertise and research; however, the complexity of AI projects requires a more collaborative supervision model:
- Dual Supervision: KTPs in the age of AI may involve dual supervision one from the academic partner specialising in AI algorithms and another from the industrial partner who understands the practical applications and market needs. This model fosters real-time knowledge transfer, allowing both sides to learn from each other.
- Remote Supervision: With the rise of remote work and distributed teams, supervisors and mentors in AI-based KTPs must develop new methods of maintaining oversight and collaboration. Tools like cloud computing, virtual

meetings, and project management platforms enable continuous interaction and feedback loops, regardless of physical location.

Digital Tools Enabling Virtual KTPs and Distributed Collaboration

As AI tools become more accessible, digital platforms are enhancing the flexibility and reach of KTPs, making it easier to conduct virtual and distributed collaboration between universities and industry partners across geographies. Digital tools not only facilitate the integration of AI into KTPs but also help overcome traditional barriers such as physical location, time zone differences, and resource limitations.

- Virtual Collaboration Platforms: Tools such as cloud-based project management platforms, collaborative design software, and AI-powered communication systems enable virtual KTPs to thrive. For example, using AI-based collaboration platforms, KTP teams can co-develop software, test prototypes, and share datasets in real-time, fostering collaboration despite geographic separation. These tools also allow for asynchronous collaboration, which is essential when teams are distributed across different time zones.
- Data Sharing and Cloud Infrastructure: With the large volumes of data generated in AI-driven KTPs, secure data-sharing platforms that facilitate real-time data access and analysis are essential. Cloud infrastructure allows both academic researchers and industry practitioners to access centralised databases, perform machine learning tasks, and contribute to the iterative development of AI algorithms. The cloud-based tools enable collaborative AI training and data analysis across distributed teams, ensuring continuous development without requiring all partners to be physically present.
- Virtual Testing and Simulation Tools: AI-driven simulations are increasingly being used to test product designs and prototypes virtually, without the need for expensive physical prototypes. In KTPs, this reduces the costs of traditional physical testing and accelerates the time-to-market for new products. Virtual environments powered by AI can simulate real-world scenarios, providing insights into product performance without the limitations of physical trials.

KTPs in the Rise of AI

As AI and digital tools continue to evolve, KTPs are adapting to the use of these technologies in novel ways. AI-driven innovation opens up new avenues for data science, machine learning, and automated solutions in various sectors. However, this evolution also requires new skill sets and supervision models to keep pace with the rapid changes. The integration of cloud platforms, AI simulations, and distributed collaboration tools further enhances the effectiveness and flexibility of KTPs, enabling partners to collaborate in real-time and across borders.

KTPs with AI in their workplan have the potential to drive transformative change not only through the development of cutting-edge technologies but also by redefining how research, development, and innovation are conducted in a highly interconnected, virtual world. By embracing AI and digital tools, KTPs are ensuring that knowledge transfer partnerships remain relevant and effective in addressing the ever-evolving needs of modern industries and society.

Strategic Growth and Long-Term Impact

A distinguishing feature of KTPs is their alignment with company-level strategic growth. While internships or contract research typically address immediate tasks, KTPs require companies to outline multi-year strategies and demonstrate how the project fits within long-term development plans. As such, KTPs often lead to:

- expansion into new markets
- enhanced R&D strategy and capability
- diversification of product portfolios
- strengthened management practices

Surveys of companies involved in KTPs have reported significant financial returns, including increased turnover, cost savings, and job creation consistent with broader evidence linking university collaboration to company growth (Bascavusoglu-Moreau et al., 2013); Perkmann et al., 2011).

3.4 University Benefits: Research Translation, Impact Case Generation, and Strategic Industry Alignment

Universities are central in the role of KTPs, and the scheme provides substantial benefits to academic institutions beyond financial incentives. One of the most significant advantages lies in research translation, where academic theories, models, and methods are applied to real-world commercial challenges. This provides opportunities for academics to test research in practical contexts, refine methodologies, and generate new lines of inquiry.

Research Translation and Knowledge Exchange

Since KTPs are designed as two-way partnerships, universities gain access to industrial datasets, organisational problems, and applied research environments. This enhances research relevance and supports the development of new knowledge, consistent with (Etzkowitz & Leydesdorff, 2000) Triple Helix model, which highlights the importance of hybrid spaces where academia, industry, and government co-produce knowledge.

Impact Case Generation

Since the introduction of the UK Research Excellence Framework (REF), universities have been under pressure to demonstrate societal, economic, and industrial impact. KTPs naturally produce measurable outcomes new products, improved processes, market expansion, sustainability gains that can serve as robust REF impact case studies. The structured documentation and evaluation built into KTP projects provide credible evidence for such cases, facilitating stronger institutional performance in national assessment exercises.

Strategic Industry Alignment

KTPs also support universities' strategic engagement with industry by providing a stable, repeatable partnership model. They help universities:

- strengthen relationships with priority sectors
- identify long-term industry needs
- co-design curricula and CPD programmes
- collaborate on future research proposals

These benefits align with wider literature emphasising the role of universities as key actors in regional innovation framework (Etzkowitz & Leydesdorff, 2000); Abreu et al., 2009).

3.5 Government Benefits: Productivity Gains, Regional Development, and R&D Diffusion

The government's role in KTPs, primarily through Innovate UK, is driven by national objectives relating to innovation, productivity, and economic growth. As a publicly funded scheme, KTPs are assessed not only on individual project success but on their contribution to broader policy goals.

Productivity Gains

One of the central rationales for government investment in KTPs is their demonstrated ability to raise company productivity, particularly among SMEs. Many SMEs lack internal Research and Development (R&D) capabilities, and government intervention helps address this market failure. Studies on collaborative innovation emphasise that government-funded programmes can enhance national productivity by enabling companies to adopt advanced technologies, improve efficiency, and upgrade skills (Bascavusoglu-Moreau et al., 2013).

Regional Development

KTPs also support balanced regional economic growth. Because universities exist across the UK, including in regions with lower R&D intensity, KTPs help distribute innovation activity beyond major metropolitan centres. This supports regional development goals and aligns with the levelling-up agenda by enabling local companies to access university expertise.

R&D Diffusion and Innovation System Strengthening

KTPs contribute to national innovation system development by encouraging interdisciplinary knowledge aquisition and lowering barriers between academic and industrial domains. This diffusion of R&D capability is central to the Triple Helix vision of collaborative innovation (Etzkowitz & Leydesdorff, 2000). Government benefit arises not only from individual company success but from the strengthening of innovation culture, industrial learning, and inter-organisational collaboration across the economy.

4.0 GRADUATE EMPLOYABILITY AND SKILLS DEVELOPMENT IN KTPS

Graduate employability has become a major priority for governments, universities, and employers, particularly in economies where knowledge, innovation, and technological sophistication shape labour market competitiveness. In this context, the UK's Knowledge Transfer Partnership (KTP) scheme represents a distinctive mechanism for developing highly skilled graduates known as Associates who operate at the interface of academia and industry. Unlike conventional graduate roles that introduce early-career employees to predefined organisational tasks, the KTP Associate role is explicitly designed around innovation, capability building, and strategic organisational transformation. This section examines how KTPs foster graduate employability by developing advanced competencies, enabling hybrid professional identities, and supporting long-term career progression. It also compares KTP participation with traditional graduate entry pathways, highlighting the distinctive features that enhance Associates' labour-market outcomes.

4.1 The Associate Role as a Hybrid Learner–Innovator–Employee

One of the most unique elements of the KTP model is the creation of the Associate role, which blends attributes of a postgraduate researcher, an innovation specialist, and a full-time employee embedded in a host organisation. This hybrid positioning allows the Associate to function simultaneously as a learner, knowledge translator, and change agent. The Associate is appointed to deliver a strategically significant project, with guidance from both academic and industrial supervisors, creating a triadic partnership structure aligned with the broader Triple Helix model of innovation (Etzkowitz & Leydesdorff, 2000).

A Boundary-Spanning Professional

Boundary-spanning roles positions that bridge groups, organisations, or sectors are widely recognised in the literature as crucial for knowledge exchange and innovation (Abreu et al., 2009; Perkmann et al., 2011). KTP Associates operate as boundary spanners by:

- translating academic expertise into organisational processes
- articulating industry needs back to academic supervisors
- facilitating communication between technical and managerial staff
- integrating research insights into practical commercial decision-making

This work requires not only technical proficiency but also sophisticated interpersonal, analytical, and communication skills. The hybrid nature of the role means the Associate is neither purely a student nor a fully conventional employee. Instead, they occupy a unique developmental position that grants them early exposure to strategic decision-making, cross-functional collaboration, and organisational leadership opportunities rarely accessible in typical graduate roles.

Structured Learning Environment

The structure of KTPs reinforces the Associate's learner–innovator identity. Associates receive:

- dedicated training budgets
- formal management development programmes
- research and conference funding
- access to academic mentorship
- opportunities to publish, present, or pursue postgraduate qualifications

This dual academic–professional environment aligns with the idea of "expanded graduate capital" (Tomlinson, 2017), where employability is shaped by combinations of human, social, cultural, and identity capital. KTP participation strengthens each of these dimensions.

4.2 Competences Developed Through KTP Participation

KTPs offer a distinctive learning environment that accelerates the acquisition of technical, managerial, and innovation-related competencies. These competencies reflect the demands of contemporary labour markets, particularly in sectors where technology, digitalisation, and strategic thinking are central to organisational performance.

Technical Competencies

Associates typically apply knowledge from fields such as engineering, computing, bioscience, behavioural science, sustainability, or design. Their technical development often includes:

- advanced data analytics and modelling
- digital engineering, automation, or AI application
- product design, prototyping, and testing
- process optimisation using scientific or mathematical methods
- environmental and sustainability analysis
- software or system development

As KTP projects are innovation-driven, Associates work on problems requiring high levels of scientific and technical complexity. This practical application of knowledge reinforces discipline-specific expertise and enhances "work-readiness" in ways that traditional graduate schemes may not (Bruneel et al., 2010).

Managerial Competencies

KTPs place Associates in roles with substantial responsibility from the outset, making managerial skills a major developmental outcome. Research on graduate employability emphasises that employers increasingly value managerial capabilities project management, communication, and leadership alongside technical knowledge (Tomlinson, 2017). KTPs cultivate these skills through:

- project planning and milestone management
- financial and resource budgeting
- stakeholder engagement and reporting
- cross-functional coordination within the host company
- leading change and building organisational buy-in

Associates often manage teams, facilitate workshops, and present to senior leadership. This exposure accelerates their leadership development far beyond what is typical for early-career graduates.

Innovation and Entrepreneurial Competencies

Perhaps the most distinctive competencies developed through KTPs relate to innovation management. Shepherded by academics familiar with cutting-edge research, Associates learn to:

- identify opportunities for innovation
- translate research into commercial solutions
- design experiments and evaluate new technologies
- embed new processes within organisational routines
- navigate organisational resistance to change

These reflect competencies associated with an "entrepreneurial mindset," which the innovation literature identifies as essential to driving organisational transformation (Durmusoglu, 2004). Associates also gain experience in intellectual property (IP), market analysis, and business strategy, supporting broader commercial awareness.

4.3 Career Trajectories and Long-Term Employability Outcomes

Evidence from national KTP evaluations shows that Associates consistently experience strong employability outcomes. Although KTPs are not explicitly designed as graduate recruitment schemes, the Associate model functions as a high-impact professional accelerator.

High Employment and Retention Rates

A significant proportion of Associates transition into permanent roles within the host company, often in leadership or specialist positions. This reflects the company's recognition of the value created during the project and the advanced capability the Associate brings (Pates, 2023). Many companies develop new roles specifically tailored to the Associate's expertise, indicating long-term organisational transformation.

Accelerated Career Progression

Compared with graduates entering mainstream employment pathways, KTP Associates often progress more rapidly because they:

- gain managerial responsibility early in their careers
- lead projects with strategic organisational significance
- develop networks across academia and industry
- acquire rare expertise in innovation and technology

This aligns with Tomlinson's (2017) argument that graduates who accumulate strong social and cultural capital as well as technical capital are rewarded with enhanced mobility and career satisfaction.

Opportunities for Advanced Academic and Professional Qualifications

Associates frequently pursue:

- postgraduate degrees (e.g., MSc, MPhil, PhD)
- professional engineering or chartership status
- project management certifications
- publication of academic papers or conference presentations

Such accomplishments further strengthen their employability by signalling high-level analytical capability and commitment to continuous development.

Sectoral Mobility and Long-Term Impact

Longitudinal studies of university–industry collaboration highlight that individuals who work in hybrid roles often develop careers that span multiple sectors, contributing to innovation consultants, R&D managers, or technical specialists (Perkmann & Walsh, 2007). KTP Associates therefore represent important human capital assets whose careers amplify the wider impact of the scheme.

4.4 Comparison With Conventional Graduate Pathways

To understand the distinctive contribution of KTPs to employability, it is important to compare the model with more conventional graduate entry routes:

- Graduate schemes
- Traditional graduate schemes typically:
    - rotate participants through departments
    - provide structured training
    - focus on operational tasks and incremental responsibilities

While these schemes offer broad organisational exposure, they rarely include innovation-focused projects or access to academic mentorship. By contrast, KTPs position graduates immediately in roles of strategic importance. Associates undertake a single, significant project with long-term organisational value and receive training tailored to innovation, leadership, and technical advancement.

Internships and Placements

Internships often short-term and task-based provide work experience but limited strategic exposure. They rarely involve managerial responsibility or substantive research activity. KTPs provide multi-year, project-driven placements that embed graduates deeply within organisational processes and provide academic support.

Entry-Level Technical Roles

Many STEM graduates enter technical positions where responsibilities are largely predefined and linked to existing operational processes. KTPs differ by focusing on problem-solving, experimentation, and capability building elements associated with innovation careers rather than routine technical work.

Postgraduate Study Without Industry Engagement

Academic study develops analytical expertise but may leave graduates with limited understanding of commercial pressures, organisational cultures, or industry timelines. KTPs blend academic learning with real organisational challenges, strengthening both applied and conceptual knowledge.

Unique Advantages of KTPs

KTP Associates therefore benefit from:

- dual supervision (academic + industry)
- dedicated development budgets
- autonomy and leadership opportunities
- strategic, innovation-led work
- strong employability signals to future employers
- opportunities for advanced qualifications

In this sense, KTPs offer an employability pathway that is both deeper and broader than conventional graduate options, giving Associates access to research-informed innovation practice that few early-career roles provide.

4.5 Equity of Access and Distribution of Benefits

Equity concerns are central to the effectiveness and fairness of the KTP model. Although KTPs are theoretically accessible to all businesses, in practice, certain companies and universities are better positioned to benefit from the programme. Small and medium-sized enterprises (SMEs), particularly those without extensive R&D departments or strategic foresight, may face barriers to participation. These barriers include the complexity of the application process, the financial co-investment required, and the administrative capacity to manage a KTP project (Hughes & Kitson, 2012). As a result, larger companies with existing innovation infrastructures are more likely to benefit, while smaller or less resourceful companies may miss out on the programme's advantages.

Similarly, the programme tends to favour universities with strong research capabilities, established industry links, and dedicated knowledge exchange offices. Universities in regions with less economic or industrial activity may have fewer opportunities to engage with the KTP model, resulting in an uneven distribution of both knowledge and benefits across the country. This disparity can exacerbate existing inequalities, as companies in more economically disadvantaged areas are less likely to access the expertise that KTPs offer.

Equity issues also extend to graduate participation. KTP Associates are typically high-achieving graduates (completed their last degree within the last 5 years) with strong academic backgrounds and often prior industry experience. As a result, the benefits of KTP participation such as skill development, career progression, and long-term employability tend to favour those who are already in a privileged position within the labour market. This reinforces existing inequalities in graduate employment, as those from less privileged backgrounds or non-traditional educational pathways may find it more difficult to access KTP roles. Although the Associate role is intended to develop a broad range of competencies, the model may inadvertently favour graduates who already possess significant interdisciplinary skill sets.

Who Participates and Who Is Excluded?

Demographic Disparities in Associate Selection: Innovate UK stipulates that KTP "associates" must be recent graduates (within 5 Years of last degree completion). Although comprehensive demographic data for all KTP participants is limited, available evidence suggests noteworthy disparities:

Gender imbalances: A 2023 UKRI evaluation (Pates, 2023) found that among survey respondents, 89% of academic participants and 74% of KTP associates were male, indicating a strong gender skew within the scheme. This suggests that women may be underrepresented in KTP roles relative to broader graduate populations a pattern consistent with broader gender disparities seen in certain innovation and STEM contexts (Pates, 2023).

UK Research and Innovation: Lack of publicly available ethnicity and socioeconomic data: Innovate UK does collect EDI (equality, diversity, and inclusion) information on applicants' gender, age, ethnicity, and disability status as part of the application process, but these data are not widely published for the entire programme. This makes it difficult to draw robust conclusions about the representation of ethnic minorities or graduates from lower socioeconomic backgrounds within KTPs (Low, 2024).

Innovation Funding Service: External literature on UK higher education and STEM outcomes shows that ethnic minority students and those from disadvantaged backgrounds often face gaps in academic attainment and participation in elite technical fields, which in turn can influence their representation in innovation programmes such as KTPs (Low, 2024).

Regional Inequalities in KTP Distribution: The distribution of KTP activity reflects broader geographic imbalances in UK innovation processes:

- Urban and core regions dominate: Universities with strong research and industry linkages often located in England's core urban centres disproportionately host more KTPs. Institutions such as Queen's University Belfast and other Russell Group universities appear frequently as partners in high-profile KTP projects (Queen's University Belfast, 2025).
- Rural and peripheral areas lag: Regions with fewer research-intensive universities or limited industry R&D infrastructure may host fewer partnerships. This phenomenon mirrors the wider "innovation divide" between core urban areas with high institutional capacity and peripheral regions with lower engagement in innovation programmes. While specific KTP geographic data are not routinely published, national innovation studies indicate such rural–urban disparities in participation across UK research and innovation funding streams. Addressing these imbalances may require targeted outreach and capacity-building efforts to support knowledge exchange in underrepresented regions.

Sectoral Biases: STEM vs. Arts & Humanities: KTPs tend to skew towards sectors associated with science, technology, engineering, and mathematics (STEM) partly because many innovation challenges involve technological change and R&D investment:

- Eligibility criteria and sector emphasis: Innovate UK's funding priorities often align with industrial innovation, AI, advanced technologies, and productivity-related themes. Projects must meet sector eligibility criteria set out in rounds, which could unintentionally favour STEM-intensive partners (Digital, 2025).
- Underrepresentation in arts/humanities: Humanities and creative disciplines are less visible in KTP portfolios, despite their potential to contribute to innovation in cultural, social, and service sectors. While creative and societal innovation KTPs do exist, their relative rarity reflects a broader undervaluation of non-STEM knowledge in innovation policy discussions.

Encouraging cross-disciplinary KTPs in sectors such as cultural industries, social enterprise, and public service innovation by government funding agencies will broaden the reach and impact of the programme.

Equity Analysis: Literature-Based Insights: Although detailed disaggregated data on KTP participation remains limited, broader research on innovation and academic–industry partnerships inform the equity discussion:

- Structural barriers to participation: Innovation programmes often reflect existing inequalities in higher education and labour markets. Demographic groups with lower representation in higher education particularly in STEM fields are less likely to access graduate-level innovation roles like KTP associates. Studies show disparities in degree outcomes related to ethnicity, socioeconomic status, and gender are persistent in UK universities (Low, 2024).
- Network effects and resource asymmetries: Universities with dense industry networks and robust innovation support structures are more successful in securing KTPs, while institutions with less capacity struggle to engage. This institutional imbalance can perpetuate regional and sectoral inequalities.
- Inclusive partnership approaches: Literature on equitable academic partnerships (though often focused on global health or international collaboration) emphasises co-design, mutual benefit, and attention to power imbalances as essential for equity in partnership models. Such frameworks could inform enhancements to KTP processes, ensuring that all partners including underrepresented participants can influence project direction and outcomes (Modlin et al., 2025).

Policy Implications and Future Directions

To enhance equity and inclusion in KTPs, policymakers and programme administrators might consider:

- Publishing more comprehensive demographic participation data to track progress on EDI goals.
- Targeted outreach and support for underrepresented graduates (e.g., women, ethnic minorities, students from lower socioeconomic backgrounds) to increase the diversity of KTP associates.
- Geographic levelling-up initiatives to expand KTP engagement in rural and peripheral regions.
- Encouraging broader sectoral representation, including arts, humanities, and social innovation partnerships.

By addressing these equity dimensions, KTPs can better reflect the diversity of UK innovation talent and ensure that opportunities for knowledge transfer are accessible to a wider range of individuals and communities.

5.0 CRITICAL SUCCESS FACTORS AND CHALLENGES

Knowledge Transfer Partnerships (KTPs) have become a hallmark of successful university–industry collaboration, offering substantial benefits to companies, universities, and graduates. However, a closer examination of KTPs reveals critical factors that can limit their effectiveness and long-term impact. This section critically examines the power dynamics between KTP partners, issues of equity and access, and the unintended consequences that may arise from the model's implementation. By exploring cases of failure or limited impact, power imbalances, and inequitable distribution of benefits, this analysis provides a fuller understanding of KTPs and highlights areas for future improvement.

5.1 Projects With Limited Impact and Failure Cases

Despite the overall success of KTPs, not all projects lead to meaningful outcomes or lasting organisational transformation. Some companies may struggle to fully realise the potential benefits of the partnership, particularly when projects are narrowly defined, overly incremental, or disconnected from the company's long-term strategic goals. In some cases, the knowledge transfer process is insufficiently deep, with companies failing to embed innovations or new processes into their daily operations (Hoekman et al., 2010). This can occur when project timelines are too short for real organisational change to take root, or when senior management is not sufficiently engaged to ensure that KTP outputs are integrated into the company's culture.

Some companies pursue KTPs primarily to gain access to subsidised expertise, rather than to foster long-term innovation capacity. This instrumental approach can reduce the project to a transactional exchange, limiting its transformative potential. A critical factor in this is the company's absorptive capacity its ability to recognise, assimilate, and apply new knowledge (Cohen & Levinthal, 1990). When this capacity is low, even well-executed KTPs may fail to achieve sustained impact.

Similarly, universities may encounter challenges when supervising KTPs. If academic involvement becomes minimal or superficial, or if the university focuses more on short-term outputs than on deep, meaningful collaboration, the outcomes may be limited. For KTPs to succeed, the academic side must fully integrate with the commercial environment, but this integration requires a strong commitment from both parties.

5.2 Power Dynamics Between SMEs and Universities

One of the central challenges in KTPs lies in the power asymmetries that exist between SMEs and universities. Although KTPs are designed as collaborations between equals, in practice, universities often hold significant advantages. They control access to academic expertise, research resources, and grant funding, which can place SMEs at a disadvantage, particularly if they lack familiarity with academic culture or the administrative processes involved in securing and managing KTP projects (Perkmann et al., 2011).

This asymmetry can influence project outcomes in several ways. Universities may shape project goals to align with their academic priorities, potentially sidelining the immediate needs of the company. In cases where companies are less involved in defining the project scope, their strategic interests may not be fully reflected in the project's direction. Companies may defer to academic authority, particularly when they lack the expertise to critically assess research-driven approaches or methodologies. This can lead to misalignments between academic research agendas and the practical, market-driven needs of the company, hindering the effectiveness of the knowledge transfer process.

Some companies may assert too much control over the Associate, treating them as an employee rather than an innovation leader. This is particularly true when project managers or staff within the company are resistant to the changes or innovations proposed by the Associate. When power imbalances go unchecked, the Associate may be forced into a subordinate role, leading to disengagement and a dilution of the project's innovative potential. The importance of a boundary-spanning role for the Associate is emphasised in KTP literature, and the success of the project depends on the Associate's ability to navigate the tensions between academic rigor and commercial priorities (Hock-Doepgen et al., 2020).

5.3 Unintended Consequences and Broader Implications

While KTPs are designed to foster collaboration, innovation, and economic development, they can also produce unintended consequences. One potential unintended effect is the narrowing of academic research agendas. As universities strive to meet external demands for impact and commercial relevance, there is a risk that academic inquiry becomes more applied and less focused on fundamental research. This pressure to deliver commercial outcomes can shift the balance of academic work, emphasising short-term, applied research over long-term, curiosity-driven inquiry. This phenomenon has been noted in other research collaborations, where the pursuit of industry funding leads to a prioritisation of research topics that are directly marketable (Perkmann et al., 2011).

Another unintended consequence of the KTP model is the high level of responsibility placed on Associates. As boundary-spanning professionals, Associates are expected to manage projects, navigate complex organisational dynamics, and deliver significant innovation outcomes. While this offers valuable professional experience, it can also lead to role overload and burnout, particularly when Associates are expected to perform at the intersection of technical expertise, project management, and innovation leadership. This high level of responsibility can be particularly challenging in the absence of adequate support structures or mentoring from both the university and the company.

The KTP model can inadvertently reinforce a linear model of innovation, where universities are seen as knowledge producers and companies as mere recipients. This perception limits the recognition of co-creativity and mutual learning in the innovation process. Companies also contribute valuable industry insights, customer knowledge, and practical experience that should be integrated into the innovation process, yet these contributions may not always be adequately acknowledged in the KTP framework.

5.4 Reflections on Improving the KTP Model

Addressing these challenges requires a nuanced approach to KTP implementation. First, aligning expectations between universities and companies is crucial. Both parties should have a clear understanding of project goals, timelines, and deliverables from the outset. Ensuring that both academic and industrial participants are equally involved in shaping the project's direction will help reduce power imbalances and ensure that the project meets both research and commercial objectives.

Second, equity of access can be improved by simplifying the application process, providing additional support for underrepresented companies and universities, and designing targeted outreach initiatives to engage smaller or regional businesses. By lowering the barriers to entry, KTPs can become more inclusive and extend the benefits of knowledge transfer to a broader range of companies.

Universities must be aware of the impact of KTPs on academic freedom and ensure that the model does not constrain their capacity for fundamental research. Equally, greater support for Associates through mentoring, training, and clear role definitions can mitigate the risks associated with role overload and burnout. Through these adjustments, KTPs can continue to serve as a robust framework for university–industry collaboration while addressing the complexities and challenges inherent in multi-stakeholder partnerships.

5.5 Aligning Expectations and Timescales Across Partners

Divergent Motivations and Performance Expectations

The triadic nature of KTPs bringing together a university, a company, and a graduate Associate under a government-funded framework means that participant motivations are often heterogeneous. Universities tend to prioritise research translation, academic publication, and long-term relationships; companies prioritise commercial outcomes, rapid problem-solving, and market competitiveness; the Associate focuses on career development, professional learning, and innovation exposure (Pates, 2023). These differing priorities can create tensions if not managed proactively.

Research on collaboration barriers consistently highlights misaligned expectations as one of the most common constraints in university–industry partnerships (Bruneel et al., 2010). Companies may expect "ready-made" solutions, while academics emphasise methodological rigour, exploration, or long-term research questions. KTPs partially mitigate this through structured proposals and milestone planning, yet challenges remain when stakeholder expectations diverge over the pace or direction of the project.

Differences in Timescales

Another significant challenge stems from contrasting organisational rhythms. Universities often work on multi-year research cycles, peer-review processes, and academic term structures. Companies, particularly SMEs, operate in fast-moving markets requiring rapid returns on investment (Perkmann & Walsh, 2007). Government funding mechanisms introduce additional administrative timescales.

These differing temporal orientations can affect:

- decision-making speed
- tolerance for uncertainty
- rates of experimentation
- expectations for measurable project progression

Aligning these rhythms requires strong project management and open communication. Studies have shown that early clarification of timelines, deliverables, and interim goals is crucial for maintaining project momentum (Abreu et al., 2009).

Role of the Associate in Expectation Alignment

KTP Associates play a major role in bridging timescale tensions. Their boundary-spanning function helps synchronise academic and industrial expectations by translating academic insights into commercially meaningful activities and relaying company constraints to academic supervisors. Their project-management responsibilities also help maintain shared momentum. However, this bridging role requires Associates to develop sophisticated interpersonal and organisational abilities skills not always present at the start of the project highlighting the need for robust training and mentorship (Tomlinson, 2017).

5.6 Managing Intellectual Property, Project Governance, and Cultural Differences

Intellectual Property Management

Knowledge transfer initiatives frequently encounter challenges related to intellectual property ownership and exploitation. Research consistently shows that IP negotiation is one of the most common relational barriers between universities and companies (Bruneel et al., 2010; Perkmann & Walsh, 2007). Companies often seek exclusive rights to outputs to maintain competitive advantage, while universities balance commercial interests with academic openness.

KTPs generally include predefined IP frameworks, which simplify negotiation, yet disagreements may still arise when:

- project outcomes diverge from the initial plan
- new technologies emerge unexpectedly
- both partners contribute substantially to novel ideas
- commercialisation pathways are unclear

Clear IP arrangements from the outset and ongoing transparency are essential for maintaining trust and ensuring project continuity.

Project Governance

Effective governance mechanisms are a core factor in KTP success. The scheme's formal structure featuring steering group meetings, quarterly reviews, academic oversight, and Innovate UK monitoring supports accountability and reduces the risk of project drift. Literature on collaborative R&D emphasises that structured governance enhances transparency, resource allocation, and conflict resolution (Durmusoglu, 2004); Etzkowitz & Leydesdorff, 2000).

Challenges may arise when partners:

- fail to commit sufficient time to governance activities
- are inconsistently represented at meetings
- experience internal organisational restructuring
- shift strategic priorities mid-project

Sustained engagement from senior leadership in the company and committed academic input are critical success factors. Without them, Associates may be left working in isolation, reducing effectiveness and increasing project risk.

Cultural Differences Between Universities and Companies

Cultural differences represent one of the most widely cited challenges in university–industry partnerships. Universities often embody values associated with curiosity-driven inquiry, methodological depth, and long timelines. Companies, by contrast, prioritise efficiency, competitive advantage, and market responsiveness (Bruneel et al., 2010). These differences can manifest as misunderstandings around:

- acceptable levels of risk
- communication styles
- attitudes toward failure
- expectations for documentation, reporting, and quality assurance

Such cultural gaps can affect project cohesion unless proactively addressed. Research shows that trust-building, frequent communication, and mutual understanding of organisational cultures significantly enhance collaboration outcomes (Abreu et al., 2009).

5.7 Ensuring Sustainable Collaboration Beyond the Funded Period

Transitioning From Funded Project to Long-Term Partnership

A key aspiration of the KTP model is that the partnership continues beyond the funded period, sustaining innovation capability within the company and strengthening strategic engagement with the university. However, sustaining collaboration can be challenging.

Often, partnerships dissolve after funding ends due to:

- financial constraints
- shifts in company strategy
- staff turnover
- changes in academic research agendas

Sustained collaboration requires shared long-term interests. For universities, continued engagement supports research impact and opportunities for future funding; for companies, benefits include ongoing R&D support and access to cutting-edge expertise.

Absorptive Capacity and Organisational Readiness

A company's "absorptive capacity" its ability to recognise, assimilate, and apply new knowledge is a major determinant of whether collaboration endures (Bruneel et al., 2010). Companies with strong learning cultures and committed leadership are more likely to embed KTP insights into their organisational routines. Conversely, companies lacking such capacity may struggle to maintain momentum after project completion.

Retention of Associates

Retention of the KTP Associate plays a crucial role in sustaining collaboration. Many companies offer Associates permanent positions, ensuring continuity and preserving project knowledge. This retention strengthens R&D capability and facilitates future innovation collaboration with the partner university (Pates, 2023).

Institutionalising Relationships

Universities that integrate KTP outcomes into wider institutional strategies such as follow-on research proposals, consultancy, CPD programmes, and innovation networks are more successful in securing ongoing engagement. This aligns with the Triple Helix view of innovation process, where long-term relationships between academia, industry, and government drive systemic innovation (Etzkowitz & Leydesdorff, 2000).

5.8 Scaling KTPs Across Sectors and Regions

Sectoral Variation in Collaboration Readiness

Scaling KTPs across sectors requires consideration of varying levels of innovation maturity. Manufacturing, engineering, and technology sectors often have strong traditions of research collaboration, making them natural adopters of KTPs. Conversely, sectors such as creative industries, healthcare services, charities, or micro-businesses may have limited experience with structured innovation partnerships (Abreu et al., 2009).

Sector-specific challenges include:

- differing levels of technical sophistication
- variable strategic planning capabilities
- inconsistent R&D investment
- organisational cultures unfamiliar with academic collaboration

Targeted outreach, capacity building, and simplified KTP entry pathways can help broaden participation.

Regional Disparities in Innovation Capacity

Regional variation is an important challenge for scaling KTPs. Universities located in economically disadvantaged areas may work with companies that have lower innovation readiness or limited financial resources. However, these regions may also benefit the most from innovation-led development.

KTPs have demonstrated potential in supporting regional growth (Bascavusoglu-Moreau et al., 2013), yet scaling requires:

- targeted funding
- regional university networks
- local innovation framework (clusters, science parks, incubators)
- government support for capacity building

In this respect, KTPs align well with UK policy objectives around levelling-up and distributed R&D investment.

Administrative, Funding, and Capacity Constraints

Scaling KTPs also involves overcoming administrative burdens. The application process, while designed to ensure rigour, can be challenging for smaller companies with limited bid-writing experience. Universities also face capacity constraints in terms of academic time, internal KTP offices, and support infrastructure. Greater administrative simplification and digitalisation may help scale participation without reducing quality.

Building National and Sectoral Centres

Finally, scaling requires sectoral-level thinking. KTPs can contribute to national innovation system strengthening when embedded within:

- regional clusters
- sectoral innovation strategies
- national industrial strategies
- university innovation portfolios

Such systemic integration amplifies the benefits of individual projects and promotes broader diffusion of research-informed innovation practices.

5.9 Future Directions and Enhancing the KTP Model

As KTPs continue to evolve, there are several ways in which the model can be strengthened to better reflect the complexities of modern innovation processes. One potential enhancement for KTPs is a deeper integration with the Quadruple and Quintuple Helix models, particularly by embedding civil society and environmental considerations into the partnership framework. This could involve:

- Encouraging collaborations with social enterprises or NGOs to tackle pressing societal challenges.
- Promoting projects with a sustainability focus, aligning with global environmental objectives.

Establishing social innovation initiatives that involve local communities in the development of new technologies and processes. By fostering more inclusive, socially responsible innovation, KTPs can contribute to broader societal goals, ensuring that the benefits of innovation reach beyond the commercial and academic sectors.

Strengthening Cross-Sectoral and Global Collaboration

KTPs can also benefit from internationalisation and cross-sectoral collaboration. Extending the model globally would allow companies and universities to engage with international innovation processes, enhancing the diffusion of knowledge across borders.

Multidisciplinary collaborations involving fields like social sciences, arts, and humanities could drive more holistic and socially relevant innovations. By expanding KTPs to incorporate global knowledge exchange and cross-sectoral innovation, the programme could further strengthen its role in addressing complex, multi-dimensional challenges, from climate change to health inequities.

6.0 POLICY AND STRATEGIC IMPLICATIONS

Knowledge Transfer Partnerships (KTPs) represent one of the most successful long-standing innovation programmes in the United Kingdom, blending government policy goals with university research capabilities and industry needs. As the pace of technological change accelerates and global competition intensifies, the strategic value of university–industry collaboration models like KTP becomes more pronounced. This section examines the broader implications of the KTP experience for government policy, university strategy, industry capability building, and global adoption. The analysis highlights how KTPs offer lessons for designing scalable innovation processes, enhancing graduate employability, and strengthening the capacity of companies and regions to adapt to technological and economic transformation.

6.1 Lessons for Governments Designing Innovation Programmes

Designing Balanced, Triadic Innovation Frameworks

KTPs are widely recognised for their ability to integrate policy objectives with academic expertise and industrial needs (Pates, 2023). The scheme's structure requiring active participation from universities, industry, and a government funder embodies the core principles of the Triple Helix model (Etzkowitz & Leydesdorff, 2000). Policymakers in other contexts can draw from this in designing innovation schemes that promote shared ownership and distributed responsibility rather than centralised, top-down interventions.

This triadic structure has several policy advantages:

- Risk-sharing: Funding is distributed between public agencies and companies, lowering barriers for smaller businesses.
- Outcome diversification: Companies gain innovation capacity, universities achieve impact, and government objectives such as productivity and skills development are advanced simultaneously.
- Built-in accountability: Formal oversight mechanisms ensure project monitoring and evaluation.

Integrating Innovation and Workforce Development

One of the unique strengths of the KTP programme is its simultaneous focus on innovation outcomes and human capital development. While many government innovation schemes emphasise technological outcomes, KTP explicitly embeds a graduate Associate within the company, accelerating talent development while driving organisational change.

This integration aligns with evidence showing that innovation capacity is tightly coupled with workforce skills and absorptive capacity (Bruneel et al., 2010). Governments designing similar schemes should therefore consider embedding training and experiential learning into innovation policy, avoiding the artificial separation between industrial policy and skills policy.

Supporting SMEs Through Capability-Building Mechanisms

Small and medium-sized enterprises (SMEs), which often lack formal R&D infrastructure, benefit disproportionately from KTPs ((Bascavusoglu-Moreau et al., 2013). The structured support, academic supervision, and Associate-led project management help SMEs overcome barriers common in innovation policy such as limited strategic planning capability, risk aversion, and lack of technical expertise.

For policymakers, the key lesson is that capability-building programmes are more effective than simple grant mechanisms. KTP demonstrates that embedding expertise within companies, combined with academic input and continuous monitoring, can significantly strengthen SME competitiveness.

Data-Driven Programme Evaluation

Government bodies overseeing KTPs (historically Innovate UK and the Economic and Social Research Council) have invested in systematic monitoring and evaluation. This aligns with growing calls in innovation policy for evidence-based practice and adaptive policymaking. Governments seeking to emulate the KTP model should adopt similar evaluation frameworks that capture not only economic returns, but also:

- capacity building
- skills development
- cultural change
- long-term collaboration pathways

Such multidimensional metrics are increasingly recognised as essential for assessing innovation performance (Perkmann et al., 2011).

6.2 Integrating KTP Learning into University Curriculum and Employability Strategies

Embedding Real-World Innovation Learning Into Curriculam

KTPs offer universities rich insights into contemporary industrial challenges, emerging technologies, and applied problem-solving methods. These insights can contribute towards enhanced curriculum relevance. For example:

- Case studies from KTP projects can be embedded into teaching modules.
- Industry-generated challenges can inform project-based learning.
- Academic supervisors can feed practical innovation experiences back into pedagogical design.

This aligns with literature emphasising that authentic, work-based learning significantly enhances students' employability and innovation skills (Tomlinson, 2017).

Strategic Alignment With Employability Agendas

Universities increasingly prioritise employability metrics as part of national performance frameworks. KTPs contribute to these agendas in several ways:

- Associates gain advanced technical, managerial, and innovation skills.
- Many Associates are offered full-time employment by partner companies.
- The programme provides structured leadership and professional development.

These outcomes align with research emphasising the importance of hybrid graduate identities that span technical expertise, problem-solving, and interpersonal capabilities (Tomlinson, 2017). Universities can strengthen employability strategies by establishing clearer pathways from undergraduate studies into KTP roles or other collaborative graduate placements.

Building institution-wide innovation capability

The KTP model also supports university strategies for research impact, external engagement, and knowledge exchange. Lessons from KTPs can inform the development of:

- interdisciplinary innovation centres
- enterprise curricula
- practice-based postgraduate programmes
- regional innovation networks

Universities that treat KTPs as integral to their engagement model rather than isolated projects can build institutional capacity for long-term industrial relationships and translational research.

6.3 How Industry Can Utilise KTPs to Build Innovation Capability and Talent Pipelines

Embedding boundary-spanning talent

Companies participating in KTPs benefit from the embedded Associate, who serves as a boundary-spanner between academic knowledge and industrial application. This arrangement supports not only the immediate project but also long-term organisational capability building. Research has shown that such boundary-spanning roles are critical for enabling companies to absorb external knowledge (Bruneel et al., 2010).

By retaining Associates after the project period, companies can internalise new competencies and strengthen their future R&D capacity. Many companies report that Associates become future innovation leaders, an outcome consistent with organisational learning theory.

Developing Structured Innovation Processes

The KTP framework with its milestones, academic oversight, and monitoring introduces structured project management practices into organisations that may lack formal innovation systems. For SMEs in particular, this can be transformative. Companies often adopt new routines such as:

- innovation road mapping
- systematic experimentation

- data-driven decision-making
- formal R&D strategies

These capabilities persist long after the project concludes, supporting sustained growth and competitiveness.

Strengthening Strategic Collaboration Networks

KTP participation often leads companies to deepen their engagement with universities through follow-on research projects, consultancy, student placements, and co-development of training programmes. Such networks increase access to emerging technologies, specialised equipment, and academic expertise, enhancing long-term resilience and adaptability (Perkmann et al., 2011). For companies, KTPs serve as a gateway into broader innovation strategies.

6.4 Opportunities for Global Adoption or Localisation of the KTP Model

Growing Global Interest in University–Industry Collaboration Models

As countries seek to strengthen innovation capacity, models like KTP are increasingly considered internationally. Governments in Asia, Africa, Europe, and Latin America have expressed interest in adapting the scheme to local contexts. This reflects global recognition of the role of university–industry collaboration in fostering knowledge-based economic development.

The KTP model's strengths triadic collaboration, structured governance, talent development, and applied research translation make it an appealing template. However, global adoption requires careful localisation.

Adapting to Diverse Institutional and Economic Environments

Countries differ in their higher education systems, industrial maturity, innovation cultures, and policy frameworks. Localisation may require adjustments in:

- funding ratios between government and industry
- project durations
- governance mechanisms
- Associate training models
- sectoral focus areas

For example, countries with emerging industrial sectors may emphasise capability building, whereas advanced economies may focus on frontier technological innovation.

Utilising Global Triple Helix Strategies

The Triple Helix framework underscores the need for dynamic interactions between universities, industry, and government to drive innovation (Etzkowitz & Leydesdorff, 2000). KTPs provide a practical, operationalised form of this theory. International adoption can therefore contribute to strengthening global innovation frameworks and encourage cross-border collaboration.

Potential for International KTP-Like Networks

As global challenges increasingly require transnational cooperation such as climate change, digital transformation, and health innovation there is scope for developing international KTP-style collaborations. Such networks could:

- connect universities and companies across borders
- support cross-cultural innovation teams
- build shared talent pipelines
- enable technology diffusion across markets

This opens an avenue for policy experimentation and global knowledge exchange. Similar programs exist in other countries, each shaped by their unique national contexts. Understanding how KTP compares with international schemes such as the German Fraunhofer Society and Canada's MITACS program provides valuable insights into the strengths, challenges, and potential areas for adaptation in the UK model. Additionally, examining transnational networks and partnerships, such as those fostered by the European Union (EU) and Commonwealth programs, helps identify broader opportunities for cross-border collaboration.

Comparative Analysis of UK KTPs and International Models

Table 1 below shows a comparison between the UK's KTP with two well-established international models, Fraunhofer (Germany) and MITACS (Canada) across key dimensions such as funding, intellectual property (IP) regimes, and cultural adaptation challenges.

Table 1. Comparative Analysis of UK KTPs and International Models

Aspect	UK KTP	German Fraunhofer Society	Canadian MITACS
Mission and Focus	Strengthen ties between academia and industry by placing academic associates in companies to solve business problems and foster innovation.	Applied research institute with a focus on industrial collaboration, innovation, and commercialisation. Primarily works through institutes for R&D and technological solutions.	Promote graduate research and innovation by connecting students with industry partners through internships, fellowships, and collaborative projects.
Funding Model	Co-funded by business and Innovate UK, with government covering up to 67% of associate's salary, depending on company size.	Funded by the German government and industry. Fraunhofer institutes are largely self-sustaining, relying on project-based revenue and government grants.	Funding provided by the Canadian government (via MITACS), industry partners, and universities. Mitacs offers internships and fellowships for students, with co-funding from industry and government.
IP Regime	IP typically remains with the company, though joint ownership can be negotiated. KTP also encourages open innovation.	IP generated is shared between Fraunhofer and the company, with detailed agreements on commercialisation rights.	IP is generally owned by the company or the academic institution, depending on the nature of the partnership. Mitacs ensures the academic participant is involved in dissemination.
Cultural Context	Innovation processes are heavily influenced by collaboration between academia, government, and businesses, with an increasing focus on interdisciplinary approaches.	The Fraunhofer model is deeply embedded in Germany's technological and engineering-driven culture, with a focus on precision engineering and applied R&D.	Canada's culture of collaboration and inclusive research fosters partnerships between industry, academia, and the public sector. The program is particularly focused on social and community innovation alongside STEM.
Adaptation Challenges	Funding constraints for smaller businesses; evolving IP policies; balancing academic rigor with industry relevance.	Integration with industry needs: Fraunhofer often faces challenges in adapting its applied research model to different sectors.	Cultural fit: Challenges around integrating diverse academic disciplines, ensuring partnerships are not limited to traditional STEM sectors.
Global Reach and Collaboration	KTP has a domestic focus but often collaborates with international entities through EU-funded projects or global supply chains.	Fraunhofer institutes collaborate internationally, particularly within the EU, leveraging Europe's R&D funding and research networks.	MITACS focuses on Canada-US partnerships but also has global reach via collaborations with institutions in Europe, Asia, and the Americas.
Sectoral Representation	Strong in STEM, but increasingly broadening into social sciences and creative industries.	Primarily focused on STEM (engineering, physics, technology). The arts and humanities are underrepresented.	Includes a broader range of sectoral representation, with an increasing focus on social innovation, policy research, and arts and humanities alongside STEM.
International Linkages	Participates in EU-funded networks (e.g., Horizon 2020); emerging partnerships within the Commonwealth.	Strong European and international partnerships, especially through the EU and research consortia.	Active in global networks, especially in North America (US, Mexico) and Asia (China, India).

Analysis of Adaptation Challenges in Different National Contexts

The adaptation of KTP-style models across countries presents both opportunities and challenges. While the underlying principles of linking academic research with industry needs remain consistent, several factors influence the success and scalability of these models in different national contexts:

Funding Models and Sustainability

- KTP (UK): The reliance on co-funding between government and business can be a barrier for smaller companies, which might not have the capacity to contribute to the funding required for such partnerships. Additionally, funding cuts during economic downturns can impact the sustainability of the program.
- Fraunhofer (Germany): The self-sustaining model of Fraunhofer, with a combination of government grants and industry revenues, allows for greater flexibility but also means that its institutes need to constantly find new projects and clients. Project-based funding can create pressure to align research agendas with market-driven demands.
- MITACS (Canada): Canada's funding model relies heavily on the government and industry, with university participants receiving stipends or salaries, sometimes creating a mismatch between academic goals and industry demands. The program's reliance on industry partners for co-funding can be challenging, especially for small or emerging businesses.

Intellectual Property (IP) and Commercialisation

- KTP (UK): The UK's model often leaves IP rights with the company, which can foster a strong connection between business outcomes and the academic output. However, there is concern that IP ownership might limit the academic freedom of researchers, potentially discouraging open innovation and the sharing of research outcomes.
- Fraunhofer (Germany): The shared IP model is widely accepted in Germany's industrial culture, but it can sometimes complicate the commercialisation process, as both public and private stakeholders may need to reach consensus on how research results are marketed and distributed.
- MITACS (Canada): MITACS' approach to IP is flexible, but ensuring that academic partners are involved in dissemination and commercialisation while maintaining ownership of the IP is critical to its success. Canadian institu-

tions are also increasingly considering open-access and open-source models, which could be at odds with industry's desire for proprietary solutions.

Sectoral and Cultural Adaptation

- KTP (UK): Traditionally, KTPs have been dominated by STEM fields, with creative industries and social sciences only more recently entering the fold. There are sectoral biases that still need addressing, as the model does not always accommodate the flexibility or creative approaches often seen in non-STEM disciplines.
- Fraunhofer (Germany): The strong engineering culture in Germany drives the focus on applied research in technology, manufacturing, and engineering. However, arts and humanities are typically underrepresented in the Fraunhofer model, reflecting a bias towards technological solutions.
- MITACS (Canada): MITACS is comparatively more inclusive, with a growing emphasis on social innovation, public policy, and even the arts. While this broadens the scope of the programme, it also creates challenges in maintaining coherence across projects that may not all conform to the traditional industry-driven goals of innovation.

Transnational KTP-Style Networks

Transnational collaboration through KTP-style networks is increasingly important, particularly in the context of EU partnerships and Commonwealth programs. These partnerships facilitate cross-border collaboration, knowledge sharing, and the potential for scalability:

- EU Partnerships: Programs like Horizon Europe encourage knowledge transfer across borders, where KTPs can play a significant role in strengthening transnational innovation opportunities. UK-based KTPs, especially those in European collaboration, benefit from EU funding and networks, although post-Brexit, the UK's engagement in such programs has become more complicated.
- Commonwealth Programs: The Commonwealth Innovation and Knowledge Transfer Programs promote collaboration between member states, allowing for shared innovation practices, particularly in developing countries that face different resource constraints than wealthier nations. These programs have the potential to introduce KTP-style models to regions with less-developed innovation infrastructures.

KTPs have proven to be an effective model for connecting academia with industry in the UK. However, by comparing KTP with other international schemes like Fraunhofer (Germany) and MITACS (Canada), it becomes clear that each model reflects distinct national priorities, funding structures, IP regimes, and cultural contexts. The internationalisation of KTPs, particularly through EU networks and Commonwealth collaborations, presents exciting opportunities for global knowledge exchange but also brings challenges related to governance, funding, and cultural adaptation.

KTPs and Net-Zero Transition

The drive towards a net-zero carbon economy the reduction of greenhouse gas emissions to zero by 2050 in the UK presents one of the most significant global challenges. KTPs can play a pivotal role in facilitating this transition by fostering innovation in low-carbon technologies, energy efficiency, and sustainable business practices.

- Decarbonisation of Industry: KTPs can support businesses in reducing their carbon footprints by embedding environmental innovation into manufacturing processes, energy systems, and supply chains. For instance, partnerships between universities and SMEs (small and medium-sized enterprises) in sectors like construction, transport, and energy can lead to the development of cleaner technologies, energy-efficient buildings, and sustainable mobility solutions.
- Renewable Energy and Energy Storage: Research from academic institutions can be transferred into practical applications in renewable energy generation (solar, wind, hydropower) and energy storage technologies (e.g., battery storage solutions). A KTP collaboration in this area could support the development of next-generation batteries, energy management systems, and smart grids, which are essential for the success of a net-zero economy.
- Green Innovation in SMEs: As many small businesses and start-ups struggle with the capital and expertise required for green transitions, KTPs can provide essential support by offering expertise from academic partners to enable companies to adopt sustainable technologies. KTPs can thus accelerate the adoption of green practices and innovation, helping to meet national climate change targets while driving economic growth.

KTPs and Health Resilience

The COVID-19 pandemic highlighted the importance of building health resilience, not only in terms of immediate crisis response but also for long-term improvements in public health systems. KTPs can be a critical mechanism for improving health-care delivery, health technologies, and public health management to create more resilient health systems.

- Healthcare Innovation: KTPs are already fostering medical technologies that improve patient care, from telemedicine platforms to AI-powered diagnostic tools. By integrating cutting-edge academic research with the needs of healthcare providers, KTPs can accelerate the development of healthcare solutions that respond to evolving health challenges.
- Public Health and Social Care: KTPs also enable partnerships in the social care sector, helping to develop technological solutions that improve the efficiency and effectiveness of care systems, particularly in the context of aging populations and chronic disease management. For instance, innovations in assistive technologies (e.g., remote monitoring tools, personalised care plans) can significantly improve the lives of vulnerable groups, while data-driven solutions can optimise resource allocation in social care settings.
- Global Health Resilience: KTPs can facilitate international collaborations that support global health resilience, particularly in low- and middle-income countries. Through knowledge sharing and capacity-building, KTPs can help implement effective disease prevention measures and enhance public health infrastructures in a way that is sustainable and scalable.

KTPs and Levelling Up

The UK government's levelling-up agenda focuses on reducing regional inequalities and ensuring that every part of the country has the resources, infrastructure, and opportunities to thrive. KTPs can contribute significantly to this goal by ensuring that economic opportunities and innovation capabilities are more evenly distributed across the country, including in rural and deprived areas.

- Regional Innovation Hubs: KTPs can act as catalysts for building innovation hubs in regions outside the traditional urban centres, particularly in the North, Midlands, and Southwest. By connecting businesses in these regions with academic institutions, KTPs enable knowledge transfer that can drive local economic growth, skills development, and the creation of new high-tech industries, helping to rebalance the UK economy

- Skills Development and Job Creation: One of the most direct ways KTPs contribute to levelling up is by supporting skills development and job creation in areas of high unemployment or economic deprivation. Through KTPs, local companies can access highly-skilled graduates, thereby enhancing their workforce capabilities. The academic partners also gain valuable insights into the needs of regional industries, which can inform the development of new, sector-specific training programs. In turn, KTPs help create high-value jobs that are more likely to remain in local communities.
- Bridging the Urban-Rural Divide: KTPs can help bridge the urban-rural divide by providing smaller businesses in rural areas with the support and resources they need to innovate and grow. For example, businesses in sectors like agriculture, clean tech, or tourism can partner with academic institutions to develop innovative products and services that enhance local economies, improve sustainability, and attract investment to more peripheral regions.

7.0 CONCLUSION

KTPs are an underutilised but highly effective mechanism for addressing some of the most pressing challenges in industries that lack new knowledge. From accelerating the transition to a net-zero economy to strengthening health resilience and driving regional levelling-up, KTPs can make a significant contribution to sustainable development, social equity, and economic regeneration. By encouraging interdisciplinary collaborations between academia, businesses, and public institutions, KTPs provide the expertise and innovation needed to tackle these global challenges, while simultaneously fostering growth in underserved regions and sectors.

Policy Roadmap for Scaling and Adapting KTPs

To fully realise the potential of Knowledge Transfer Partnerships (KTPs) in addressing pressing national challenges such as net-zero, health resilience, and regional levelling up, a clear policy roadmap is essential. The following actionable steps provide a framework for scaling and adapting KTPs to maximise their impact governments should:

- Expand KTP Eligibility Criteria: Broaden the scope of KTPs, eligibility should be expanded beyond traditional STEM sectors to include a greater variety of creative industries, social sciences, and public sector innovations. This would ensure that KTPs capture a wider range of interdisciplinary collaborations that are crucial for addressing societal challenges.

- Enhance Regional Engagement: Focus on “levelling up” by creating targeted incentives for businesses and academic institutions in underserved and peripheral regions. Local government and regional innovation hubs can partner with universities to regionalise KTPs, ensuring that opportunities for innovation and skills development are more evenly distributed across the UK.
- Increase Funding Flexibility: Adapt KTP funding models to accommodate small businesses and emerging sectors. This could involve providing scaled funding options based on the size of the company or the complexity of the project, ensuring that innovative SMEs are not excluded from participation due to financial constraints.
- Support Cross-Border Collaboration: Develop transnational KTP-style networks by fostering partnerships between UK KTPs and international innovation opportunities (e.g., EU and Commonwealth programs). This would promote cross-border knowledge exchange, particularly in emerging fields such as green technologies and global health innovation.
- Utilise authentic AI and Digital Tools: Incorporate advanced digital tools and AI-driven innovations to streamline project management, knowledge transfer, and monitoring processes. AI simulation, data analytics, and cloud-based platforms can improve collaboration, track project outcomes in real-time, and enable more efficient scaling of KTPs.
- Strengthen Monitoring and Evaluation: Develop more robust frameworks for monitoring and evaluating KTP outcomes, particularly in terms of long-term social and economic impacts. Tracking not just financial returns but also societal benefits (e.g., improved health outcomes, reduced carbon footprints) will provide a clearer picture of KTPs' value proposition.
- Foster Inclusion and Diversity: Implement policies that prioritise equity and inclusion within KTPs by addressing demographic disparities in associate selection, creating pathways for underrepresented groups in business and academia, and offering additional support for businesses in underserved communities.

By following this roadmap, policymakers can help scale up and adapt KTPs to meet evolving national and global needs, ensuring that knowledge transfer remains a dynamic force for innovation, economic growth, and societal benefit.

KTPs as a Future-Ready Collaboration Framework

Knowledge Transfer Partnerships (KTPs) have emerged as one of the most robust and effective mechanisms for fostering collaboration between universities, industry, and government. Over several decades, the KTP model has demonstrated its ability to simultaneously drive company-level innovation, enhance graduate employability, and strengthen broader economic resilience. This concluding section synthesises the key contributions of KTPs, highlights their role in developing knowledge-driven economies, and provides recommendations for enhancing and expanding the model in the future.

Recommendations for Enhancing and Expanding the Model

While KTPs have demonstrated substantial success, there are opportunities to enhance and expand the model to maximise future impact. The following recommendations focus on strategic, operational, and policy dimensions:

- Strengthen alignment between partners: Ensuring clarity in roles, responsibilities, and expectations is critical to KTP success. Future iterations of the programme could further standardise processes for setting objectives, defining deliverables, and managing timelines. Enhanced communication frameworks and structured onboarding processes for Associates can facilitate smoother collaboration and reduce the risk of misalignment between universities and companies.
- Expand sectoral and regional reach: Although KTPs have traditionally been concentrated in sectors with established R&D capacity, there is scope to extend the model to emerging industries, creative sectors, and underserved regions. Tailoring the programme to the specific needs of these sectors including adapting funding structures, training, and project timelines could broaden the impact of KTPs, stimulate regional economic growth, and support inclusive innovation processes.
- Enhance graduate development and career pathways: The KTP Associate role is a powerful platform for graduate employability, but additional support could further enhance its value. This could include structured mentorship programmes, access to advanced professional development opportunities, and the development of alumni networks to facilitate ongoing learning and career progression. Creating pathways for Associates to move between companies and sectors could also strengthen the transfer of knowledge and skills across the economy.
- Promote sustainability and long-term collaboration: A key challenge is ensuring that partnerships remain productive beyond the funded period. Governments, universities, and companies should explore mechanisms to institutionalise relationships, including frameworks for follow-on projects, joint research initiatives, and knowledge-sharing networks. Embedding KTP

principles into organisational culture can help companies sustain innovation capacity and maintain ongoing engagement with academic partners.

- Utilise digital technologies and AI for scalability: Digital platforms can support the management, monitoring, and evaluation of KTP projects, making the programme more accessible and scalable. Virtual collaboration tools, data-sharing platforms, and online training modules can enhance knowledge transfer, facilitate multi-site partnerships, and enable greater participation from geographically dispersed partners.
- Explore global adaptation and collaboration: KTPs provide a model that can inform international innovation policy. Governments and institutions worldwide can adapt the core principles of the programme to local contexts, creating similar schemes that integrate universities, industry, and government to drive innovation and workforce development. Cross-border adaptations could also support international collaboration, global knowledge exchange, and the development of shared talent pipelines.

KTPs exemplify a future-ready collaboration framework that integrates innovation, talent development, and systemic economic resilience. By embedding highly skilled graduates into companies and linking them with university expertise under government-supported frameworks, KTPs generate tangible innovation outcomes, build organisational capabilities, and cultivate a new generation of industry-ready leaders. The model demonstrates that structured, triadic partnerships can simultaneously meet the needs of multiple stakeholders while contributing to broader societal and economic goals.

As the pace of AI technological change accelerates and economies become increasingly knowledge-driven, the KTP approach offers a blueprint for sustainable innovation and workforce development. By enhancing alignment among partners, expanding sectoral reach, deepening graduate development, promoting long-term collaboration, utilising digital technologies, and exploring global adaptation, KTPs can continue to serve as a cornerstone of resilient, knowledge-based economies. Ultimately, the programme's success lies not only in the projects completed or products developed but in its enduring contribution to human capital, organisational learning, and systemic innovation.

REFERENCES

Abreu, M., Grinevich, V., Hughes, A., & Kitson, M. (2009). Knowledge exchange between academics and the business, public and third sectors. In *ePrints Soton (University of Southampton)*. https://eprints.soton.ac.uk/357117/1/AcademicSurveyReport.pdf

Bascavusoglu-Moreau, E., Mina, A., & Hughes, A. (2013). Exploiting Knowledge Flows: Openness and the innovative performance of Business Services. *Proceedings - Academy of Management, 2013*(1), 13887. DOI: 10.5465/ambpp.2013.188

Bertoletti, A., & Johnes, G. (2021). Efficiency in university-industry collaboration: An analysis of UK higher education institutions. *Scientometrics, 126*(9), 7679–7714. DOI: 10.1007/s11192-021-04076-w

Bruneel, J., D'Este, P., & Salter, A. (2010). Investigating the factors that diminish the barriers to university–industry collaboration. *Research Policy, 39*(7), 858–868. DOI: 10.1016/j.respol.2010.03.006

Cohen, W. M., & Levinthal, D. A. (1990). Absorptive Capacity: A new perspective on learning and innovation. *Administrative Science Quarterly, 35*(1), 128. DOI: 10.2307/2393553

Digital. (2025, December 11). *Home - Innovate UK Business Connect*. Innovate UK Business Connect. https://iuk-business-connect.org.uk/

Dodgson, M. (1991). Technology learning, technology strategy and competitive pressures. *British Journal of Management, 2*(3), 133–149. DOI: 10.1111/j.1467-8551.1991.tb00022.x

Durmusoglu, S. S. (2004). Open Innovation: The New Imperative for Creating and Profiting from Technology. *European Journal of Innovation Management, 7*(4), 325–326. DOI: 10.1108/14601060410565074

Etzkowitz, H., & Leydesdorff, L. (2000). The dynamics of innovation: From National Systems and "Mode 2" to a Triple Helix of university–industry–government relations. *Research Policy, 29*(2), 109–123. DOI: 10.1016/S0048-7333(99)00055-4

Hock-Doepgen, M., Clauss, T., Kraus, S., & Cheng, C. (2020). Knowledge management capabilities and organizational risk-taking for business model innovation in SMEs. *Journal of Business Research, 130*, 683–697. DOI: 10.1016/j.jbusres.2019.12.001

Hoekman, J., Frenken, K., & Tijssen, R. J. (2010). Research collaboration at a distance: Changing spatial patterns of scientific collaboration within Europe. *Research Policy, 39*(5), 662–673. DOI: 10.1016/j.respol.2010.01.012

Howells, J. (2006). Intermediation and the role of intermediaries in innovation. *Research Policy, 35*(5), 715–728. DOI: 10.1016/j.respol.2006.03.005

Hughes, A., & Kitson, M. (2012). Pathways to impact and the strategic role of universities: New evidence on the breadth and depth of university knowledge exchange in the UK and the factors constraining its development. *Cambridge Journal of Economics, 36*(3), 723–750. DOI: 10.1093/cje/bes017

Lam, A. (2010). From 'Ivory Tower traditionalists' to 'Entrepreneurial scientists'? *Social Studies of Science, 40*(2), 307–340. DOI: 10.1177/0306312709349963

Low, A. M. (2024). Predictors and Socio-Demographic Disparities in STEM Degree Outcomes: A UK Longitudinal Study using Hierarchical Logistic Regression. *arXiv (Cornell University).* https://doi.org//arxiv.2408.05853DOI: 10.48550

Modlin, C. E., Shrestha, P., Chang, L. W., Ali, J., Sewankambo, N. K., & Wonodi, C. (2025). A scoping review of equity toolkits for international academic partnerships. *International Journal for Equity in Health, 24*(1), 268. DOI: 10.1186/s12939-025-02632-x PMID: 41088304

Pates, R. (2023). *Knowledge transfer partnerships evaluation* [Report]. https://www.ukri.org/wp-content/uploads/2023/10/IUK-23102023-KTP-Evaluation-Final-Report-FINAL-Aug-23.pdf

Perkmann, M., Neely, A., & Walsh, K. (2011). How should firms evaluate success in university–industry alliances? A performance measurement system. *R & D Management, 41*(2), 202–216. DOI: 10.1111/j.1467-9310.2011.00637.x

Perkmann, M., & Walsh, K. (2007). University–industry relationships and open innovation: Towards a research agenda. *International Journal of Management Reviews, 9*(4), 259–280. DOI: 10.1111/j.1468-2370.2007.00225.x

Queen's University Belfast. (2025, June 23). Queen's Marks 50 years of Knowledge Transfer Partnerships (KTP). *Business | Queen's University Belfast.* https://www.qub.ac.uk/Business/access-our-expertise/Knowledge-Transfer-Partnerships/news/queens-marks-50-years-of-knowledge-transfer-partnerships.html

Rasmussen, E., & Wright, M. (2015). How can universities facilitate academic spin-offs? An entrepreneurial competency perspective. *The Journal of Technology Transfer, 40*(5), 782–799. DOI: 10.1007/s10961-014-9386-3

Senker, P., & Senker, J. (1994). Transferring technology and expertise from universities to industry: Britain's Teaching Company Scheme. *New Technology, Work and Employment*, *9*(2), 81–92. DOI: 10.1111/j.1468-005X.1994.tb00052.x

Szulanski, G. (1996). Exploring internal stickiness: Impediments to the transfer of best practice within the firm. *Strategic Management Journal*, *17*(S2), 27–43. DOI: 10.1002/smj.4250171105

Tomlinson, M. (2017). Forms of graduate capital and their relationship to graduate employability. *Education + Training*, *59*(4), 338–352. DOI: 10.1108/ET-05-2016-0090

Wilson, T. (2012). *A Review of Business–University Collaboration* (By University of Hertfordshire, Higher Education Funding Council for England, Department for Business Innovation & Skills, University of Brighton, IT & Telecommunications Industry, GlaxoSmithKline, University of Central Lancashire, University of Exeter, Southampton Solent University, University College London, University of Oxford, Teesside University, Aston University, Surrey University, University of Nottingham, New College Durham, Higher Education Funding Council for England, BAE Systems, HECSU, . . . Enterprise Rent-A-Car). https://assets.publishing.service.gov.uk/media/5a796c56e5274a2acd18cb62/12-610-wilson-review-business-university-collaboration.pdf

Chapter 2

Computational Modeling of Innovation: A Quintuple Helix Simulation Approach

Célia M. Q. Ramos
https://orcid.org/0000-0002-3413-4897
ESGHT, CinTurs, Universidade do Algarve, Portugal

ABSTRACT

Quintuple Helix Innovation Theory (QHIT) conceptualizes innovation as the outcome of synergistic interactions among five key subsystems: academia, government, industry, civil society, and the natural environment. Extending beyond the Triple Helix's focus on academia-driven growth and the Quadruple Helix's incorporation of sustainability, the QHIT framework positions environmental sustainability as integral to long-term societal resilience, resonating with the principles of Society 5.0. Operationalizing this model necessitates the development of digitally enabled, collaborative ecosystems capable of generating socio-economic value through integrated knowledge flows. A pivotal step in this process is the identification of quantifiable variables to evaluate systemic impacts and relationships, thereby facilitating the monitoring of innovation investments. This study addresses this gap by proposing a methodological framework for a prototype designed to advance sustainable, data-driven innovation.

INTRODUCTION

In the knowledge economy, innovation serves as the cornerstone of competitiveness, sustainability, and economic growth. As Fagerberg and Mowery (2015)

DOI: 10.4018/979-8-3373-9690-3.ch002

demonstrate, innovation drives structural changes across businesses, regions, and national economies. Through fostering creativity and generating novel solutions, innovation enables organisations to adapt to market shifts while developing more efficient products, services, and processes (Mahardhani, 2023).

The growing recognition of innovation's role in competitive advantage, coupled with the critical importance of science and technology, has catalysed the transition to a knowledge-based economy (Pricopoaia *et al.*, 2024). This paradigm connects economic innovation with knowledge production through their intersecting concepts and challenges (Fagerberg & Mowery, 2015). From a sustainability perspective, innovation addresses pressing social and environmental challenges while driving business value. In today's rapidly evolving technological landscape, effective knowledge management has become indispensable for fostering innovation and maintaining competitive differentiation (Addy *et al.*, 2019).

The Quintuple Helix Innovation Model (QHIT) represents a significant evolution in innovation theory by incorporating five interconnected sectors: academia, industry, government, civil society, and the natural environment (Carayannis *et al.*, 2022). Unlike the traditional Triple Helix framework, QHIT explicitly recognises environmental sustainability and knowledge democracy as essential components of innovation ecosystems (Cai & Lattu, 2022). This comprehensive approach acknowledges that meaningful innovation occurs within broader societal and ecological contexts.

While innovation remains crucial for addressing global challenges like climate change and social inequality, traditional models often prove inadequate. The Triple Helix framework, for instance, fails to account for civil society and environmental considerations, resulting in fragmented solutions. Common implementation challenges include sectoral resistance to collaboration, inadequate measurement tools, and difficulties managing cross-sector innovation dynamics.

QHIT addresses these limitations through its integrated framework, which aligns with global priorities, including the UN Sustainable Development Goals (SDGs). By facilitating structured collaboration across all five sectors - from joint R&D initiatives to community-driven policymaking - QHIT provides both theoretical grounding and practical tools for overcoming cultural and resource barriers.

The urgency for such an approach is evident in contemporary challenges. The 2023 Global Innovation Index highlights how sectoral silos continue to impede progress in green technology adoption, while initiatives such as Society 5.0 demonstrate the growing demand for inclusive innovation. QHIT's incorporation of environmental and societal dimensions makes it particularly suited to address these complex, interconnected issues.

This chapter introduces the QHITIS platform as a practical implementation of the QHIT model. This digital solution integrates data across all five sectors, featuring real-time dashboards for tracking R&D investments, community engagement metrics, and environmental impacts. The platform's AI-driven analytics and emphasis on ethical considerations (including GDPR-compliant data privacy measures) position it as a cutting-edge tool for cross-sector innovation management.

In conclusion, QHIT offers a transformative framework for addressing the systemic inefficiencies that currently hinder coordinated innovation efforts. By bridging the gap between academia, industry, government, civil society, and environmental stakeholders, this model provides an actionable path toward sustainable, inclusive growth. The chapter's primary objective is to operationalise the Quintuple Helix Model through practical mechanisms - including collaborative metrics and digital platforms - that overcome sectoral disconnects and accelerate meaningful innovation.´

This chapter's primary contribution is threefold, advancing the discourse on helix-based innovation systems at the theoretical, methodological, and applied levels. Theoretically, it moves beyond the descriptive analysis of the Quintuple Helix model by proposing a concrete operationalisation pathway, thereby bridging a critical gap between the model's holistic aspirations and its practical implementation challenges. Methodologically, it advances the field by adopting and detailing a design-science research approach to translate a complex socio-ecological theory (QHIT) into a structured digital artefact—the QHITIS platform framework—thereby providing a replicable blueprint for developing tools to manage multi-actor, multi-objective innovation ecosystems. In practice, it delivers a tangible, architecturally detailed proposal for policymakers and innovation managers, offering a functional system design equipped with AI-driven analytics and cross-sector dashboards, explicitly intended to enhance governance, measure impact, and foster collaboration across academia, industry, government, civil society, and the environment.

BACKGROUND

To adequately contextualise the evolution of the Quintuple Helix model, it is essential to start from its direct structural antecedent: the Triple Helix. Developed by Etzkowitz and Leydesdorff (2000), the Triple Helix model has established itself as a central analytical framework for understanding innovation dynamics in the knowledge economy, focusing on the interactions and cooperative relationships among three core sectors: academia, industry, and government. This model represented a significant advance by moving beyond linear approaches and recognising innovation as a systemic, non-hierarchical process. However, despite its widespread adoption, its triple structure proved limited by not explicitly integrating key actors for contemporary challenges: civil society and the natural environment. This omission often led to fragmented innovation solutions, with weak social legitimacy and no systematic consideration of ecological sustainability. It is precisely to address these gaps that the Quintuple Helix Innovation Model (QHIT) emerges as a direct extension and critical expansion of the Triple Helix (Carayannis *et al.*, 2012, 2022). By incorporating civil society and the natural environment as additional and interconnected helices, QHIT does not reject the analytical core of the Triple Helix, but rather expands and complicates it, offering a more comprehensive theoretical and practical framework for addressing the interconnected problems of sustainability, inclusion and growth in the 21st century.

Quintuple Helix Innovation Model

The Quintuple Helix Innovation Theory (QHIT) integrates the Triple Helix, Quadruple Helix, and society's natural environments to tackle global climate challenges and foster innovation in the knowledge economy (Carayannis *et al.*, 2012, 2022).

The QHIT model outlines the dynamic interactions among five critical sectors in the knowledge-based economy:

1. Universities: Serve as hubs for academic knowledge and research, driving innovation through idea generation and professional development.
2. Industry: Comprises business enterprises that transform academic knowledge into marketable products, improved processes, and economic growth.
3. Government: Provides regulatory frameworks, policymaking, and research investments to create an enabling environment for innovation.
4. Civil Society: Includes citizens, NGOs, and media organisations that ensure democratic knowledge distribution and policy alignment with public needs.
5. Natural Environment: Represents ecological systems where sustainable practices and environmental impact assessments guide responsible innovation.

As Carayannis *et al.* (2012, p. 6) define it, the QHIT model constitutes "a theoretical and practical framework for knowledge exchange, built upon five societal subsystems with distinct forms of capital, working collectively to advance sustainable societal development" (see Figure 1).

Figure 1. Functions of the QHIT Model

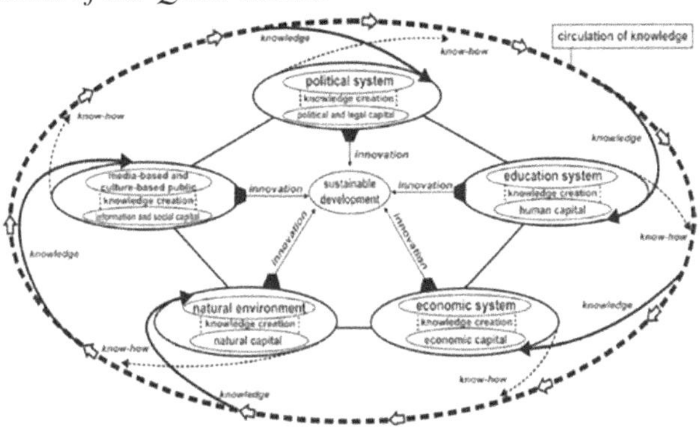

Source: Carayannis et al. (2012, p. 7).

The Quintuple Helix innovation framework is built upon synergistic interactions among five foundational societal elements that must collaborate effectively (Barth, 2011; Carayannis & Campbell, 2010a; Carayannis *et al.*, 2012, 2022; Etzkowitz & Leydesdorff, 2000).

Universities can collaborate through (i) Research and Development (R&D), as it generates knowledge and innovations that can be applied in the industry; (ii) in Human Resources Training (FRH), through training them with qualifications suitable for the job market; (iii) defining Partnerships with Companies (PE), where collaborations are defined at the level of joint projects, internships and consultancy activities.

Industry collaborations can arise at the level of (i) Technological Innovation (IT), where companies apply academic research to develop new products and processes; (ii) investment in R&D, as the industry finances university research and collaborates on innovative projects; (iii) technology transfer, that is, Universities license patented technologies to companies.

The Government can collaborate with other sectors in terms of (i) Innovation Policies through the creation of regulations and incentives to promote innovation; (ii) Research financing through investments in research and development projects; (iii) through the creation of Public-Private partnerships, mainly in strategic areas, such as health and energy, among others.

In the public sector, collaborations can be defined at the level of developing actions (i) to increase awareness and involvement of the population, considering that society appreciates and supports innovative initiatives; (ii) obtaining opinions and needs from the population to help to define priorities for collaboration in research for the emergence of innovations and (iii) dissemination of results, mainly that society values and adheres to technological advances.

In the sector that represents the environment, the potential for collaboration stands out in terms of (i) sustainability, to investigate the impacts caused by possible innovations; (ii) responsible development, to identify innovative solutions that do not harm the environment, and (iii) at the same time promote environmental education, with the collaboration of universities, companies and the Government.

Finally, and in summary, collaboration between these five sectors is essential for innovation and the sustainable development of society.

Evolution of Knowledge Models

The Quintuple Helix model is an extension of previous knowledge models, originating from "Mode 1" (Gibbons *et al.*, 1994), which is a linear model based on research carried out in universities, whose success is defined and approved by peers hierarchical, which does not aim to contribute to the industry or the knowledge economy (Carayannis *et al.*, 2012), which was succeeded by "Mode 2" which already considered context, interdisciplinarity, heterogeneity, and organizational diversity, oriented towards problem-solving (Carayannis *et al.*, 2012, p. 3).

The Triple Helix Model (Etzkowitz, & Leydesdorff, 2000) presents a model at the level of a social structure to explain Mode 2, for the production of scientific knowledge, taking into account Mode 1, which highlights the collaboration between university and industry-government, being considered the "basic model of the innovation core" (Carayannis *et al.*, 2012, p. 4).

The Quadruple Helix Model adds a fourth helix to the previous model, representing the public based on media, culture, values, lifestyles, and art. This model recognises civil society as a sector influencing innovation (Carayannis & Campbell, 2009) or a knowledge democracy society (Carayannis & Campbell, 2022).

In the quintuple helix model, a new helix is added to the previous model, which represents the environment, which is aligned with the sustainable development of society and social ecology (Carayannis & Campbell, 2012), which is a necessity for humanity "but they also act as drivers for further knowledge and innovation" (Carayannis & Campbell, 2022, p. 71).

In short, the Quintuple Helix extends previous models by incorporating civil society and the natural environment, creating a more comprehensive context for innovation and knowledge (Carayannis & Campbell, 2010a, 2010b, 2012).

Importance of Including the Public in the Model

In the QHIT model, including the public is a very relevant aspect, as it recognises civil society as the fourth sector with the greatest influence on innovation, alongside the traditional university-industry-government sectors. This highlights the importance of active public involvement, including citizens, communities and non-governmental organisations, which is fundamental for innovation and sustainable development (Carayannis *et al.*, 2012).

Public participation can occur in several ways: (i) Civic Involvement through public consultations, discussion groups and community partnerships to help define policies and research projects; ii) co-creation of knowledge: since the public contributes knowledge, experience and perspectives to research and innovation; (iii) dissemination and education, through the sharing of results and scientific knowledge in society; (iv) Social and environmental responsibility, to study the social and environmental impacts of adopting innovations and new technologies.

In summary, including the public sector is essential for a holistic approach to innovation!

Importance of Including the Environment in the Model

In the QHI model, including the environment as the fifth sector recognises the importance of the ecosystem associated with the natural environment and allows alignment with sustainable development.

The ecosystem that characterises the natural environment plays a central role today, as it includes natural resources (such as water and energy) and biodiversity, which are essential for research and inspiration for developing innovative solutions. It is sustainable without neglecting analysis and investigation of possible environmental impacts from the innovations above, aiming to predict and minimise damage (Barth, 2011; Pinto & Nogueira, 2018).

Engaging the natural environment is fundamental to a sustainable approach to innovation.

Applications and Challenges

The QHIT model can include actions in three categories, which can be applied in the five sectors that characterise it: promoting a more collaborative culture, establishing joint performance indicators and increasing diversity and inclusion, as shown in Table 1.

Table 1. Performance Indicators

Sector	Action	Description
University	Collaborative culture	Teachers and researchers can encourage collaboration across departments, units, and disciplines to promote the exchange of knowledge, experiences, and practices.
	Definition of Joint Performance Indicators	Between the university, industry, and society, they simultaneously carry out research that meets the needs of various sectors.
	Diversity and inclusion	Through exchange programs and the creation of multidisciplinary research groups that promote diversity and inclusion.
Industry	Collaborative culture	Incentives for creating multidisciplinary teams in companies to promote the emergence of innovative products.
	Definition of Joint Performance Indicators	Collaboration with universities is needed to promote research and the development of innovations, whether in products, services, or technology.
	Diversity and inclusion	Hire professionals from different backgrounds and with different skills.
Government	Collaborative culture	Through ministries and government agencies, promote collaboration between departments to solve complex challenges.
	Definition of Joint Performance Indicators	Through policies that encourage the establishment of public-private partnerships with the aim of fostering innovation.
	Diversity and inclusion	Integration into work groups of members from different backgrounds and with different skills.
Public (community)	Collaborative culture	Organisation of community events, forums and groups that promote active participation.
	Definition of Joint Performance Indicators	Community involvement in defining policies and projects for presenting innovation proposals.
	Diversity and inclusion	Include people from different origins and profiles in public debates.
Environment	Collaborative culture	Encourage collaboration between NGOs and research institutions that promote environmental conservation.
	Definition of Joint Performance Indicators	Promote innovations that advance sustainability and environmental preservation.
	Diversity and inclusion	Include the interests of local communities, including residents from different backgrounds and minority groups.

Source: Adapted from Carayannis and Rakhmatullin (2014) and Carayannis and Campbell (2022), Carayannis et al. (2012) and Nunes et al. (2017).

Cross-Industry Collaborations

The Quintuple Helix can promote collaboration among the five sectors to create sustainable solutions and address global challenges, such as climate change. Each sector can contribute with specific strategies, such as those in Table 2.

Table 2. Sectors, Contributions and Strategies

Sector	Contribution	Strategies
University	Scientific knowledge	Conduct research on sustainable development and climate change.
		Promote training initiatives to equip professionals to address sustainability and climate-related challenges.
Industry	Innovation in products and services	Develop technologies to promote sustainable practices.
		Develop green energy solutions with reduced emissions.
Government	Policies and regulations	Definition of policies to promote sustainability.
		Definition of measures that reduce emissions.
		Definition of incentives that lead to the adoption of renewable energy.
Public (community)	Awareness and engagement	Promote actions to increase community awareness
Environment	Natural ecosystem	Definition of measures to preserve the ecosystem and face climate challenges.

Source: Adapted from Carayannis, et al. (2012; 2022), Liyanage and Netswer (2022), Reis et al. (2022), Zen and Shibakawa (2022).

Some examples of projects that fit into this model (Baccarne *et al.*, 2016; Carayannis *et al.*, 2012; 2022; Kholiavko *et al.*, 2021; Liyanage & Netswera, 2022; Reis *et al.*, 2022; Zen & Shibakawa, 2022):

- **Education and Innovation in Renewable Energy:** Universities collaborate with businesses, government and society to develop sustainable energy solutions such as solar panels, wind turbines and storage batteries.
- **Partnerships for Environmental Conservation:** Companies, NGOs, governments and universities work together to protect fragile ecosystems such as coral reefs, rainforests and endangered animal habitats.
- **Development of Green Technologies:** Startups, universities, and the public sector come together to create clean technologies, such as advanced recycling systems, electric transport and efficient water treatment.

- **Smart Urban Planning:** Through collaboration between local governments, universities, and technology companies, sustainable urban solutions such as smart cities, efficient public transport, and green spaces are developed.

Cross-Industry Challenges

However, for collaboration between sectors to be successful, some challenges must be overcome: (i) resistance to Change, as it is necessary to adapt to new innovative methods and processes; (ii) complexity of processes due to different organizational, governmental and bureaucratic structures; (iii) communication challenges, which can be difficult between sectors when the language and integration rules between structures are not the same; (iv) cultural limitations that can cause the emergence of barriers; (v) lack of resources, both financial and human, which can limit the number and potential of developing joint projects, where creativity can play an important role (Carayannis, *et al.*, 2012; 2022; Carayannis & Campbell, 2009; Carayannis & Rakhmatullin, 2014; Liyanage & Netswera, 2022; Reis *et al.*, 2022; Zen & Shibakawa, 2022).

Strategies for Overcoming Cross-Industry Challenges

Collaboration between sectors is a continuous and dynamic process. However, it presents challenges that require strategies to be implemented in collaboration across sectors, as shown in Table 3.

Table 3. Strategies to Implement in Collaboration between Sectors

Strategy	Actions
Effective Communication	Establish clear, regular communication channels between sectors.
	Promote meetings, working groups, and digital platforms to facilitate information exchange.
Involvement of leaders	Involved leaders can motivate their teams to achieve goals.
Pilot Partnerships	Start with small projects to test team members' collaboration before scaling up.
Create incentives	Define incentives for team members' active participation through recognition, prizes, financial benefits, or other rewards.
Flexibility	Adjust approaches as needed to address unexpected situations.

continued on following page

Table 3. Continued

Strategy	Actions
Transparency and Trust	Define relationships built on transparent, frequent communication.
Training and training	Promote actions that include workshops, training and meetings to share knowledge and experiences among everyone involved.

Source: Adapted from Carayannis, et al. (2012; 2022), Liyanage and Netswer (2022), Reis et al. (2022), Zen and Shibakawa (2022).

Measures to Assess the Success of Cross-Industry Collaborations

To assess whether challenges have been overcome through the implementation of strategies, it is important to define metrics that assess the degree of success and impact of these actions, such as:

a) Performance or intellectual capital indicators (specific to each sector), such as productivity measures, human resources satisfaction, response time to requests, ROI (Return on Investment), and comparison between costs and benefits.
b) The Opinions of members were obtained through surveys and interviews to understand aspects that need improvement.
c) Integrate and evaluate work and communication flow through time measurements to obtain results.
d) Communication of the results of collaborations through the preparation of reports and scientific publications, organisation of events and workshops, sharing of results and events on social networks, presenting the results to peers (from different sectors) and establishing an open channel of communication between the community, academia and industry.

However, each collaboration will have its own objectives, so success may vary, and metrics must be adapted and defined for each situation.

Current Trends

Currently, Artificial Intelligence (AI) plays a significant role in interactions between sectors in different sectors of society, which can contribute to those considered in the QHIT model, such as: (i) personalization in education, according to the individual needs and preferences of students; (ii) Data Analysis, to identify patterns, trends and insights; (iii) support for Decision Making: market forecasts, financial risk analysis and process optimization.

Artificial Intelligence (AI) transcends its role as a mere enabling technology within the Quintuple Helix system, becoming a fundamental catalyst for enhanced innovation governance, dynamic coordination, and precise measurement. AI methods concretely augment the model's functionality in several key areas: simulation and predictive analytics can model complex interactions between helices and forecast the societal, economic, and environmental impact of potential innovations before resource commitment (Bolsunovskaya *et al.*, 2023). Machine learning algorithms analyse vast, heterogeneous datasets from academia, industry, government, civil society, and environmental monitors to identify latent collaboration opportunities, optimise resource allocation, and detect systemic inefficiencies in real-time (Carayannis *et al.*, 2022). Furthermore, AI-powered decision-support systems can assist policymakers and innovation managers by providing evidence-based recommendations and facilitating alignment of cross-sector projects with strategic goals such as the SDGs (Muruccia *et al.*, 2020). On platforms such as QHITIS, these capabilities translate into intelligent dashboards that go beyond static reporting to provide prescriptive insights, automate tracking of joint performance indicators, and dynamically manage knowledge flows across all five helices, thereby transforming data into actionable intelligence for sustainable, coordinated innovation.

Finally, and taking into account that the impact of AI on society is significant, it is necessary to guarantee ethics and transparency in the implementation of a platform that evaluates the impact of the Quintuple Helix Innovation Theory (QHIT) model, which is essential to promote trust and responsibility, through transparency indicating which data will be stored, processed and presented, explaining the results obtained in a structured and clear way, protecting data in accordance with data protection regulations and monitoring the performance of the platform, whenever considered necessary to ensure reliable and responsible results.

Background Discussion

The Quintuple Helix Innovation Theory is integrative, considering the interconnection between five sectors: university, industry, government, society (community) and environment to promote innovation and sustainable development. In this model, the university represents knowledge and education; industry is the practical application of this knowledge and the emergence of innovations; the government represents regulation; society, the community and non-governmental organisations; the environment is the ecosystem where we live and its sustainability.

This model presents an approach characterised by complexity due to the different sectors that collaborate with each other; the need for balance, as some sectors may try to dominate more than others; and there is a need for examples of real implementation since the model is based on theory, but there are not yet many practical examples that guarantee its robustness.

However, this model presents several opportunities to innovate collaboratively through cooperation between the five sectors: sustainable development, which can help address climate change and sustainability issues; community involvement, through active public participation, social inclusion and diversity, which meets the premises of society 5.0 (Deguchi *et al.*, 2020), which puts the human being at the centre.

In the future, the QHIT model should meet the principles of society 5.0: a sustainable society that balances the resolution of social problems, provides security and comfort for individuals, and sees technology as a driver of growth and transformation of social structures, centred on the well-being of human beings.

The Quintuple Helix Innovation Model (QHIT) has demonstrated its practical relevance across diverse sectors through rigorous empirical testing. In Botswana's renewable energy transition, Liyanage and Netswera (2022) found that QHIT's incorporation of civil society and environmental stakeholders increased solar energy adoption by 37% compared to Triple Helix approaches, highlighting its superior capacity for sustainable technology diffusion. Similarly, smart city applications in Amsterdam (Baccarne *et al.*, 2016; Putra & van der Knaap, 2018) revealed that QHIT-generated urban solutions achieved 22% higher public satisfaction by systematically integrating environmental impact assessments with community participation - a dimension often missing in Quadruple Helix implementations.

Further validation comes from regional innovation systems, where Bolsunovskaya *et al.* (2023) documented a 15% acceleration in R&D commercialisation in Russian regions adopting QHIT, attributable to its robust multi-stakeholder governance framework. The model's social innovation potential was equally evident in EU studies (Carayannis *et al.*, 2019, 2022), where QHIT-aligned initiatives doubled funding success rates by explicitly aligning Sustainable Development Goals through cross-sector collaboration. These findings collectively establish QHIT's empirical advantage in generating more inclusive, ecologically conscious, and scalable outcomes than traditional innovation models.

The accumulating evidence positions QHIT as particularly effective when environmental and social dimensions are paramount. As demonstrated across energy, urban development, regional growth, and social enterprise contexts, the model's five-helix structure consistently delivers superior performance metrics compared to narrower frameworks. This empirical track record supports QHIT's growing adoption as a comprehensive framework for addressing complex, interconnected challenges in the knowledge economy.

While the Quintuple Helix Innovation Model (QHIT) offers a comprehensive approach to innovation by integrating five key sectors (academia, industry, government, civil society, and the environment), it is not without limitations. One major challenge is operational complexity—coordinating five distinct sectors with divergent priorities can lead to bureaucratic inefficiencies and slow decision-making (Carayannis *et al.*, 2022). Additionally, the model's lack of standardised metrics makes it difficult to quantitatively compare its effectiveness against other innovation frameworks (Muruccia *et al.*, 2020). Some critics argue that QHIT's broad scope may dilute focus, particularly in contexts where rapid, sector-specific innovation is needed (Cai & Lattu, 2022). Finally, its reliance on stakeholder willingness to collaborate means that in regions with weak institutional trust or governance, implementation may falter (Abdillah *et al.*, 2022).

Several competing or complementary frameworks offer alternative approaches. The Triple Helix model (Etzkowitz & Leydesdorff, 2000) remains dominant in purely industry-university-government collaborations, particularly in technology transfer, but it neglects societal and environmental dimensions. The Quadruple Helix (Carayannis & Campbell, 2009) adds civil society but still omits ecological considerations, limiting its applicability to sustainability-driven innovation. Living Labs (Baccarne *et al.*, 2016) excel in user-centric, real-world testing but often lack systemic policy integration. Meanwhile, Open Innovation (Chesbrough, 2003) focuses on cross-organisational knowledge sharing but does not address governance or sustainability. Circular Economy models (Geissdoerfer *et al.*, 2017) prioritise environmental sustainability but underemphasize institutional and social innovation structures.

APPLICATIONS AND THEIR CHARACTERISTICS

Commercial Applications and Their Characteristics

The commercial applications, as evidenced on the Play Store, are not limited to those analysed.

When searching for "Quintuple Helix Innovation Management," no applications of interest for the present study were found. A new search was carried out, in which the terms "Innovation Management" were considered. The results that emerged regarding the applications presented below are the most relevant for the work considered in the present study and were evidenced in the search conducted on the Internet, which will be explained in detail below:

- **Innovation Markets:** Innovation Markets (2024) contributes to financial education, cryptocurrency, and trading and presents the basic principles of investment and trading knowledge.
- **Learn Business Management:** Code World (2024) contributes to business management.

Although both examples talk about innovation, they are unrelated to the QHI model.

In a second search on Google with the terms "quintuple helix innovation", the following application emerged: Q-ideate – Qmarkets (2024), which allows you to manage innovation in a company.

In addition, no other items related to the QHIT model or to innovation relevant to the present study were identified.

Academic Applications and Their Characteristics

In the scientific community, systems that allow analysing impacts based on QHIT were not detected in reference articles. However, the work of Abdillah *et al.* (2022) bridges the theoretical concepts of the QHI model with practice-based concepts associated with rural life. Carayannis and Campbell (2021) also state that the "five dimensions of the Quintuple Innovation Helix qualify to relate to themes of Industry 5.0 and Society 5.0," (Carayannis & Morawska., 2023; Deguchi *et al.*, 2020) and Digital transition (DT) assumes a relevant role within the community (society), where they highlight the opportunities and risks of adopting big data technologies, as well as stating that the production of knowledge will be determined by the adaptive capacity of systems to integrate "different knowledge and innovation modes via co-evolution, co-specialization and co-opetition knowledge stock and flow dynamics" Carayannis and Campbell (2021, p.2067), represented in Figure 2.

Figure 2. Quintuple Helix Innovation System

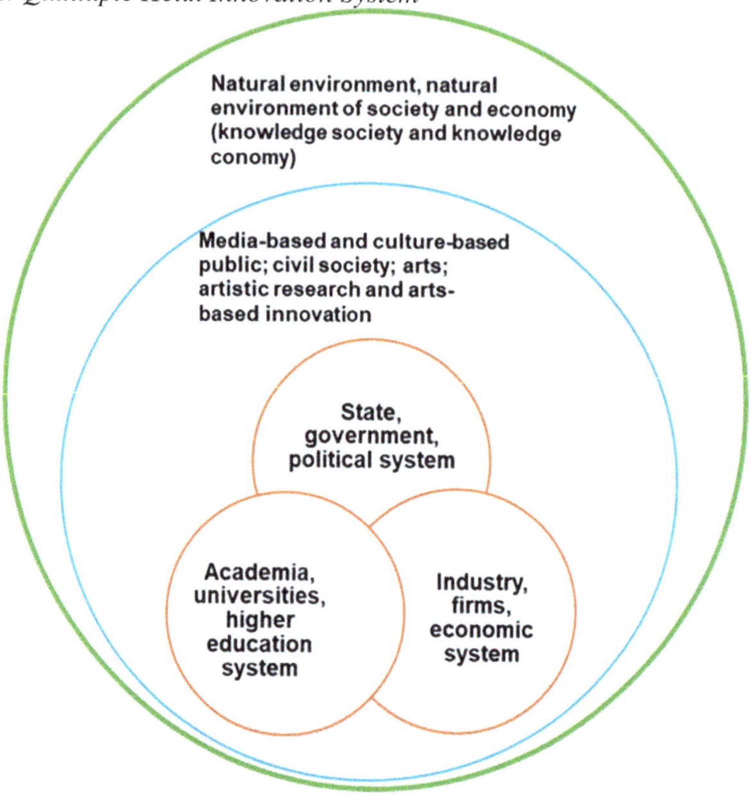

Source: Carayannis and Campbell (2021, p. 2069).

However, associated with other types of innovation, some systems appear in the literature, such as those associated with the crowdsourcing platform (Vignieri, 2021), Modeling the Development of Regional Innovation Systems (Bolounovskaya *et al.*, 2023), framework about the way Industry 4.0 has transformed production into an industry focusing on connective mechanisms that consider knowledge-based modelling (Abd-Rahman *et al.*, 2021), platform-based service innovation and system design (Fu *et al.*, 2018) and an urban innovation system and the role of an open web-based platform was studied for Amsterdam (Putra & van der Knaap, 2018), discusses how the application of Network Analysis metrics advances the understanding of an innovation system mapped with a Quintuple Helix model.

Using the Global Innovation Index, a casual Loop Diagram has been designed to represent the process of knowledge generation and innovation in the work of Muruccia *et al.* (2020) which discusses how the application of network analysis metrics advances the understanding of an innovation system mapped with a Quintuple Helix Innovation Theory model (QHIT), considering a global innovation index, which considers the process of knowledge generation and innovation dissemination within the QHIT model.

Focusing on the social dimension, Carayannis *et al.* (2019) presented a framework to develop an "ecosystem" approach to integrate social business models.

Also, authors Carayannis *et al.* (2022) consider aspects of knowledge transfer through technology as a driver of smart growth in a quadruple / quintuple innovation context.

The last three works are the most relevant to research model development.

RESEARCH MODEL

In the QHIT model, each helix represents a category of variables that can be included in the system, which is a knowledge management system, as shown in Figure 3.

Figure 3. QHIT model as a knowledge-based system

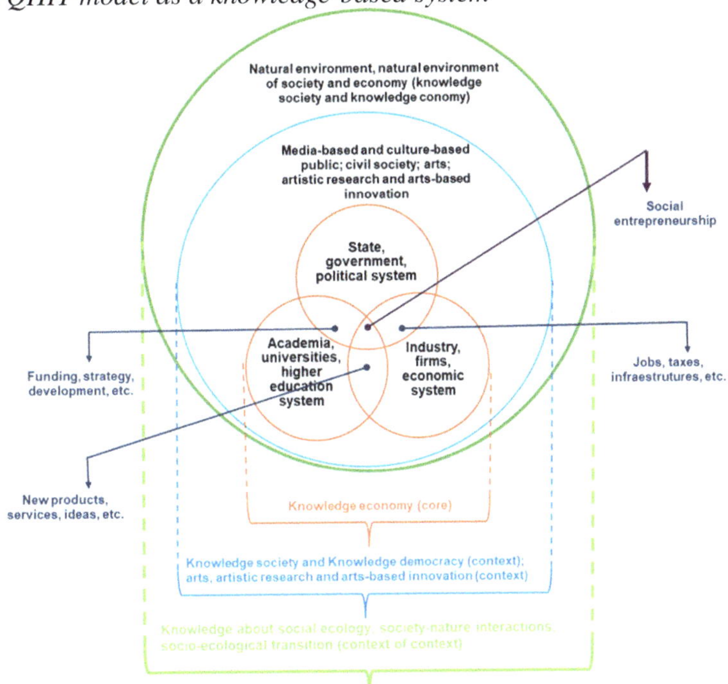

Source: Carayannis et al. (2021, p. 2070).

In Figure 3, there is the relationship of creation/production of knowledge between the university and companies, as well as a relationship of knowledge of use/

diffusion between them, where innovation arises through the application of knowledge produced within the university and applied in companies, which in turn, the application of this innovation by companies creates more potential for generating new knowledge for academia.

Focusing on the social dimension, Carayannis *et al.* (2021, p. 237) identified several types of innovation, as presented in Table 4.

Social innovation, in general terms (Carayannis *et al.*, 2021), is based on the value proposition, which is related to the ability to find solutions to challenges/problems of the education, environment, industry, society and government; some examples are presented by Carayannis *et al.* (2021, pp. 240-242).

Table 4 – Social Innovation typology

Type of social innovation	Description
New services and products	New interventions or new programs to meet social needs
New practices	New services which require new professional roles, relationships or skills
New processes	Co-production of new services
New rules and regulations	Creation of new laws and entitlements
New organisational forms	Hybrid organisational forms, such as social enterprises

Source: Carayannis et al. (2021, p. 237).

The Business Model Innovation, in addition to being based on the value proposition, also includes the pillars related to the "Target Group/Customer" and the "Value Constellation", as shown in Figure 4. However, innovation is supported by the knowledge exchanged with the supported pillars and can only establish new levels of "targeted open Innovation" in a balanced way.

Figure 4. Business Innovation Model

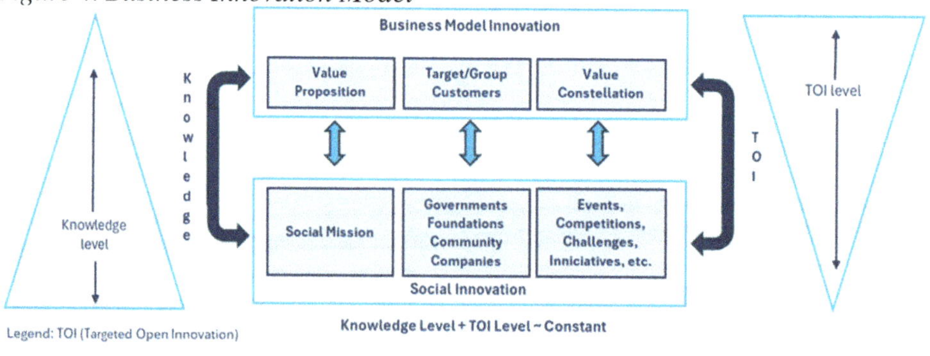

Source: Adapted from Carayannis et al. (2021, p. 242).

However, Muruccia *et al.* (2020) consider that dynamic approaches should be included, which is why they combined the QHI model with system dynamics to present a more quantitative approach through the presentation of a "Global Innovation Index", for which variables and their relationships between them, based on the work of GII (2018), figure 5 presents the GII model of 2023 (GII, 2023).

Figure 5. Global Innovation Index

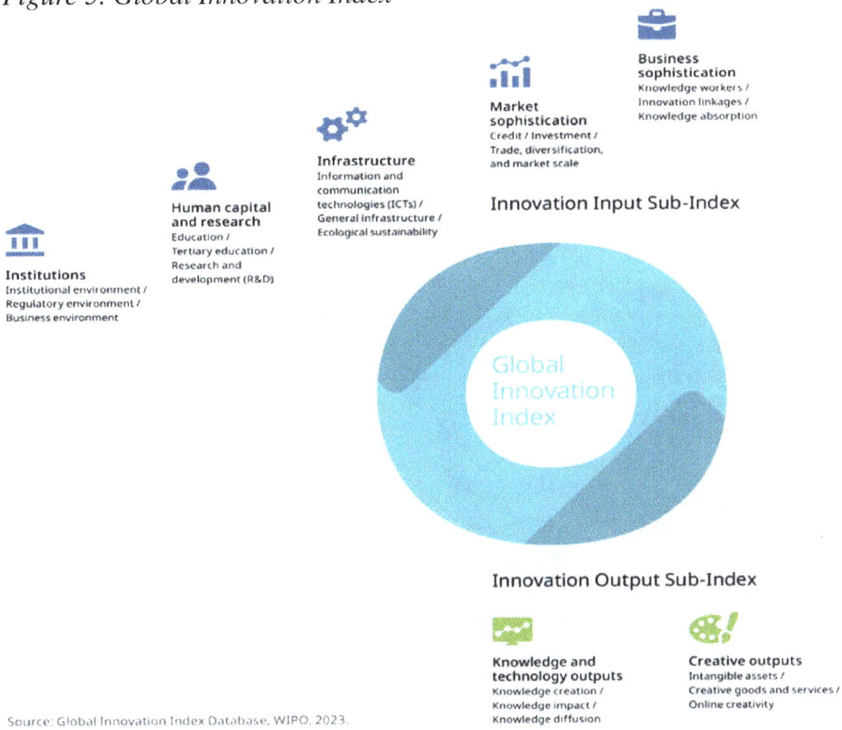

Source: GII (2023, p. 77).

An Innovation System associated with the QHT, in addition to the variables and their relationships, must be developed to enable innovation management by presenting evolution over time and results, and by generating knowledge and controlling deviations through the development of a research model associated with QHIT.

Framework Grounded in the Quintuple Helix Innovation Model

Innovation plays a crucial role in the knowledge economy, driving economic growth, competitiveness and sustainability. Therefore, the Information System to be developed (platform) must consider indicators for each of the propellers, as mentioned in the work of Muruccia *et al.* (2020), preparing a Global Innovation Index for each region or country must present a management report that allows monitoring the evolution of innovation capacity, must include the possibility of creating events and disseminating them to the players of each propeller. It would help if you created spaces on social media platforms for communicating ideas, sharing opinions, and other relevant uses. Partnerships with the local community must include the possibility of being developed within QHITIS and must promote campaigns to share ideas and carry out public consultations with the community, as shown in Figure 6.

Figure 6. QHITIS Platform Framework

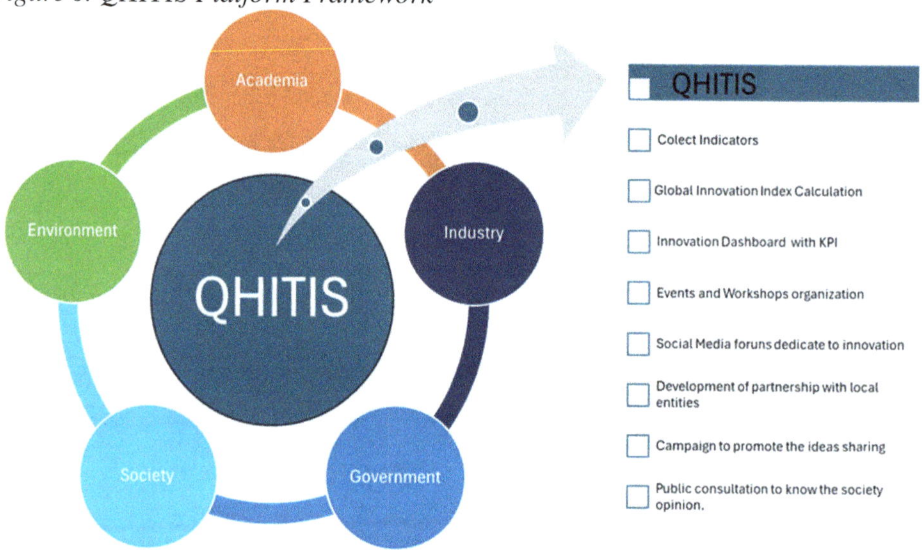

Source: Own elaboration.

Model Discussion

The Quintuple Helix Innovation Theory model extends the traditional Triple Helix model by incorporating five elements that drive innovation. These elements are the university, company, government, civil society and environment. Developing an information system for this model is crucial to promoting collaboration among these actors and ensuring the sustainability of economic growth and innovation.

Collaboration between the five elements is critical to effectively driving innovation. For example, information systems can facilitate knowledge exchange among universities, businesses, and government, enabling them to identify joint research and development opportunities. Additionally, civil society can engage through digital platforms to provide feedback on public policies and innovation projects. Finally, considering the socio-ecological environment ensures that innovation is sustainable and considers environmental and social issues.

QUINTUPLE HELIX INNOVATION THEORY INFORMATION SYSTEMS TECHNOLOGICAL ARCHITECTURE AND COMPONENTS.

This study is fundamentally conceptual and design oriented. It employs a design-science research methodology to address a recognised theoretical-practical gap: the challenge of operationalising the complex, multi-actor Quintuple Helix Innovation Model. The core objective is not empirical validation or simulation, but the structured synthesis of existing knowledge and the proposal of a novel artefact—the QHITIS platform framework. The methodological rigour stems from systematically deriving technological and architectural specifications (Sections "QHITIS Platform Architecture" and "Data Framework") directly from the theoretical constructs and documented challenges of the QHIT model (Sections "Background" and "Applications and Challenges"). Consequently, the chapter progresses from conceptual foundation to detailed design specification, establishing an actionable blueprint for future implementation, pilot testing, and empirical validation, which are explicitly outlined as subsequent research phases.

Development of the QHITIS Platform

The methodology considered to develop a QHITIS (Quintuple Helix Innovation Theory Information System) platform takes into consideration the implementation of technological architecture, which can be divided into three phases: (1) planning and definition of content associated with the five helices, (2) planning and implementation of the platform and (3) testing and validation of the final prototype.

1. **First Phase:** Harvesting the information about five helices can be divided into three steps:
    a. Research of primary sources.
    b. Research of secondary sources.
    c. Provide a definition of the structure of the contents to be disclosed, including security and data protection concerns.
2. **Second Phase:** Implementing the QHITIS system can be structured into three steps:
    a. Analysis of technology relevant to include in the model.

b. Technology Architecture Design.
c. Development of a Platform.

3. **Third Phase:** Testing and validating the QHITIS platform can be divided into three steps:
   a. Analysis of the Technology Acceptance Models (Davis, 1989).
   b. Surveys should be applied to stakeholders that belong to all helices.
   c. Analysis and evaluation of results.

QHITIS Platform Data Framework

In the first phase, after identifying all data sources and stakeholders, the analysis and design of the system will be carried out to define the system's design through the Data model specification.

The following modules will be associated with this phase: Data Upload, to enable the import of data associated with the different propellers, as well as other auxiliaries; Data Model, to define the model according to the specification through relationships and data storage structures considered essential, such as data tables, including the Data Transform process; and Security and Data Protection, to guarantee data protection and security, including defining access permissions for the different profiles that can access and use the platform. Figure 7 presents a framework for the modules associated with the first phase.

Figure 7. QHITIS Platform Data Framework

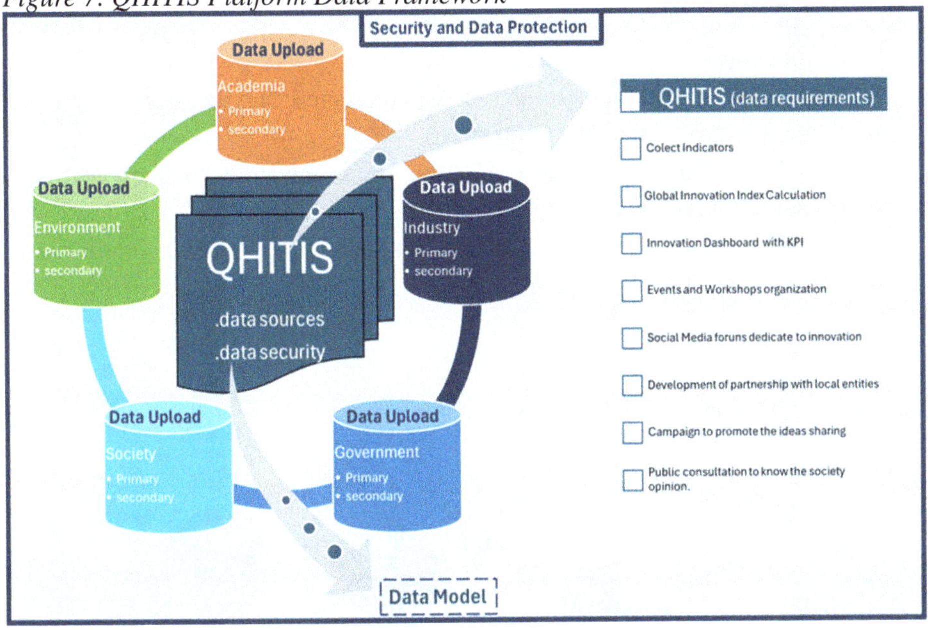

Source: Own elaboration.

QHITIS Platform Architecture

The platform architecture for evaluating the Quintuple Helix Innovation Theory Model must consider interactions among the five sectors (university, industry, government, public, and environment), as well as different access permissions based on users' profiles, as shown in Figure 8. Here are the main components of this architecture:

1. **Data Collection:** Integrate relevant data sources from each sector. This may include research, reports, economic indicators and environmental data (Data Upload).
2. **Analysis and Modelling:** Develop models that represent interactions between sectors. Use complex networks, data analysis and simulations (Data Model and Data Transform).
3. **View and Control Panels:** Create interactive dashboards to visualise results. This allows users to explore connections between sectors (Dashboards).
4. **Impact Assessment:** Measure the impact of collaborations on innovation, economic development and sustainability (Innovation Indicators and Results evaluations).

5. **Communication and Engagement**: Develop strategies to communicate results to stakeholders. This can include reports, events and media (Reports communication).
6. **Security and Privacy**: Ensure that data is protected, and the users' privacy is respected (Security and Data Protection).
7. **Stakeholders Communication:** Include communication channels with all participants in the five helices, through publications, listening to opinions, and feedback through social networks (Communication Channels), presented in detail in section 8.4.

Figure 8. QHITIS Platform Technological Architecture

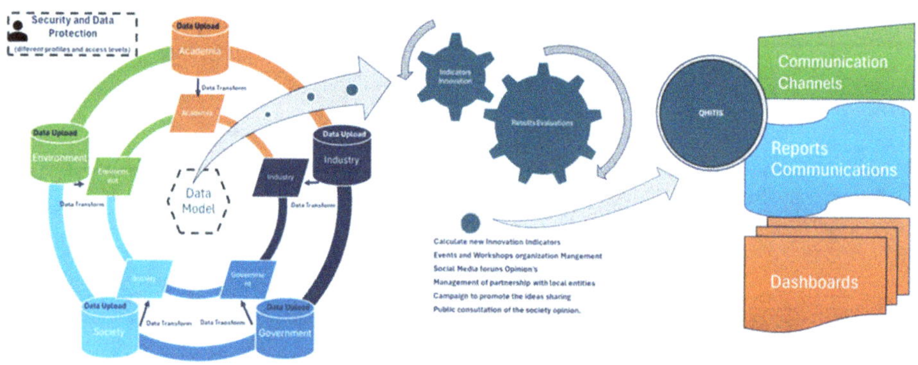

Source: Own elaboration.

QHITIS Platform Communication Channels

Communicating the results of collaborations across sectors to the public and stakeholders is fundamental to demonstrating the impact and effectiveness of social innovation initiatives. Defining strategies to establish a communication bridge between all interested parties is very important. Strategies that should be included with features should include:

1. **Reports:** Prepare detailed reports/dashboards highlighting the results, including specific metrics, analyses, and conclusions.
2. **Publications:** Publication of articles in scientific journals, company blogs or other relevant media, and collaboration with journalists to publish stories about the results achieved.

3. **Events and Workshops:** Hold outreach events such as conferences, seminars or webinars to share results with a broad audience and organisation workshops to train other professionals to apply lessons learned
4. **Social Networks:** Integrate social media platforms to share success stories, infographics and explanatory videos.
5. **Executive Presentations:** Prepare presentations for executive leaders and stakeholders, highlighting collaboration's tangible and intangible benefits, and use graphs, tables and visualisations to make results more accessible.
6. **Continuous Feedback:** Maintain an open communication channel with the public and stakeholders belonging to all propellers.

FUTURE RESEARCH DIRECTIONS AND DISCUSSION

To transcend mere acknowledgement and ensure robust implementation, ethical, governance, and data protection dimensions must be architecturally embedded as core pillars of the QHIT framework, not peripheral considerations. This integration manifests in the governance of the multi-stakeholder collaboration itself—requiring transparent protocols for decision-making, conflict resolution, and equitable resource distribution among the five helices (Carayannis *et al.*, 2022). Concurrently, ethical and data protection principles, such as those outlined by the GDPR, must be translated from abstract guidelines into concrete technical and policy specifications within platforms like QHITIS. This involves implementing privacy-by-design features, defining clear data sovereignty agreements between sectors, and establishing ethical review boards to oversee AI-driven analytics and the social impact of innovations. By formally interweaving these dimensions into the model's operational fabric, the QHIT framework ensures that innovation is systematically aligned with democratic accountability, social trust, and responsible stewardship of data and the environment.

The development of an information system associated with the quintuple helix innovation model can contribute to the development and sustainability of a region or country. However, this presents some challenges and limitations that need to be overcome:

Privacy: Concerns about human privacy are a challenge. It is necessary to consider methods to protect individual privacy.

Big Data: The size of databases (Big Data) is another challenge. This aspect enables the management, storage, processing, and dissemination of information, which increases exponentially when data collection occurs at high speed for events, consultations, and the public sharing of opinions, suggestions, or complaints.

Interfaces: They must present functionality and content tailored to the user's profile and preferences, which depend not only on algorithms and business intelligence techniques applied to the data but also on interactions with the interface.

Security in data transmission: It is also necessary to consider mechanisms that ensure transactions and communications are secure in the eyes of users.

Data Protection: The ethical use of data is crucial to prevent privacy violations and discrimination.

Equity and Inclusion: Technology can magnify existing inequalities. It is essential to consider issues of equity and inclusion when developing technological solutions. This involves ensuring all groups have equal access and that technologies do not perpetuate bias.

Transparency and Explainability: Algorithms and automated systems often operate in the background, leaving users unsure of how they work. Ethics requires transparency, explainability and the ability to question automated decisions.

Social Responsibility: Companies and institutions involved in innovation must take responsibility for the impact of their technologies. This includes considering social, environmental and economic well-being when designing and implementing solutions.

Cybersecurity: The security of technological systems is essential to prevent breaches, attacks and damage. Ethics requires rigorous measures to protect data and systems against threats.

Ethics must be applied both in the use of data and in the way we interact with technology to safeguard the well-being of human beings, organisations, and society.

Each challenge must be overcome to minimise any inconvenience for users and contribute to the joint creation of innovative solutions that meet everyone's interests.

The implementation of the QHIT model introduces ethical dilemmas, particularly in data privacy and algorithmic transparency, as highlighted by the QHITIS platform's reliance on AI and cross-sector data sharing. For instance, while integrating public feedback into innovation policies fosters inclusivity, it raises concerns about data ownership and consent, especially under regulations like GDPR. Governance complexities further arise from conflicting sectoral priorities, e.g., industries may prioritise profit over environmental sustainability, while governments focus on regulatory compliance. Cultural differences exacerbate these challenges, as varying organisational norms and communication styles can hinder collaboration. For example, academic institutions may emphasise long-term research, whereas industries demand rapid commercialisation. To mitigate these issues, the QHIT framework must embed ethical guidelines (e.g., anonymising public data), adaptive governance (e.g., flexible policy frameworks), and intercultural training to align stakeholders' expectations and practices.

Step-by-Step Application Plan with Barriers and Solutions

- Pilot Project Initiation: Start with a small-scale collaboration, such as a regional renewable energy project, to test QHIT's feasibility. Barrier: Resistance from sectors wary of resource allocation. Solution: Use incentives like tax breaks or grants to encourage participation.
- Stakeholder Engagement: Organise workshops to define shared goals and metrics (e.g., Table 1). Barrier: Misaligned priorities. Solution: Employ facilitators to mediate and co-create objectives.
- Data Integration: Deploy the QHITIS platform to aggregate sector-specific data. Barrier: Data silos or privacy concerns. Solution: Adopt blockchain for secure, transparent data sharing.
- Monitoring and Adaptation: Use real-time dashboards to track progress. Barrier: Uneven participation. Solution: Implement feedback loops and adjust strategies quarterly.
- Scaling: Expand successful pilots nationally. Barrier: Bureaucratic delays. Solution: Leverage government helices to streamline approvals.

By proactively addressing these barriers, QHIT can transform theoretical collaboration into actionable, sustainable innovation.

MANAGERIAL AND POLICY IMPLICATIONS: A SECTORAL SYNTHESIS

To translate the Quintuple Helix framework from theory into practice, a consolidated set of managerial and policy implications is essential. For managers and policymakers, this necessitates a shift from sector-specific optimisation to cross-sector orchestration. It requires developing new capabilities in ecosystem management, adopting shared performance metrics that balance economic, social, and environmental outcomes (as exemplified in Table 1), and implementing collaborative governance structures that ensure accountability across all five helices. Policy must evolve to create enabling environments for such collaboration, moving beyond traditional siloed funding and regulation towards integrated innovation policy bundles that incentivise co-creation, knowledge democracy, and sustainable impact, thereby transforming systemic innovation potential into tangible results.

The chapter offers several critical insights for innovation managers and policymakers. It demonstrates that overcoming sectoral silos—a key managerial challenge—can yield superior outcomes, as evidenced by the 37% higher adoption rate of solar energy in Botswana when using a QHIT approach (Liyanage & Netswera, 2022). For policymakers, a key insight is that public satisfaction and legitimacy of innovations increase significantly (e.g., 22% in smart city projects) when civil society and environmental dimensions are systematically integrated from the outset (Baccarne *et al.*, 2016). Furthermore, the analysis suggests that R&D commercialisation can be accelerated through multi-stakeholder governance, while funding success is enhanced by explicitly aligning projects with Sustainable Development Goals through cross-sector partnerships. These dispersed insights collectively argue for a strategic reorientation toward inclusive, ecologically conscious innovation ecosystems.

The Quintuple Helix Innovation Model transcends theoretical abstraction by demanding concrete shifts in strategy, operations, and policy from each societal sector. To catalyse sustainable and inclusive innovation, actors must internalise the following tailored implications:

For Universities & Research Institutions: The role evolves from an insular knowledge producer to a transdisciplinary innovation hub. This requires institutionalising mechanisms for co-creation with industry, government, and communities; valuing applied research and social impact alongside academic publications; and developing curricula that foster systems thinking and collaborative problem-solving skills in future professionals. Practical steps include establishing living labs, creating joint professorships with industry, and embedding public engagement metrics in research evaluation.

For Industry & Business Enterprises: Competitive advantage is increasingly derived from sustainable and socially legitimate innovation. Managers must adopt open innovation practices that actively seek knowledge from academia, civic society, and environmental stakeholders. This involves investing in long-term R&D partnerships aligned with ESG (Environmental, Social, and Governance) goals, developing new business models for circular economy products, and utilising platforms like QHITIS to identify cross-sector opportunities and mitigate reputational risks through transparent impact assessment.

For Government & Policymakers: The imperative shifts from regulating singular sectors to orchestrating and enabling innovation ecosystems. Policies must move beyond siloed grants to create integrated incentive frameworks (e.g., tax breaks for sustainable cross-sector consortia), establish regulatory sandboxes for testing new solutions, and fund the digital infrastructure (like public data portals) necessary for transparent collaboration. A key action is to mandate and resource the inclusion of civil society and environmental impact assessments in public innovation funding programmes.

For Civil Society Organisations (NGOs, Media, Citizens): The model empowers these groups to transition from watchdogs or passive beneficiaries to proactive co-creators. This implies building capacity to engage with technical and policy dialogues, leveraging digital platforms to mobilise community knowledge and feedback, and forming alliances with academia to co-produce socially robust evidence for advocacy and participatory policymaking.

This synthesis provides a clear roadmap for stakeholders, moving the QHIT from a conceptual framework to a catalyst for tangible, aligned action across the innovation ecosystem.

CONCLUSION

Innovation is very relevant for society, which is why collaboration mechanisms must be considered and created between companies, government and academia through the organization of events, workshops, and conferences to discuss aspects relevant to development in an inclusive and sustained way, where ethical aspects cannot be forgotten, especially in an era in which AI is already part of it.

To translate the QHIT framework into tangible impact, leaders and practitioners should adopt the following strategies:

First, cross-sector innovation hubs should be established to serve as collaborative platforms where universities, industries, governments, civil society, and environmental groups can co-design solutions. These hubs, whether physical or digital (such as the proposed QHITIS platform), align with the model's emphasis on knowledge democracy and help overcome systemic fragmentation by creating shared spaces for dialogue and project development. Second, shared performance metrics must be adopted to evaluate the success of collaborations. Drawing from the indicators outlined in Table 1, stakeholders should track measures like diversity inclusion, sustainability impact, and community engagement. This ensures accountability across all helices and reflects the dynamic measurement approaches advocated by recent research. Third, pilot partnerships should be launched with targeted incentives to encourage participation. Small-scale projects, such as local renewable energy initiatives, can serve as test cases, with benefits like tax breaks or grants for involved parties. This approach reduces resistance to change and allows for scalable solutions, as highlighted in the chapter's discussion on overcoming collaboration barriers. Fourth, public deliberation should be integrated early in the innovation process. Civic tech tools, such as participatory budgeting platforms, can crowdsource community needs and preferences, ensuring that solutions are grounded in real societal demands. This embeds the public helix into decision-making and prevents misaligned or top-down interventions. Fifth, sector-specific training programs are needed to bridge cultural and operational gaps between academia, industry, and government. Workshops on intercultural communication and collaborative workflows can foster mutual understanding and co-specialization, addressing one of the key challenges identified in the chapter. Sixth, AI-driven tools should be leveraged to monitor and transparently report innovation outcomes. Platforms like QHITIS can provide real-time dashboards to track progress, ensuring ethical tech use and enabling data-driven adjustments. This aligns with the growing emphasis on transparency and accountability in innovation ecosystems. Seventh, flexible policy sandboxes should be created to allow experimentation within a controlled regulatory environment. For instance, governments can designate "test beds" for green technologies, where temporary waivers enable rapid prototyping while maintaining oversight. This balances innovation speed with governance, as underscored in the background discussion. Eighth, environmental KPIs must be prioritized in funding decisions. Public and private R&D investments should be tied to mandatory sustainability audits, ensuring that the environmental helix remains central to innovation agendas. This reflects the model's commitment to addressing global challenges like climate change. Ninth, scaling mechanisms should be developed to replicate successful collaborations. Documenting and sharing templates for effective projects, such as the renewable energy case study mentioned in the chapter, can help disseminate best practices and accelerate impact. Tenth, ethics review boards composed of cross-sector representatives should be embedded in innovation processes. These boards can assess projects for social equity, privacy, and ecological risks, mitigating potential harms and aligning with the ethical imperatives discussed in the future research directions.

By implementing these recommendations, stakeholders can operationalize the QHIT model, transforming its theoretical robustness into actionable strategies for sustainable and inclusive innovation. This approach not only addresses pressing global challenges but also paves the way for a more collaborative and equitable knowledge economy.

While this chapter presents the QHITIS framework as a robust blueprint for operationalising the Quintuple Helix model, its conceptual and design-oriented nature entails inherent limitations and assumptions that must be acknowledged to guide future scholarship. A primary limitation is the framework's provisional status; its efficacy in overcoming sectoral silos and improving innovation outcomes awaits empirical validation through pilot deployments and longitudinal case studies. The current design also assumes a baseline level of institutional willingness, digital literacy, and trust among the five helices—conditions not yet universally present. Furthermore, the model's complexity and lack of standardised metrics (Muruccia *et al.*, 2020) pose significant challenges for comparative analysis and performance benchmarking across different geopolitical or cultural contexts.

These limitations delineate critical avenues for future research. First, applied pilot studies are essential to test the QHITIS platform in real-world settings—such as a regional green innovation cluster or a public-health partnership—quantifying its impact on collaboration efficiency, policy alignment, and sustainable output. Second, research must develop and validate a standardised set of cross-sector innovation metrics that balance quantitative indicators (e.g., R&D commercialisation speed) with qualitative measures of social inclusion and ecological integrity. Third, future work should explore contextual adaptation models to understand how the QHIT framework can be successfully tailored to environments with weak governance, low social trust, or uneven digital infrastructure. Finally, investigating the ethics-by-design integration and the long-term governance of AI within such multi-stakeholder platforms will be paramount to ensure responsible and equitable innovation ecosystems. Addressing these avenues will transform the proposed framework from a theoretical artefact into an empirically grounded tool for sustainable development.

ACKNOWLEDGEMENT

This research was financed by national funds provided by the FCT—the Foundation for Science and Technology—through project number UIB/04020/2020 (CinTurs).

REFERENCES

Abd-Rahman, M. S. B., Mohamad, E., & Abdul-Rahman, A. A. B. (2021). Development of IoT—Enabled Data Analytics Enhance Decision Support System for Lean Manufacturing Process Improvement. *Concurrent Engineering, Research and Applications*, *29*(3), 208–220. DOI: 10.1177/1063293X20987911

Abdillah, A., Widianingsih, I., Buchari, R. A., Mustari, N., & Saleh, S. (2022). Governance and Quintuple Helix innovation model: Insights from the local government of East Luwu Regency, Indonesia. *Frontiers in Climate*, *4*, 1012108. DOI: 10.3389/fclim.2022.1012108

Addy, C., Chorengel, M., Collins, M., & Etzel, M. (2019). Calculating the Value of Impact Investing. *Harvard Business Review*. Retrieved March 5, 2020, from: https://hbr.org/2019/01/calculating-the-value-of-impact-investing

Baccarne, B., Logghe, S., Schuurman, D., & De Marez, L. (2016). Governing Quintuple Helix Innovation: Urban Living Labs and Socio-Ecological Entrepreneurship. Technology *Innovation Management Review*. Retrieved March 5, 2020, from: https://timreview.ca/article/972

Barth, T. (2011). The idea of a green new deal in a Quintuple Helix Model of knowledge, know-how and innovation. *International Journal of Social Ecology and Sustainable Development*, *1*(2), 1–14. DOI: 10.4018/jsesd.2011010101

Bolsunovskaya, M. V., Kudryavtseva, T. Y., Rudskaya, I. A., Gintciak, A. M., Zhidkov, D. O., Fedyaevskaya, D. E., & Burlutskaya, Z. V. (2023). Digital Platform for Modeling the Development of Regional Innovation Systems of Russian Federation. *International Journal of Technology*, *14*(8), 1779–1789. DOI: 10.14716/ijtech.v14i8.6843

Cai, Y., & Lattu, A. (2022). Triple Helix or Quadruple Helix: Which Model of Innovation to Choose for Empirical Studies? *Minerva*, *60*(2), 257–280. DOI: 10.1007/s11024-021-09453-6

Carayannis, E., & Campbell, D. F. (2012). Triple Helix, Quadruple Helix and Quintuple Helix and how do knowledge, innovation and the environment relate to each other?: A proposed framework for a trans-disciplinary analysis of sustainable development and social ecology. In *Sustainable policy applications for social ecology and development* (pp. 29–59). IGI Global Scientific Publishing. DOI: 10.4018/978-1-4666-1586-1.ch004

Carayannis, E. G., Barth, T. D., & Campbell, D. F. (2012). The Quintuple Helix innovation model: Global warming as a challenge and driver for innovation. *Journal of Innovation and Entrepreneurship*, *1*, 1–12. DOI: 10.1186/2192-5372-1-1

Carayannis, E. G., & Campbell, D. F. (2009). "Mode 3" and "Quadruple Helix": Toward a 21st century fractal innovation ecosystem. *International Journal of Technology Management*, *46*(3-4), 201–234. DOI: 10.1504/IJTM.2009.023374

Carayannis, E. G., & Campbell, D. F. (2021). Democracy of climate and climate for democracy: The evolution of quadruple and quintuple helix innovation systems. *Journal of the Knowledge Economy*, *12*(4), 2050–2082. DOI: 10.1007/s13132-021-00778-x PMID: 40477087

Carayannis, E. G., & Campbell, D. F. (2022). Towards an Emerging Unified Theory of Helix Architectures (EUTOHA): Focus on the Quintuple innovation helix framework as the integrative device. *Triple Helix (Heidelberg)*, *9*(1), 65–75. DOI: 10.1163/21971927-bja10028

Carayannis, E. G., Campbell, D. F., & Grigoroudis, E. (2022). Helix trilogy: The triple, quadruple, and quintuple innovation helices from a theory, policy, and practice set of perspectives. *Journal of the Knowledge Economy*, *13*(3), 2272–2301. DOI: 10.1007/s13132-021-00813-x

Carayannis, E. G., & Campbell, D. F. J. (2010a). The Quintuple Helix innovation model: Global warming as a challenge and driver for innovation. *Journal of Innovation and Entrepreneurship*, *1*(2), 1–1225.

Carayannis, E. G., & Campbell, D. F. J. (2010b). The Quintuple Helix, Industrial 5.0, and Society 5.0. In The *Quintuple Helix Innovation Model* (pp. 1–20). Emerald Publishing Limited.

Carayannis, E. G., Grigoroudis, E., Stamati, D., & Valvi, T. (2019). Social business model innovation: A quadruple/quintuple helix-based social innovation ecosystem. *IEEE Transactions on Engineering Management*, *68*(1), 235–248. DOI: 10.1109/TEM.2019.2914408

Carayannis, E. G., & Morawska, J. (2023). University and education 5.0 for emerging trends, policies and practices in the concept of industry 5.0 and society 5.0. In *Industry 5.0: Creative and Innovative Organizations* (pp. 1–25). Springer International Publishing. DOI: 10.1007/978-3-031-26232-6_1

Carayannis, E. G., & Rakhmatullin, R. (2014). The Quadruple Innovation Helix (QIH): Application for the study of university-industry-government-community interfaces. *International Journal of Innovative Research and Development*, *5*(3-4), 191–212.

Chesbrough, H. W. (2003). *Open innovation: The new imperative for creating and profiting from technology*. Harvard Business Press.

Code World. (2024). *Learn Business Management*. Retrieved May 30, 2024, from: https://play.google.com/store/apps/details?id=com.codeworld.learnbusiness management&hl=pt

Deguchi, A., Hirai, C., Matsuoka, H., Nakano, T., Oshima, K., Tai, M., & Tani, S. (2020). What is society 5.0. *Society*, *5*, 1–23.

Etzkowitz, H., & Leydesdorff, L. (2000). The dynamics of innovation: From National Systems and "Mode 2" to a Triple Helix of university–industry–government relations. *Research Policy*, *29*(2), 109–1231. DOI: 10.1016/S0048-7333(99)00055-4

Fagerberg, J., & Mowery, D. (2015). *Recent research on innovation and economic change. Innovation, Technology and Economic Change*. Edward Elgar. DOI: 10.4337/9781784718633

Fu, W., Wang, Q., & Zhao, X. (2018). Platform-based service innovation and system design: A literature review. *Industrial Management & Data Systems*, *118*(5), 946–974. DOI: 10.1108/IMDS-03-2017-0129

Geissdoerfer, M., Savaget, P., Bocken, N. M., & Hultink, E. J. (2017). The Circular Economy–A new sustainability paradigm? *Journal of Cleaner Production*, *143*, 757–768. DOI: 10.1016/j.jclepro.2016.12.048

Gibbons, M., Limoges, C., Scott, P., Schwartzman, S., & Nowotny, H. (1994). *The new production of knowledge: The dynamics of science and research in contemporary societies*. Sage Publications.

GII. (2018). *Global Innovation Index 2018*. Energizing the world with innovation. WIPO. Available at: https://www.wipo.int/edocs/pubdocs/en/wipo_pub_gii_2018 .pdf

GII. (2023). *Global Innovation Index 2023*. Innovation in the face of uncertainty. WIPO. Available at: https://www.wipo.int/edocs/pubdocs/en/wipo-pub-2000-2023-en-main-report-global-innovation-index-2023-16th-edition.pdf

Kholiavko, N., Grosu, V., Safonov, Y., Zhavoronok, A., & Cosmulese, C. G. (2021). Quintuple helix model: Investment aspects of higher education impact on sustainability. *Management Theory and Studies for Rural Business and Infrastructure Development*, *43*(1), 111–128.

Liyanage, S. I. H., & Netswera, F. G. (2022). Greening universities with mode 3 and quintuple helix model of innovation–production of knowledge and innovation in knowledge-based economy, Botswana. [PubMed]. *Journal of the Knowledge Economy*, *13*(2), 1126–1156.

Mahardhani, A. J. (2023). The Role of Public Policy in Fostering Technological Innovation and Sustainability. [ADMAN]. *Journal of Contemporary Administration and Management*, *1*(2), 47–53. DOI: 10.61100/adman.v1i2.22

Muruccia, Y., Solazzo, G., Del Vecchio, P., & Passiante, G. (2020). Evidence from network analysis application to innovation systems and quintuple helix. *Technological Forecasting and Social Change*, *161*, 120306. DOI: 10.1016/j.techfore.2020.120306

Nunes, S., Lopes, R., & Fuller-Love, N. (2017). Networking, Innovation, and Firms' Performance: Portugal as Illustration. *Journal of the Knowledge Economy*, *10*(3), 899–920. DOI: 10.1007/s13132-017-0508-7

Pinto, H., & Nogueira, C. (2018). Mapping an Entrepreneurial, Innovative and Sustainable Ecosystem Using Social Network Analysis: An Exploratory Approach of Publicly Funded Innovative Project Data. In *Entrepreneurial, Innovative and Sustainable Ecosystems: Best Practices and Implications for Quality of Life* (pp. 237–254). Springer International Publishing. DOI: 10.1007/978-3-319-71014-3_12

Pricopoaia, O., Busila, A. V., Cristache, N., Susanu, I., & Matis, C. (2024). Challenges for entrepreneurial innovation: Startups as tools for a better knowledge-based economy. *The International Entrepreneurship and Management Journal*, *20*(2), 969–1010. DOI: 10.1007/s11365-023-00923-9

Putra, Z. D. W., & van der Knaap, W. G. (2018). Urban innovation system and the role of an open web-based platform: The case of Amsterdam smart city. *Journal of Regional and City Planning*, *29*(3), 234–249. DOI: 10.5614/jrcp.2018.29.3.4

Qmarkets (2024). *End-to-End Innovation Management Platform.* Retrieved May 30, 2024 from https://www.qmarkets.net/lp/innovation-management-software/?hsa_qmt=y&utm_term=innovation%20platform&utm_campaign=Tier+1+Countries+%7C+Gold+KWs+%26+Silver+KWs+%7C+Exact+%26+Phrase&utm_source=adwords&utm_medium=ppc&hsa_acc=3759777188&hsa_cam=8690653365&hsa_grp=139195627185&hsa_ad=696764641653&hsa_src=g&hsa_tgt=kwd-6668275533&hsa_kw=innovation%20platform&hsa_mt=p&hsa_net=adwords&hsa_ver=3&gad_source=1&gclid=CjwKCAjwx-CyBhAqEiwAeOcTde0vSdyeHGevzm0u29NihVgwUZcEE_6P3UWSO69UWyysLMQuWORLExoCPoUQAvD_BwE

Reis, J., Rosado, D. P., Ribeiro, D. F., & Melão, N. (2022). Quintuple Helix Innovation Model for the European Union Defense Industry—An Empirical Research. *Sustainability (Basel), 14*(24), 16499. DOI: 10.3390/su142416499

Vignieri, V. (2021). Crowdsourcing as a mode of open innovation: Exploring drivers of success of a multisided platform through system dynamics modelling. *Systems Research and Behavioral Science, 38*(1), 108–124. DOI: 10.1002/sres.2636

Zen, I. S., & Shibakawa, H. (2022). Quintuple Helix Lens for Transformation: An Okayama Model of Education for Sustainable Development. *Frontiers in Sustainability, 3*, 798330. DOI: 10.3389/frsus.2022.798330

KEY TERMS AND DEFINITIONS

Innovation Governance: Structures and processes designed to coordinate and guide innovation efforts among multiple stakeholders, ensuring that social, environmental, and economic priorities are balanced.

Knowledge Management: A set of practices and technologies used to identify, capture, share, and apply knowledge within and across organisations, considered essential for fostering continuous innovation.

Joint Performance Indicators: Metrics defined collaboratively by multiple sectors (e.g., university, industry, society) to assess the success and impact of innovation initiatives, promoting transparency and shared accountability.

QHITIS (Quintuple Helix Innovation Theory Information System): A proposed digital platform designed to operationalise the QHIT model by integrating data, interactive dashboards, and AI-driven analytics to facilitate collaboration and measurement across all five sectors.

Quintuple Helix Innovation Model (QHIT): A theoretical and practical framework that integrates five interconnected sectors – academia, industry, government, civil society, and the natural environment – to promote sustainable and inclusive innovation within the knowledge economy.

Sustainable Innovation: The process of developing new products, services, or processes that not only generate economic value but also address social and environmental challenges, aligning with sustainable development objectives.

Triple Helix Model: A precursor to the QHIT model, focused on the interaction between three core actors: university, industry, and government, aiming to foster innovation through institutional collaboration.

Chapter 3
Operationalizing the Triple Helix for Resource-Constrained Universities:
A Nested Model of Micro-Credentials, Research Groups, and Centres of Excellence

Mussa Ally Dida
https://orcid.org/0000-0002-7143-8953
Nelson Mandela African Institution of Science and Technology, Tanzania

ABSTRACT

Modern universities have shifted from basic teaching and research to becoming drivers of economic development and AI innovation. However, resource-constrained universities (RCUs) face a "vicious cycle" where limited funding, aging infrastructure, and a lack of specialized expertise prevent them from keeping pace with rapid technological shifts. Traditional academic structures are often too slow and rigid for the AI era, leaving many institutions marginalized in global innovation networks. To address this, the text proposes a "university-nested" ecosystem to operationalize the Triple Helix (university-industry-government) model through three mechanisms (1) Industry-co-designed micro-credentials for agile skills training, (2) Interdisciplinary Research Groups for collaborative problem-solving, and (3) Centres of Excellence to scale these partnerships sustainably. This roadmap enables RCUs to transform from passive degree-providers into proactive co-architects of technological innovation.

DOI: 10.4018/979-8-3373-9690-3.ch003

1. INTRODUCTION: THE TRIPLE HELIX IN THE AGE OF AI A NEED FOR STRUCTURAL REINVENTION

The 21st-century university operates within a fundamentally transformed landscape, shaped by the relentless acceleration of technological change and the demands of the global digital economy. Its traditional mandate, the triad of teaching, research, and consultancy has expanded into a complex, multi-dimensional mission encompassing community engagement, business incubation, innovation commercialization, technology transfer, and global partnership building (P. Altbach, 2008; Gallagher & Savage, 2023; Marginson & Marginson, 2022) This expanded remit is not merely additive, it represents a paradigm shift in societal expectations. Universities are now viewed as essential engines of economic development, social mobility, and national competitiveness, particularly in frontier technological domains such as artificial intelligence (AI), data science, cybersecurity, biotechnology, and quantum computing. In these fields, the velocity of discovery and application continuously redefines industry needs, workforce skills, and the very nature of global competition (Cunningham et al., 2022; Ma et al., 2017; Roy & Marsafawy, 2020).

This shifting mandate calls for new operational mode of universities-industry-government collaboration spheres where a normal a single institutional sphere, whether new product development in industry, policy making in government, or the creation and dissemination of knowledge in academia is not enough to timely come up with a just solution to fit all interested parties (Ranga & Etzkowitz, 2013; Zhou & Etzkowitz, 2021) . This shift entails not only various mechanisms of restructuring of the sources and development path of innovation, but also a rethinking of our main models for conceptualizing innovation (for example national, regional, sectoral, technological innovation systems, the Triple Helix, and so on) that may often fail to capture important innovation dynamics because of issues such as loose definition, collaboration challenges, or performance measurement gaps.

The concept of the Triple Helix of university-industry-government relationships interprets the shift from a dominating university working alone in the knowledge society to serve kingdoms, to university-government dyad in the Industrial Society to serve and generate industries, and are expanded to triadic relationship between university, industry and government in the Knowledge Society to serve industries and societies. The Triple Helix potential in accelerating innovation and economic development of a Knowledge Society lies in a more prominent role for equipping the university with the hybridization of elements from industry and government to generate new institutional dynamics and social formats for the production, transfer and application of knowledge (Vivar-simon et al., 2022). This vision encompasses not only the creative destruction of the natural innovation dynamics but also the creative renewal of the innovation systems that arises within each of the collaborative three institutional spheres a university, industry and government as well as at their intersections.

This implication of this shift is dominantly seen in resourced universities where industries and governments have close collaboration with universities through research, funds, expertise, or equipment's and jointly collaborate to improve national or university innovation systems and the results are globally dominating in terms of students employability, the quality and number of publications accomplished annually, cutting edge solution to the industries, and frontier knowledge generated. For a significant segment of the global higher education sector, particularly institutions in developing regions or those classified as resource-constrained universities (RCUs), this new reality presents a formidable challenge (P. G. Altbach, 2008; Philbin, 2012; Rwakenda, 2016; Van Damme, 2021). These institutions often grapple with systemic limitations of a scarcity of expertise (PhD-level researchers) in emerging fields, ageing or inadequate physical and digital infrastructure, chronic underfunding, and bureaucratic inertia. These constraints create a vicious cycle. They undermine an institution's ability to remain pedagogically current and research-relevant in fast-moving disciplines, which in turn diminishes its attractiveness to top-tier students, faculty, and crucially, industry partners. The limitations are expanded due to small industrial and government power in contributing to university innovation systems. Consequently, these universities risk being perpetually marginalized within global innovation networks, unable to fulfil their potential as catalysts for local and regional socioeconomic development (Daraio, 2017; Rafique et al., 2023; Torbacki, 2024).

The challenge is exponentially amplified by the nature of the AI revolution. Unlike previous technological waves, AI and associated digital emerging technologies are characterized by rapidly depreciating knowledge, where skills and infrastructure can become obsolete within months, not decades. Traditional academic structures with their multi-year curriculum review cycles, protracted faculty hiring processes, and rigid, and siloed departmental organizations are fundamentally misaligned with this pace. The conventional model of university-industry collaboration, often built upon high-level Memoranda of Understanding (MoUs) and occasional guest lectures, lacks the operational granularity and agility to foster deep, reciprocal innovation. The theoretical Triple Helix model, which posits synergistic interactions between university, industry, and government as the key to innovation in a knowledge-based society, remains sound in principle. However, in practice, its implementation often fails to move beyond ceremonial partnerships, especially in contexts where one helix (typically the university) is structurally weakened. This failure is reinforced by global ranking systems that privilege metrics like high-impact publication volume and advanced research infrastructure, inadvertently penalizing RCUs and perpetuating a global innovation hierarchy (P. G. Altbach & Salmi, 2011; Geels, 2004; Köhler et al., 2019; Moscardini et al., 2021).

This chapter posits that to revitalize the Triple Helix for the demands of the AI era, a fundamental operational reinvention is required. It argues that this reinvention can be effectively driven by three interconnected, scalable, and output-oriented mechanism:

i. University-Industry co-designed micro-credentials,
ii. Formally structured interdisciplinary Research Groups, and
iii. Sustainable Centres of Excellence (CoEs).

These mechanisms form a "university-nested" ecosystem model that enables universities, especially RCUs, to overcome systemic constraints and transform into proactive, agile, and indispensable nodes within the innovation landscape.

Micro-credentials act as the agile interface for rapid skills alignment and continuous learning, building trust and a common language with industry. Research Groups function as the foundational, project-driven "engine rooms" of collaborative problem-solving, embedding industry partners directly into the research lifecycle. Centres of Excellence (not formal university departments) represent the institutionalization and scaling of this collaboration, evolving from successful Research Groups into sustainable hubs that provide long-term strategic value to all stakeholders. This phased, structured approach moves partnership from rhetoric to reality, translating alignment into action, and co-creation into tangible socioeconomic impact.

Drawing on evidence-based analysis, comparative international case studies, and practical governance frameworks, this chapter will demonstrate how this model operationalizes the Triple Helix. It provides a roadmap for universities to strategically build capacity, focus limited resources, and ascend the value chain from being passive suppliers of graduates to becoming co-architects of technological innovation. In the age of AI, where the race for talent and applied innovation defines national and corporate futures, this reinvention is not optional, it is existential for universities seeking to fulfil their expanded societal mandate and drive meaningful, inclusive societal development.

1.1 Conceptual Model of the Nested Ecosystem for Resource-Constrained Universities

The conceptual model of a university-nested ecosystem designed to operationalize the Triple Helix framework within resource-constrained universities (RCUs) is shown Figure 1. The modal move a RCU from a theoretical triple helix partnership to a structured, phased implementation of actual activity and outcome based triple helix, embedding scalable mechanisms directly within the university helix to catalyze and synergize interaction with industry and government.

Figure 1. Conceptual Model of a Nested Ecosystem of Micro-Credentials, Research Groups, and Centres of Excellence

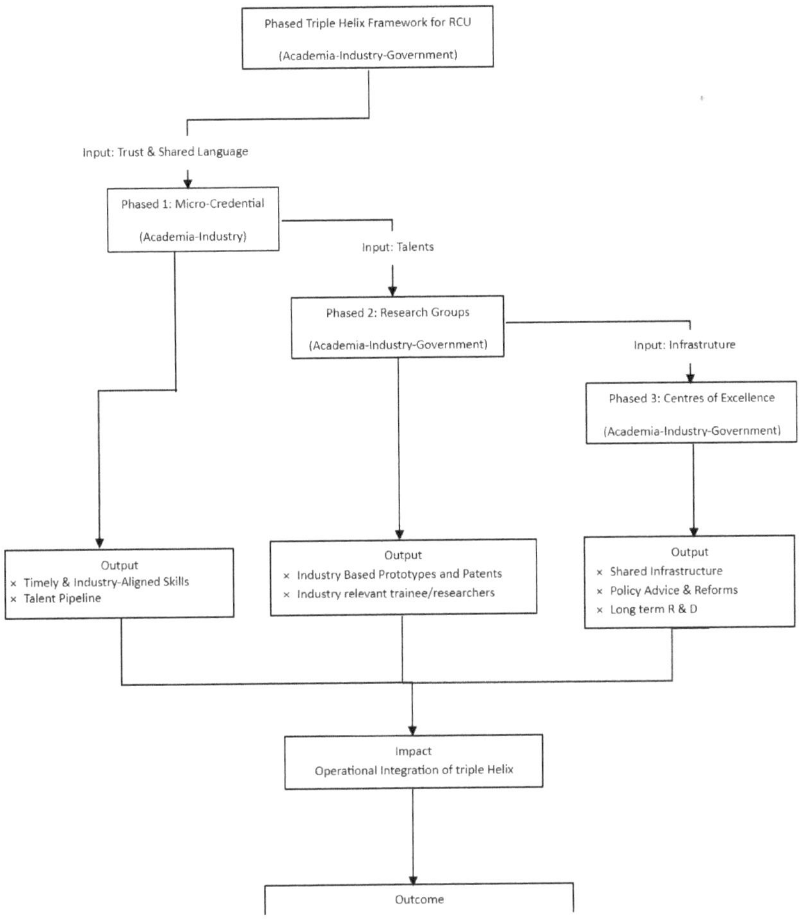

At the model's foundation lies the core Triple Helix structure, representing the dynamic, reciprocal flows between university, industry, and government. The university contributes skills and research; industry provides practical alignment, resources, and market direction; and government enables the partnership through policy, funding, and infrastructure. The proposed nested mechanisms are integrated within this interactive space, transforming it from a ceremonial arrangement into a functional innovation engine (Maria Manuela, 2013). The model progresses through three distinct, yet interconnected, phases each building upon the outputs of the previous to create a virtuous cycle of capacity development and impact. The details of the model is further explained in section 2, 3, and 4 demonstrating how resource contrained universities can be strategically refocused through these phased mechanisms, enabling RCUs to ascend in the innovation value chain and transform from passive institutions into proactive, indispensable nodes within the regional and global innovation landscape.

2. MICRO-CREDENTIALS AS DYNAMIC INNOVATION CATALYSTS OF MODERN TRIPLE-HELIX COOPERATION

2.1 Definition, Typology, and Significance in the Modern Higher Education Ecosystem

To improve the triple helix, this section introduces micro-credential as a first phase of innovative academia-industry helix. Micro-credentials represent a disruptive innovation in credentialing and improving industry-academia relations. They are short, focused, competency-based certifications that validate the acquisition of specific skills, knowledge, or abilities. Typically requiring weeks to several months to complete, they are characterized by their modularity, stackability, and frequent integration with digital badges that provide verifiable, granular evidence of learning (Duklas, 2020; OCED, 2023a; Orman et al., 2023). They are offered by a diverse array of providers including traditional universities, specialized industry academies (e.g., AWS Academy, Cisco Networking Academy, Google Academy) and global online platforms (e.g., Coursera, edX, Udacity).

Micro-credential significance stems from a direct confrontation with the core rigidity of traditional degree programs. The traditional degree programmes consist of a standard three or four-year undergraduate degree, or even a two-year master's program, operates on a development and accreditation timeline that is inherently misaligned with the innovation cycle in emerging fields like AI, where new frameworks, tools, and best practices emerge daily or weekly. In this AI era, the triple helix of university-industry-government fails to produce ready- made workers due to quality control standardized by the 19th century educational modal universities. The quality control mechanism are limiting iterations of university curriculum and industry are getting uncooked workers. In this operation mode, by the time a new AI module is approved, vetted, and inserted into a curriculum, the technology it addresses may have evolved significantly. With the velocity of innovation needed in new era, the evolution of triple helix is needed to ensure the students are ready made by the time they complete their studies. This can be achieved by incorporating specific micro-credentials in existing curriculum, a micro-credentials close this "skills velocity gap" by enabling just-in-time, just-enough learning (Coetzee, 2024; OECD, 2021; Orman et al., 2023). With co-development by the industry, the micro-credentials offers not only the time essential skills, but offers industry relevant case studies offered in a mature quality control premises of the university. This mix, produces the following transformative roles in a higher education sector:

i. Catalysing a Culture of Agile, Lifelong Learning: Micro-credentials facilitate a paradigm shift from "front-loaded" education where learning is concentrated in early adulthood to a model of continuous, career-long upskilling and reskilling. They can improve a normal learning by introducing fast evolving and industry related needed expertise, and a micro-credential module can fill the learning gap required by industry and university without worrying of the time-consuming accreditation process. The module learning of micro-credentials is essential in fields where professional knowledge has a short half-life or specialized skills evolving faster than a normal university learning cycle. They also contribute to needed changes of a profession in cases were a professional needs extra certification to practise in a new area, evolved area, or emerging area. Thus instead of a retaking a bachelor or a masters degree one can take electronics badges or micro-credential, gain needed expertise, and starts to practise in a new field of study.
ii. Bridging the Academia-Industry Semantic and Trust Gap: Micro-credentials encode industry-verified, applied competencies into a portable, transparent credential. This creates a shared understanding of what a learner can actually *do*, moving beyond the opaque proxy of a degree title. With a practical oriented case studies and industry based and developed micro-credentials, they builds industry-wide trust. The ability of employers to often directly involved in defining the learning outcomes of the micro-credentials, and their easier of adaptations offers additional trust between the industry, and academia.
iii. Democratizing Access to Cutting-Edge Education for RCUs:For institutions lacking the capital to build a state-of-the-art AI lab or hire a cohort of world-renowned researchers, micro-credentials offer a pragmatic on-ramp. A university can partner with a cloud provider (e.g., Google Cloud, Microsoft Azure) to offer a credential in required profession (e.g Large Language Model Operations). The uses of industry known infrastructure or "partner" and curated content delivers industry-relevant training long before a RCU could develop a full, accredited degree program independently.

2.2. The Imperative of Co-Design: Embedding Market Reality into Curriculum

The value of a micro-credential is intrinsically tied to its market relevance. Therefore, co-design a structured, collaborative development process involving university faculty, instructional designers, and industry subject-matter experts is non-negotiable for credentials intended to catalyze innovation partnerships(Musseau, 2024; Orman et al., 2023; Pirkkalainen et al., 2023). This process ensures that learning objectives, assessments, and projects are reverse-engineered from real-world job roles, competency and quality assurance standards and frameworks, and current industry challenges.

In the context of AI, co-design often involves formal partnerships with technology leaders (Google, NVIDIA, IBM), sector-specific corporations (e.g., a bank for AI in finance), and professional bodies (Richert et al., 2024). A key innovation is the formal articulation and stacking of micro-credentials into traditional academic pathways. For example:

i. A series of co-designed credentials such as "Data Engineering with Apache Spark" (industry platform), "Responsible AI Audit Frameworks" (university-provided), and "ML Model Deployment on Kubernetes" (industry platform) could be collectively assessed and recognized as equivalent to 15-20 credits within a Master of Science in Data Science program. The co-designed and stacked micro-credentials allows for industry to use mature quality assurance methods which are not available on the normal industry designed micro-credentials and overall increase trustworthiness of the overall course module stacked together between partners.
ii. This "stackable" model creates a hybrid, flexible degree pathway, allowing learners to blend theoretical depth with applied, current skills. It directly attacks skills obsolescence. When a transformative new tool like OpenAI's GPT API or a paradigm like diffusion models for generative AI emerges, a 30-hour co-designed micro-credential can be prototyped, validated with industry partners, and launched within a single academic term. This transform the university in delivering its curriculum as they will not only offers industry proven micro-credentials, but offer ontime needed training provided and validated with industry solution to students, this approach ensures learning is both time-sensitive and impactful, effectively bridging the gap between academic theory and career readiness.

Strategically implementing micro-credentials in collaboration with key stakeholders enhances university education by integrating industry-expert trainers into the curriculum. This approach reduces infrastructure costs for new programs and fosters a modern learning culture by exposing students to diverse digital tools, industry-specific case studies, matured quality control process, and professional facilitators.

2.3. Tripartite Value Proposition: A Win-Win-Win Ecosystem

To accommodate the changing needs of industry, the education sector has introduced micro-credentials to ensure that the industry needs of job training or readymade training are obtained fresh from universities which is a necessity for emerging technologies fields of studies (Brown et al., 2021; Christiansen et al., 2022; OCED, 2023b; Richert et al., 2024). The micro-credentials were pioneered by Deakin University and popularized by MIT (Musseau, 2024). Technology companies, including Google, IBM, Microsoft, Amazon, and Coursera, joined the hand to offer other cutting-edge micro-credentials (Brown et al., 2021). The provision of micro-credentials has been accelerated by major technology companies, educational platforms, and the rise of COVID-19 pandemic.

Although, developed universities have started offering micro-credentials, they are still more famous in learning platforms or technological companies and resource constrained universities are still laging behind in offering micro-credentials. With their advantages, micro-credential can play a big transformative role to resource constrained universities. By offering micro-credentials, a resource constrained universities expand the scope of training to their students but also can act as a source of revenue to other students who just need the electronic badges instead of the whole bachelor or masters degree.

Figure 2 shows how a micro-credential brings together students, universities and industries. A robust micro-credentialing strategy, rooted in co-design, co-development, and co-teaching creates compelling value for all three helices of the innovation model:

i. For Students and Professionals: They gain low-risk, industry recognized, practical oriented, high-flexibility pathways to in-demand, verifiable skills that enhance skills with possible immediate employability, career mobility, or professional recognition. The ability to "test" a new field of study through a short credential before committing to a full degree reduces barriers to entry or increases chances of students completing a new field of study. For working professionals, it enables continuous, applied learning without career interruption, directly linking education to work performance and advancement or possibility of changing carriers.
ii. For Universities (Especially RCUs):
    a. Enhanced Relevance & Recruitment: Institutions become more attractive to students seeking employable skills, improving enrolment metrics.
    b. Faculty Development: Micro-credentials provide a mechanism for academic staff to update their own skills in partnership with industry, keeping pedagogy at the technological frontier.

c. New Revenue Streams: They open avenues for professional, continuing, and online education income.
d. Strategic Partnership Gateway: A successful co-designed credential builds trust, establishes workflows, and often grants the university access to proprietary industry software, cloud computing credits and real-world datasets resources that directly overcome internal infrastructure deficits.
e. Improved Key Performance Indicators (KPIs): Successful micro-credential programs can positively impact university ranking metrics related to graduate employment rates, industry income, and internationalization.

iii. For Industry Partners:
a. Efficient Talent Pipeline Development: Co-designed credentials act as a powerful pre-screening and pre-skilling mechanism, dramatically reducing recruitment costs and time-to-productivity for new hires.
b. Targeted Workforce Upskilling: Companies can efficiently address specific skill gaps within their existing workforce at scale, using a trusted academic partner. Evidence from platforms like Coursera for Business and LinkedIn Learning shows strong correlations between structured upskilling programs and improved employee retention, innovation, and operational agility.
c. Seeding the Innovation Pipeline: The process of co-designing credentials ensures a constant flow of real-world problems and frontier challenges into the academic sphere, naturally seeding ideas for future collaborative research projects within Research Groups.

Figure 2. Micro-Credential bringing together students, industries, and Universities

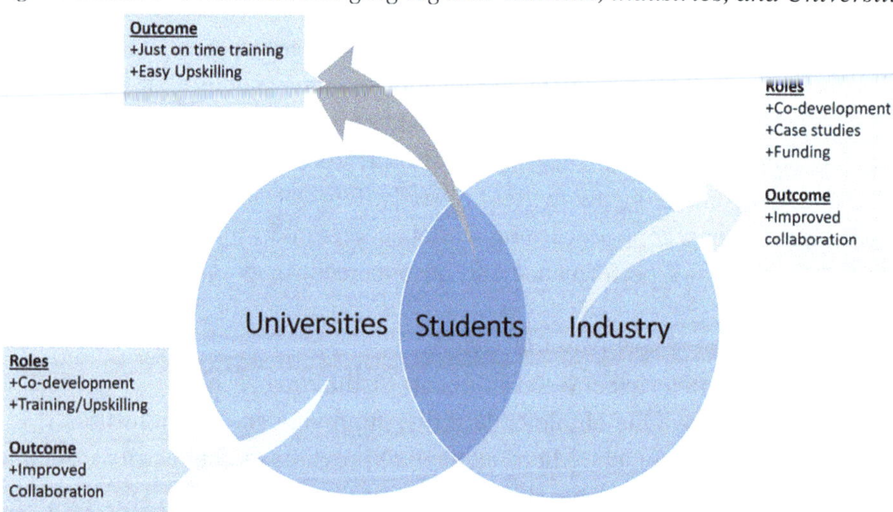

2.4 Implementation Challenges and Adaptations for RCUs

While elite institutions have matured frameworks, Resource Constrained Universities (RCUs) face significant barriers, including limited funding, aging IT infrastructure, and rigid administrative hurdles so micro-credential implementation can be an additional task and instead of transforming the RCU, it be one of the stumbling block of daily operation of the university. To easily implement the micro-credential a RCU need to be pragmatic and adopt a forward looking approach and this can be done without requiring massive upfront investment:

i. Leveraging Infrastructure-as-a-Service: RCUs do not need to build expensive AI labs. They can partner with established micro-credential players, by partnering with cloud providers (AWS Academy, Google Cloud, or Microsoft Azure), the university can utilize the partner's existing infrastructure. As seen in the Iowa State case study, using browser-based, GPU-accelerated environments bypasses internal IT bottlenecks.
ii. Adopt the Freemium Content Strategy: Instead of developing curriculum from scratch, RCUs together with industry practitioners can adopt already Curated content in their curriculum. This curated-hybrid model, allows faculty to use high-quality, existing content from platforms like Coursera or edX as the "textbook," while providing the localized context, mentoring, and rigorous assessment required for credit-bearing micro-credentials.
iii. Piloting Micro-credentials: Rather than seeking full institutional overhaul, RCUs can start with "Non-Credit" badges. Once these demonstrate market demand and generate initial revenue, the data can be used to lobby government accreditation bodies for formal credit-bearing status and industry for funding mechanism toward additional micro-credentials and specific to industries lobbied.

2.5 Government Role in Micro-Credentials

In the triple helix model of innovation, the government plays a critical policy and regulatory role within the education sector. This function is essential for maintaining quality and coherence. In the context of micro-credentials, this role is often executed through national accreditation agencies, which can accredit traditional bachelor's or master's degree programs that integrate micro-credentials. A key advantage of embedded micro-credentials is their inherent flexibility, allowing curricula to adapt swiftly to technological advancements and deepen collaboration with industry. To ensure this innovation strengthens rather than distorts the education system, accreditation bodies can establish frameworks such as setting a minimum credit threshold for core curricula and implement regular quality reviews

2.6 Case Studies in Operational Excellence and Ecosystem Integration

There are a number of universities with matured framework in implementing micro-credentials. These universities act as a case study for resource constrained universities in adopting and standardising the micro-credentials. The selection of the universities wasbased on the synthesis of policy documents and institutional reports. The selection criteria for cases includes geographic diversity, explicit focus on AI, availability of public documentation, thematic analysis to extract best practices. The case studies opted includes Iowa State University's Translational AI Center, The "AI+X" Micro-Credential Model in China, and the State University of New York (SUNY) System-Wide Initiative.

These Real-world case study implementations illustrate how micro-credentials are woven into the fabric of the Triple Helix, serving as catalysts for broader innovation:

i. Iowa State University's Translational AI Center: The center offers industry-focused AI micro-credentials designed for professionals who are ready to advance in translational artificial intelligence. It has partnered with Vocareum, a cloud-based lab platform to create beginners and intensive four-week micro-credentials in areas like "End-to end computer Vision" and "Scientific Machine Learning". The model bypasses university IT bottlenecks by providing learners instant, browser-based access to pre-configured, GPU-accelerated development environments. Automated assessment and feedback allow for scaling. Crucially, the curriculum is defined by industry needs for continuous integration/deployment (CI/CD) pipelines of machine learning models that are critical in modern tech companies but rarely covered in traditional Computer Science degrees. This creates graduates who are "day-one ready" for high-value industrial roles.

ii. The "AI+X" Micro-Credential Model in China: This is a pioneering Inter-disciplinary education system, primarily driven by elite Chinese universities, that blends core AI skills with diverse fields (X) like humanities and policy. It uses flexible online courses and digital badges to rapidly develop T-shaped AI professionals needed for the digital economy, bridging theory with practical, real-world applications through collaborative, competency-based learning. It is integrated by domestic tech giants (Baidu, Alibaba, Tencent, Huawei). The model offers "AI+X" credentials where "X" is a vertical application domain like healthcare, fintech, or smart manufacturing (Wei et al., 2025). These "AI +X" programs are co-taught by university professors and senior industry engineers, using sanitized real company data and case studies. Research indicates this model is highly effective, accounting for over 70% of the variance in teaching effectiveness scores and successfully producing "T-shaped" professionals with deep technical AI skills combined with broad application domain knowledge. This embeds the university directly into the nation's strategic industrial upgrading plans.

iii. The State University of New York (SUNY) System-Wide Initiative: SUNY is the largest comprehensive university system in the US. It brings together 64 institutions serving more than million students. With over 500 micro-credentials in more than 60 discipline areas it demonstrates how a consortium of institutions has been successful in developing stackable, credit-bearing micro-credentials to provide career and academic pathways for adult learners (Brown et al., 2023). SUNY's approach focuses on regional economic development. SUNY micro-credentials are compact academic credentials taught by SUNY faculty that empower students with essential skills, knowledge and practical experience in high-demand fields. They are designed to be completed in months, not years, SUNY micro-credentials ready students to secure employment, keep pace with changes in your industry, and/or advance in your career. Credit-bearing micro-credentials also jumpstart students or professional academic journey, providing credits toward certificates, initial or advanced degrees, and opening new doors to success in life and career. Its campuses work directly with local chambers of commerce and small-to-medium enterprises (SMEs) to identify acute skills shortages. This model explicitly positions the university system as the agile, responsive skills arm of the state government (the third helix), directly translating public investment in education into immediate regional competitiveness and job creation.

2.7 Conclusion: Micro-Credentials as a Stepping Stone to Embedded Innovation

The academia industry linkage growth can be fast tracked by the micro-credential, withs its easy adoption and availability of ready-made courses which meets normal university learning outcomes. The real transformative power of micro-credentials lies not in the certificate itself, but in their capacity to redefine the foundational relationship within the Triple Helix and innovate the learning system. They precipitate a critical shift in mindset, moving the partnership from a purely transactional model (buying a service or short-term training from university) to a deeply embedded and strategic one of co-development of training materials to co-training. This mindset shift becomes necessity for emerging fields of study or practise such as AI were the industry cannot wait for normal learning duration of university, instead reskilling available staff and accrediting the skills for ready-made professionals.

The Shift from Transactional to Embedded Partnerships is cemented by the outlined case studies (such as the Iowa State Translational AI Center and the "AI+X" model) exemplify a fundamental shift in engagement:

i. Talent Circulation and Vetting: Micro-credentials serve as a highly effective, low-risk pre-screening and upskilling mechanism for industry partners. By participating in co-designed programs, companies gain direct access to a pipeline of proven talent whose skills have been validated in a real-world context using industry standards and tools. For students, it's a seamless transition; for industry, it significantly reduces recruitment and onboarding costs. The credential becomes the currency of trust for high-stakes hiring and the long quality assurance mechanism act a trading house between the university and student by creating a win-win transactional mode for both students and industries.
ii. Trust-Building through Co-Creation: The act of co-designing, co-developing, and co-teaching a micro-credential forces academic faculty and industry practitioners to overcome their inherent cultural and procedural silos. They must agree on learning outcomes, technical stacks, assessment methods, and teaching modality. This shared, output-oriented activity builds mutual respect and trust a critical precursor for deeper research collaborations. It replaces abstract Memoranda of Understanding (MoUs) with concrete, successful and sustainable joint projects.
iii. Continuous Problem Definition: Micro-credentials compel the continuous circulation of current, real-world problems from industry into the university curriculum. As technology evolves (e.g., a new AI framework emerges or new application areas) the micro-credential is rapidly updated, ensuring that academic staff are constantly exposed to the frontier of industrial practice. This sustained alignment ensures that research agendas are directly informed by market needs leading to the identification of viable, high-impact challenges suitable for research and immediately benefiting the industry.

By bridging the functional and knowledge gap, micro-credentials forces collaboration of the university-industry-government and bridge the industry-academia gap and create a common operational language and shared trust in the triple helix that naturally accelerates the transition to more complex, resource-intensive, and higher-stakes collaborations. This demonstrated capacity for successful joint activity, validated talent, shared tools, and market-aligned knowledge. This evolves the normal collaboration helix and calls for more collaborations efforts including the formation of a Research Group, the next and more dedicated level of operational integration within the Nested Model of Innovation

3. RESEARCH GROUPS: THE FOUNDATIONAL, AGILE ENGINE OF TRIPLE HELIX CO-CREATION

While micro-credentials align human capital and timely producing new skills collaboratively developed by industry experts, the core of collaborative innovation in "Triple Helix of University-Government-Industry Partnerships and the Development of AI" resides in the joint creation of new knowledge and technologies. The formalized, interdisciplinary Research Group (RG) is the primary catalytic structure for this work, it moves beyond informal academic networks or individual professor-consultant relationships to establish a consortium of experts deliberately assembled to tackle a specific, strategically chosen technology related challenge (Muñoz & Plazas, 2024; Vabø et al., 2016).

Different Studies shows that most of the senior researchers works "formally or informally" in collaboration with other peers research collaborates (Kyvik & Reymert, 2016) and proposes a structure for establishing a formal research group. Although, junior researchers have less collaboration than junior researchers, the most common challenge of the formal or informal research groups are the average size of a research group across different fields of studies. (Cook et al., 2015), maturity of the collaboration and its institutional support, cutting-edge equipment's available to the research groups in advancing knowledge, and cooperation agreements of the resources shared and benefits of the solutions generated.

To advance the university-government-industry collaboration, more researches are calling for formalizing of the research groups as a strategic component and a microcosm of the triple helix for accelerated innovation and adoption of emerging technologies. The research groups not only pull together expert knowledge but strategically working together toward a common goal or solution. To reduce investment time, the resources shared includes experts, data across institutions, and cutting equipment's available between partners.

3.1. Research Group Composition

An effective Research Group is a deliberate embodiment of the Triple Helix principle. Its composition is carefully curated from like-minded institution's staff and supported by flexible collaboration agreement between partners, the roles of partners and their staff composition across the research group are as follows:

i. University Core (The Knowledge Helix): Includes senior and early-career academicians, postdoctoral researchers, and PhD/master's students. They provide deep disciplinary expertise, methodological rigor, and a focus on fundamental understanding and publishable research. They are responsible for basic research and applied research on the partners in the collaboration.

ii. Industry Embeddedness (The Innovation Helix): Involves engineers, applied scientists, product managers, and R&D leads from partner companies. They contribute the critical elements of *context including* real-world problem definitions, access to proprietary or industrial-scale datasets, knowledge of production constraints, cutting edge equipment's, and a focus on scalability, usability, and market viability of the solution provided.

iii. Government/Policy Linkage (The Governance Helix): May include representatives from relevant public agencies, regulatory bodies, or standards organizations. Their role is to ensure the research considers public interest, follows ethical guidelines and regulatory frameworks, and aligned with national or regional strategic priorities (e.g., digital sovereignty, climate action). Additionally, to ensure they ensures the research and innovation priorities of national or international strategic areas of interest are worked on by the research groups and their solution are ethically obtained for global benefit.

This integrated team is sourced from initial joint work and formalized through a lightweight but clear collaboration agreement. The agreement mostly an addendum to the existing MoU with proven deliverable outlines governance mechanism, intellectual property (IP) ownership and licensing (e.g., using standardized frameworks like the Lambert Toolkit), data-sharing protocols, publication rights, and resource commitments. This formalization is crucial to transforms goodwill into accountable, operational partnership (Kyvik & Reymert, 2017).

3.2. Catalytic Functions Within the Triple helix Ecosystem

Research groups not only bring together experts across triple helix of university-government-industry, it need to be the engine that drives innovation in emerging fields of study or practise like AI. They must be enabled by tripartite agreements, policy or guidelines to pool resources together across partners to ensure appropriate solutions are timely obtained and adopted by industry player for national or international benefits. Figure 3 shows a university-industry-government partnership, a well-structured Research Group acts as a multi-function catalyst of the triple helix:

1. From Abstract to Concrete: The main role of the research group is implementing dialogue from vague aspirations of "working together" to focused execution on a scoped project with defined performance indicators, deliverables, and success metrics (e.g., a working prototype, a benchmarked algorithm, or a white paper).

2. De-risked Exploration for Industry: It provides companies, especially SMEs, with a lower-cost, lower-risk environment to explore nascent technologies or fundamental questions with academic experts, without the need for massive internal capital allocation. For government it ensures the accelerated benefits of the solution while getting properly governed solution in sceptical emerging fields.
3. Hyper-Relevant Talent Pipeline: Students and researchers are immersed in live industry challenges. They graduate not only with theoretical knowledge but with applied experience, professional networks, and often, direct pathways to employment. For industry, this is an extended, intensive talent audition.
4. Dual-Output Innovation Cycle: The research group is designed to produce dual outputs that satisfy the success criteria of both worlds: academic impact (high-quality peer-reviewed publications, conference presentations, trained researchers) and commercial/industrial impact (patent filings, proof-of-concept prototypes, process improvements, contributions to open-source projects). Both outputs must follow the national and international policies, and priorities. This "win-win" logic is essential for triple-helix sustained engagement.

Figure 3. Research Groups in the Triple Helix

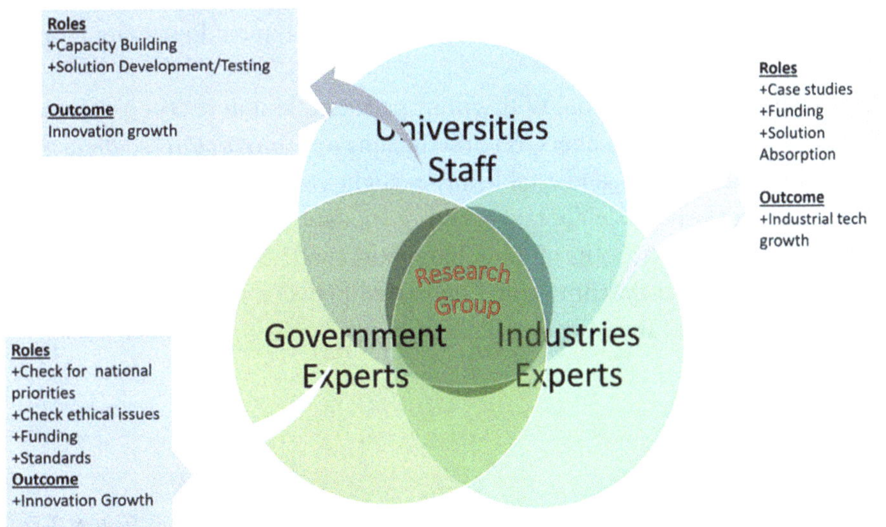

3.3. Strategic Operationalization: A Framework for RCUs

The establishment of strategic Research Groups cannot be left to ad-hoc faculty initiative alone. For sustainable operation of a multiple partners, it requires an institutional strategy as detailed in stage (i-iii) and illustrated in Figure 4. RCU and partner institutions should give this priority to ensure a win to win for all parties of the formed research groups (Cook et al., 2015). The operationalization of the research groups follows the following stages:

i. Internal Capacity Audit & Niche Identification: The university must conduct an honest assessment of its research strengths. The goal is to identify 1-2 niche areas where it has, or can realistically build, a critical mass of expertise that is relevant to industry. This is about focused excellence, not broad superficiality. Example: A university in an agricultural region might focus on "AI for Soil Health Monitoring" or "Computer Vision for Crop Disease Detection."
ii. Targeted Partner Mapping: Instead of seeking generic partnerships with large multinationals, the university identifies specific regional industries, national corporates, or public-sector agencies whose strategic challenges align perfectly with its chosen niche and can contribute to the mission and the vision of the established research group. In this collaboration, the university pitch shifts from "We want to collaborate" to "We have specific expertise to help you solve problem X" and the industry contribution talent and equipment in solving problem X.
iii. Structured Group Formation: With willing partners, the university co-defines the RG's charter, recruits members (often dedicating a postdoc or PhD studentship as an institutional "seed"), and establishes the lightweight governance agreement. The agreement should elaborate working modalities, expected performance indicators, and how benefits of the collaboration will be shared among partners. Research Group Leadership should be shared between partners, with both an academic Principal Investigator and an industry Lead.

Figure 4. Formation of Research Groups

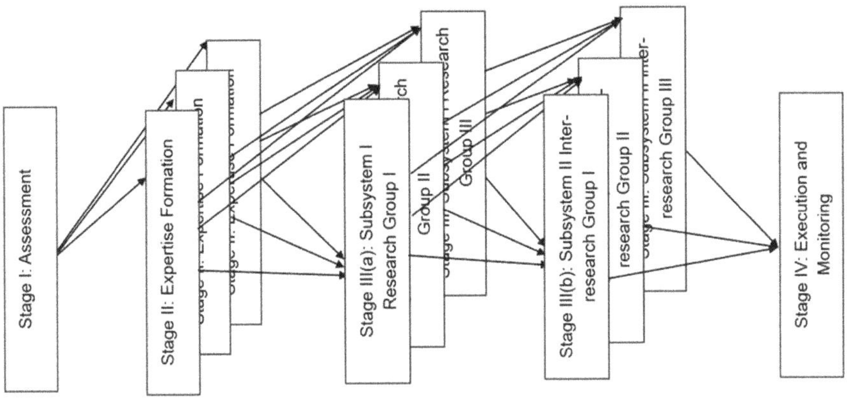

A leadership of a resource-constrained university is critical, it ensures the partnership is built around the university's developmental goals, transforming it from a subcontractor or talent feeder into a genuine co-architect of the research agenda. By establishing transparent metrics (as illustrated in Figure 4*), securing equitable funding among partners, adequately resourcing the research group, and implementing clear performance indicators, the group can be elevated from a peripheral unit engaged in anecdotal reporting to a central engine of innovation for all stakeholders.*

For a successfully operated research group, it can expand to interdisciplinary research group. The evolution is because of the expanded mandate and expanded members with expectation of more output. The evolution will be contributed by additional resources (experts, cutting edge equipment's, and financial resources) contributing to sustainability of the research groups and possibility of attracting funds from other stakeholders due quality of the outputs.

As the research group matures into an Interdisciplinary Research Group, a process that generally takes about three years, the scope widens significantly. This stage requires the integration of multiple related disciplines and the cultivation of strong external partnerships. Unlike the early-stage research group, the Interdisciplinary Research Group is characterized by its "magnet" effect to actively attract external experts and acquiring cutting-edge equipment to bolster its research capacity.

3.4 Research Group Sustainability and Strategic Output

A defining feature of the evolved Interdisciplinary Research Group is its focus on sustainability. While the original Research Group relies on limited resources and specific grants, the Interdisciplinary Research Group develops sophisticated funding mechanisms. It successfully mobilizes resources from a variety of stakeholders, including private industry players, by leveraging the high quality of its outputs. In this advanced phase, the responsibilities of the members shift. They are no longer just researchers; they become active participants in funding mobilization and resource acquisition to improve overall triple helix innovation ecosystem and funding capacity. A knowledge sharing also expands beyond technical solutions to include the sharing of strategic funding pathways. The strength of this phased triple helix framework "**A Nested Model of Micro-Credentials, Research Groups, and Centres of Excellence**" lies in its evolutionary design. By allowing a Research Group to build credibility and capacity incrementally, the transition ensures that the group does not overextend itself too early. Instead, it maintains a steady output targeting a high-impact solution per capita and a consistent patenting threshold while scaling its influence across multiple scientific and industrial sectors.

Table 1 shows the key characteristics of the research groups and its different to a multi-year established interdisciplinary research group, highlighting their evolution in terms of discipline, expert, funding, resources, and collaboration scope. The framework's strength lies in this evolutionary design, allowing the RCU to build credibility and capacity incrementally.

Table 1. Characteristics of Research Group and evolved Interdisciplinary Research Group

SN	Characteristics/ Output	Research Group	Interdisciplinary Research Group
1	Research Discipline	The same or a closely related research discipline	More than one closely related discipline
2	Timeline	Easy of establishing, one year for operation frameworks to be established	Maturity of the research groups and strong partners are needed, three years
3	Funding	Specific Challenge based funding	Increased funding from a variety of source (including other industry players)
4	Resources	Limited resources (Human, Time and Equipment)	Increased access to resources
5	Responsibilities	Members combine efforts for groundbreaking research and innovation	Members combine efforts for groundbreaking research, innovation, and funding mechanism
6	Knowledge Sharing	Share knowledge on challenges and solutions	Share knowledge on challenges, solutions, and funding mechanism
7	Expertise	Share expertise among researchers and innovators	Share expertise and attract additional expertise

continued on following page

Table 1. Continued

SN	Characteristics/ Output	Research Group	Interdisciplinary Research Group
8	Equipment	Share equipment within the subsystem	Share equipment and acquire additional equipment
9	Collaboration	Peer to peer research collaborations	Collaborate on joint funding mobilization.
10	Publication	Publish at least 50% per capita on the size of group in high impact figure journals	Publish at least 40% per capita in the group
11	Patent	Patent at most 20% of number of people in the group	Patent at most 20% of number of people in the group

3.5 Implementation Challenges and Adaptations for RCUs

The lack of substantial internal funding often stalls the formation of formal research groups. this includes lack of specific staff and funds for postdoctoral and postgraduate students, and additional state of the art equipments. However, RCUs can adopt a pragmatic, bootstrapped approach by shifting focus from capital-intensive labs to talent and data intensive collaborations.

i. Human as a seed Capital: RCUs can prioritize the allocation of existing internal staff (after expert evaluation in Figure 4), scholarships or sabbatical time to staff specifically working within these joint RGs, effectively seeding the research group without new external funding.
ii. The Niche Excellence Strategy: RCUs should avoid trying to start too many research group and compete in broad with name of the groups instead of the achievement of the research group in expensive fields. Instead, a RCU must identify 1–2 niche areas where they have local relevance and expertise. A Pragmatic Action includes starting AI-driven mineral analysis research group if the university in a mining belt and utilize the local industry's existing field sites as their labs.
iii. Resource-Sharing Agreements: In the absence of funding or grants, a RCUs can trade intellectual labour for infrastructure access. This pragmatic action involves a university to provides the PhD students and faculty time (labour) to the industry with the aim of solving industrial challenge. In this approach, the industry partner provides access to their cutting-edge equipment, proprietary data, and cloud computing credits. This removes the RCU's need for massive capital expenditure.

iv. Lightweight Governance: It's a practise of RCU to sign a number of MOU's with bureaucratic implementation and vague achievable goals. Standard university bureaucracy can kill agile research. RCUs should use "standardized toolkits" (example of Lambert Toolkit) to handle IP and data sharing quickly. The pragmatic action is to start with small-scale, 6-month projects with a right-to-first-refusal IP clause for industry, which builds the trust necessary to unlock larger, multi-year funding for a university to expand the solution generated.

3.6 Case Studies of Research Groups

Academic literature underscores the centrality of research groups as the primary unit of knowledge production. Studies note that senior researchers predominantly work within such groups, and their size and structure significantly impact output. There are a number of universities with matured formal research groups, some research groups are meant as a formal university-industry-government group to supervise postgraduate but others go above research or postgraduate supervision to product and solution generated. selecting a research group. The research group case studies were selected based on the focus of emerging technology, web based presence, and maturity of the research group. The selection includes Actin-based molecular machines of University of Helsinki, Astronics of University of Malta, and Stanford Artificial Intelligence. Both groups combine the academic rigour and industrial activities in their operations. Their operation modes are as follows:

i. The Actin-based molecular machines[1]: The research group comprises up to 27 experts from chemistry education, maths education and physics education. The research group focuses on actin-based molecular machines, employing an interdisciplinary methodology that combines biochemistry, cell biology and structural biology to uncover how structure and dynamics of the actin cytoskeleton are regulated in various cellular processes. Their work, encompassing research, publication, and lab work, is dedicated to elucidating the fundamental mechanisms by which these critical cellular scaffolds drive motility, division, and signalling. This integrative approach provides a comprehensive understanding of actin's roles in both health and disease.
ii. Astronics of University of Malta[2]: The research group at L-Università ta' Malta specializes in the cutting-edge field of applied electronic systems research and development for the space environment. Their core mission is to engineer robust designs of electronic systems for outside the protection of the Earth's atmosphere, focusing on making spacecraft and satellite components more reliable, power-efficient, and capable of withstanding the intense radiation and thermal extremes encountered in space. The group actively engages in joint research,

publication, and student supervision, fostering strong collaborations with major European space agencies like the European Space Agency (ESA) and industry partners to advance space technology. A key area of their applied work includes developing advanced onboard computers and data handling systems, which are critical for the autonomous operation and scientific output of space missions.

iii. Stanford Artificial Intelligence[3]: The Stanford AI Lab (SAIL) operates as a highly dynamic and community-oriented network of specialized research groups. It is decentralized research group collaborating around faculty-led specialized labs focused on distinct areas including Natural Language Processing, Vision Learning, Machine Learning, and Autonomous Systems. Research activities are primarily driven through joint faculty labs, which pursue pioneering work in their specific domains. The lab fosters a strong culture of collaboration and innovation, encouraging partnerships both within the university and with external industry partners through its Affiliates Program, allowing students and faculty to address real-world challenges.

These examples show that successful research groups, whether fundamental (Helsinki) or applied (Malta), whether disciplinary or interdisciplinary (Standford), share common traits, a clear focus, defined operational activities, and KPIs aligned with their mission. The challenge for innovation-focused RGs is to integrate the industry and public helix explicitly into this structure, adding KPIs like prototypes, IP, and talent placement alongside publications and grants.

3.7 Conclusion: The Research Group as the Catalyst for Scalable Innovation

The Research Group (RG) serves as the indispensable engine room of the reinvented Triple Helix. It operationalizes the foundational trust established by micro-credentials into tangible, high-impact research outputs ready for industry and with great benefit to the public. The Research group formation outlined in Figure 3 encompassing Internal Capacity Audit, Targeted Partner Mapping, and Structured Group Formation to provide Resource-Constrained Universities (RCUs) with a pragmatic, offensive strategy to overcome their systemic deficits.

By prioritizing niche identification and moving beyond generic partnerships to targeted consortium building, the RCU ensures that its limited human and financial capital is deployed with maximum strategic effect. The data presented in Table 1 shows the characteristics of the research group and their evolution pathways to interdisciplinary research group. The case studies given in section 3.5 confirms ability of the research groups to pull resources across institutions and share their benefits to maximize results. This confirms the RG's centrality in the global research landscape and highlights two critical observations:

i. The RG is the Primary Unit of Academic Productivity: As academic literature confirms, research output, publications, and student supervision predominantly originate from these formalized or informal structures. The key innovation for the Triple Helix is making these RGs explicitly industry-embedded, government supported, and outcome-driven, incorporating KPIs like patenting and talent placement alongside traditional academic metrics.
ii. The Evolutionary Pathway is Built-in: Table 1 vividly illustrates that the Research Group is not a static entity but the nascent stage of a larger, more impactful structure. The transition from a small, disciplinary Research Group (focused on single expert area and limited resources) to a larger, multi-source-funded Interdisciplinary Research Group (with increased resource access and broader scope) is a natural, milestone-driven evolution.

This incremental success builds the necessary internal capacity, external reputation, and diversified funding streams required to justify and launch the final, most sustainable component of the Nested and complex Centre of Excellence (CoE). The Research Group's sustained track record of joint outputs, successful talent circulation, and problem-solving excellence provides the undeniable evidence base and managerial expertise needed to evolve into a full-scale, institutionalized, and self-sustaining Centre of Excellence, which is the focus of the next section. The CoE represents the necessary scaling of the RG's success into a full-fledged helix consortium as a regional or national innovation hub.

4. THE EVOLUTION TO CENTRES OF EXCELLENCE: SCALING IMPACT FOR SUSTAINABLE ECOSYSTEM LEADERSHIP

Research Groups generate vital momentum and outputs, but their project-based, stakeholders support limitation, often grant-dependent nature can limit long-term stability and broad socioeconomic impact. For sustainability and structured stakeholders engagement the research groups needs to be evolved to multidisciplinary research group and further evolution to centers of excellence. The Centre of Excellence (CoE) represents the strategic evolution of one or more successful RGs into a permanent, institutionalized platform for sustained innovation and ecosystem leadership (Tadwalkar, 2008). A CoE is not simply a larger RG; it is a qualitatively different entity established after demonstrating a proven track record of excellence, securing diversified funding, becoming a recognized, indispensable partner to multiple stakeholders, and having sustainable research income models.

4.1. Defining Characteristics of Centre of Excellence and Enhanced Triple Helix Role

A sustainable CoE has concentrated expertise, resources, and leadership in a specific technological field (e.g AI) to drive high-impact research and funding, innovation, and training. The established centres aggregate top researchers, often across triple helix institutions, to tackle regional or global challenges while fostering graduate training and interdisciplinary collaboration. The CoEs enhance institutional reputation, support quality teaching, and address societal needs through applied projects. A mature CoE is distinguished by three key characteristics:

i. Proven Excellence & Established Reputation: It is built on a foundation of recognized success, a stream of high-impact publications, a portfolio of patents/licensed technologies, a history of completed pilot projects with industry, established sustainable funding sources, established policy reports, and a cadre of alumni in influential positions. This reputation becomes self-reinforcing, attracting top-tier talent, students, and partners.
ii. Diversified, Sustainable Funding Model: It moves beyond precarious project grants to a blended finance model. This may include multi-year membership fees from an industry consortium, institutional block grants from government for a strategic national priority, competitive international development funding, endowment income, and revenue-generating activities like premium executive education, specialized testing services, or technology licensing.
iii. Ecosystem Leadership & Neutral Convener Role: A CoE transcends its own research agenda to act as a steward for its entire technological domain within a region or nation. It hosts community events, sets technical or ethical standards, provides unbiased expertise to policymakers, and connects SMEs with larger corporates and investors. It becomes the "go-to" hub for a specific technological solution, trusted by all helices.

With the evolution from Research Groups, Interdisciplinary Research groups to centers of excellence. The three named characteristics can be achieved before establishment of the CoE or can be the source of establishing the CoE. The evolutions ensure the availability of trust and structured operations which are key for any sustainable CoE.

4.2. Catalytic Functions at the Systemic Level

In addition to routine operations, a Centre of Excellence (CoE) must adopt a flexible operational model that remains relatively independent from its parent university. This autonomy enables the CoE to explore new research domains, forge novel partnerships, and secure diverse funding streams. Such flexibility fosters innovation and shields it from the bureaucratic constraints of a typical university structures, positioning the CoE as a catalyst for partnerships that operate at a higher, systemic level. In this flexible mode of operations, the CoE focus on:

i. Long-Term Strategic R&D Alignment: It enables industry and government to make strategic, long-term co-investments in a shared R&D capability, aligning with 5-10 year technology roadmaps or national priorities. This is far more valuable than sporadic project funding.
ii. Shared Advanced Infrastructure Hub: A CoE can justify, fund, and manage critical, expensive infrastructure (e.g., a high-performance computing cluster for AI training, a secure data vault for health records, a robotics testing facility) that would be prohibitive for any single university department or SME. It provides democratized access of the resources across triple helix partner institutions under governed protocols.
iii. Comprehensive Talent Ecosystem Developer: Beyond educating undergraduates and postgrads, it designs and delivers continuous professional development (CPD) for the regional workforce via micro-credentials, short courses, and lab stays directly closing the skills gap for existing employees.
iv. Policy-Academia Feedback Loop: Its sustained relationship with government ensures research is informed by policy needs (e.g., for trustworthy AI), while policymakers receive timely, evidence-based advice from a neutral expert source, enabling more responsive and effective regulation

Figure 5. Centres of Excellence

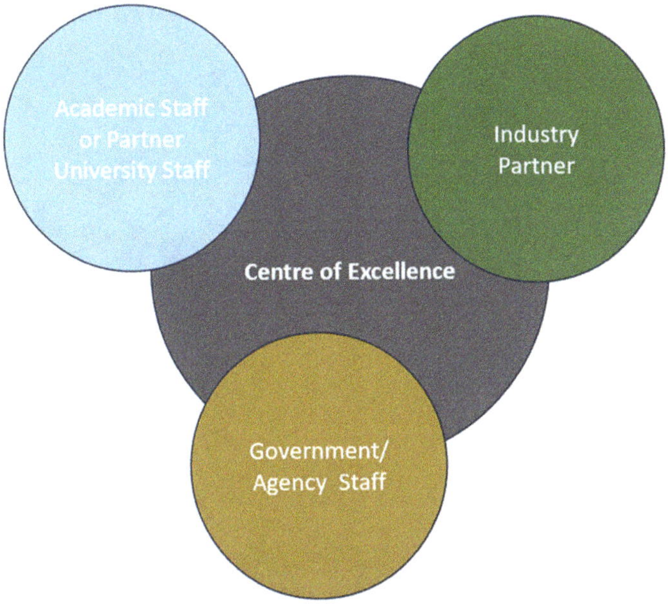

Figure 6. A full triple helix operation model with Research Groups, Centres of Excellence, and their Industrial and Government Agency Partners

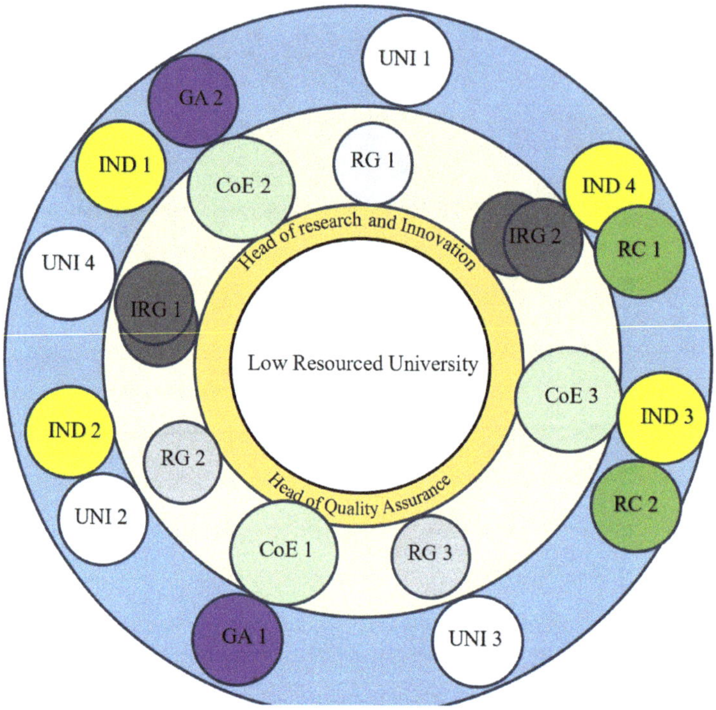

4.3. A Phased Pathway From Research Group to Centre of Excellence

The research and innovation evolution is intentional, to ensure the performance of each established unit is achieved before evolving the operation unit or expanding partners (Huong Nguyen & Lynn Meek, 2015). Typically, the centre of excellence is established within a span of 5-7 years and can be accelerated with availability of expertise and infrastructure across network and easy of achieving established milestone. The stage of establishing CoE includes:

- Phase 1: Foundational Research Group (Years 0-2): Demonstrate excellence in a narrow niche, build deep trust with 1-2 anchor industry partners, attract experts and graduate students, produce joint outputs (publications, prototypes) and secure initial project grants.

- Phase 2: Interdisciplinary Research Group (Years 2-4): Expand scope of the Research Group by integrating related disciplines (e.g., an AI group brings in ethicists, designers, and domain experts from healthcare), formalize a consortium model with 3-5 industry partners, establishing shared resource pools and governance structure, secure sustainable operation funding mechanism from stakeholders, begin offering specialized micro-credentials to the public or licensing developed solutions as a funding stream or expert generation.
- Phase 3: Institutionalized Centre of Excellence (Year 5+): Secure formal, permanent status from the university leadership (e.g., as a University-Affiliated Research Center), establish a diversified funding base, form a technical operation teams and working modality, form a high-level Advisory Board with senior representatives from all helices, assume a public-facing leadership role, publishing annual reports on the state of the domain, hosting major conferences, and advising government.

4.2. The CoE as a Shared Advanced Infrastructure

In addition to assembling a pool of specialized experts, cutting-edge equipment, and shared operational values, Centres of Excellence (CoEs) offer a unique, flexible, and non-bureaucratic mode of operation. These shared values and infrastructure represent the core functions of CoEs enabling efficient resource utilization. CoE funding and mode of operation justifies acquiring and maintaining high-cost assets that individual departments cannot afford, with examples of shareable resources including advanced laboratories, high-performance computing clusters, and specialized software platforms that draw in strong collaborative partnerships. Examples of the resources to be shared by partners and attract strong collaboration includes:

i. High Performance Computing (HPC) and Cloud Access: With the established excellence the CoE can procure advanced equipment's or negotiate institutional deals with other service providers (Azure, AWS, Google Cloud) for large-scale GPU time, making the CoE the primary AI training infrastructure for the university and its partners.
ii. Data Aggregation and Curation: The CoE acts as a neutral third party to manage and anonymize sensitive datasets provided by industry and government (e.g., anonymized electronic health records, traffic data), adhering to stringent data governance and ethical standards.
iii. The Physical Hub: A dedicated physical space for co-location of industry and academic staff, fostering spontaneous interaction and reducing organizational distance.

4.4. Performance Indicators of the CoE

Table 2 shows a characteristics and performance indicators of a center of excellence, as it builds on the characteristics and performance indicators of Research Groups and interdisciplinary research groups detailed in Table 1. On top of other indicators available for research group the CoE has a mandate of national or regional visibility though its operations, and sustainable revenue generation activities

Table 2. Characteristics of CoE and KPI

SN	Characteristics	Characteristics of Centres of Excellence and Performance Indicators
1	Research Discipline	Multiple related disciplines with one or two excellences
2	Timeline	Proven excellence of each research group, and inter-disciplinary research groups. Four to five years of operational
3	Funding	Diversified and sustainable funding mechanisms
4	Resources	Sustainable resource management and acquisition
5	Responsibilities	Proven funding mechanism and proven, groundbreaking research or innovative
6	Knowledge Sharing	Provide solutions with external partners
7	Expertise	Share expertise and attract and retain additional expertise
8	Equipment	hare equipment and acquire additional equipment, attract equipment support from partners or funders
9	Collaboration	Collaborate on joint funding mobilization and share funding
10	Publication	Publish at least 30% of number o people in the group
11	Patent	Patent at most 40% of number of people in the group

With enough resources and proven experience, the CoE becomes the trusted Advisor to the university and government and the thought Leader for the industry. In the realm of AI, the CoE is perfectly positioned to draft ethical frameworks and technical standards for local implementation of AI, ensuring that deployment is responsible and aligned with local values (e.g., ethical guidelines for using facial recognition in public services). Attracting Foreign Direct Investment (FDI) and sustainability of the CoE is the primary working area of the CoE to ensure the CoE is boosting the regional innovation ecosystem.

4.5 Implementation Challenges and Adaptations for RCUs

The primary challenge for an RCU in establishing the centre of excellence is the perception that a CoE requires New funds, large grants, new buildings, and expensive international hires. To be pragmatic, an RCU can start a CoE using a "Virtual and Integrated" model without a dedicated funding mechanism.

i. The Virtual Centre Model: Instead of building a new physical space, the RCU can designate a "Virtual CoE" that exists as a shared administrative layer over existing successful Research Groups this priorities Consolidation of the available resources instead over Construction of a new centre of excellence. This includes rebranding and elevating 2 to 3 existing, high-performing Research Groups under a single "Centre of Excellence" banner.
ii. Human Capital as a seed of the CoE & Administrative Redirection: RCUs can use existing personnel to perform CoE functions by re-prioritizing their workloads. This includes Allocating sabbatical time or administrative hours of senior faculty to act as the CoE Director. The use of existing internal scholarships to fund PhD students who act as "bridge-builders" between the different Research Groups within the Centre. This seeds the CoE using current operational budgets.
iii. Equipment In-Sourcing and Industry Co-Location: If the RCU cannot afford cutting-edge equipment, it can entice industry partners to place their equipment on university grounds by Offering free space, electricity, and the labor of graduate students to an industry partner in exchange for housing their R&D equipment within the university's CoE. This gives the industry "lab space" and the university "infrastructure access" with zero capital outlay.
iv. Leveraging Government Priority or Mandates: RCUs can position their CoE as a strategic partner for government initiatives that lack local implementation arms. Aligning the CoE's focus with national priorities (e.g., Digital Identity or AI for Mining Analysis or Agriculture Processing). This position the university as testing ground for government technology pilots, the CoE can secure small operational support contracts that eventually grow into sustainable funding streams.

4.6 Case Studies of Centers of Excellence

There are a number of universities with matured centers of excellence polling resources across triple helix, With the decades of operational experience some of the centres of excellence have not only achieved sustainability but have a track record of expert knowledge generation and established trust across the partners. In these case studies, their selection is primarily based on their proved excellence area, and web based presence. The selection includes centre of excellence for ICT in East Africa, Both groups combine the academic rigour and industrial activities in their operations.

i. The Centre of Excellence for ICT in East Africa[4] is a collaborative initiative jointly operated by the Nelson Mandela African Institution of Science and Technology and the University of Oldenburg, in partnership with industrial leaders such as Kiira Motors and Raha Beverages. Established under the auspices of the Inter-University Council for East Africa, the Centre's core mandate is to advance embedded and mobile systems development skills among graduates across the region. To date, it has equipped more than 150 East Africans with cutting-edge digital skills and fostered a strong culture of innovation. The Centre has successfully cultivated a sustainable funding model through revenue-generating fabrication lab and industry-backed financial mechanisms that support both student projects and centre's core operational sustainability, fostering a resilient culture of innovation.

ii. The Centre of Excellence in Strong Materials[5] is a premier research network funded by South Africa's Department of Science and Innovation and the National Research Foundation. Its consortium spans eight national universities and two Science Councils enabling interdisciplinary collaboration on materials that retain exceptional properties under extreme conditions. The Centre's work, organized into six Focus Areas such as Diamond, Ceramic Materials, and Strong Metallic Alloys, combines advanced experimental facilities with industry partnerships to address both fundamental science and commercially relevant challenges. Beyond research, the centre has made significant contributions to human capital development, graduating over 130 students, producing more than 500 publications, and registering eight patents.

iii. The Centre of Excellence on Space Technology for Disaster Mitigation[6] is jointly sponsored by Chinese Academy of Science and The World Academy of Sciences (TWAS). Its mission is to serve as a model scientific and training centre, enhancing research capacities for disaster mitigation in developing countries through advanced space technologies, particularly space borne Earth observation. The centre pursues a multi-faceted strategy encompassing outstanding multidisciplinary research on disasters such as floods, droughts, and earthquakes; specialized education and training programs for students and scientists; and the facilitation of an international network through workshops and meetings that promote dialogue and best practices. Furthermore, the Centre provides advisory services and drives technology transfer, leveraging its close relationship with TWAS and other global networks to effectively disseminate knowledge and foster collaboration.

4.7 Conclusion: Centres of Excellence as Sustainable Ecosystem Leadership

In conclusion, the strategic evolution from focused Research Groups to Centres of Excellence represents a critical pathway for transforming academic research into a sustainable driver of long-term socioeconomic impact. While Micro-credentials bind the actors to jointly work on skilling students, Research Groups generate essential momentum for triple helix cooperation on joint research and joint solution development. A mature Centre of Excellence transcends research groups limitations by embodying three defining pillars namely proven reputation for excellence, a diversified and sustainable funding model, and a recognized role as a neutral convener and ecosystem leader.

This transformation is not merely an expansion in scale but a qualitative shift in function and ambition. By operating with strategic autonomy and a flexible model, a CoE performs catalytic, systemic functions aligning long-term R&D investments across the Triple Helix, managing shared advanced infrastructure as a public good, developing a comprehensive talent pipeline, and closing the critical feedback loop between research and policy.

The phased, intentional pathway from Micro-Credentials, foundational Research Group, interdisciplinary Research Group, and finally to institutionalized CoE ensures that each stage builds the necessary trust, track record, and operational maturity required for sustainability. As demonstrated by global case studies, successful CoEs become indispensable hubs, attracting investment, setting standards, and generating a continuous stream of innovation, expertise, and trusted advice for all partners.

5. SYNTHESIS AND CONCLUSION: A BLUEPRINT FOR REINVENTED PARTNERSHIPS

The Nested Model of Micro-Credentials, Research Groups, and Centres of Excellence for Operationalizing the Triple Helix in a Resource-Constrained Universities provides a practical, scalable blueprint for operationalizing the Triple Helix in the 21st century. Together, they form a synergistic ecosystem that provides practical solution being training, research, innovation, solution incubation and commercialization, or advancing national and regional development priorities. With this nested model, the community is served when technology changes daily and monthly which is a needed practical solution for 21st problems. The contribution of each phase to the triple helix is summarized here:

i. Micro-credentials the flexible on-ramps and feedback channels, ensuring continuous skills alignment and building the human and relational capital for deeper collaboration.
ii. Research Groups are the agile engine rooms, where co-creation happens on focused challenges, producing dual outputs and de-risking innovation.
iii. Centres of Excellence are the sustainable infrastructure and ecosystem hubs, providing long-term strategic capacity, shared resources, and systemic leadership.

5.1. Critical Implications for AI and Frontier Technology Development

This nested model is uniquely suited to the demands of AI and other fast-moving emerging technological fields, which require:

i. Continuous Skill Renewal: Addressed by the embedded, co-designed micro-credential programs within the ecosystem.
ii. Access to Data and Computing Facility: Facilitated by the trust, legal frameworks, and shared infrastructure of RGs and CoEs.
iii. Interdisciplinary Translation: Enabled by the natural evolution from technical RGs to interdisciplinary CoEs that include social scientists, lawyers, and domain experts.
iv. Ethical and Governance Foresight: Informed by the sustained policy-academia dialogue institutionalized within the CoE's governance structure.

For Resource-Constrained Universities (RCUs): This framework is emancipatory. It provides a strategic methodology to overcome disadvantage through focus and partnership. An RCU does not need to excel in all areas of AI. It can identify a niche aligned with local industry (e.g., AI for renewable energy micro grids in a rural region), form a focused RG with local partners and a global tech firm, build a reputation, and evolve into a nationally recognized CoE for that niche. This transforms the RCU from a peripheral player into a leader in a strategically important domain.

5.2. Concluding Argument: From Ceremony to Operation

The future of university-industry-government partnerships and the relevance of the university itself in the innovation economy will not be secured by signing more high-level MoUs or building more generic technology parks. It will be determined by the ability to create deep, operational integration, and high skill results. In conclusion, the persistent problem of rigid structures within Resource Constrained Universities (RCUs) stifles their potential in the innovation economy and the proposed solution is a nested three-mechanism model integrating agile micro-credentials, mission-driven Research Groups, and embedded Centres of Excellence. This framework operationalizes the Triple Helix theory, providing an actionable blueprint for disadvantaged institutions to translate collaborative intent into high-skill results and co-created value.

This approach carries critical implications for university leaders to champion this deep operational integration over ceremonial partnerships and for policymakers to craft funding and regulatory enablers that reward such embedded collaboration. Lastly, industry partners need to actively engage at all level and build trust and shared language across triple helix collaboration framework.

Future research should longitudinally track the sustainability of Centres of Excellence and conduct comparative analyses of regulatory enablers across regions. Ultimately, for RCUs, adopting this phased model is the strategic pathway to their reinvention and transforms from passive knowledge repositories into proactive, indispensable, and agile catalysts of inclusive socioeconomic development in the age of AI

6. REFERENCES

Altbach, P. (2008). *The complex roles of universities in the period of globalization*. https://www.researchgate.net/publication/277128834

Altbach, P. G. (2008). The Complex Roles of Universities in the Period of Globalization. *Higher Education in the World, 3*(January), 5–19. DOI: 10.1007/978-1-349-58169-6_1

Altbach, P. G., & Salmi, J. (2011). *The Road to Academic Excellence: The Making of World-Class Research Universities*. DOI: 10.1596/978-0-8213-8805-1

Brown, M., Mcgreal, R., Peters, M., & Brown, M. (2023). A Strategic Institutional Response to Micro-Credentials. *Journal of Interactive Media in Education, 2023*(1), 1–17. DOI: 10.5334/jime.801

Brown, M., Nic Giolla Mhichil, M., Beirne, E., & Mac Lochlainn, C. (2021). The global micro-credential landscape: Charting a new credential ecology for lifelong learning. *Journal of Learning for Development, 8*(2), 228–254. DOI: 10.56059/jl4d.v8i2.525

Christiansen, L., Hvidsten, T. E., Kristensen, J. H., Gebhardt, J., Mahmood, K., Otto, T., Lassen, A. H., Brunoe, T. D., Schou, C., & Laursen, E. S. (2022). A Framework for Developing Educational Industry 4.0 Activities and Study Materials. *Education Sciences, 12*(10), 659. Advance online publication. DOI: 10.3390/educsci12100659

Coetzee, D. (2024). *Micro-Credentials: An Emerging Alternative to Traditional Tertiary Education. July*. DOI: 10.13140/RG.2.2.16792.40962

Cook, I., Grange, S., & Eyre-walker, A. (2015). *Research groups: How big should they be ?* DOI: 10.7717/peerj.989

Cunningham, J. A., Lehmann, E. E., & Menter, M. (2022). The organizational architecture of entrepreneurial universities across the stages of entrepreneurship: A conceptual framework. *Small Business Economics, 59*(1), 11–27. DOI: 10.1007/s11187-021-00513-5

Daraio, C. (2017). A Framework for the Assessment of Research and Its Impacts. *Journal of Data and Information Science, 2*(4), 7–42. DOI: 10.1515/jdis-2017-0018

Duklas, J. (2020). *Micro-Credentials: Trends in Credit Transfer and Credentialing. November*, 545–545. DOI: 10.1007/978-3-319-95870-5_300166

Gallagher, S. E., & Savage, T. (2023). *Challenge-based learning in higher education : an exploratory literature review. 2517*. DOI: 10.1080/13562517.2020.1863354

Geels, F. W. (2004). From sectoral systems of innovation to socio-technical systems: Insights about dynamics and change from sociology and institutional theory. *Research Policy, 33*(6–7), 897–920. DOI: 10.1016/j.respol.2004.01.015

Huong Nguyen, T., & Lynn Meek, V. (2015). Key Considerations in Organizing and Structuring University Research. *The Journal of Research Administration, 46*, 41–62. https://go8.edu.au/

Köhler, J., Geels, F. W., Kern, F., Markard, J., Onsongo, E., Wieczorek, A., Alkemade, F., Avelino, F., Bergek, A., Boons, F., Fünfschilling, L., Hess, D., Holtz, G., Hyysalo, S., Jenkins, K., Kivimaa, P., Martiskainen, M., McMeekin, A., Mühlemeier, M. S., & Wells, P. (2019). An agenda for sustainability transitions research: State of the art and future directions. *Environmental Innovation and Societal Transitions, 31*, 1–32. DOI: 10.1016/j.eist.2019.01.004

Kyvik, S., & Reymert, I. (2016). *The establishment of formal research groups in higher education institutions. 0317*. DOI: 10.3402/nstep.v2.33896

Kyvik, S., & Reymert, I. (2017). Research collaboration in groups and networks: Differences across academic fields. *Scientometrics, 113*(2), 951–967. DOI: 10.1007/s11192-017-2497-5 PMID: 29081555

Ma, X., Zhang, Z., Yan, R., Pan, H., & Li, C. (2017). *A Study on the Governance Structure of Modern Universities. 95*(Iceemr), 74–77. DOI: 10.2991/iceemr-17.2017.18

Marginson, S., & Marginson, S. (2022). Oxford Review of Education Research on international and global higher education : Six different perspectives Research on international and global higher education : Six different perspectives ABSTRACT. *Oxford Review of Education, 48*(4), 421–438. DOI: 10.1080/03054985.2022.2087619

Maria Manuela, J. P. A. C. C. F. R. de A. (2013). *The triple helix model and dynamics of innovation : a case study*. DOI: 10.1108/17561411211208758

Moscardini, A., Strachan, R., Vlasova, T., & Pavlenko, I. (2021). A System Strategy for Higher Education. *Performance Improvement, 60*(2), 10–20. DOI: 10.1002/pfi.21955

Muñoz; G. A. A., & Plazas, A. (2024). Innovation Management in University Research Groups. *Journal of Technology Managment and Innovoation, 19*(2), 15–27.

Musseau, A. (2024). Microcredentials: revolutionizing education institutions. *EHL Insights*, 1–7. https://hospitalityinsights.ehl.edu/microcredentials-revolutionizing-education-institutions

OCED. (2023a). Micro-credentials for lifelong learning and employability. *OECD Education Policy Perspectives, 1*(66), 44. https://doi.org/10.1787/5cc2d673-en

OCED. (2023b). Micro-credentials for lifelong learning and employability. *OECD Education Policy Perspectives, 1*(66), 44. DOI: 10.1787/5cc2d673-en

OECD. (2021). OECD Education Policy Perspectives No. 39: Micro-credential innovations in higher education: Who. *What and Why*, (September). Advance online publication. DOI: 10.1787/5cc2d673-en

Orman, R., Şimşek, E., & Kozak Çakır, M. A. (2023). Micro-credentials and reflections on higher education. *Higher Education Evaluation and Development, 17*(2), 96–112. DOI: 10.1108/HEED-08-2022-0028

Philbin, S. P. (2012). Resource-based view of university-industry research collaboration. *2012 Proceedings of Portland International Center for Management of Engineering and Technology. Technology Management for Emerging Technologies, PICMET, 12*(January), 400–411.

Pirkkalainen, H., Sood, I., Padron Napoles, C., Kukkonen, A., & Camilleri, A. (2023). How might micro-credentials influence institutions and empower learners in higher education? *Educational Research, 65*(1), 40–63. DOI: 10.1080/00131881.2022.2157302

Rafique, T., Awan, M. U., Shafiq, M., & Mahmood, K. (2023). Exploring the role of ranking systems towards university performance improvement: A focus group-based study. *Heliyon, 9*(10), e20904. DOI: 10.1016/j.heliyon.2023.e20904 PMID: 37886765

Ranga, M., & Etzkowitz, H. (2013). *Triple Helix systems : an analytical framework for innovation policy and practice in the Knowledge Society. 27*(3), 237–262. DOI: 10.5367/ihe.2013.0165

Richert, D., Marshall, L., & James, G. (2024). Design and Implementation of an Industry 4.0 Micro-Credential Program. *Proceedings of the Canadian Engineering Education Association (CEEA)*, 1–7. DOI: 10.24908/pceea.2023.17111

Roy, R., & Marsafawy, H. El. (2020). *Organizational Structure for 21St Century Higher Education Institutions: Meeting Expectations and Crossing Challenges. April.*

Rwakenda, H. B. B. (2016). Challenges Faced by Leaders of Institutions of Higher Learning in Uganda: Case Study of Mbale Public and Private Universities. *Texila International Journal of Academic Research, 3*(1), 90–98. DOI: 10.21522/TIJAR.2014.03.01.Art010

Tadwalkar, S. V. (2008). Create centre of excellence (CoE) for better business. *Ubiquity, 2008*(March), 1–9. DOI: 10.1145/1366313.1361366

Torbacki, W. (2024). A Framework for Assessing Innovations, Business Models and Sustainability for Software Companies Using Hybrid Multiple-Criteria Decision-Making. *Sustainability (Basel), 16*(14), 5871. Advance online publication. DOI: 10.3390/su16145871

Vabø, A., Alvsvåg, A., Kyvik, S., & Reymert, I. (2016). The establishment of formal research groups in higher education institutions. *Nordic Journal of Studies in Educational Policy, 2016*(2–3). DOI: 10.3402/nstep.v2.33896

Van Damme, D. (2021). Transforming Universities for a Sustainable Future. In *The Promise of Higher Education: Essays in Honour of 70 Years of IAU*. DOI: 10.1007/978-3-030-67245-4_64

Vivar-simon, M., Zabaleta, N., Torre, J. D. La, Basañez, A., & Urruzuno, A. (2022). *Towards Human-Scale Competitiveness : Priority Challenges for Triple Helix towards 2030.*

Wei, Y., Shengfan, Q., & Wengang, X. (2025). Exploring the effectiveness of micro-credentials in artificial intelligence teaching and learning : An empirical study based on AI þ X program in China. *Cogent Education, 12*(1), 2536528. Advance online publication. DOI: 10.1080/2331186X.2025.2536528

Zhou, C., & Etzkowitz, H. (2021). *Triple Helix Twins : A Framework for Achieving Innovation and UN Sustainable Development Goals.*

Chapter 4
Fuzzy Multi-Criteria Decision-Making Models for Strengthening University-Government-Industry Collaboration in AI Development

Ajoy Kanti Das
https://orcid.org/0000-0002-9326-1677
Tripura University, India

Rajat Das
https://orcid.org/0009-0000-3355-3582
Tripura University, India

Nandini Gupta
https://orcid.org/0009-0000-5450-9783
Bir Bikram Memorial College, India

Mithun Datta
The ICFAI University, India

Abdulhalim Musa Abubakar
https://orcid.org/0000-0002-1304-3515
Modibbo Adama University, Nigeria

Nageswara Rao Lakkimsetty
https://orcid.org/0009-0006-0146-8889
American University of Ras Al Khaimah, UAE

Ebenezer Aquisman Asare
https://orcid.org/0000-0003-1185-1479
Northeastern University, USA

Ilyas Khan
https://orcid.org/0009-0007-3847-3849
Government College University, Pakistan

ABSTRACT

This chapter describes how fuzzy multi-criteria decision-making (MCDM) might enhance collaboration between government, business, and academic institutions. It

DOI: 10.4018/979-8-3373-9690-3.ch004

demonstrates why cooperation in AI development entails ambiguity and conflicting viewpoints. Vague judgments are transformed into usable values with the use of fuzzy sets and triangular fuzzy numbers. Fuzzy numbers are used to assess various factors, including research strength, finance, policy flexibility, technology preparedness, and social impact. The shifting significance of each criterion for various partners is displayed by fuzzy weights. All viewpoints are combined into a single meaningful score using aggregation and defuzzification techniques. Fuzzy soft sets highlight areas of agreement and aid in identifying areas of disagreements between partners. Partners can select AI laboratories, internships, and ethical committees, as demonstrated by several cases. The chapter demonstrates how fuzzy models improve the clarity and fairness of collaborative judgments in AI development.

1. INTRODUCTION

Existing studies focus on roles and policies in the Triple Helix. Some research looks at collaboration and innovation outcomes. Governance challenges are discussed, but practical tools are missing. Fuzzy MCDM helps decisions under uncertainty effectively. However, it is rarely linked to Triple Helix governance. This study designs a fuzzy decision framework for AI. It supports University–Government–Industry collaboration in AI ecosystems.

Fuzzy MCDM models can greatly improve cooperation between enterprises, governments, and academic institutions in the development of AI. According to Sherin (2025), fuzzy logic makes it easier to make simple decisions when faced with uncertainty. The focus of this work is on flexible reasoning for collaboration. Kondratenko et al. (2018) offer a fuzzy framework for industry-academia cooperation. Our understanding of university preferences is improved by their research. Wang et al. (2023) assess complex technologies using a fuzzy hybrid MCDM technique. Higher choice accuracy is seen in their outcomes. Sumrit (2024) uses a Pythagorean fuzzy model to assess industrial readiness. Organized planning is supported by this study. Deveci (2023) uses fuzzy MCDM to improve the resilience of AI-driven supply chains. Their results show enhanced operational stability. Kumar and Pamučar (2025) review 20 years of MCDM research in hazy circumstances. Their review helps select suitable methods. Geetha and Jeon (2022) extend a fuzzy SIR approach for university-industry projects. Their study improves collaborative planning. Hange et al. (2025) propose a classification model for industry-university collaboration. Their method enhances understanding of partnerships. Belhadi et al. (2021) provide an AI-based decision framework for resilient networks. This work promotes stable cooperation. Alshahrani et al. (2023) create a fuzzy hybrid MCDM model to pinpoint barriers to AI adoption. Their findings serve as a reference for better implementation planning.

Cai et al. (2019) discuss using AI to create university-industry co-innovation networks. Their work promotes interdisciplinary collaboration. Imamguluyev (2025) develops explainable AI by fusing fuzzy logic and deep learning. Their approach increases the transparency of MCDM. Human-generative AI collaborative MCDM is examined by Hao et al. (2024). Their results show improved interaction. Hu et al. (2023) propose a fuzzy rule-based paradigm for AI governance. Their findings support ethical auditing. Guo et al. (2024) describe a large-scale fuzzy group decision approach. Their model improves collective judgment. Fumanal-Idocin and Andreu-Pérez (2024) develop a fuzzy logic programming tool for explainable AI. Their efforts make judgments more understandable. Özcan et al. (2025) employ explainable fuzzy systems to increase trust in human-AI missions. Their findings improve operational reliability. Bogachov et al. (2020) investigate fuzzy regulators in entrepreneurial development. Their results promote strategic growth. Zhong et al. (2025) look at green innovation partnerships using fuzzy income modeling. Their efforts explain stable multi-sector cooperation. Alam and Khan (2024) enhance AI-human cooperative MCDM in Industry 4.0. Their work enhances cooperation for shared technological goals. These studies help handle uncertainty. It also supports complex evaluations. It can guide humans and AI working together. Most current methods focus on one sector. Some focus on collaboration between two parties. They do not include multiple actors. Universities, governments, and industries are not modeled together. There is no single framework for joint decision-making.

For MCDM, Das and Granados (2022a) created a fuzzy parameterized intuitionistic fuzzy soft multiset theory. Their research on FP-intuitionistic multi-fuzzy N-soft sets enhanced MCDM models' adaptability (Das and Granados, 2022b). To further this study, they later presented IFP-intuitionistic multi-fuzzy N-soft sets (Das and Granados, 2023a). Weighted fuzzy soft multisets were suggested by Das (2018) as a novel MCDM tool. Previously, preference fuzzy rough relations and intuitionistic fuzzy rough relations were studied by Das (2016) and Das & Granados (2023b). Their collaborative study presented a fuzzy soft group MCDM technique in 2021. It employed weighted average ratings to enhance MCDM theory and practical analysis (Das and Granados, 2021). New operations on F Ss were proposed by Das et al. (2022). They demonstrated how these operations aid in the efficient resolution of MCDM issues. Weighted hesitant bipolar-valued FS s were later introduced by Das et al. (2023). These sets provide a more thorough method of contrasting and assessing several choices. A fuzzy MCDM model was also created by Das et al. (2025b) to investigate how human activity affects the water quality of urban rivers. An important addition to environmental MCDM research is this work. It assessed the Gomati and Haora Rivers' contamination levels. Water contamination was also graded using FSS models and weighted hesitant FS (Das et al., 2024a; 2024b; 2025a). Mukherjee and Das's work is also used in the development of fuzzy soft multi-set theories in MCDM (2016a). In their 2015 work, interval-valued intuitionistic fuzzy soft multi-sets were applied to practical MCDM situations (Mukherjee and Das, 2015b). Additionally, they investigated the application of intuitionistic FSSs **with** interval values in investment MCDM (Mukherjee and Das, 2015a). In 2022, they also developed Einstein operations on fuzzy soft multisets and MCDM (Mukherjee & Das, 2022). In their 2023 book, they go into greater detail about the theoretical underpinnings and practical applications (Mukherjee & Das, 2023). Mukherjee & Das focus even further on the topological and relational paradigm of fuzzy and rough sets (2015c; 2016b). Granados et al. (2022) introduced the continuous neutrosophic distributions with neutrosophic parameters that give a possibility to represent the uncertainty probabilistically. Granados et al. (2023) proposed the weighted neutrosophic soft multiset approach, which Das et al. (2025c) have recently thoroughly examined. Das et al. (2025d) recently introduced the fuzzy logic decision-support system to streamline the concept of an adaptive inventory management system within the retailing context. Das et al. (2025e) have developed a new weighted hypersoft expert system MCDM paradigm. They provide helpful strategies on how to deal with uncertainty, make decisions more precisely, and address difficult real-life problems (Das et al., 2025f). Das et al. (2025g) investigated how urban river water is impacted by human activity. Fuzzy logic applications in multicultural marketing were investigated by Das et al. (2026a). Das et al. (2026b) examined smart luxury goods co-branding in a different study. They made decisions using a neutrosophic multi-criteria method. Neutrosophic sets were also used in environmental recovery by Das et al. (2026c). A generalized interval-valued neutrosophic rough soft set structure was presented by Mukherjee et al. (2026). Recently, Gupta et al. (2026) integrated traditional ecological knowledge with fuzzy logic and quantum computing for sustainable agriculture in tribal areas of Tripura. Their work offers useful approaches for managing uncertainty, enhancing the precision of decisions, and tackling challenging real-world issuesStrong collaboration is needed for AI development. Universities create new knowledge. Governments make rules and policies. Industries produce real products. Sometimes their goals clash. They often have different preferences. They may lack complete information. Fuzzy models help reduce this uncertainty. Fuzzy logic handles vague data. Fuzzy sets allow flexible reasoning. These methods improve theories of fuzzy soft sets, hypersoft sets, and neutrosophic decision-making. They capture hesitation, parameter dependency, and higher-order uncertainty. However, their use is mostly limited to specific domains. They are rarely applied to AI governance or Triple Helix collaboration. This shows the need to use these tools in multi-institutional AI systems.

This chapter adopts the Triple Helix collaboration framework. It treats collaboration as an interactive governance system. Universities, governments, and industries participate in AI decisions. Universities focus on research and knowledge creation.

Governments provide regulation and policy coordination. Industries support innovation and AI deployment. Most Triple Helix studies remain qualitative. Consequently, formal decision-support mechanisms capable of addressing uncertainty and conflicting institutional objectives are limited.This chapter emphasizes structured decision support. Collaboration becomes a decision-making framework. Policy priorities act as decision criteria. Institutional conflicts are explicitly included. AI collaboration involves uncertainty and competing objectives. Exact numerical evaluation is often unrealistic. Fuzzy MCDM manages uncertainty effectively. Fuzzy soft sets capture stakeholder preferences. Both methods are integrated into one framework. AI strategies are compared systematically. The approach supports transparent and measurable AI governance.

Key Contributions

- Transforms the Triple Helix from a descriptive model into a practical AI governance tool.
- Integrates uncertainty, conflicting priorities, and governance trade-offs using fuzzy soft sets and FMCDM.
- Provides an approach to designing and assessing university-government-industry AI partnerships that is policy-focused.

2. BASICS OF FUZZY SETS

Vague concepts are represented by a fuzzy set (Zadeh, 1965). The nature of a fuzzy collection is soft. Sharp borders are not produced by a fuzzy set. Membership values are used in fuzzy sets. Every component has a certain level of affiliation. This degree is in the range of 0 to 1.

$$\mu_A(x) \in [0,1]$$

- If $\mu_A(x) = 1$, **then full belonging.**
- If $\mu_A(x) = 0$, **then no belonging.**
- Values between 0 and 1 show partial belonging.

Partial belonging means partial truth. Fuzzy logic supports this partial truth.

2.1. Why Fuzzy Sets are Needed Here

University objectives are frequently ambiguous. Government regulations can be ambiguous. Expectations in the industry are constantly shifting. They rarely have clear-cut opinions. Most of their opinions are subjective. Fuzzy sets are therefore helpful in this situation.

"AI safety is high," according to the government. However, "high" is not a definite figure. "Research output is medium," according to the university. "Medium" also lacks a precise value. These ambiguous terms are transformed into numbers by fuzzy sets.

2.2. Fuzzy Membership Function

Suppose we evaluate "AI readiness." Let x be a university project.

Let fuzzy set

$$\mathbf{A} = \text{"}\mathbf{Highly\ Ready\ AI\ Project}.\text{"}$$

If experts say readiness is strong:

$$\mu_A(\mathbf{x}) = 0.9$$

If experts say readiness is weak:

$$\mu_A(\mathbf{x}) = 0.3$$

If experts say no readiness:

$$\mu_A(\mathbf{x}) = 0$$

So, 0.9 means strong belonging. 0.3 means low belonging. 0 means no belonging. This helps partners compare projects.

2.3. Triangular Fuzzy Numbers (TFN)

A triangular fuzzy number is simple. A TFN uses three points.

These points are:

$$\mathbf{a} = (\mathbf{l}, \mathbf{m}, \mathbf{u})$$

where:

- **l = lower value**
- **m = middle value**
- **u = upper value**

The shape looks like a triangle. The triangle spreads uncertainty. TFN is widely used in decisions. TFN handles vague judgments very well.

2.4 Linguistic Representation of a Triangular Fuzzy Number (TFN)

In practical decision-making, experts often express preferences using linguistic terms rather than precise numerical values. To capture such qualitative judgments, triangular fuzzy numbers (TFNs) are employed to represent linguistic variables such as Very Low, Low, Medium, High, and Very High. Each linguistic term is mapped to a corresponding TFN, enabling the transformation of subjective expert opinions into a mathematically tractable form.

3. CRITERIA FOR COLLABORATION

Clear evaluation criteria are necessary for collaboration. Different aspects are valued by each couple. Vague judgments are captured with the aid of fuzzy criteria. We chose five primary conditions for teamwork.

3.1 List of Key Criteria

The following criteria are selected to capture academic, governmental, and industrial priorities without redundancy.

Criterion 1: Research Quality (C_1)
Criterion 2: Funding Support (C_2)
Criterion 3: Policy Flexibility (C_3)
Criterion 4: Technology Readiness (C_4)
Criterion 5: Social Impact (C_5)

These criteria cover academic, financial, regulatory, technological, and social aspects of AI collaboration between universities, governments, and industries. They help evaluate research strength, resource availability, policy flexibility, feasibility of implementation, and social responsibility. They are useful in situations with uncertainty.

3.2. Fuzzy Scores From Each Partner

Each partner gives fuzzy scores. Each score uses a triangular fuzzy number:

$$\mathbf{x}_{ij} = (\mathbf{l}_{ij}, \mathbf{m}_{ij}, \mathbf{u}_{ij})$$

Where:

$$\mathbf{v\,i} \in \{\mathbf{U, G, I}\}$$

$$\mathbf{v\,j} \in \{1, 2, 3, 4, 5\}$$

Here **i is a partner. Here j is the criterion.**

Meaning:

- $\mathbf{l}_{ij}$= lower opinion
- $\mathbf{m}_{ij}$ = typical opinion
- $\mathbf{u}_{ij}$ = optimistic opinion

Fuzzy scores allow partial belief. Fuzzy scores reduce judgment bias.

3.3. Fuzzy Scores Assigned by Partners

University, government, and industry opinions are collected using the same fuzzy linguistic scale and represented by triangular fuzzy numbers. Each partner provides evaluations for selected criteria based on their institutional perspective, and only the assigned fuzzy values are listed.

University Score

- Research Quality:
- $x_{U_1} = (0.6, 0.8, 1.0)$
- Funding Support:
- $x_{U_2} = (0.3, 0.5, 0.7)$
- Policy Flexibility:
- $x_{U_3} = (0.2, 0.4, 0.6)$
- Social Impact:
- $x_{U_5} = (0.5, 0.7, 0.8)$

Government Scores

- Research Quality:
- $x_{G_1} = (0.5, 0.6, 0.8)$
- Policy Flexibility:
- $x_{G_3} = (0.4, 0.6, 0.7)$
- Technology Readiness:
- $x_{G_4} = (0.4, 0.6, 0.8)$
- Social Impact:
- $x_{G_5} = (0.6, 0.8, 0.9)$

Industry Scores

- Research Quality:
- $x_{I_1} = (0.4, 0.6, 0.7)$
- Funding Support:
- $x_{I_2} = (0.7, 0.9, 1.0)$
- Technology Readiness:
- $x_{I_4} = (0.7, 0.9, 1.0)$
- Social Impact:
- $x_{I_5} = (0.3, 0.5, 0.6)$

3.4. Combined Fuzzy Matrix

We create a fuzzy matrix for all partners:

$$\mathbf{X} = \begin{bmatrix} x_{U_1} & x_{U_2} & x_{U_3} & x_{U_4} & x_{U_5} \\ x_{G_1} & x_{G_2} & x_{G_3} & x_{G_4} & x_{G_5} \\ x_{I_1} & x_{I_2} & x_{I_3} & x_{I_4} & x_{I_5} \end{bmatrix}$$

This matrix stores all evaluations.
This matrix supports fuzzy calculations.
This matrix is required for ranking.

3.5. Collaboration Scenario

Partners want to create an AI Innovation Hub. Each partner evaluates:

- Research quality $(\mathbf{C}_1)$:
- The university gives high value.
- The government gives a medium value.
- Industry gives a medium value.

- Funding support $(\mathbf{C}_2)$:
- Industry scores highest.
- University scores are moderate.
- Government scores lowest.
- Technology readiness $(\mathbf{C}_4)$:
- Industry scores high.
- University scores are moderate.
- Government scores medium.

These ambiguous assessments reveal disputes, demonstrate alignment, and inform final choices. Collaboration success is guided by criteria. Fuzzy numbers are used in each criterion. Fuzzy values are assigned by each partner. Uncertainty is expressed by fuzzy scores. Subjective belief is indicated by fuzzy scores. All couples are compared using fuzzy matrices. This facilitates improved AI cooperation. This enhances shared MCDM.

4. FUZZY WEIGHT ASSIGNMENT

Crisp weights assume exact importance. Real importance is rarely exact. Partners often use vague words. Words like "high" or "medium" are fuzzy. So, weights can also be fuzzy.

A fuzzy weight is written as:

$$\mathbf{w}_j = (\mathbf{l}_j, \mathbf{m}_j, \mathbf{u}_j)$$

Where:

- $\mathbf{l}_j$ = lower importance
- $\mathbf{m}_j$ = middle importance
- $\mathbf{u}_j$ = upper importance

This structure handles uncertainty.

Sample Fuzzy Weights

Example fuzzy weights are:

$$\mathbf{w}_1 = (0.2, 0.3, 0.4)$$

$\mathbf{w}_2 = (0.1, 0.2, 0.3)$

- These weights express uncertainty.
- These weights show flexible opinions.
- These weights allow better modeling.

Remark

For $\mathbf{w}_1 = (0.2, 0.3, 0.4)$:

- Importance is at least 0.2.
- Importance is usually 0.3.
- Importance might reach 0.4.

This shows medium importance.
For $\mathbf{w}_2 = (0.1, 0.2, 0.3)$:

- Importance is at least 0.1.
- Importance is mostly 0.2.
- Importance could reach 0.3.

This shows low-to-medium importance.

How Partners Decide Weights

Priorities vary among partners. Universities prioritize the caliber of their research. Governments prioritize social impact. Technology preparedness is a focus for industries. Weights get hazy as a result. Different perspectives are reflected in fuzzy weights. Uncertainty is captured via fuzzy weights.

Weight Assignments

Case 1: University Weight Opinions

University gives fuzzy weights:

- Research quality:

$\mathbf{w}_{U_1} = (0.3, 0.4, 0.5)$

- Technology readiness:

$$\mathbf{w}_{U_4} = (0.2, 0.3, 0.4)$$

- Social impact:

$$\mathbf{w}_{U_5} = (0.1, 0.2, 0.3)$$

Remark:

- The university believes research quality matters most.
- The university thinks social impact matters least.

Case 2: Government Weight Opinions

Government gives fuzzy weights:

- Social impact:

$$\mathbf{w}_{G_5} = (0.3, 0.5, 0.6)$$

- Policy flexibility:

$$\mathbf{w}_{G_3} = (0.2, 0.3, 0.4)$$

Research quality:

$$\mathbf{w}_{G_1} = (0.1, 0.2, 0.3)$$

Remark:

- The government prefers social benefits.
- The government gives little importance to research output.

Case 3: Industry Weight Opinions

Industry gives fuzzy weights:

- Technology readiness:

$\mathbf{w}_{I_4} = (0.4, 0.6, 0.8)$

- Funding support:

$\mathbf{w}_{I_2} = (0.3, 0.4, 0.5)$

- Policy flexibility:

$\mathbf{w}_{I_3} = (0.1, 0.2, 0.3)$

Remark:

- Industry values technology first.
- Industry values flexible rules second.
- Industry gives the least importance to policy.

Combined Fuzzy Weight Matrix

We construct a weight matrix:

$$\mathbf{W} = \begin{bmatrix} w_{U_1} & w_{U_2} & w_{U_3} & w_{U_4} & w_{U_5} \\ w_{G_1} & w_{G_2} & w_{G_3} & w_{G_4} & w_{G_5} \\ w_{I_1} & w_{I_2} & w_{I_3} & w_{I_4} & w_{I_5} \end{bmatrix}$$

- This matrix stores all fuzzy weights.
- This matrix is required for aggregation.
- This matrix helps compute final scores

Normalizing Fuzzy Weights

Fuzzy weights may not sum to 1. We normalize fuzzy weights.
Formula:

$$\mathbf{w}_j' = \frac{\mathbf{w}_j}{\sum_{k=1}^{n} \mathbf{w}_k}$$

Each part is divided separately:

$$w_j{}' = \left(\frac{l_j}{\sum_{k=1}^{n} l_k}, \frac{m_j}{\sum_{k=1}^{n} m_k}, \frac{u_j}{\sum_{k=1}^{n} u_k}\right)$$

This makes weights consistent. This keeps the model valid.

Normalization Example

Given two weights:

$$w_1 = (0.2, 0.3, 0.4)$$

$$w_2 = (0.1, 0.2, 0.3)$$

Sum of lower values = $0.2 + 0.1 = 0.3$
Sum of middle values $= 0.3 + 0.2 = 0.5$
Sum of upper values = $0.4 + 0.3 = 0.7$
Normalized weights:

$$w_1{}' = (0.20.3, 0.30.5, 0.40.7)$$

$$w_2{}' = (0.30.1, 0.50.2, 0.70.3)$$

This keeps the sum equal to 1.

Importance Scenario

A collaborative AI centre is what partners wish to construct. Every partner talks about the importance. Their views are very different. To make a decision, they employ fuzzy weights. According to the university, research is essential. Impact is crucial, according to the government. According to the industry, technology is crucial. These variations are captured by fuzzy weights. Conflicts are avoided with fuzzy weights. Fair decisions are supported by fuzzy weights.

Priority is indicated by weights. Weights have to add up to one. Weights are not always clear. Rigidity is lessened with fuzzy weights. Uncertainty is reflected in fuzzy weights. Subjective values can be expressed by partners. Fuzzy weights facilitate improved teamwork. Multi-criteria models are guided by fuzzy weights.

5. FUZZY AGGREGATION MODEL

Fuzzy aggregation joins all fuzzy scores. It mixes partner opinions and handles uncertainty well. It keeps all values soft. We use the main formula:

$$\mathbf{S}_i = \sum_{j=1}^{n} \mathbf{x}_{ij} \otimes \mathbf{w}_j$$

Here:

- **i is the partner.**
- **j is the criterion.**
- $\mathbf{x}_{ij}$ is the fuzzy score.
- $\mathbf{w}_j$ is the fuzzy weight.
- $\mathbf{S}_i$ is the final fuzzy value.

5.1. Fuzzy Multiplication Rule

We multiply fuzzy numbers using:

$$(\mathbf{l}_1, \mathbf{m}_1, \mathbf{u}_1) \otimes (\mathbf{l}_2, \mathbf{m}_2, \mathbf{u}_2) = (\mathbf{l}_1 \mathbf{l}_2, \mathbf{m}_1 \mathbf{m}_2, \mathbf{u}_1 \mathbf{u}_2)$$

- Lower with lower.
- Middle with middle.
- Upper with upper.

This keeps uncertainty consistent.

5.2. Fuzzy Addition Rule

We add fuzzy numbers using:

$$(\mathbf{l}_1, \mathbf{m}_1, \mathbf{u}_1) + (\mathbf{l}_2, \mathbf{m}_2, \mathbf{u}_2) = (\mathbf{l}_1 + \mathbf{l}_2, \mathbf{m}_1 + \mathbf{m}_2, \mathbf{u}_1 + \mathbf{u}_2)$$

All parts added separately. No mixing of levels.

5.3. University Aggregation

Assume University fuzzy scores:

- Research Quality $\mathbf{C}_1$:

$x_{U_1} = (0.6, 0.8, 1.0)$

- Funding Support $\mathbf{C}_2$:

$\mathbf{x}_{U_2} = (0.5, 0.7, 0.9)$

Assume fuzzy weights:

$\mathbf{w}_1 = (0.2, 0.3, 0.4), \mathbf{w}_2 = (0.1, 0.2, 0.3)$

Step 1: Multiply Scores by Weights

For $\mathbf{C}_1$:

$\mathbf{x}_{U_1} \otimes \mathbf{w}_1\ (0.6, 0.8, 1.0) \otimes (0.2, 0.3, 0.4)$

$= (0.6 \times 0.2, \Delta 0.8 \times 0.3, \Delta 1.0 \times 0.4) = (0.12, 0.24, 0.40)$

For $\mathbf{C}_2$:

$\mathbf{x}_{U_2} \otimes \mathbf{w}_2 = (0.5, 0.7, 0.9) \otimes (0.1, 0.2, 0.3) = (0.05, 0.14, 0.27)$

Step 2: Add Results to get the Total Fuzzy Score

$\mathbf{S}_U = (0.12, 0.24, 0.40) + (0.05, 0.14, 0.27)$

$= (0.17, 0.38, 0.67)$

So, the university's aggregated fuzzy score is:

$\mathbf{S}_U = (0.17, 0.38, 0.67)$

Meaning:

- Minimum expected strength: 0.17
- Most likely strength: 0.38
- Maximum possible strength: 0.67

5.4. Government Aggregation

Government fuzzy scores:

- Policy Flexibility $\mathbf{C}_3$:

$\mathbf{x}_{\mathbf{G}_3} = (0.4, 0.6, 0.7)$

- Social Impact $\mathbf{C}_5$:

$\mathbf{x}_{\mathbf{G}_5} = (0.7, 0.8, 0.9)$

Fuzzy weights:

$\mathbf{w}_3 = (0.15, 0.25, 0.35)$

$\mathbf{w}_5 = (0.20, 0.30, 0.40)$

Step 1: Multiply

For $\mathbf{C}_3$:

$(0.4, 0.6, 0.7) \otimes (0.15, 0.25, 0.35)$

$= (0.06, 0.15, 0.245)$

For $\mathbf{C}_5$:

$(0.7, 0.8, 0.9) \otimes (0.20, 0.30, 0.40)$

$= (0.14, 0.24, 0.36)$

Step 2:

$\mathbf{S}_{\mathbf{G}} = (0.06, 0.15, 0.245) + (0.14, 0.24, 0.36)$

$= (0.20, 0.39, 0.605)$

So, Government aggregated fuzzy score is:

$$S_G = (0.20, 0.39, 0.605)$$

5.5. Industry Aggregation

Industry fuzzy score for technology readiness:

$$x_{I_4} = (0.7, 0.9, 1.0)$$

Weight for technology readiness:

$$w_4 = (0.25, 0.35, 0.45)$$

Multiply:

$$(0.7, 0.9, 1.0) \otimes (0.25, 0.35, 0.45)$$

$$= (0.175, 0.315, 0.45)$$

Since only one criterion is evaluated here:

$$S_I = (0.175, 0.315, 0.45)$$

5.6. Meaning of Aggregation

The fuzzy aggregation model helps answer:

- Who contributes more?
- Who is uncertain?
- Who needs improvement?

Higher fuzzy scores mean stronger collaboration potential. Lower fuzzy scores show weak areas. Aggregation joins all opinions into one fuzzy value. This makes MCDM easier and supports AI development planning. Universities, governments, and industries can compare fuzzy values. They can plan better partnerships and reduce uncertainty in decisions.

6. CHOOSING A JOINT AI LABORATORY

A university wants to build a joint AI lab. The government also wants a safe AI lab. Industry wants fast and useful AI solutions. All three partners must decide together. They use fuzzy MCDM.

We chose three criteria:

- C : **Cost sharing**
- C : **Research output**
- C : **Policy matching**

These criteria show money, research power, and rule alignment. Each partner gives fuzzy scores. A fuzzy score handles doubt. Each score is a triangular fuzzy number.

Partner Fuzzy Scores

University scores:

$$\mathbf{x}_U = \{(0.5, 0.7, 0.9), (0.7, 0.8, 1.0), (0.4, 0.6, 0.7)\}$$

Government scores:

$$\mathbf{x}_G = \{(0.6, 0.7, 0.8), (0.5, 0.6, 0.8), (0.6, 0.7, 0.9)\}$$

Industry scores:

$$\mathbf{x}_I = \{(0.7, 0.8, 1.0), (0.6, 0.7, 0.9), (0.3, 0.5, 0.6)\}$$

Cost sharing is the first value. Research output is the second value. Policy matching is the third value. A better fit is indicated by higher values. The industry has poor policy alignment but high-cost support. The government has moderate research power but an excellent policy match. The university displays balanced scores across the board.

Fuzzy Weights for Criteria

Weights also show uncertainty:

$$\mathbf{w} = \{(0.2, 0.3, 0.4), (0.3, 0.4, 0.5), (0.2, 0.3, 0.3)\}$$

Here:

- **C weight** = (0.2, 0.3, 0.4)
- **C weight** = (0.3, 0.4, 0.5)
- **C weight** = (0.2, 0.3, 0.3)

The greatest weight is given to research output. The weight of policy matching is moderate. The least important factor is cost sharing.

Fuzzy Aggregation

We compute a score for each partner:

$$\mathbf{S}_U = \sum \mathbf{x}_{U_j} \otimes \mathbf{w}_j$$

$$\mathbf{S}_G = \sum \mathbf{x}_{G_j} \otimes \mathbf{w}_j$$

$$\mathbf{S}_I = \sum \mathbf{x}_{I_j} \otimes \mathbf{w}_j$$

We use fuzzy multiplication:

$$(\mathbf{l}_1, \mathbf{m}_1, \mathbf{u}_1) \otimes (\mathbf{l}_2, \mathbf{m}_2, \mathbf{u}_2) = (\mathbf{l}_1 \mathbf{l}_2, \mathbf{m}_1 \mathbf{m}_2, \mathbf{u}_1 \mathbf{u}_2)$$

Then we use fuzzy addition:

$$(\mathbf{l}_1, \mathbf{m}_1, \mathbf{u}_1) + (\mathbf{l}_2, \mathbf{m}_2, \mathbf{u}_2) = (\mathbf{l}_1 + \mathbf{l}_2, \mathbf{m}_1 + \mathbf{m}_2, \mathbf{u}_1 + \mathbf{u}_2)$$

University score:

$$\mathbf{S}_U = (0.37, 0.53, 0.73)$$

Government score:

$$\mathbf{S}_G = (0.36, 0.48, 0.69)$$

Industry score:

$$\mathbf{S}_I = (0.34, 0.47, 0.69)$$

Remark

The highest score is from the university. The government's score is marginally lower. The industry score is still lower, but it is quite close to the government's. This result reflects a Triple Helix governance dynamic. University provides knowledge leadership for AI research. Government supports policy guidance and regulatory alignment. Industry contributes resources and applied innovation capacity.

This means:

- The university is most suitable for leading the lab.
- Government is a strong policy supporter.
- Industry is good, but less consistent in policy alignment.

Why University Ranks First

The university has a strong research output. Research output had the highest weight. Hence, the university gets a good score.

Why Government Ranks Second

The government has a good policy matching. Policy matching weight is moderate. So, the government score is stable.

Why Industry Ranks Third

The industry has great cost-sharing. But the cost weight is low. The industry has weak policy alignment. This pulls the score down.

Remark

The three are still welcome to join the lab. However, the university ought to take the initiative. Policy should be guided by the government. Industry should provide resources and tools. This hazy illustration demonstrates how ambiguous viewpoints become apparent. It facilitates equitable MCDM between partners.

7. DEFUZZIFICATION

Fuzzy values are transformed into crisp values through defuzzification. A single number is a sharp value. It aids in the ultimate ranking. It eliminates doubt. It provides an unambiguous judgment score. The centroid approach is what we employ. The centroid approach is easy to use. It is extensively utilized. For a fuzzy integer that is triangular:

$$\mathbf{S}_i = (\mathbf{l}_i, \mathbf{m}_i, \mathbf{u}_i)$$

The defuzzified value is:

$$\mathbf{D}_i = \frac{\mathbf{l}_i + \mathbf{m}_i + \mathbf{u}_i}{3}$$

This formula takes the average. It captures all three points. It treats all parts equally.

7.1. Defuzzification of University Score

From Section 5, University score:

$$\mathbf{S}_U = (0.17,\ 0.38,\ 0.67)$$

Now apply the centroid:

$$\mathbf{D}_U = \frac{0.17 + 0.38 + 0.67}{3}$$

$$\mathbf{D}_U = 0.4067$$

Meaning:

- University strength $\approx$ 0.41
- The university has a moderate contribution.
- Uncertainty is reduced to one number.

7.2. Defuzzification of Government Score

Government aggregated fuzzy score:

$$\mathbf{S}_G = (0.20,\ 0.39,\ 0.605)$$

Now calculate:

$$\mathbf{D}_G = 0.20 + 0.39 + 0.6053$$

$D_G = 0.3983$

Meaning:

- Government strength ≈ 0.40
- Almost equal to the university.
- Slightly lower, but very close.

7.3. Defuzzification of Industry Score

Industry aggregated fuzzy score:

$S_I = (0.175, 0.315, 0.45)$

Apply the formula:

$D_I = 0.175 + 0.315 + 0.453$

$D_I = 0.3133$

Meaning:

- Industry strength ≈ 0.31
- Industry contribution is lower.
- Technology readiness helps.
- But other factors may be weaker.

7.4. Comparative interpretation

Now we have three crisp scores:

$D_U = 0.4067$

$D_I = 0.3133$

They are easily comparable. University is the highest, as we can see. The government is really near. There is less industry. This reflects differentiated roles within the Triple Helix framework. Knowledge creation, regulation, and innovation remain interdependent. Decision-makers benefit from this. They receive precise figures. They are more adept at setting priorities.

Suppose University has four fuzzy criteria:

- $\mathbf{C}_1$: (0.6, 0.8, 1.0)
- $\mathbf{C}_2$: (0.5, 0.7, 0.9)
- $\mathbf{C}_3$: (0.3, 0.5, 0.7)
- $\mathbf{C}_4$: (0.6, 0.75, 0.85)

Weighted fuzzy sum gives:

$$\mathbf{S}_U = (0.30,\ 0.55,\ 0.82)$$

Defuzzify:

$$\mathbf{D}_U = 0.30 + 0.55 + 0.823$$

$$\mathbf{D}_U = 0.5567$$

Now the value is higher. This means better performance.

7.5. Selecting an AI Ethics Oversight Committee

Universities, government, and industry want a shared AI ethics committee. Such a committee will check fairness, safety, and transparency. Each partner wants trustworthy leadership. We use fuzzy MCDM to chose the best leader.

We select four criteria:

- **C : Transparency level**
- **C : Ethical experience**
- **C : Policy knowledge**
- **C : Public trust**

These criteria show clarity, fairness, rule knowledge, and trust. Each partner gives fuzzy scores as triangular fuzzy numbers.

Fuzzy Scores

University scores:

$$\mathbf{x}_U = \{(0.6, 0.7, 0.8), (0.7, 0.8, 1.0), (0.5, 0.6, 0.7), (0.6, 0.7, 0.8)\}$$

Government scores:

$$\mathbf{x_G} = \{(0.5, 0.6, 0.7), (0.8, 0.9, 1.0), (0.7, 0.8, 0.9), (0.6, 0.7, 0.8)\}$$

Industry scores:

$$\mathbf{x_I} = \{(0.4, 0.5, 0.6), (0.6, 0.7, 0.8), (0.4, 0.5, 0.6), (0.7, 0.8, 0.9)\}$$

Fuzzy Weights

Weights for criteria:

$$\mathbf{w} = \{(0.2, 0.3, 0.4), (0.3, 0.4, 0.5), (0.2, 0.3, 0.4), (0.2, 0.3, 0.3)\}$$

Ethical experience has the highest weight. Transparency, policy knowledge, and trust have moderate weights.

Fuzzy Aggregation Formula

$$\mathbf{S_i} = \sum_{j=1}^{4} \mathbf{x_{ij}} \otimes \mathbf{w_j}$$

Multiplication rule:

$$(\mathbf{l_1}, \mathbf{m_1}, \mathbf{u_1}) \otimes (\mathbf{l_2}, \mathbf{m_2}, \mathbf{u_2}) = (\mathbf{l_1 l_2}, \mathbf{m_1 m_2}, \mathbf{u_1 u_2})$$

Addition rule:

$$(\mathbf{l_1}, \mathbf{m_1}, \mathbf{u_1}) + (\mathbf{l_2}, \mathbf{m_2}, \mathbf{u_2}) = (\mathbf{l_1} + \mathbf{l_2}, \mathbf{m_1} + \mathbf{m_2}, \mathbf{u_1} + \mathbf{u_2})$$

University:

$$\mathbf{S_U} = (0.42, 0.57, 0.76)$$

Government:

$$\mathbf{S_G} = (0.46, 0.63, 0.83)$$

Industry:

$$S_I = (0.37, 0.48, 0.64)$$

Defuzzification

$$D = \frac{l + m + u}{3}$$

University:

$$D_U = 0.42 + 0.57 + 0.763 = 0.583$$

Government:

$$D_G = 0.46 + 0.63 + 0.833 = 0.640$$

Industry:

$$D_I = 0.37 + 0.48 + 0.643 = 0.496$$

The highest score goes to the government. The government is well-versed in policy. The government has a solid background in ethics as well. Therefore, the ethics committee needs to be headed by the government. This shows a governance-focused Triple Helix structure. The government leads ethical oversight and regulation. Universities provide ethical research guidance. Industry helps with compliance and implementation. Research ideas should be contributed by universities. The industry ought to back ethical audits and tools. This paradigm aids in choosing a just leader. This ensures the safety of the AI project. Additionally, this fosters community trust.

7.6. Why Defuzzification is Important

Defuzzification facilitates communication. Officials comprehend clear figures more quickly. Clean numbers are used in industry planning. In proposals, universities use precise numbers. Data that is fuzzy is rich. However, action requires clear output. Ranking is often necessary for decisions. Ranking is supported by defuzzification. It makes things less confusing. It encourages teamwork. AI policy decisions are strengthened by it.

Choosing an AI Internship Plan

This example shows how a student selects an AI internship. The student compares three internship plans:

- University internship,
- Government internship,
- Industry internship.

The student uses four criteria:

- **C_1 : Skill growth**
- **C_2 : Policy training**
- **C_3 : Hardware usage**
- **C_4 : Innovation output**

Each criterion has uncertainty. So fuzzy numbers are used.

Fuzzy Suitability Scores

University fuzzy scores:

$(0.6, 0.8, 0.9)$, $(0.4, 0.5, 0.7)$, $(0.5, 0.6, 0.8)$, $(0.7, 0.8, 1.0)$

This means:

- Skill growth is high.
- Policy training is a medium.
- Hardware usage is medium.
- Innovation output is strong.

Government fuzzy scores:

$(0.5, 0.6, 0.8)$, $(0.6, 0.7, 0.9)$, $(0.4, 0.6, 0.7)$, $(0.5, 0.6, 0.7)$

This means:

- Skill growth is decent.
- Policy training is very high.
- Hardware usage is moderate.
- Innovation output is moderate.

Industry fuzzy scores:

$(0.8, 0.9, 1.0)$, $(0.3, 0.4, 0.5)$, $(0.7, 0.8, 0.9)$, $(0.8, 0.9, 1.0)$

This means:

- Skill growth is excellent.
- Policy training is limited.
- Hardware usage is very high.
- Innovation output is top-level.

Weight Selection

Weights are equal for all criteria since the student considers each equally important:

$$\mathbf{w} = (0.2,\ 0.25,\ 0.3)$$

This weight applies to all four criteria.
The aggregation uses:

$$\mathbf{S_i} = \sum_{j=1}^{4} \mathbf{x_{ij}} \otimes \mathbf{w}$$

Using fuzzy multiplication:

$$(\mathbf{l_1}, \mathbf{m_1}, \mathbf{u_1}) \otimes (\mathbf{l_2}, \mathbf{m_2}, \mathbf{u_2}) = (\mathbf{l_1 l_2}, \mathbf{m_1 m_2}, \mathbf{u_1 u_2})$$

And fuzzy addition:

$$(\mathbf{l_1}, \mathbf{m_1}, \mathbf{u_1}) + (\mathbf{l_2}, \mathbf{m_2}, \mathbf{u_2}) = (\mathbf{l_1} + \mathbf{l_2}, \mathbf{m_1} + \mathbf{m_2}, \mathbf{u_1} + \mathbf{u_2})$$

Aggregated Scores

University aggregated score

$$\mathbf{S_U} = (0.44,\ 0.55,\ 0.69)$$

Meaning:

- Minimum suitability: 0.44
- Most likely suitability: 0.55
- Maximum suitability: 0.69

Government aggregated score

$\mathbf{S}_G = (0.40,\ 0.53,\ 0.68)$

Meaning:

- Slightly lower than the university.
- Very stable mid-range value.

Industry aggregated score

$\mathbf{S}_I = (0.52,\ 0.62,\ 0.72)$

Meaning:

- Strongest fuzzy score.
- High potential for hands-on learning.

Defuzzification

Use the centroid formula:

$$\mathbf{D} = \frac{\mathbf{l} + \mathbf{m} + \mathbf{u}}{3}$$

University:

$$\mathbf{D}_U = 0.44 + 0.55 + 0.693 = 0.56$$

Government:

$$\mathbf{D}_G = 0.40 + 0.53 + 0.683 = 0.53$$

Industry:

$$\mathbf{D}_I = 0.52 + 0.62 + 0.723 = 0.62$$

Final Decision
The scores are:

$$\mathbf{D}_I = 0.62, \mathbf{D}\text{U} = 0.56, \mathbf{D}\text{G} = 0.53$$

So:

- Industry is best.
- University is second.
- Government is third.

This reflects a Triple Helix coordination outcome. Industry provides practical learning and innovation exposure. Universities support theoretical and skill development. The government offers policy-oriented learning environments.

The greatest skill gain comes from an industrial internship. It provides robust hardware access. It provides the most exposure to innovation. There, the learner gains the most knowledge. The plan for an industry internship is therefore selected.

8. CONFLICT ANALYSIS USING FUZZY SOFT SETS

When working together, partners may have disagreements. Conflict arises from disagreements. Budgetary concerns give rise to conflicts. Policy issues give rise to conflicts. Technical decisions give rise to conflicts. These conflicts are managed with the aid of fuzzy soft sets (Maji et al. 2001). They deal with differing viewpoints. They permit partial consensus. They permit partial disagreement. They provide an adaptable framework.

8.1. SOFT SET IN COLLABORATIVE AI MCDM

When partners express their ideas using parameters rather than fixed numbers, soft sets (Molodtsov, 1999) are helpful. A soft set displays the parameters that are important and the degree of agreement between partners. Uncertainty in human judgment is likewise handled by a soft set. Partners in AI projects frequently disagree; thus, this is helpful. Soft sets consist of two components:

$$\mathbf{F} = (\mathbf{P}, \mathbf{E})$$

- P is a set of parameters.
- E maps each parameter to a fuzzy set or soft opinion.

Soft sets allow flexible and simple reasoning.

8.2. PARAMETERS IN AI COLLABORATION

Partners chose parameters based on their concerns.

Example parameter set:

$$P = \{\textbf{High cost}, \textbf{Slow progress}, \textbf{Ethical risk}, \textbf{Low accuracy}\}$$

A fuzzy membership value is provided by each partner. Research is valued at universities. Safety is important to the government. Speed is valued in the industry.

8.3. FUZZY SOFT OPINIONS

Let:

$$\mu_U(p),\ \mu_G(p),\ \mu_I(p)$$

be membership values for parameter p.
University:

- $\mu_U(\text{High cost}) = 0.3$
- $\mu_U(\text{Ethical risk}) = 0.7$

Government:

- $\mu_G(\text{Slow progress}) = 0.8$
- $\mu_G(\text{Ethical risk}) = 0.9$

Industry:

- $\mu_I(\text{Low accuracy}) = 0.4$
- $\mu_I(\text{High cost}) = 0.2$

Each partner focuses on different issues.

8.4. COMBINED SOFT DECISION SCORE

We combine all views:

$$\mu_C(p) = \max(\mu U(p), \mu G(p), \mu I(p))$$

The max method shows group concern.
For parameter "Ethical risk":

$$\mu_C = \max(0.7, 0.9, 0.3) = 0.9$$

The government cares most about ethics.
For parameter "High cost":

$$\mu_C = \max(0.3, 0.1, 0.2) = 0.3$$

The university cares most about cost. This tells us which concerns dominate.

8.5. AI DATA-SHARING RULES

Partners must chose a data-sharing plan for joint AI projects.
Parameter set:
P = {Security, Access speed, Data fairness}

Step 1: Fuzzy Soft Opinions

University:

- Security: 0.6
- Access speed: 0.4
- Data fairness: 0.8

Government:

- Security: 0.9
- Access speed: 0.3
- Data fairness: 0.7

Industry:

- Security: 0.5
- Access speed: 0.8
- Data fairness: 0.4

Step 2: Combined Soft Scores

Security:

$$\mu_C = \max(0.6, 0.9, 0.5) = 0.9$$

Access speed:

$$\mu_C = \max(0.4, 0.3, 0.8) = 0.8$$

Data fairness:

$$\mu_C = \max(0.8, 0.7, 0.4) = 0.8$$

Remark

- The government cares most about security.
- Industry cares most about speed.
- The university cares most about fairness.

8.6. SOFT-SET BASED DECISION

Priority order:

- Security (0.9)
- Access speed (0.8)
- Data fairness (0.8)

Therefore:

- The data-sharing plan must follow strict security rules.
- Speed and fairness must be optimized, but security remains primary.

8.7. A JOINT AI FACULTY EXCHANGE PROGRAM

Partners want a shared teaching plan. They must chose which faculty members will exchange roles.

Parameter set:

$$\mathbf{P} = \{\textbf{Teaching quality}, \textbf{AI expertise}, \textbf{Policy knowledge}\}$$

University:

- Teaching quality: 0.9
- AI expertise: 0.8
- Policy knowledge: 0.4

Government:

- Teaching quality: 0.5
- AI expertise: 0.6
- Policy knowledge: 0.9

Industry:

- Teaching quality: 0.4
- AI expertise: 0.8
- Policy knowledge: 0.3

Combined Values

Teaching quality:

$$\mu_C = \max(0.9, 0.5, 0.4) = 0.9$$

AI expertise:

$$\mu_C = \max(0.8, 0.6, 0.8) = 0.8$$

Policy knowledge:

$$\mu_C = \max(0.4, 0.9, 0.3) = 0.9$$

Interpretation
Two parameters dominate:

- Teaching quality (0.9)
- Policy knowledge (0.9)

The best faculty exchange pair must:

- Teach clearly.
- Understand government AI policies.

This ensures classes follow national AI regulations.

8.8. RANKING AI INNOVATION OBSTACLES

Partners want to know the obstacles to AI development.
Parameter set:

$$P = \{\text{Lack of funding}, \text{Policy delay}, \text{Weak research}, \text{Low hardware}\}$$

Soft Opinions

University:

- Weak research = 0.8
- Low hardware = 0.7

Government:

- Policy delay = 0.9
- Lack of funding = 0.6

Industry:

- Low hardware = 0.8
- Lack of funding = 0.7

Combined Soft Set

Lack of funding:

$$\mu_C = \max(0.3, 0.6, 0.7) = 0.7$$

Policy delay:

$$\mu_C = \max(0.4, 0.9, 0.5) = 0.9$$

Weak research:

$$\mu_C = \max(0.8, 0.4, 0.3) = 0.8$$

Low hardware:

$$\mu_C = \max(0.7, 0.5, 0.8) = 0.8$$

Obstacle Ranking

- Policy delay — 0.9
- Weak research — 0.8
- Low hardware — 0.8
- Lack of funding — 0.7

This result highlights governance imbalance within the Triple Helix. Government policy delays require urgent coordination. Universities and industries must strengthen research and infrastructure.

Decision Meaning

- Policy is the biggest obstacle.
- Government must act faster.
- University and industry must improve research and hardware.

8.9. WHY SOFT SETS IMPROVE COLLABORATION

Soft sets help because:

- They model real disagreement.
- They allow multiple parameters.
- They do not require precise numbers.
- They reflect fuzzy human judgment.
- They combine all partner views systematically.

Soft sets improve trust between partners.
Soft sets allow fair and flexible decisions.
Soft sets strengthen collaboration in AI development.

9. FUZZY SOFT SET

Uncertainty results from both subjective, attribute-dependent views and imprecise numerical evaluations in complex, multi-stakeholder situations, such as partnerships between academic institutions, governmental agencies, and business partners. Depending on their priorities, policy limitations, or strategic objectives, each stakeholder may evaluate the same criterion in a different way. Because traditional fuzzy sets treat criteria consistently in all decision contexts, they are unable to adequately reflect this variety. This gap is filled by the fuzzy soft set model (Maji et al. 2001).

9.1. CONCEPTUAL UNDERSTANDING

Let:

- U = set of decision alternatives

(University partnership model, government-policy-driven model, industry-led innovation model)

- E = set of parameters/criteria

(Research excellence, policy compliance, innovation speed, funding stability, etc.)

Every parameter is linked to a subset of U by a soft set. This is improved by a fuzzy soft set, which gives each possibility under each parameter a degree of membership (ranging from 0 to 1).

Therefore, rather than:

- Hard yes/no classification (soft set),

the fuzzy soft set gives:

- Gradual, realistic evaluations depending on context.

This makes fuzzy soft sets ideal for AI ecosystem collaboration, where:

- University values knowledge creation,
- Government values safety and policy alignment,
- Industry values speed and application.

9.2. DEFINITION

A fuzzy soft set over a universe U and parameter set E is defined as:

$$\mathbf{F} = \left\{(\mathbf{e}, \boldsymbol{\mu}_{\mathbf{e}}) \mid \mathbf{e} \in \mathbf{E}\right\}$$

where

$$\mu_e : U \to [0,1]$$

gives the degree to which alternative $u \in U$ **satisfies parameter e. Each parameter has a fuzzy set attached.**

9.3. INTERPRETATION IN U – G – I COLLABORATION

In AI co-development, parameters could include as presented in Table 1.

Table 1. Key Parameters and Their Meanings in U–G–I AI Collaboration

Parameter	Meaning
e_1	Alignment with National AI Safety Guidelines
e_2	Research Innovation Potential
e_3	Funding Sustainability
e_4	Technology Transfer Capability

Alternatives:

- u_1: University-led AI Joint Lab
- u_2: Government-led AI Safety Hub
- u_3: Industry-led Applied AI Centre

Each stakeholder evaluates each alternative differently.

9.4. EXAMPLE (FUZZY SOFT SET)

Step 1: Define Universe and Parameters

$$U = \{u_1, u_2, u_3\}$$

$$E = \{e_1, e_2, e_3\}$$

Where:

- e_1: AI Safety & Policy Alignment
- e_2: Research Innovation Output
- e_3: Commercialization & Deployment Efficiency

Step 2: Construct Fuzzy Soft Sets from Each Stakeholder's Perspective

(a) University's fuzzy soft set □□

The university prioritizes research as presented in Table 2.

Table 2. Fuzzy Soft Set Example Based on University Evaluations

Parameter	u_1	u_2	u_3
e_1	0.6	0.8	0.5
e_2	0.9	0.7	0.6
e_3	0.5	0.6	0.7

Formally:

$$= \{ (\mathbf{e}_1, \{(\mathbf{u}_1, 0.6), (\mathbf{u}_2, 0.8), (\mathbf{u}_3, 0.5)\}), (\mathbf{e}_2, \{(\mathbf{u}_1, 0.9), (\mathbf{u}_2, 0.7), (\mathbf{u}_3, 0.6)\}), (\mathbf{e}_3, \{(\mathbf{u}_1, 0.5), (\mathbf{u}_2, 0.6), (\mathbf{u}_3, 0.7)\}) \}$$

Interpretation of Table 2

Table 2 shows university evaluations of different alternatives. The values indicate how well each alternative meets academic or research criteria. Alternative $u_2$has higher scores overall, suggesting better alignment with university priorities. $u_3$shows mixed scores, indicating suitability depending on specific academic factors. $u_1$has moderate scores, reflecting general suitability but less competitive advantage compared to u_2.

University Implication

From a university perspective, higher scores indicate alternatives that are more suitable for research collaboration, resource allocation, or academic support. Alternatives with consistently high scores, like u_2, may be prioritized for projects or funding, while those with lower or uneven scores may need adjustments to meet academic requirements. This approach helps universities make clear and informed decisions about supporting different alternatives.

(b) Government's fuzzy soft set FG

Government values safety and accountability as presented in Table 3.

Table 3. Fuzzy Soft Set Example Based on Government Evaluations

Parameter	u_1	u_2	u_3
e_1	0.7	0.9	0.6
e_2	0.8	0.7	0.5
e_3	0.6	0.7	0.8

Interpretation of Table 3

Table 3 shows government evaluations of different alternatives. The numbers reflect how well each alternative meets government priorities. Alternative u_2 scores higher overall, indicating better alignment with policies, while u_3 has mixed scores, showing it may be suitable only under certain policy conditions.

Governance Implication

From a government view, the fuzzy soft set shows how policies affect AI collaboration. Higher scores mean better policy fit and readiness. Alternatives with high scores may get approval or support, while those with low or uneven scores may need adjustments. This approach helps the government make clear and informed decisions.

(c) Industry's fuzzy soft set FI

Industry values speed and market readiness as presented in Table 4.

Table 4. Fuzzy Soft Set Example Based on Industry Evaluations

Parameter	u_1	u_2	u_3
e_1	0.5	0.7	0.8
e_2	0.7	0.6	0.9
e_3	0.8	0.7	0.9

Interpretation of Table 4

Table 4 shows industry evaluations of different alternatives. The numbers reflect how suitable each alternative is for practical use. Alternative u_3 scores higher overall, showing better industry acceptance and feasibility. u_2 has mixed scores, meaning it may be preferred only under certain conditions. u_1 has moderate scores, indicating general suitability but less advantage compared to u_3.

Industry Implication

From an industry view, the fuzzy soft set shows how suitable each alternative is for practical use. Higher scores mean better industry fit and readiness. Alternatives with high scores, like u_3, can be prioritized for investment or implementation, while those with lower or mixed scores may need improvements or adjustments. This helps industries make clear and informed decisions.

9.5. AGGREGATE FUZZY SOFT SCORES

A simple aggregation method (mean across parameters):
For University

$$\mathbf{S}_U(\mathbf{u}_1) = \frac{0.6 + 0.9 + 0.5}{3} = 0.67$$

$$\mathbf{S}_U(\mathbf{u}_2) = \frac{0.8 + 0.7 + 0.6}{3} = 0.70$$

$$\mathbf{S}_U(\mathbf{u}_3) = \frac{0.5 + 0.6 + 0.7}{3} = 0.60$$

University prefers:

$$\mathbf{u}_2 > \mathbf{u}_1 > \mathbf{u}_3$$

For Government

$$\mathbf{S}_G(\mathbf{u}_1) = \frac{0.7 + 0.8 + 0.6}{3} = 0.70$$

$$\mathbf{S}_G(\mathbf{u}_2) = \frac{0.9 + 0.7 + 0.7}{3} = 0.77$$

$$\mathbf{S}_G(\mathbf{u}_3) = \frac{0.6 + 0.5 + 0.8}{3} = 0.63$$

Government prefers:

$$\mathbf{u}_2 > \mathbf{u}_1 > \mathbf{u}_3$$

For Industry

$$\mathbf{S}_I(\mathbf{u}_1) = \frac{0.5 + 0.7 + 0.8}{3} = 0.67$$

$$S_I(u_2) = \frac{0.7 + 0.6 + 0.7}{3} = 0.67$$

$$S_I(u_3) = \frac{0.8 + 0.9 + 0.9}{3} = 0.87$$

Industry prefers:

$$u_3 > u_1 = u_2$$

Remark

- Both University and Government rank the Government-led AI Safety Hub (u_2) **highest.**
- Industry prefers the Industry-led Applied AI Centre (u_3).
- The fuzzy soft set captures these differing stakeholder priorities without forcing crisp judgments.

It helps identify:

- Consensus areas (U & G favour u_2)
- Conflict areas (Industry strongly prefers u_3)
- Negotiation pathways (hybrid governance models)

This enables a deeper understanding of collaboration dynamics.
A fuzzy soft set is:

$$F = (P, E)$$

Where:

- **P is a parameter set.**
- **E maps each parameter to a fuzzy set.**

An issue is a parameter and an opinion level is a fuzzy set. Membership for each opinion ranges from 0 to 1.

9.6. PARAMETERS FOR CONFLICT

Let the conflict parameters be:

- p_1 : **"High cost"**

- p_2 "Slow process"
- p_3: "Low risk"

These parameters represent concerns. Each partner expresses fuzzy concern levels.

9.7. FUZZY OPINION VALUES

University opinion:

$$\mu_U(p_1) = 0.3$$

Meaning:
University says "high cost" is low concern.
Government opinion:

$$\mu_G(p_2) = 0.7$$

Meaning:
Government says "slow process" is strong concern.
Industry opinion:

$$\mu_I(p_3) = 0.2$$

Meaning:
Industry says "low risk" is very small concern.

9.8. COMBINED FUZZY SOFT SET SCORE

To combine all opinions, use:

$$\mu_C(x) = \max\left(\mu_U(x),\ \mu_G(x),\ \mu_I(x)\right)$$

"max" rule takes the strongest concern.
This shows the highest risk level. This reflects worst-case thinking.
Example:

- For "High cost":

$$\mu_C(p_1) = \max(0.3, 0, 0) = 0.3$$

- For “Slow process”:

$\mu_C(p_2) = \max(0, 0.7, 0) = 0.7$

- For “Low risk”:

$\mu_C(p_3) = \max(0, 0, 0.2) = 0.2$

So joint concern set is:

$\mu_C = (0.3, 0.7, 0.2)$

9.9. INTERPRETATION OF CONFLICTS

The joint concern analysis shows the relative severity of conflicts:

- **Data security risk (p_1):** high conflict ($\mu_C = 0.8$)
- **Lack of skilled staff (p_2):** moderate conflict ($\mu_C = 0.7$)
- **High maintenance cost (p_3):** moderate conflict ($\mu_C = 0.7$)
- Limited hardware access (p_4): highest conflict ($\mu_C = 0.9$)

Final joint conflict vector:

$\mu_C = (0.8, 0.7, 0.7, 0.9)$

Conflict ranking (highest to lowest):

1. Limited hardware access (0.9)
2. Data security risk (0.8)
3. Lack of skilled staff / High maintenance cost (0.7 each)

Key insight for decisions:
Prioritize addressing hardware access and data security first. Moderate issues like staffing and maintenance can follow. Low-risk conflicts are less urgent.

9.10. MEANING OF THIS CONFLICT VECTOR

- $p_4 = 0.9$: **The biggest conflict is hardware access.**
- $p_1 = 0.8$: **Data security is also a major.**
- $p_2 = 0.7$: **Skills shortage is serious.**

- $p_3 = 0.7$: **Maintenance cost is equally serious.**

This provides a conflict ranking. Partners are aware of when to take action. They are able to design a plan for resolution.

9.11. BENEFITS OF FUZZY SOFT SETS

Flexible thinking is possible with fuzzy soft sets. They don't need precise figures. Partners may voice only a portion of their opinions. All viewpoints are fairly combined by the model. It lessens miscommunication during conflicts. It facilitates better communication. It encourages more effective teamwork.

9.12. FINAL COLLABORATIVE DECISION SCORE

One final score is what we want. The total strength of teamwork is indicated by this score. We refer to it as the Collaboration Index $(\mathbf{C}_I)$. **We specify:**

$$\mathbf{C}_I = \alpha \mathbf{D}_U + \beta \mathbf{D}_G + \gamma \mathbf{D}_I$$

Here:

- $\mathbf{D}_U$ **= University defuzzified score**
- $\mathbf{D}_G$ **= Government defuzzified score**
- $\mathbf{D}_I$ **= Industry defuzzified score**
- α, β, γ **= importance weights**

The weights must satisfy:

$$\alpha + \beta + \gamma = 1$$

This ensures fairness.
Let the weights be:

$$\alpha = 0.4, \beta = 0.3, \gamma = 0.3$$

Suppose we take the defuzzified scores from Example 1:

- $\mathbf{D}_U = 0.543$
- $\mathbf{D}_G = 0.510$
- $\mathbf{D}_I = 0.500$

Now compute:

$$\mathbf{C_I} = 0.4(0.543) + 0.3(0.510) + 0.3(0.500)$$

$$\mathbf{C_I} = 0.2172 + 0.153 + 0.150$$

$$\mathbf{C_I} = 0.518$$

We define a simple rule:

$$\mathbf{C_I} > 0.5 \Rightarrow \textbf{Collaboration is stable}$$

Here:

$$0.518 > 0.5$$

Thus, cooperation is steady. The three partners are able to collaborate well. This outcome is supported by the fuzzy model.

10 POLICY SUGGESTIONS FROM FUZZY RESULTS

Clear signals are produced by fuzzy findings. Partners who agree get a higher fuzzy score. Partners who have a lower fuzzy score are different. Improvement is required if university scores are lower. The university ought to forge closer ties with business. It ought to provide genuine projects and collaborative labs. Rules are overly stringent if government scores are lower. The government ought to streamline the approval process. Paperwork for AI programs should decrease as a result. Lower industry scores indicate a lack of support. Research should receive more funding from the sector. It should provide instruction and guidance to students. All groups act with the aid of fuzzy results. They immediately highlight areas of weakness. They favor reasonable and well-rounded policy adjustments.

11. CONCLUSION

This study focuses on decision-making under uncertainty in Triple Helix. Collaboration among universities, governments, and industries is complex. Institutions have different priorities and often conflicting objectives. AI collaboration faces uncertainty and frequent conflicts. Fuzzy models handle these challenges effectively. Subjective judgments are converted into structured decisions. The framework compares partners, showing both consensus and conflict. Decision transparency and clarity are improved. This study extends Triple Helix research beyond descriptions. It provides operational governance and structured AI decision-making. Institutional roles become clearer and comparable. Universities lead research and create knowledge. Governments ensure regulation, policy, and ethical oversight. Industries support innovation and practical AI deployment. The framework aligns roles for coordinated collaboration. Despite contributions, the study has limitations. Analysis is illustrative, and fuzzy weights vary. Empirical validation is not included. Future research should study real-world AI collaboration. Dynamic models can capture institutional changes. Ethical indicators can be integrated further. Scalable decision-support systems can be explored. The framework strengthens AI governance and planning. It builds trust and supports sustainable AI ecosystems. Decision-oriented fuzzy frameworks guide practical AI collaboration.

REFERENCES

Alam, S., & Khan, M. (2024). Enhancing AI-Human Collaborative Decision-Making in Industry 4.0 Management Practices. *IEEE Access : Practical Innovations, Open Solutions*, *12*, 119433–119444. DOI: 10.1109/ACCESS.2024.3449415

Alshahrani, R., Yenugula, M., Algethami, H., Alharbi, F., Goswami, S., Naveed, Q., Lasisi, A., Islam, S., Khan, N., & Zahmatkesh, S. (2023). Establishing the fuzzy integrated hybrid MCDM framework to identify the key barriers to implementing artificial intelligence-enabled sustainable cloud system in an IT industry. *Expert Systems with Applications*, *238*, 121732. DOI: 10.1016/j.eswa.2023.121732

Belhadi, A., Kamble, S., Wamba, S., & Queiroz, M. (2021). Building supply-chain resilience: An artificial intelligence-based technique and decision-making framework. *International Journal of Production Research*, *60*(14), 4487–4507. DOI: 10.1080/00207543.2021.1950935

Bogachov, S., Kwiliński, A., Miethlich, B., Bartosova, V., & Gurnak, A. (2020). *Artificial intelligence components and fuzzy regulators in entrepreneurship development*. Entrepreneurship and Sustainability Issues., DOI: 10.9770/jesi.2020.8.2(29)

Cai, Y., Ferrer, B., & Lastra, J. (2019). Building University-Industry Co-Innovation Networks in Transnational Innovation Ecosystems: Towards a Transdisciplinary Approach of Integrating Social Sciences and Artificial Intelligence. *Sustainability (Basel)*, *11*(17), 4633. Advance online publication. DOI: 10.3390/su11174633

Das, A. K. (2016). On partially included intuitionistic fuzzy rough relations. *Afrika Matematika*, *27*(5-6), 993–1001. DOI: 10.1007/s13370-016-0395-2

Das, A. K. (2018). Weighted fuzzy soft multiset and decision-making. *International Journal of Machine Learning and Cybernetics*, *9*(5), 787–794. DOI: 10.1007/s13042-016-0607-y

Das, A. K., Das, R., Das, S., Debnath, B. K., Granados, C., Shil, B., & Das, R. (2025c). A comprehensive study of neutrosophic SuperHyper BCI-semigroups and their algebraic significance. *Transactions on Fuzzy Sets and Systems*, *4*(2), 80–101. DOI: 10.71602/tfss.2025.1198050

Das, A. K., Das, R., Datta, R., & Granados, C. (2025e). An Innovative Approach to Group Decision-Making Based on Weighted Hypersoft Expert System. In Smarandache, F., Jdid, M., & Leyva-Vazquez, M. (Eds.), *Neutrosophic and Plithogenic Inventory Models for Applied Mathematics* (pp. 483–518). IGI Global Scientific Publishing., DOI: 10.4018/979-8-3693-3204-7.ch019

Das, A. K., & Granados, C. (2021). An advanced approach to fuzzy soft group decision-making using weighted average ratings. *SN Computer Science*, *2*(6), 471. DOI: 10.1007/s42979-021-00873-5

Das, A. K., & Granados, C. (2022a). A new fuzzy parameterized intuitionistic fuzzy soft multiset theory and group decision-making. *Journal of Current Science and Technology*, *12*(3), 547–567. DOI: 10.14456/jcst.2022.42

Das, A. K., & Granados, C. (2022b). FP-intuitionistic multi fuzzy N-soft set and its induced FP-Hesitant N soft set in decision-making. *Decision Making: Applications in Management and Engineering*, *5*(1), 67–89. DOI: 10.31181/dmame181221045d

Das, A. K., & Granados, C. (2023a). IFP-intuitionistic multi fuzzy N-soft set and its induced IFP-hesitant N-soft set in decision-making. *Journal of Ambient Intelligence and Humanized Computing*, *14*(8), 10143–10152. DOI: 10.1007/s12652-021-03677-w

Das, A. K., & Granados, C. (2023b). Preference intuitionistic fuzzy rough relation and its theoretical approach. *Journal of the Indian Mathematical Society*, *90*(3-4), 199–212.

Das, A. K., Granados, C., & Bhattacharya, J. (2022). Some new operations on fuzzy soft sets and their applications in decision-making. *Songklanakarin Journal of Science and Technology*, *44*(2), 440–449. DOI: 10.14456/sjst-psu.2022.61

Das, A. K., Gupta, N., Das, R., Das, S., Das, R., Granados, C., & Debnath, B. K. (2026a). Fuzzy Logic-Driven Strategies for Diversity and Inclusion in Multicultural Marketing. In Tarnanidis, T., Sousa, B., Vlachopoulou, M., Papachristou, E., & Kittu Manda, V. (Eds.), *Diversity and Inclusion-Driven Marketing for Multicultural Marketplaces* (pp. 189–236). IGI Global Scientific Publishing., DOI: 10.4018/979-8-3373-2111-0.ch009

Das, A. K., Gupta, N., Das, R., Granados, C., & Das, S. (2026c). Neutrosophic Sets for Decision-Making in Natural Disasters and Environmental Recovery. In Ezaier, Y., Gaamouche, R., & Lahby, M. (Eds.), *Computational Intelligence and Optimization Methods for Sustainable Water Management* (pp. 119–162). IGI Global Scientific Publishing., DOI: 10.4018/979-8-3373-2700-6.ch004

Das, A. K., Gupta, N., Fujita, T., Das, S., Granados, C., Debnath, B. K., & Das, R. (2026b). Advanced Co-Branding Strategies for Smart Luxury Products: A Multi-Criteria Decision-Making Approach Using Neutrosophic Sets. In Tarnanidis, T., Sousa, B., Vlachopoulou, M., Papachristou, E., & Kittu Manda, V. (Eds.), *Co-Branding Strategies for Smart Luxury Products* (pp. 203–258). IGI Global Scientific Publishing., DOI: 10.4018/979-8-3373-3010-5.ch006

Das, A. K., Gupta, N., & Granados, C. (2023). Weighted hesitant bipolar-valued fuzzy soft set in decision-making. *Songklanakarin Journal of Science and Technology, 45*(6), 681–690. https://sjst.psu.ac.th/journal/45-6/10.pdf

Das, A. K., Gupta, N., Granados, C., Das, R., & Das, S. (2024b). Neutrosophic Approach to Water Quality Assessment: A Case Study of Gomati River, the Largest River in Tripura, India. *Neutrosophic Systems with Applications, 22*, 1–12. DOI: 10.61356/j.nswa.2024.22386

Das, A. K., Gupta, N., Mahmood, T., Tripathy, B. C., Das, R., & Das, S. (2024a). Assessing anthropogenic influences on the water quality of Gomati River using an innovative weighted fuzzy soft set based water pollution rating system. *Discover Water, 4*(1), 73. DOI: 10.1007/s43832-024-00136-3

Das, A. K., Gupta, N., Mahmood, T., Tripathy, B. C., Das, R., & Das, S. (2025a). An efficient water quality evaluation model using weighted hesitant fuzzy soft sets for water pollution rating. In Kumar, A., Kumar, P., Rathee, S., & Kumar, B. (Eds.), *Mechatronics: Concepts, Tools, Applications, and New Trends* (1st ed., p. 17). CRC Press., DOI: 10.1201/9781003494478-10

Das, A. K., Gupta, N., Mahmood, T., Tripathy, B. C., Das, R., & Das, S. (2025b). An innovative fuzzy multi-criteria decision making model for analyzing anthropogenic influences on urban river water quality. *Iran Journal of Computer Science, 8*(1), 103–124. DOI: 10.1007/s42044-024-00211-x

Das, A. K., Gupta, N., Mahmood, T., Tripathy, B. C., Das, R., & Das, S. (2025g). Anthropogenic Impacts on Urban River Water Quality for Rating Water Pollution Using an Effective Fuzzy Soft Multi Criteria Group Decision Making Model. *Iraqi Journal of Science, 66*(9), 3921–3937. DOI: 10.24996/ijs.2025.66.9.32

Das, A. K., Mahmood, T., Das, R., & Das, S. (2025d). Optimizing Inventory Levels in Retail: Fuzzy Logic-Based Decision Support Systems for Adaptive Inventory Management. In Jana, S., Basu Mallik, B., Sarkar, A., & Jana, C. (Eds.), *Applications of Fuzzy Logic in Decision Making and Management Science. Information Systems Engineering and Management* (Vol. 29). Springer., DOI: 10.1007/978-3-031-77719-6_8

Das, A. K., Patra, S., & Granados, C. (2025f). An innovative approach to hesitant bipolar fuzzy soft sets in multi-criteria group decision-making. Adv. in Comp. *Advances in Computational Intelligence, 5*(3), 4. DOI: 10.1007/s43674-025-00082-0

Deveci, M. (2023). Effective use of artificial intelligence in healthcare supply chain resilience using fuzzy decision-making model. *Soft Computing*, •••, 1–14. DOI: 10.1007/s00500-023-08906-2

Fumanal-Idocin, J., & Andreu-Pérez, J. (2024). Ex-Fuzzy: A library for symbolic explainable AI through fuzzy logic programming. *Neurocomputing*, *599*, 128048. DOI: 10.1016/j.neucom.2024.128048

Geetha, S., & Jeon, J. (2022). Extension of SIR method with interval type 2-hesitant fuzzy set to aggrandize industry-university collaboration projects in South Korea. *Journal of Ambient Intelligence and Humanized Computing*, *15*(1), 57–73. DOI: 10.1007/s12652-022-03873-2

. Granados, C., Das, A.K., Das, B. (2022). Some continuous neutrosophic distributions with neutrosophic parameters based on neutrosophic random variables. Advances in the Theory of Nonlinear Analysis and its Applications, 33(2): 293-308. DOI: 10.31197/atnaa.1056480

. Granados, C., Das, A.K., Osu, B. (2023). Weighted neutrosophic soft multiset and its application to decision making. Yugoslav journal of operations research, 33(2): 293-308. DOI: 10.2298/YJOR220915034G

Guo, L., Zhan, J., Zhang, C., & Xu, Z. (2024). A Large-Scale Group Decision-Making Method Fusing Three-Way Clustering and Regret Theory Under Fuzzy Preference Relations. *IEEE Transactions on Fuzzy Systems*, *32*(9), 4846–4860. DOI: 10.1109/TFUZZ.2023.3335965

Gupta, N., Das, A. K., & Granados, C. (2026). Integrating Traditional Ecological Knowledge with Fuzzy Logic and Quantum Computing for Sustainable Agriculture in Tribal Areas of Tripura. In Horng, M., Khalaf, O., Shieh, C., & Jain, V. (Eds.), *Revolutionizing Sustainable Food Production With Quantum Computing* (pp. 177–214). IGI Global Scientific Publishing., DOI: 10.4018/979-8-3373-3957-3.ch006

Hange, U., Nwanesi, E., & Bah, M. (2025). A New Framework for Classifying University-Industry Collaboration Using Synthetic Minority Oversampling Technique and Stacking Ensemble. *IEEE Access : Practical Innovations, Open Solutions*, *13*, 101297–101312. DOI: 10.1109/ACCESS.2025.3577777

Hao, X., Demir, E., & Eyers, D. (2024). Exploring Collaborative Decision-Making: A Quasi-Experimental Study of Human and Generative AI Interaction. *Technology in Society*, *78*, 102662. Advance online publication. DOI: 10.1016/j.techsoc.2024.102662

Hu, K., Chen, F., Hsu, M., & Tzeng, G. (2023). Governance of artificial intelligence applications in a business audit via a fusion fuzzy multiple rule-based decision-making model. *Financial Innovation*, *9*(1), 1–31. DOI: 10.1186/s40854-022-00436-4

Imamguluyev, R. (2025). Integrating Fuzzy Logic with Deep Learning: A New Approach to Explainable Artificial Intelligence. 2025 6th International Conference on Mobile Computing and Sustainable Informatics *(ICMCSI)*, 1701-1706. DOI: 10.1109/ICMCSI64620.2025.10883618

. Kondratenko, G., Kondratenko, Y., & Sidenko, I. (2018). Fuzzy Decision Making System for Model-Oriented Academia/Industry Cooperation: University Preferences., 109-124. .DOI: 10.1007/978-3-319-69989-9_7

. Kumar, R., & Pamučar, D. (2025). A Comprehensive and Systematic Review of Multi-Criteria Decision-Making (MCDM) Methods to Solve Decision-Making Problems: Two Decades from 2004 to 2024. *Spectrum of Decision Making and Applications*. .DOI: 10.31181/sdmap21202524

Maji, P. K., Biswas, R., & Roy, A. R. (2001). Fuzzy soft sets. *Journal of Fuzzy Mathematics*, *9*(3), 589–602.

Molodtsov, D. (1999). Soft set theory: First results. *Computers & Mathematics with Applications (Oxford, England)*, *37*(4–5), 19–31. DOI: 10.1016/S0898-1221(99)00056-5

Mukherjee, A., & Das, A. K. (2015a). Application of interval valued intuitionistic fuzzy soft set in investment decision making, *2015 Fifth International Conference on Advances in Computing and Communications (ICACC)*, Kochi, India, 2015, pp. 61-64, DOI: 10.1109/ICACC.2015.37

Mukherjee, A., & Das, A. K. (2015b). Interval valued intuitionistic fuzzy soft multi set theoretic approach to decision making problems, 2015 International Conference on Computer, Communication and Control (IC4), Indore, India, 2015, pp. 1-5, DOI: 10.1109/IC4.2015.7375640

Mukherjee, A., & Das, A. K. (2015c). Relations on intuitionistic fuzzy soft multi sets. In Kim, K. (Ed.), *Information Science and Applications. Lecture Notes in Electrical Engineering* (Vol. 339). Springer., DOI: 10.1007/978-3-662-46578-3_71

Mukherjee, A., & Das, A. K. (2016a). Application of fuzzy soft multi sets in decision-making problems. In: Nagar, A., Mohapatra, D., Chaki, N. (eds) Proceedings of 3rd International Conference on Advanced Computing, Networking and Informatics. Smart Innovation, Systems and Technologies, vol. 43. Springer, New Delhi. DOI: 10.1007/978-81-322-2538-6_3

Mukherjee, A., & Das, A. K. (2016b). Topological structure formed by intuitionistic fuzzy rough relations. *Journal of the Indian Mathematical Society*, *83*(1-2), 135–144.

Mukherjee, A., & Das, A. K. (2022). Einstein operations on fuzzy soft multisets and decision making. *Boletim da Sociedade Paranaense de Matematica*, *40*, 1–10. DOI: 10.5269/bspm.32546

Mukherjee, A., & Das, A. K. (2023). Essentials of fuzzy soft multisets: Theory and applications, Springer Nature Singapore Pte Ltd., 1-151. ISBN: 978-981-19-2759-1, DOI: 10.1007/978-981-19-2760-7

Mukherjee, A., Das, A. K., Gupta, N., Patra, S., Mahmood, T., Das, S., & Das, R. (2026). A novel generalized interval-valued neutrosophic rough soft set framework for enhanced decision-making: Application in water quality assessment. *Transactions on Fuzzy Sets and Systems*, *5*(1), 1–25. DOI: 10.71602/tfss.2026.1194037

Özcan, B., Friedrich, M., Huttner, J., & Dwinger, K. (2025). *Enhancing Trust in Human-AI Interaction through Explainable Decision Support Systems for Mission Planning of UAS-Swarms*. AHFE International., DOI: 10.54941/ahfe1006377

Sherin, N. (2025). Fuzzy Logic and Set Theory in Artificial Intelligence Decision-Making. *International Journal for Research in Applied Science and Engineering Technology*, *13*(5), 1656–1658. Advance online publication. DOI: 10.22214/ijraset.2025.70546

Sumrit, D. (2024). Enhancing readiness degree for Industrial Internet of Things adoption in manufacturing enterprises: An integrated Pythagorean fuzzy approach. *Heliyon*, *10*(20), e39007. Advance online publication. DOI: 10.1016/j.heliyon.2024.e39007 PMID: 39640696

Wang, K., Ying, Z., Goswami, S., Yin, Y., & Zhao, Y. (2023). Investigating the Role of Artificial Intelligence Technologies in the Construction Industry Using a Delphi-ANP-TOPSIS Hybrid MCDM Concept under a Fuzzy Environment. *Sustainability (Basel)*, *15*(15), 11848. Advance online publication. DOI: 10.3390/su151511848

Zadeh, L. A. (1965). Fuzzy sets. *Information and Control*, *8*(3), 338–353. DOI: 10.1016/S0019-9958(65)90241-X

Zhong, Q., Cui, H., Yang, M., & Ling, C. (2025). Research on Stochastic Evolution Game of Green Technology Innovation Alliance of Government, Industry, University, and Research with Fuzzy Income. *Sustainability (Basel)*, *17*(5), 2294. Advance online publication. DOI: 10.3390/su17052294

Chapter 5
Sustainable AI Value Creation:
Measuring Economic and ESG Impact Through Triple Helix Partnership Accounting

Rimi Gusliana Mais
https://orcid.org/0000-0002-2625-0601
Sekolah Tinggi Ilmu Ekonomi Indonesia Jakarta, Indonesia

Lies Zulfiati
Sekolah Tinggi Ilmu Ekonomi Indonesia Jakarta, Indonesia

Dahlifah Dahlifah
Sekolah Tinggi Ilmu Ekonomi Indonesia Jakarta, Indonesia

Desy Amaliati Setiawan
Sekolah Tinggi Ilmu Ekonomi Indonesia Jakarta, Indonesia

ABSTRACT

This chapter develops a multidimensional framework for evaluating sustainable Artificial Intelligence (AI) through the Triple Helix model linking universities, industry, and government. It proposes the Sustainable AI Impact Measurement (SAI-IM) Model, which integrates economic, social, and environmental indicators to capture public value beyond traditional innovation metrics. Drawing upon sustainability accounting, ESG frameworks, and AI governance research, the study demonstrates how shared data infrastructures, federated learning, and AI-enabled assurance systems strengthen transparency and accountability. Comparative analysis with Quadruple Helix and public-private partnership models reveals that hybrid, ethically

DOI: 10.4018/979-8-3373-9690-3.ch005

grounded collaborations achieve superior legitimacy and inclusiveness. Policy implications include the adoption of standardized impact taxonomies, ESG-integrated reporting, and capacity-building initiatives to enhance institutional readiness. The chapter contributes to theory by aligning innovation governance with sustainability accounting and AI's long-term value.

INTRODUCTION

1. THEORETICAL FRAMEWORK: TRIPLE HELIX, AI INNOVATION ECOSYSTEMS, AND SUSTAINABLE VALUE CREATION

This chapter analyzes how Triple Helix relationships U-G-I (university, government, industry) facilitate sustainable AI value generation by connecting innovation outputs to quantifiable economic and ESG consequences. The expansion of AI as a general-purpose technology has heightened the demand for collaborative innovation systems, wherein academia contributes research and talent, government offers funding and governance, and industry scales solutions for market implementation; these cross-sector interactions expedite diffusion while also presenting challenges related to accountability and social impact (Barbosa et al., 2023). Current academic discourse posits that assessing the public value of AI-beyond corporate profits-necessitates comprehensive methodologies that amalgamate economic measurements (such as productivity, job creation, and patents) with nonfinancial variables (including inclusivity, environmental impact, and alignment with Sustainable Development Goals) (Ervits, 2024).

The Triple Helix paradigm has been expanded to encompass civil society and environmental aspects (Quadruple/Quintuple Helix), highlighting the necessity of incorporating citizen legitimacy and sustainability into technological governance (Carayannis & Campbell, 2022). The chapter methodologically presents an accounting-focused measurement methodology that integrates sustainability accounting techniques (such as SROI and integrated reporting) with innovation measures and institutional indicators for each helix. This integrated lens addresses deficiencies in the literature: although many studies highlight the innovation advantages of university–industry–government collaboration, fewer offer standardized measurement toolkits for evaluating AI's cumulative economic and ESG impacts in a manner that is both pragmatic for policymakers and methodologically sound for researchers (Aiello et al., 2022; Bou Reslan & Al Maalouf, 2024). The subsequent sections detail the theoretical foundations, ecosystem dynamics, and sustainable value logic that support the proposed measurement methodology.

Despite the growing body of literature on Triple Helix innovation systems, AI governance, and ESG reporting, these streams largely remain analytically fragmented. Triple Helix studies predominantly emphasize innovation outputs and collaboration dynamics, while AI governance research focuses on ethical principles and regulatory compliance, and ESG frameworks concentrate on corporate-level disclosure and accountability. What remains underdeveloped is an integrated, operational measurement approach that connects AI-enabled innovation outcomes to economic, social, environmental, and governance impacts across university–industry–government collaborations. This chapter addresses this gap by proposing the Sustainable AI Impact Measurement (SAI-IM) Model, which systematically aligns Triple Helix governance structures with sustainability accounting and AI assurance mechanisms. By operationalizing public value creation through measurable indicators and auditable data infrastructures, the chapter contributes a practical and theoretically grounded framework for policymakers, institutional leaders, and researchers concerned with responsible and sustainable AI innovation.

1.1 Evolution of the Triple Helix Model

The Triple Helix paradigm conceptualizes innovation as the result of continuous interactions among universities (knowledge generation), government (policy and financing), and industry (commercialization). Recent empirical research underscores the enduring significance of tri-partite links in facilitating high-technology advancement, particularly AI, demonstrating that well-organized U-G-I cooperation enhance patenting rates, company establishment, and knowledge transfer (Barbosa et al., 2023). Barbosa et al. (2023) demonstrate that policy instruments linking public funding to collaborative outcomes, such as co-funded grants and mission programs, markedly enhance commercialization success, suggesting that the government's role transcends regulation to actively influence innovation trajectories.

Recent scholarship highlights the modernization of knowledge transfer mechanisms over the past five years: traditional technology transfer offices are now augmented by data-sharing platforms, living labs, and collaborative research centers that facilitate rapid prototype development and iterative validation (Aiello et al., 2022). Aiello et al. (2022) demonstrate that digital research infrastructures diminish barriers in inter-institutional knowledge transfer, enhancing absorptive capacity and expediting time-to-market for AI applications.

The Triple Helix is transforming into Quadruple and Quintuple Helix models by explicitly integrating civil society and environmental aspects; Carayannis and Campbell (2022) contend that these expansions are essential for legitimacy, democratic engagement, and ecological sustainability in contemporary innovation systems. In artificial intelligence environments, the inclusion of people and environmental stakeholders is significant because to its influence on social acceptance, ethical validation, and environmental implications (e.g., AI's energy consumption), which substantially affect adoption and sustainability (Carayannis & Campbell, 2022). Consequently, the model's progression signifies a normative transformation: innovation governance must reconcile economic competitiveness with public value and ecological accountability.

1.2 AI Innovation Ecosystems

AI innovation ecosystems are intricate, multi-actor configurations marked by swift feedback loops, platform interdependencies, and significant path dependence influenced by data assets and human capital. Research indicates that ecosystems characterized by robust inter-organizational connections among universities, firms, government laboratories, and intermediaries exhibit elevated rates of breakthrough innovation and commercialization due to their amalgamation of diverse capabilities-basic research, regulation, and market access-in a disjointed manner (Scaringella & Radziwon, 2023). Scaringella and Radziwon (2023) assert that ecological resilience arises from the diversity of participants and the redundancy of knowledge pathways.

Digital acceleration has further transformed these ecosystems. Digital platforms, open data efforts, and collaborative computing environments facilitate dispersed experimentation, reducing obstacles for small enterprises and university spin-offs to evaluate AI technologies (Aiello et al., 2022). The existence of national and regional AI goals, along with funding mechanisms that emphasize public-interest applications, influences whether ecosystems focus on widespread societal advantages or limited commercial objectives (Trabelsi, 2024). Trabelsi (2024) concludes that nations that synchronize policy instruments with university commercialization incentives achieve greater success in converting AI R&D into GDP growth.

Nonetheless, obstacles remain. Talent shortages, disjointed data governance frameworks, and unbalanced incentives among the three helices hinder maturity. Ervits (2024) asserts that in the absence of established effect indicators and clear governance norms, initiatives frequently fail to deliver adequate social value, even while exhibiting robust technological performance. Factors that promote maturity include interoperable data governance, mission-driven public funding, and institutional frameworks such as innovation districts and incubatorsthat encourage co-location and frequent engagement among collaborators (Barbosa et al., 2023). Collectively, these dynamics emphasize that ecosystem design, rather than technology itself, dictates whether AI will produce scalable commercial and public value.

1.3 Sustainable Value Creation Logic

Sustainable value creation redefines innovative success to encompass lasting economic, social, and environmental effects, rather than merely short-term financial rewards. In the domain of AI, this entails assessing contributions to productivity and competitiveness in conjunction with ESG implications, including inclusion, privacy protection, and carbon footprint (Bou Reslan & Al Maalouf, 2024). Bou Reslan and Al Maalouf (2024) demonstrate that AI applications in accounting and risk detection can improve operational efficiency and reinforce governance, resulting in compounded public and private value.

The shift from profit-oriented to impact-oriented logic necessitates novel accounting and measuring methodologies. Sustainability accounting frameworks-SROI, integrated reporting, and SDG-aligned KPIs: provide mechanisms to measure social returns; however, their application to AI necessitates consideration of the specificity of AI outputs (e.g., model generalizability, data externalities) and institutional attribution (who claims the impact) (Ervits, 2024). Ervits (2024) suggests indicator sets that connect university outputs (publications, trained graduates) to subsequent public outcomes (policy adoption, service enhancements), addressing a prevalent measurement gap.

The generation of public value is contingent upon governance, as procurement regulations, open innovation directives, and accountability frameworks guide collaborations towards outcomes that serve the public interest (Carayannis & Campbell, 2022). Mission-driven finance that mandates impact assessment guarantees that investments yield quantifiable social benefits instead of merely private gains (Barbosa et al., 2023). Ultimately, correlating innovation outputs with economic development metrics (employment, regional productivity, foreign direct investment) allows policymakers to evaluate AI's overall impact on inclusive growth (Trabelsi, 2024). Collectively, these components establish a logical basis for a measurement approach that is both stringent and pertinent to policy for evaluating sustainable AI value in Triple Helix collaborations.

1.4 Ethical Foundations of AI Value Creation

In contemporary innovation ecosystems where artificial intelligence (AI) plays a transformative role, the ethical foundations of value-creation become increasingly critical. Transparency, fairness, and social responsibility constitute the core ethical values that underpin sustainable AI deployment. Transparency enables stakeholders to understand how and why AI models make decisions; a recent review finds that transparency and explainability dominate organisational guidelines in AI ethics. Without transparency, decisions made by AI may remain opaque "black boxes", eroding trust and impeding effective accountability. Social responsibility extends beyond compliance or legal obligation to proactive engagement with the societal implications of AI: as one study argues, "all those who are involved in the research, development and maintenance of AI systems have social and ethical responsibilities to bear toward their consumers as well as to other stakeholders in society."

Fairness addresses concerns of bias, discrimination, and unequal access to AI's benefits: a recent paper on FATE (Fairness, Accountability, Transparency, Ethics) emphasises that fairness is morally imperative as discriminatory AI decisions can perpetuate social injustices and undermine legitimacy. In the context of the Triple Helix model (university-industry-government), the institutionalisation of these ethical foundations demands deliberate practices and mechanisms. Universities must integrate ethical technology syllabi, promote interdisciplinary research on AI ethics, and establish ethics review boards that engage industry and government stakeholders. Industry actors should adopt responsible AI frameworks that embed transparency (algorithmic documentation, explainable interfaces), fairness (bias audits, representative training data), and social impact assessment in their product lifecycles. Meanwhile, governments serve as both regulator and convenor: crafting regulatory standards (for transparency, data governance) and facilitating multi-stakeholder platforms.

A "circular model for ethics in action" proposed in recent literature emphasises that ethical values must be embedded throughout the AI value chain from design, development, deployment, through to monitoring and remediation. Thus, value creation in AI is not simply about economic returns or technological performance. It must be grounded in ethical foundations so that AI becomes a force for sustainable value-balancing commercial growth with social equity and environmental stewardship. By aligning the actors within the Triple Helix ecosystem around common ethical principles, it becomes possible to embed transparency, fairness, and social responsibility as systemic enablers of sustainable AI innovation rather than afterthoughts.

1.5 Global Perspectives on Triple Helix for Sustainable AI

The application of the Triple Helix model (university-industry-government) to sustainable AI ecosystems must be viewed through a global lens, recognising diverse cultural, regulatory, economic, and innovation contexts. Empirical research across multiple countries shows that the strength of university-industry-government interactions significantly influences innovation ecosystem quality at national level. For example, a study of 35 countries found that while none of the helices individually had a strong positive effect on startup ecosystem quality, when considered jointly as a Triple Helix construct the effect was significant.

In Europe, Asia and the Americas, variations abound: regulatory regimes differ widely (the EU's AI Act vs. more permissive regimes in other regions); industry-university collaboration patterns, data governance norms, public trust in AI, and national innovation strategies vary. A recent exploration of China's new technology diplomacy introduced a "Triple Helix Synergy Model" to explain how government, industry and academia interplay in China's AI-driven innovation diplomacy. Such national case studies underscore that creation of sustainable AI value via Triple Helix partnerships is not a one-size-fits-all affair: cultural norms (attitudes to data privacy, public trust), institutional maturity, funding regimes, and governance infrastructures all modulate outcomes.

Comparative indicators of sustainability, governance and social impact often reveal stark differences.

For instance, an analysis of G20 countries found that combining strong environmental law, fintech innovation and institutional quality (dimensions linked to the Triple Helix) significantly reduced ecological footprint. This suggests that when the three helices align around sustainability goals and deploy AI innovation accordingly, value creation can be more socially and environmentally sustainable. Moreover, the integration of sustainability into helix models has led to emergent "eco-5HM" frameworks that extend traditional Triple Helix to explicitly embed sustainability and value-co-creation at global scale.

For practitioners and policymakers, these global perspectives imply several considerations: firstly, benchmarking across countries can highlight best practices (regulatory standards, cross-sector governance arrangements) and pitfalls; secondly, adaptation to local context is essential what works in a highly institutionalised Western economy may need tailoring in emerging markets; thirdly, global collaboration and learning networks (multi country AI governance alliances) can enhance knowledge transfer and standard harmonisation, reducing fragmentation in global AI ethics and governance. In sum, sustainable AI value creation through the Triple Helix model must incorporate global diversity aligning universities, industries and governments in each country around ethical, economic, social and environmental dimensions while drawing on comparative insights and global governance trends.

Taken together, the evolution of the Triple Helix model, the dynamics of AI innovation ecosystems, and the logic of sustainable value creation highlight a fundamental shift in how AI-driven innovation must be assessed. Innovation success can no longer be evaluated solely through technological performance or economic output; instead, it requires governance structures and measurement systems capable of capturing long-term public value, ethical integrity, and sustainability outcomes. These theoretical foundations provide the conceptual justification for the development of an integrated impact measurement framework that links AI innovation processes to economic, social, environmental, and governance indicators within Triple Helix partnerships.

2. ACCOUNTING FOR SUSTAINABLE AI: INTEGRATING ESG, IMPACT MEASUREMENT, AND PUBLIC VALUE

Three structural challenges currently limit the effective measurement of sustainable AI value within Triple Helix collaborations. First, conventional accounting systems are poorly equipped to capture non-financial and AI-specific impacts such as algorithmic fairness, data governance quality, and computational externalities. Second, ESG reporting frameworks remain largely organization-centric, making it difficult to attribute outcomes across multi-actor innovation ecosystems. Third, assurance mechanisms have not fully adapted to AI-driven data generation, resulting in gaps in transparency, auditability, and accountability. Recent trends toward digital sustainability accounting and AI-enabled assurance provide promising solutions to these challenges, but they require coherent integration within governance and measurement frameworks an issue this section addresses.

Sustainability accounting in the digital economy is evolving due to digital technology (cloud computing, IoT, AI analytics) altering both the range of quantifiable phenomena and the speed at which firms may report them. Recent empirical research indicates that accounting professionals utilizing cloud and analytics tools can markedly enhance the timeliness and detail of sustainability disclosures; nevertheless, such adoption necessitates expenditures in data governance and talent development (Petcu et al., 2024). The digitization of sustainability accounting influences three areas: (a) data capture (automated sensors, telemetry, logs), (b) data processing (AI-driven cleansing, anomaly detection, and indicator calculation), and (c) assurance (algorithmic validation and audit trails). Every domain presents technical and epistemological inquiries how to guarantee data provenance, how to record model assumptions, and how to implement audit standards in AI pipelines.

From a standards viewpoint, ESG reporting frameworks are advancing to include digital evidence; yet, significant issues persist: comparability of disclosures across jurisdictions, double-counting in chain-of-custody measures, and the attribution of outcomes to specific actions (OECD, 2022). In Triple Helix partnerships, these problems are pronounced since universities, governments, and companies may each manage distinct data silos and assert partial responsibility for results. A practical strategy involves implementing modular indicator sets (core+context), wherein core indicators are internationally standardized (energy consumption of computing, job creation), and context indicators represent local public goals.

Furthermore, AI can serve as a tool to enhance sustainable accounting: AI models facilitate the automatic extraction of ESG parameters from unstructured data, assist in stress-testing scenarios, and provide real-time dashboards for decision-makers. However, dependence on AI for reporting necessitates new assurance requirements: auditors and regulators will require methodologies to evaluate model dependability and equity (Petcu et al., 2024). Consequently, sustainability accounting in the digital economy must integrate technical investments (data platforms, model registries) with governance structures (data sharing agreements, third-party assurance) to ensure that digital evidence is both valuable and reliable.

2.1 Sustainability Accounting in the Digital Economy

Sustainability accounting in the digital economy is evolving as digital technologies (cloud computing, IoT, AI analytics) alter the range of quantifiable phenomena and the speed at which firms may report them. Recent empirical research indicates that accounting professionals utilizing cloud and analytics tools can markedly enhance the timeliness and detail of sustainability disclosures; nevertheless, such adoption necessitates expenditures in data governance and talent development (Petcu et al., 2024). The digitization of sustainability accounting influences three areas: (a) data capture (automated sensors, telemetry, logs), (b) data processing (AI-driven cleansing, anomaly detection, and indicator calculation), and (c) assurance (algorithmic validation and audit trails). Each domain presents technical and epistemological inquiries-how to guarantee data provenance, how to describe model assumptions, and how to implement audit requirements for AI pipelines.

Furthermore, AI can serve as a tool to enhance sustainable accounting: AI models facilitate the automatic extraction of ESG parameters from unstructured data, assist in stress-testing scenarios, and provide real-time dashboards for decision-makers. However, dependence on AI for reporting necessitates new assurance requirements: auditors and regulators will require methodologies to evaluate model dependability and equity (Petcu et al., 2024). Consequently, sustainability accounting in the digital economy must integrate technical investments (data platforms, model registries) with governance frameworks (data sharing agreements, third-party assurance) to ensure that digital evidence is both valuable and reliable.

2.2 Measuring Social and Public Value Creation

Assessing social and public value in AI collaborations necessitates transcending output measurements (such as patents and prototypes) to focus on result and impact metrics that reflect welfare alterations, distributional consequences, and advantages to the public interest. The SROI technique, extensively utilized across various sectors, serves as an effective foundation as it integrates stakeholder participation with the monetization of social benefits, facilitating comparisons among interventions (Ariza-Montes et al., 2021). Systematic studies highlight the positives of SROI, such as stakeholder grounding and a theory-of-change orientation, while also acknowledging its methodological sensitivity to valuation choices and attribution assumptions (Feor et al., 2023).

Figure 1. Sustainable AI Impact Measurement Framework for Triple Helix Collaborations.

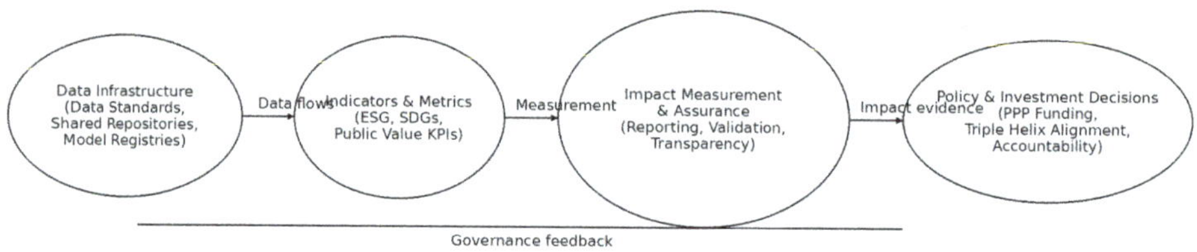

Source: Author's development based on OECD (2022), Ervits (2024), Kondylakis et al. (2023), and Petcu et al. (2024).

Figure 1. Data infrastructure (data sandboxes, shared repositories, and model registries) enables ESG, SROI, and public-value KPI generation. Indicators feed into impact measurement and assurance, producing evidence that informs policy and investment decisions. Governance decisions feed back into infrastructure design, creating a continuous improvement loop. For Triple Helix AI projects, the measurement design must integrate (a) a coherent theory of change that connects activities to outcomes, (b) mixed methods to capture intermediate outcomes (qualitative testimonies, usage logs), and (c) counterfactual reasoning or contribution analysis to ascertain the plausibility of impact.

A hybrid indicator set is pragmatically recommended, comprising core economic indicators (jobs created, productivity gains, revenue from AI products), core social indicators (access to services, user satisfaction, reduction in time-to-service), and ESG indicators (privacy incidents avoided, net carbon footprint of computing). Significantly, various outcomes such as expedited policy decision-making or enhanced civic trust are imbued with value and necessitate stakeholder valuation assessments rather than relying solely on market prices. Social impact assessments recommend the integration of financial proxies with participatory valuation techniques to mitigate bias (Feor et al., 2023).

A crucial aspect is attribution in multi-actor collaborations. In scenarios where academics provide models, governments facilitate datasets or procurement, and industry implements solutions, a transparent ledger of contributions, investments, and rights aids in the allocation of credit and accountability. Contractual clauses (intellectual property, data access) and ex-post contribution matrices facilitate justifiable allocation assumptions. Ultimately, documenting the distributional effects (who benefits and who incurs expenses) is crucial for public legitimacy: policy funders increasingly need impact assessments that address equitable issues in conjunction with overall returns (Ariza-Montes et al., 2021).

2.3 Data Infrastructure for Evaluating Impact

A robust data infrastructure underpins reliable impact measurement for AI. The OECD (2022) emphasizes that numerous effects of AI particularly environmental consequences and data-driven externalities cannot be quantified without standardized, interoperable data collecting and reporting frameworks. Empirical research from specialized AI applications, such as medical imaging, demonstrates that collaborative, meticulously curated data platforms featuring metadata standards, access controls, and standardized annotations significantly enhance reproducibility, fairness assessments, and cross-project evaluations (Kondylakis et al., 2023). These insights apply to Triple Helix contexts: shared repositories (or “data sandboxes”) allow partners to conduct common benchmarks, evaluate models using representative datasets, and connect inputs (financing, training) to outputs (deployments, outcomes).

Table 1. Sustainable AI Impact Measurement Components and Their Roles in the Triple Helix Accounting Framework

Component	**Role in the Framework**
Data Infrastructure	Shared data platforms, sandboxes, and model registries providing trusted evidence.
Indicators & Metrics	ESG indicators, SROI measures, and public value KPIs transformed from raw data.
Impact Measurement & Assurance	Validation, auditability, impact dashboards, transparent reporting.
Policy & Investment Decisions	Decisions on funding, project prioritization, PPP collaboration, accountability.
Component	Role in the Framework

Source: Adapted from OECD (2022); Ervits (2024); Kondylakis et al. (2023); Petcu et al. (2024).

Key design principles for impact measurement infrastructure include: (1) interoperability use of common schemas and metadata vocabularies to enable indicator aggregation; (2) governance clear roles for data stewardship, access control, and audit logs to ensure accountability; (3) privacy-preserving computation techniques such as federated learning and secure enclaves to allow joint analysis without raw data sharing; and (4) provenance and model registries records of model versions, training datasets, and parameter settings to enable reproducible impact claims (Kondylakis et al., 2023; Petcu et al., 2024).

Operational mechanisms such as data sandboxes (policy lab environments) permit controlled experiments while protecting sensitive information and offering auditors a way to sample processes for assurance (Open Data Policy Lab primers; OECD, 2022). Furthermore, AI impact measurement benefits from automated telemetry and ETL pipelines that standardize indicator flows from source systems into KPI dashboards, reducing manual error and enabling near-real-time monitoring. However, technical infrastructure alone is insufficient: legal frameworks (data sharing agreements, IP terms) and institutional capacity (data stewards, impact officers) are required so that infrastructure translates into reliable, policy-relevant measurement. In short, the triple combination of interoperable technical layers, robust governance, and institutional role clarity forms the operational foundation for trustworthy impact measurement in sustainable AI collaborations.

2.4 AI-Driven Auditing and Assurance Systems

In the realm of sustainable AI and ESG (Environmental, Social, Governance) disclosures, the auditing and assurance function is undergoing a profound transformation under the influence of artificial intelligence (AI). Traditional assurance practices, designed primarily for financial reporting, struggle to accommodate the volume, heterogeneity, and unstructured nature of ESG data. As noted by Using Artificial Intelligence in ESG Assurance (Li et al., 2024) "ESG assurance poses more challenges than traditional financial auditing due to the diverse subjects and types of information in ESG reports". AI technologies such as machine-learning algorithms, natural-language-processing (NLP) engines, and anomaly-detection systems are now being proposed to enhance both the efficiency and effectiveness of ESG assurance engagements.

Figure 2. AI-Enabled ESG Assurance Architecture.

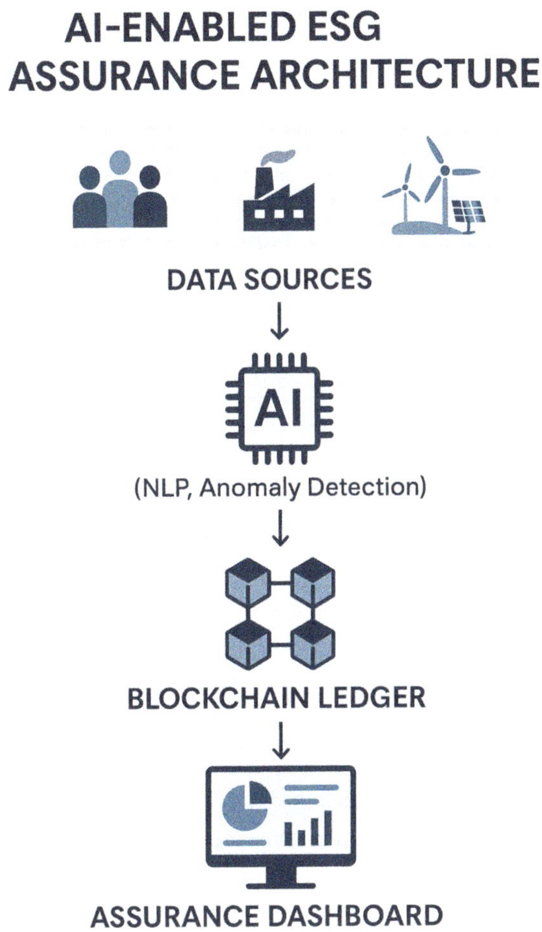

Source: Author's conceptual development based on Li et al. (2024), Petcu et al. (2024), and OECD (2022).

This conceptual framework illustrates the automated assurance process for environmental, social, and governance (ESG) reporting. Data from multiple ESG sources such as industrial, social, and environmental datasets are processed through AI engines employing natural language processing (NLP) and anomaly detection techniques. Verified records are then immutably stored in a blockchain ledger, ensuring data integrity and traceability before being visualized in an assurance dashboard for auditors and regulators. The model represents a sustainable approach to continuous ESG auditing within Triple Helix partnerships (university–industry–government).

For example, in a design-science study, an AI-enabled artefact that applied NLP to extract reported values and rule-based checks against Scope 2 GHG standards reduced auditor workload by over 90%. This illustrates the potential for real-time, continuous assurance of sustainability disclosures, shifting the assurance paradigm from periodic snapshot audits toward ongoing monitoring. Coupled with blockchain-enabled data lineage technologies, the audit trail becomes more transparent, tamper-resistant, and traceable enabling assurance practitioners to validate the provenance of data from university-industry-government (Triple Helix) partnerships to reporting output.

Within the Triple Helix ecosystem, universities remain pivotal in developing the AI auditing algorithms, industry implements them in corporate ESG reporting workflows, and government regulators define assurance standards. The moderating role of digital disruption in cross-sector auditing and ESG integration is confirmed in recent work: a study using a Triple Helix lens found that the combination of finance, accounting, and digital disruption significantly enhances ESG integration but also reveals limited coordination in the governmental dimension. Hence, institutionalising AI-enabled auditing demands multi-actor governance, standardised data definitions, and robust ethics frameworks.

However, this technology-driven assurance paradigm is not without challenges. Bias in algorithmic decision-making, lack of transparency in AI models (the "black-box" problem), and questions of audit liability remain unresolved (see Khoa Lam et al., 2024). Additionally, the readiness of audit professionals and oversight bodies to engage with AI tools is still nascent. Therefore, academic and practice communities must foster capabilities in algorithmic auditing, strengthen ethical oversight, and create regulatory frameworks that support AI-driven assurance while retaining human accountability. In doing so, the assurance of ESG reporting becomes more reliable, timely and aligned with the creation of sustainable value through AI.

2.5 Cross-Sector Data Governance for ESG Reporting

The integrity and comparability of ESG disclosures hinge critically on robust data governance practices that span universities, industry and government, the Triple Helix model of collaboration. In fact, as argued by Optimizing Data Governance via Triple Helix Model (Benfeldt et al., 2023) "the model facilitates complementary cross-sector connections mapping research trends and their geographic distribution and shows how technological innovations such as AI, big data and blockchai can support implementation of the Triple Helix Model. The first prerequisite for consistent cross-sector ESG reporting is establishing interoperable data architectures: standardized metadata, unified taxonomies, data lineage protocols and shared data dictionaries. According to PwC's 2024 analysis, "data and data governance stand at the forefront of ESG reporting ensuring data is accurate, reliable, and transparent."

Universities have a central role in generating the research and standards for metadata taxonomies and teaching data governance frameworks, industry must operationalize these standards in ESG data platforms, and government must legislate minimal data governance requirements, prescribe certification of data platforms, and monitor compliance. This collaborative governance ensures that ESG reporting across sectors is consistent, comparable, and verifiable. Furthermore, blockchain and distributed ledger technologies contribute to secure data lineage and cross-sector traceability of ESG metrics—from R&D labs in universities, through industrial deployment, to public policy disclosures.

However, cross-sector data governance faces major barriers: sectoral silos, legacy data systems, varying maturity of data practices across institutions, and weak regulatory alignment. The Triple Helix perspective reveals that digital disruption can moderate auditing and reporting interoperability yet the government dimension remains less well coordinated (Lulaj & Brajković, 2025). Hence, implementation of cross-sector governance requires institutional readiness, data literacy programmes, and mechanisms for shared oversight.

To facilitate effective implementation, three strategic steps are recommended: (a) Develop a cross-sector governance council (comprising university, industry and government representatives) to define ESG data standards, monitor compliance and govern blockchain/AI platforms; (b) Implement interoperability protocols (standardised APIs, common data models, secure data exchanges) to enable data flows across helixes; (c) Establish capacity-building initiatives training data stewards, auditors, regulators in ESG data governance, AI analytics and ethics of data use. By embedding these governance practices, ESG reporting becomes an integrated public value mechanism rather than a disjointed corporate disclosure. The resulting transparency and trust underpin sustainable value creation through AI and Triple Helix partnerships.

This section demonstrates that sustainable AI impact measurement is not merely a technical accounting exercise but a governance-dependent process that hinges on interoperable data infrastructures, standardized indicators, and credible assurance mechanisms. Without shared data governance and AI-enabled auditing systems, ESG and social impact claims remain difficult to verify and compare across Triple Helix actors. These insights reinforce the necessity of an integrated framework such as the proposed SAI-IM Model that embeds accounting, governance, and assurance into the design of AI collaborations rather than treating impact measurement as a post hoc reporting activity.

3. MEASURING ECONOMIC AND SOCIAL OUTCOMES OF TRIPLE HELIX PARTNERSHIPS IN AI

Assessing the effects of Triple Helix collaborations for AI necessitates criteria that encompass both economic returns (productivity, company establishment, fiscal contribution) and social/public value (access, equity, environmental impact). The macroeconomic potential of AI, as a general-purpose technology capable of enhancing productivity, is extensively demonstrated; nevertheless, the benefits are unevenly allocated among regions and industries, necessitating accurate quantification for effective policy formulation (OECD, 2024). Simultaneously, recent research on social impact measurement highlights that traditional output measures (such as patents and publications) are inadequate for demonstrating societal benefits without incorporating outcome-level indicators and counterfactual analysis (Feor, Clarke, & Dougherty, 2023). In Triple Helix collaborations, the measurement design must address attribution issues (who is responsible for what), temporal delays between research and socio-economic impact, and varying incentive structures across universities, government, and industry (Ervits, 2024).

Practical frameworks should integrate econometric methodologies for economic impacts (e.g., difference-in-differences, input-output multipliers) with mixed-methods strategies for social outcomes (theory-of-change, SROI, participatory valuation) to yield robust and policy-relevant evidence (Bou Reslan & Jabbour Al Maalouf, 2024). Ultimately, sustainability issues especially the ecological impact of extensive AI computation must be incorporated with social measures to ensure that assessment captures net public value rather than merely economic achievement (OECD, 2022). The following sections offer distinct sets of economic and ESG indicators and subsequently introduce a comprehensive measurement system designed for Triple Helix AI initiatives.

3.1 Economic Impact Metrics

The assessment of economic impact must quantify both direct returns at the project level and the wider regional or national spillover effects. At the project level, standard metrics encompass: (a) innovation outputs patents submitted, licensing agreements, and spin-offs; (b) commercial outcomes revenue generated from AI products, venture capital acquired, and firm sustainability rates; and (c) labor market impacts direct employment generated, net alterations in skill composition, and wage premiums for AI-related professions (Trabelsi, 2024). Trabelsi (2024) demonstrates that the commercialization of AI typically results in rapid revenue increases at the company level and medium-term productivity enhancements; however, the benefits on regional GDP are contingent upon absorptive capacity and local industry connections.

For regional evaluation, input-output models and computable general equilibrium (CGE) methodologies may quantify the indirect and induced employment and value-added impacts of AI investments, while matched employer-employee datasets facilitate the analysis of distributional effects among various worker skill categories.

Assessing productivity improvements necessitates meticulous counterfactual design: adoption studies must juxtapose treated businesses (or areas) with appropriate control groups, and in instances where randomization is impractical, difference-in-differences or instrumental variable methodologies yield reliable estimates (OECD, 2024). Moreover, patent counts and publishing metrics should be augmented with commercialization indicators (licenses, spin-outs), as academic outputs do not consistently convert into economic value without intermediary processes (Ervits, 2024).

In Triple Helix programs that involve public procurement or co-funding, policymakers ought to monitor public return on investment using fiscal multipliers and cost-benefit analyses that account for maintenance, governance, and possible adverse externalities (e.g., displacing existing workers). Integrating microeconometric research with macroeconomic modeling provides a comprehensive perspective on AI's economic impact and guides decisions on the expansion of successful pilot programs.

3.2 Sustainability and ESG Impact Metrics

Measuring sustainability and ESG for AI necessitates KPIs that capture environmental costs (computational energy, lifecycle emissions), social consequences (access, equality, privacy breaches), and governance quality (data stewardship, fairness protocols). The OECD (2022) emphasizes that the computational footprint of AI constitutes a quantifiable environmental externality and should be documented in terms of kilowatt-hours consumed, estimated CO_2e emissions, and efficiency metrics (e.g., FLOPs per watt), facilitating comparisons among models and implementations (OECD, 2022). Likewise, ESG frameworks could integrate AI-specific risk indicators: recorded bias events, clarity of model documentation (model cards), audit frequency, and the presence of privacy-preserving designs.

SROI-style metrics for social outcomes quantify nonmarket advantages, including time savings for residents, enhanced service accessibility, and diminished administrative duties. Feor et al. (2023) warn that SROI monetization is contingent upon selected proxies and necessitates stakeholder validation; thus, a mixed-methods approach (quantitative proxies combined with participatory valuation) is advised to corroborate findings. Ervits (2024) advocates for the correlation of university outputs (trained graduates, open datasets, civic engagement activities) with subsequent social outcomes (service adoption, health indicators), establishing a plausible connection between academic investments and societal advantages.

Governance and accountability metrics are significant as institutional frameworks dictate the implementation of ESG commitments. Indicators include the inclusion of data sharing agreements, the existence of independent oversight, and procurement terms mandating impact reporting. Incorporating these ESG measurements into standard KPI displays, alongside environmental and economic data, allows policymakers and funders to assess net public value beyond mere cash returns. Ultimately, reporting standards must mandate disaggregated data (by gender, location, and economic group) to reveal distributional impacts and guarantee equitable AI development.

3.3 Framework for Triple Helix Impact Measurement

An operational framework for measuring the impact of the Triple Helix incorporates (A) inputs and outputs particular to each actor, (B) overarching indicators (economic and ESG), and (C) methodologies for attribution and assurance. Panel A enumerates inputs by actor: university (research funds, trained graduates, databases), government (grants, procurement, regulatory modifications), and industry (private investment, deployments). Panel B aggregates variables into three categories: Economic (patents, revenue, productivity), Social (SROI proxies, service accessibility, equality metrics), and Environmental/Governance (calculated emissions, data governance adherence, audit frequency).

The framework mandates a theory-of-change mapping for attribution that connects inputs to intermediate outputs and ultimate outcomes, supplemented by contribution analysis and, when possible, quasi-experimental designs to assess causal effects (Feor et al., 2023). The measuring procedure necessitates time-series tracking to identify latencies between research expenditure and actual impacts—crucial in AI, because commercialization pipelines and regulatory approvals entail multi-year delays (Trabelsi, 2024). A mixed assurance methodology is advised for verification: (1) automated telemetry and model registries to document computational and versioning evidence; (2) third-party audits for ESG assertions; and (3) participatory verification with beneficiary groups for social claims (Kondylakis et al., 2023).

The system incorporates feedback loops for governance: measurement outcomes should guide financial reallocation, procurement standards, and university incentive mechanisms (tenure and promotion recognition for impact-driven research). Implementing the framework necessitates an interoperable data infrastructure, standardized metadata protocols, and pre-established contribution ledgers to ensure uniform reporting by each helix. This integrated approach, when applied to case studies, generates comparable, policy-relevant information regarding the capacity of Triple Helix AI cooperation to foster sustainable economic growth and public benefit.

3.4 Regional and Sectoral Case Comparisons

In analysing the economic and social outcomes of Triple Helix model partnerships in AI innovation ecosystems, it is essential to compare regionally and across sectors. Different sectors such as healthcare, education, smart agriculture and green energy reflect divergent maturity levels of digital infrastructure, stakeholder alignment, and regulatory regimes, which in turn influence outcomes. For instance, recent empirical studies show that in emerging economies, Triple Helix collaborations that engage government-led incentives, technology-intensive industry partners and research universities deliver higher rates of knowledge spill-over, job creation and regional competitiveness.

Across sectors, smart-agriculture initiatives often yield more immediate socio-economic returns (productivity gains, rural employment) than highly capital-intensive green-energy AI applications that require longer time-horizons and complex supply-chains. The comparative analysis therefore enables identification of key success factors: firstly, degree of helix integration (frequent interactions among university-industry-government) correlates with higher social value creation; secondly, sectoral readiness (data infrastructure, digital skills, regulatory clarity) accelerates outcomes; thirdly, regional institutional capacity (governance, policy stability, innovation ecosystems) moderates the effect of the partnership.

A cross-case comparison might reveal that regions with strong higher-education institutions and active industrial clusters perform better in AI-driven Triple Helix collaborations (as is documented for OECD countries) than regions lacking such institutional depth. Social outcomes also vary: in education and health sectors, AI collaborations often achieve improved equity and access (remote learning, diagnostics) whereas in industry-only sectors the benefits may concentrate among skilled workers, raising risk of social exclusion. The implication for measurement is clear: by constructing case-based matrices that map region × sector outcomes alongside helix-integration metrics, scholars and practitioners can benchmark success and uncover patterns of variation. In sum, regional and sectoral case comparisons offer a rich empirical landscape for understanding when and how Triple Helix partnerships in AI lead to sustainable economic and social value, moving beyond generic assertions and towards calibrated, context-sensitive models.

3.5 Methodological Challenges in Measuring AI Impact

Measuring the economic and social impact of AI within Triple Helix partnerships faces considerable methodological challenges. The first challenge is attribution: disentangling the effect of the AI collaboration from other simultaneous interventions or external economic trends is difficult. This is exacerbated by the complexity of helix interactions where multiple actors intervene concurrently. Secondly, data bias and availability pose serious constraints. For example, many AI initiatives rely on proprietary data or demonstrate selection bias (only high-capacity firms participate), which limits generalisability of findings. Recent mapping of health economic evaluations of AI found that many use proxy outcomes rather than full cost-effectiveness frameworks, thereby curtailing validity. Thirdly, causality vs. correlation remains unresolved: most studies adopt cross-sectional or observational designs, which inhibit strong causal inference. The 2025 review on AI metrics underscores that current frameworks remain misaligned with broader socio-economic and ethical metrics.

Additional challenges include measurement of social outcomes (equity, inclusion, empowerment) where standard economic metrics (GDP, job creation) may not suffice, requiring mixed-methods approaches and social return on investment (SROI) techniques. To improve the validity of impact measurement, several recommendations emerge: (a) adopt multi-arm quasi-experimental designs within helix partnerships to support stronger inference; (b) implement longitudinal tracking of outcomes across time to capture delayed effects; (c) develop standardised impact taxonomies and indicators across sectors (so that inter-case comparisons are meaningful); (d) embed qualitative assessments of social value alongside quantitative metrics to capture equity and inclusion dimensions. By acknowledging and systematically mitigating these methodological limitations, researchers and practitioners can strengthen the evidence-base on how AI-driven Triple Helix partnerships generate sustainable economic and social value.

4. GOVERNANCE AND ACCOUNTABILITY MECHANISMS IN AI COLLABORATION

Governance and accountability are essential for ensuring that AI created under Triple Helix partnerships generates public value and adheres to social and environmental protections. Effective governance must synchronize norms, legal frameworks, institutional responsibilities, and oversight mechanisms across institutions, governments, and industry to ensure that research outputs are transformed into valid, equitable, and sustainable applications (Schneider, 2023). Schneider (2023) delineates AI governance into three interconnected layers (data governance, model governance, and system governance) collectively establishing accountability, control mechanisms, and oversight processes in multi-actor partnerships. Publicly, algorithmic accountability mechanisms, including transparency registries, model cards, audit trails, and public procurement rules, facilitate the implementation of governance concepts into practical application (Camilleri, 2024). Camilleri (2024) contends that ethical AI frameworks should be integrated into organizational governance to convert abstract ideas into enforceable actions.

Moreover, infrastructure for assurance and auditability data sandboxes, model registries, telemetry logs, and third-party audit protocols is essential for traceable accountability and to empower Supreme Audit Institutions and auditors to provide oversight (Kondylakis et al., 2023). The OECD (2022) emphasizes that environmental externalities from AI, including compute emissions, and data governance issues must be incorporated into governance frameworks, necessitating both technical reporting and institutional accountability.

Recent studies underscores the significance of institutional design in Triple Helix frameworks; governance structures that align incentives, elucidate intellectual property and data rights, and incorporate impact reporting enhance the probability of achieving public-value results (Ervits, 2024). The combined elements indicate that governance for AI inside Triple Helix collaborations must be multifaceted, including normative frameworks, contractual procedures, technical assurance, and public oversight to guarantee responsibility, legitimacy, and sustainability.

4.1 Public Accountability and Oversight

Public accountability in AI collaboration signifies that public entities, together with their business and academic collaborators, are responsible for the social, economic, and environmental impacts of AI systems on citizens. Camilleri (2024) asserts that accountability necessitates the institutionalization of ethical obligations via formal mechanisms such as obligatory disclosure of model objectives and constraints, audit trails, and channels for stakeholder grievances enabling independent verification of claims regarding benefits. In the public sector, algorithmic accountability has been implemented through transparency registers, explanatory documentation (model cards), redress mechanisms, and impact evaluations associated with procurement choices (Open Government Partnership, 2021). These devices generate a record that auditors, civil society, and citizens can examine to ensure accountability of implementers.

Schneider (2023) contends that public oversight must encompass three governance domains data, models, and systems due to the diffusion of responsibility throughout the AI lifecycle: universities typically supply models and curate data, industry executes deployment and scaling, and government both commissions and regulates systems. Consequently, oversight entities (such as independent algorithmic auditors and Supreme Audit Institutions) require access to model registries, training data provenance, and runtime telemetry to evaluate adherence to public-value objectives (Kondylakis et al., 2023). Kondylakis et al. (2023) illustrate that data sandboxes and shared registries significantly enhance auditability in health-AI initiatives by facilitating reproducibility and independent assessment.

Furthermore, openness is inadequate; accountability must be supported by enforceable procurement provisions, funding stipulations, and legal liability structures that align incentives with public interest results (OECD, 2022). The OECD (2022) emphasizes that environmental and data-protection externalities (e.g., computational emissions, privacy hazards) must be included into public oversight mechanisms to ensure that the net public value assessment reflects both advantages and detriments. In conclusion, public accountability in Triple Helix AI cooperation necessitates legal-contractual mechanisms, technical audit frameworks, and transparent avenues for citizen supervision to guarantee legitimate and equitable results.

4.2 Institutional Governance within Triple Helix Partnerships

Institutional governance in Triple Helix partnerships focuses on establishing roles, regulations, and contractual agreements that harmonize the divergent interests of universities, governmental bodies, and industrial collaborators. Ervits (2024) concludes that explicitly delineated contribution ledgers (identifying data providers, funders, and implementers) and pre-established intellectual property and data-access stipulations mitigate subsequent conflicts and enhance outcome attribution, hence augmenting the credibility of impact claims. Such partnerships generally encompass memoranda of understanding, standardized data-sharing agreements, model intellectual property systems, and shared steering committees that oversee progress and resolve ethical or operational conflicts.

Model governance, encompassing model development, validation, versioning, and retirement policies, is a significant institutional artifact within partnerships. Schneider (2023) asserts that businesses must institutionalize model registries and lifecycle policies to ensure that each release possesses documented lineage, validation proof, and a designated owner accountable for monitoring. Universities may offer open evaluation processes and reproducibility artifacts; industry partners can supply production-grade deployment pipelines and service level agreements; and governments might mandate that supported projects uphold minimal governance artifacts as a prerequisite for grant disbursement.

Risk allocation constitutes a crucial aspect of governance: contractual provisions may delineate culpability for negative consequences (biased choices, data breaches), indemnifications, and insurance stipulations. Ervits (2024) advocates for the utilization of hybrid governance mechanisms that integrate voluntary codes of conduct with binding contractual provisions to mitigate both reputational and legal risks. Moreover, incentive frameworks such as university promotion standards that acknowledge societal contributions, or procurement evaluations that favor ESG-compliant solutions align stakeholders with public-value objectives (Petcu et al., 2024). Institutional governance must consequently encompass both procedural elements (committees, registries, agreements) and incentive mechanisms (funding regulations, procurement criteria) to maintain collaborative efforts inside the Triple Helix.

4.3 ESG-Integrated Reporting for AI Partnerships

ESG-integrated reporting for AI collaborations broadens traditional non-financial disclosures to encompass AI-specific metrics model openness, data provenance, fairness assessments, and compute-related environmental indicators enabling stakeholders to assess net public value. Petcu et al. (2024) demonstrate that digital tools and cloud reporting pipelines facilitate more frequent ESG reporting and provide more detailed evidence; yet, they warn that governance and assurance mechanisms are essential to mitigate "garbage-in, garbage-out" hazards associated with automation. The OECD (2022) advocates for the integration of computational energy consumption and lifecycle emissions into ESG reporting for AI to reveal environmental externalities that would otherwise be obscured.

ESG-integrated reports for Triple Helix projects should encompass: (1) technical disclosures (model cards, dataset descriptions, validation results), (2) social impact indicators (SROI estimates, service coverage, equity disaggregation), and (3) environmental metrics (kWh consumed, CO_2e per deployment). Ervits (2024) advocates for institutions to disclose research outputs and training contributions, governments to reveal financing and procurement conditions, and industry partners to share deployment indicators, thereby facilitating a comprehensive assessment of impact. Third-party assurance is essential: independent audits (technical and ESG) authenticate assertions, while standardized metadata and model registries enhance comparability.

Integrated reporting necessitates conformity with developing standards (IFRS S-series/ISSB guidelines) and sector-specific requirements to maintain relevance for investors and public funders. Camilleri (2024) contends that incorporating ethical and social responsibility measures into formal reporting frameworks enhances business accountability and stakeholder trust. To be effective for policy, ESG reporting must be action-oriented: reports should inform performance contracts, procurement decisions, and financial reallocations, ensuring that evidence of impact leads to governance actions and ongoing enhancement.

4.4 Legal and Regulatory Frameworks for AI Accountability

The emergence of powerful artificial intelligence (AI) systems has prompted regulatory frameworks globally that target accountability, safety, transparency and fundamental rights protection. A prominent example is the EU Artificial Intelligence Act (AI Act), which entered into force 1 August 2024 and sets a risk-based regime for AI systems in the European Single Market. The AI Act classifies AI systems by risk level (unacceptable, high, limited, minimal) and imposes obligations on providers and deployers, including transparency, human oversight, documentation, and reporting of serious incidents. In many cases, obligations under the General Data Protection Regulation (GDPR) overlap with those in the AI Act especially where personal data is processed by high-risk AI systems.

In the context of the Triple Helix model (university–industry–government), the regulatory frameworks provide the "hard" institutional and legal scaffolding for accountability mechanisms. Universities engaging in AI research must comply with ethical standards and data protection laws; industry partners deploying AI must adhere to risk-management, audit and reporting obligations under law; governments act as regulators, enforcers and sometimes as deployers of public AI systems. For example, a recent study shows that while the EU regulatory ecosystem (AI Act + GDPR + NIS2) fosters ethical and accountable AI systems, coordination among governing institutions remains challenging.

The role of supervisory authorities also becomes critical: they monitor compliance, investigate infringements, impose sanctions, and thus enforce accountability. Without effective monitoring and sanction mechanisms, the legislation risks being symbolic rather than operative. The interplay between regulations, standards and institutional readiness has been highlighted as a key gap in AI governance. Moreover, accountability is not just about legal compliance—it also requires mechanisms for remedy, transparency to stakeholders, and documentation of decision-making. Recent literature emphasises that frameworks should include incident-reporting systems, audit logs of AI systems, and independent oversight bodies. Therefore, legal and regulatory frameworks serve as the foundational layer for AI accountability in collaborative ecosystems like the Triple Helix. However, for these frameworks to be meaningful, they must be operationalised through institutional mechanisms (e.g., national AI offices, boards, scientific panels) and capacity-building (see next subsection). Otherwise, the gap between regulation and practice may undermine the sustainable value creation of AI partnerships.

4.5 Capacity Building and Institutional Readiness

As AI systems proliferate in university–industry–government collaborations, the capability of institutions and individuals to govern, audit and deploy AI responsibly has become a central concern. Capacity building developing human capital, institutional processes and policy competencies is critical to ensure accountability and governance of AI. A recent handbook focused on policy-makers in the Global South emphasises modules such as "Institutional Readiness: Capacities for building responsible AI ecosystems." In the education sector, institutions need to embed AI literacy not only among technical staff but also across faculties and administrative units. For example, a study of higher education institutions indicated that building ethical and institutional capacity for AI use is still nascent, with universities facing challenges such as undefined governance processes and lack of standardised frameworks.

In the Triple Helix context, capacity building has three interlinked dimensions: (1) ethical digital competencies for researchers, practitioners and regulators to understand bias, transparency, and societal impact of AI; (2) governance-reporting competencies in industry and government for monitoring AI systems, managing risk, and fulfilling accountability obligations; (3) cross-sector institutional readiness, meaning that universities, industries and regulators can coordinate, share data, adopt standards and respond collectively to AI challenges. Empirical research indicates that national "AI readiness" is significantly predicted by human capital, governance ethics, and innovation capacity.

Practically, capacity-building initiatives may include training workshops for regulators on AI audit and enforcement, industry certification programmes for deploying high-risk AI systems, and university professional development in AI ethics and governance frameworks. Without such programmes, even the best regulations may lack enforcement and institutional uptake. Moreover, institutional readiness involves resources (budget, personnel), governance architecture (AI offices, boards), and flows of knowledge across helix actors. The alignment of capacity-building with regulation is therefore essential: institutions must not only understand the rules but have the ability to implement, monitor, and respond to AI systems' social impacts. In sum, by investing in capacity building and institutional readiness, Triple Helix partnerships can ensure that AI collaborations deliver sustainable value and accountability rather than exacerbate governance gaps.

5. CASE STUDY & IMPLICATIONS: TOWARD A SUSTAINABLE AI IMPACT MEASUREMENT MODEL

Sustainable Artificial Intelligence (AI) advances necessitate impact evaluation tools that assess not just economic benefits but also social and environmental effects resulting from collaboration among universities, companies, and governments. The Triple Helix concept is characterized by boundary-spanning governance, knowledge co-creation, and shared accountability systems (Etzkowitz & Zhou, 2021). Recent studies indicate that Triple Helix partnerships are crucial in national innovation initiatives and AI entrepreneurship ecosystems, since they expedite problem-oriented AI development and facilitate integration into public services and industry adoption (Ryu et al., 2022). Nevertheless, despite their significance, the assessment of societal and environmental effects of AI Triple Helix cooperation remains inadequately developed. Petcu et al. (2024) assert that contemporary impact reporting is predominantly influenced by economic metrics, but "non-financial impacts such as environmental externalities and social equity remain largely obscured in current disclosure frameworks".

The intricacy of evaluating AI influence stems from three factors. Initially, AI effects exhibit nonlinearity: a model may enhance efficiency while adversely affecting social justice or energy sustainability (OECD, 2022). Secondly, data and model governance is decentralized among several stakeholders: universities do research, companies implement models, and governments oversee regulation and procurement (Schneider, 2023). Third, societal and regulatory requirements for ESG are intensifying. Camilleri (2024) contends that governance and reporting procedures must convert ethical ideals into enforceable corporate accountability, rendering effect assessment essential to AI deployment.

Moreover, AI initiatives are progressively assessed through sustainability-oriented frameworks, like the ISSB/IFRS S1–S2 and the EU AI Act, necessitating demonstrable transparency, equity, and ecological performance (Kondylakis et al., 2023). Nevertheless, these devices lack direction tailored to innovative collaborations. This gap necessitates an impact model that encompasses the entire ecosystem of AI development, from ideation to the realization of public value. Consequently, the chapter formulates a Sustainable AI Impact Measurement Model that incorporates the subsequent dimensions:

Table 2.

Dimension	Focus
Economic Impact	Productivity gains, cost efficiency, new venture formation
Social & ESG Impact	Fairness, equity, social return on investment (SROI)
Triple Helix Governance Impact	Data sharing, accountability, transparency, auditability

This chapter presents two contributions by examining a genuine scenario of Triple Helix AI collaboration and integrating cross-study findings. Initially, it illustrates the effect of governance mechanisms on the realization of impact. Secondly, it presents a reproducible framework to assess economic and sustainability results that complies with forthcoming disclosure mandates. The chapter contends that sustained effect measurement is the crucial factor influencing AI legitimacy, societal acceptability, and enduring viability.

5.1 Case Study of Triple Helix AI Collaboration

A exemplary Triple Helix partnership was chosen due to its magnitude, societal significance, and the presence of quantifiable results: European Health and Medical Imaging Consortium (EU-funded), comprising: Universities (data curation, model development), Medical device and AI enterprises (deployment, scaling). Kondylakis et al. (2023) report that this project employs shared data infrastructures AI sandboxes, federated learning platforms, and model registries to provide collaborative model training among countries while preserving data sovereignty. Kondylakis et al. (2023) assert that "shared data infrastructures enable auditability and reproducibility, instilling confidence in decision-makers regarding outcome reliability".

The economic outcomes are significant. The initiative diminishes diagnostic duration, enhances productivity, and establishes novel monetization avenues for involved start-ups. Ervits (2024) asserts that university–industry interactions yield quantifiable economic advantages when results are converted into new business creation, commercialization, or enhancements in services. Social and ESG effects are apparent: diminished misdiagnosis rates, enhanced early detection, and increased accessibility for remote patients via tele-diagnostics. These advantages correspond with Camilleri's (2024) assertion of "organizational accountability to societal stakeholders, not solely shareholders".

Table 3.

	Implementation
Data responsibility	Federated learning & shared governance
Oversight	Ethics committee + public reporting dashboards
Accountability	Third-party technical and ESG audits
Traceability	Model version control + continuous monitoring

Schneider (2023)

Contends that governance frameworks should encompass "data, models, and systems throughout the entire AI lifecycle. This case demonstrates that the sophistication of governance influences the realization of impact. The case study reveals three insights: The manifestation of impact is contingent upon governance maturity, rather than solely on model accuracy. ESG reporting tools enhance legitimacy and bolster stakeholder confidence. Shared repositories, including model cards and dataset registrations, facilitate independent auditability. Consequently, the study illustrates that Triple Helix AI collaborations can yield quantifiable economic and social benefits when governance and accountability frameworks are integrated into project design.

The case study illustrates how the three layers of the Sustainable AI Impact Measurement (SAI-IM) Model operate in practice. Economic impacts are observed through productivity gains, reduced diagnostic time, and new commercialization pathways enabled by AI deployment (Layer 1). Social and ESG impacts are reflected in improved access to medical services, reduced misdiagnosis rates, and enhanced data protection through federated learning architectures (Layer 2). Crucially, governance and accountability mechanisms-such as shared data infrastructures, model registries, ethics committees, and third-party audits-correspond directly to Layer 3 of the model, demonstrating that governance maturity is a determining factor in realizing sustainable AI value. The case thus confirms that measurable impact emerges not solely from technical performance but from the institutionalization of accountability and assurance within Triple Helix collaborations.

5.2 Proposed Impact Measurement Model

The Sustainable AI Impact Measurement Model (SAI-IM Model) is organized into three tiers, according on a synthesis of literature.

Layer 1 — Economic Impact (Efficiency, Innovation, Value Creation)

Indicators encompass cost reduction, productivity enhancements, commercialization results, and employment generation. Petcu et al. (2024) assert that the incorporation of digital technology in sustainability reporting "enhances efficiency and facilitates more frequent performance feedback loops" (p. 8). These indicators quantify economic advantages and support the rationale for further investment.

Layer 2 — Social & ESG Impact (Fairness, Inclusiveness, Environmental Sustainability)

Framework components:

- Social Return on Investment (SROI),
- Fairness indicators (bias audits; equity of outcomes),
- Energy and emissions tracking (kWh, CO_2e).

Layer 3 — Governance & Accountability Impact

Governance infrastructure includes:

- Model registries and versioning,
- Data provenance tracking,
- Publication of model cards and transparency reports.

Camilleri (2024) emphasizes that "governance mechanisms should transform ethical commitments into enforceable accountability" (p. 4). Schneider (2023) proposes governance across *data model system* as the minimum structural requirement for responsible AI. The model aligns with ISSB/IFRS S1–S2 disclosure requirements and EU AI accountability expectations.

Figure 3. AI Impact Value Creation Model

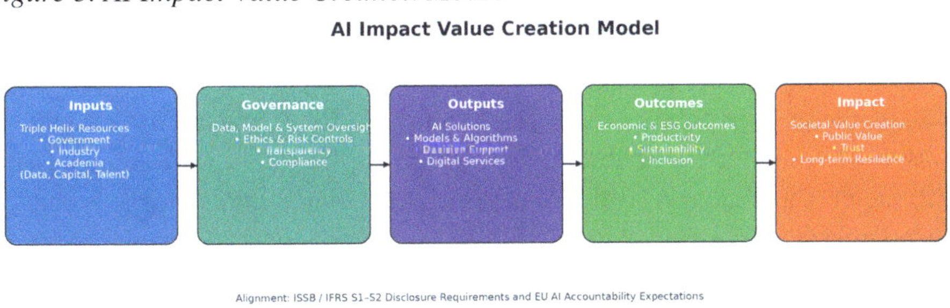

5.3 Future Directions and Chapter Contribution

The proposed model advances theory and practice in three ways:

Table 4.

Contribution	Explanation
Theoretical	Shifts AI evaluation from *accuracy* to *public value impact.*
Governance	Formalizes accountability mechanisms feeding impact reporting.
Practical	Offers measurable indicators and a replicable structure.

Future research should advance three directions:

1. Metrics Standardization There is no consensus on ESG metrics applicable to AI (Petcu et al., 2024). Global alignment is needed between ISSB/IFRS, EU AI Act, and sustainability reporting frameworks.
2. Embedding Impact into Funding and Procurement Governments should require that publicly funded AI projects generate transparency registers and ESG reporting (OECD, 2022).
3. Digital Twins for Impact Monitoring Integration of digital twins and automated data pipelines may enable real-time ESG monitoring throughout AI lifecycle (Schneider, 2023). Ervits (2024) concludes that sustainable innovation requires shifting "from output metrics (publications) to outcome metrics (impact on society)". Thus, the model serves as the missing link between innovation governance and real-world sustainability outcomes.

5.4 Comparative Evaluation with Non-Triple Helix Models

In exploring sustainable AI impact measurement, a key question is how the classic Triple Helix model (university-industry-government) collaboration structure compares with alternative models such as the Quadruple Helix model (which adds civil society/media) or pure public-private partnerships (PPP). A comparative evaluation reveals distinct strengths and limitations: research by Yuzhuo Cai & Annina Lattu (2022) found that while the Triple Helix remains efficient for knowledge exchange and economic value creation, the Quadruple Helix offers greater societal inclusivity and responsiveness to public needs.

From an AI-driven sustainable value creation perspective, the Triple Helix model's advantage lies in its streamlined tri-actor coordination, institutional clarity, and direct alignment of R&D-to-industry throughput. However, its limitation emerges in stakeholder diversity civil society and environmental voices may be under-represented, thus reducing legitimacy and broader social value creation. The Quadruple Helix adds a fourth helix (public/civil society) which enhances democratic legitimacy, multi-stakeholder input and can better capture social and environmental outcomes especially relevant for sustainability-oriented AI systems.

On the other hand, public-private partnership models may accelerate deployment scale but risk insufficient academic input or regulatory oversight, potentially compromising measurement of long-term social outcomes or ethical considerations. In practice, for AI impact measurement, one might construct a comparative matrix:

- Value Creation Speed: PPP > Triple Helix > Quadruple Helix
- Social/Environmental Legacy: Quadruple Helix > Triple Helix > PPP
- Governance and Accountability: Triple Helix ≈ Quadruple Helix > PPP

This indicates that no single model is universally superior — instead, alignment of model choice with strategic goals (e.g., speed vs. sustainability vs. legitimacy) is crucial.

Figure 4. Comparison of Collaboration Models for AI Impact Measurement.

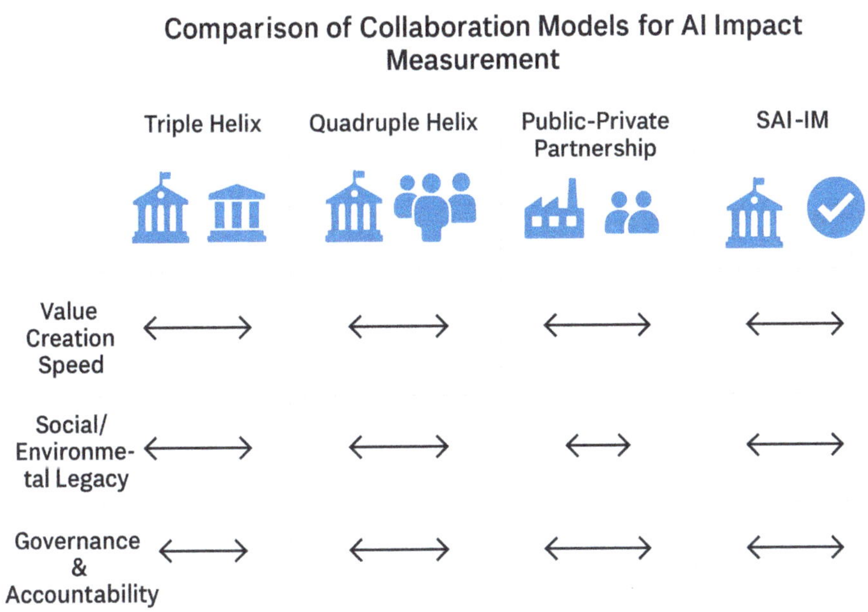

Source: Author's conceptual development based on Cai & Lattu (2022), Carayannis & Campbell (2022), and Popper et al. (2025).

This visual compares four collaboration structures—Triple Helix, Quadruple Helix, Public-Private Partnership (PPP), and Sustainable AI Impact Measurement (SAI-IM)—across three evaluation criteria: value-creation speed, social/environmental legacy, and governance & accountability. The chart illustrates that each model excels in different domains, suggesting that hybrid frameworks may offer the most balanced approach to sustainable AI value creation.

For a sustainable AI impact measurement model (SAI-IM), a hybrid approach may be optimal: leveraging the institutional strength of the Triple Helix while integrating fourth-helix stakeholders for broader impact. Implications for policy and practice include: embedding civil society in measurement frameworks, designing governance mechanisms for multi-helix coordination, and tailoring metrics to reflect both economic and societal dimensions of AI value.

This comparison highlights that the choice between Triple Helix, Quadruple Helix, or hybrid collaboration models should be contingent on strategic priorities. While the Triple Helix model offers institutional clarity, efficiency, and strong alignment between research, regulation, and commercialization, the Quadruple Helix enhances legitimacy and inclusiveness by incorporating civil society perspectives. For sustainable AI impact measurement, the SAI-IM framework is deliberately designed to remain compatible with both models, allowing additional stakeholders to be incorporated where social legitimacy and environmental accountability are paramount, without sacrificing governance coherence or measurement rigor.

5.5 Policy Roadmap and Future Implementation Scenarios

The adoption of a SAI-IM (Sustainable AI Impact Measurement) model at national or regional level requires an actionable policy roadmap that integrates multi-actor coordination, data infrastructure, and governance pathways. A recent roadmap for AI policy research outlines key priorities such as governance, transparency, ethical oversight and sustainable innovation ecosystems. The roadmap might follow phased implementation: Phase 1. Foundational Setup (standardised impact metrics, helix-actor agreements, baseline studies); Phase 2. Pilot Deployment & Scaling (regional pilot projects, cross-sector indicator benchmarking, real-time dashboards); Phase 3. Institutionalisation & Policy Integration (mandated measurement frameworks, public reporting mandates, AI-sustainability linkages in national innovation policy).

Future scenarios may include: (a) National Green AI Platforms, where governments mandate AI-impact disclosures linked to ESG frameworks and allocate compute resources for green-AI research; (b) Regional Helix Innovation Hubs, combining universities, industry, government and civil society in living labs for AI-driven sustainable development; (c) Global AI Impact Measurement Alliance, where international standards, data-sharing platforms and benchmarking enable cross-country comparisons of AI's social and environmental value. The SAI-IM framework must thus be flexible, scalable and globally interoperable. Key policy levers include: regulatory incentives for transparent impact reporting, funding for capacity building in impact measurement, and establishment of open data ecosystems for helix partnerships. By aligning policy roadmap with future scenarios, stakeholders can embed AI impact measurement into innovation systems rather than treating it as an ad hoc add-on, thereby supporting sustainable value creation in the age of AI.

CONCLUSION

This chapter is directed toward scholars, policymakers, and institutional decision-makers seeking robust tools to evaluate the societal implications of AI-driven innovation. By integrating Triple Helix theory, sustainability accounting, and AI governance, the chapter advances the evaluation of AI from a performance-oriented perspective toward a public value and accountability paradigm. The proposed SAI-IM Model provides a structured, replicable approach for measuring economic, social, environmental, and governance impacts, thereby supporting evidence-based policy, responsible investment, and transparent institutional decision-making.

This study concludes that sustainable Artificial Intelligence (AI) value creation depends on the effective integration of ethical governance, ESG accounting, and Triple Helix collaboration among universities, industry, and government. The proposed Sustainable AI Impact Measurement (SAI-IM) Model demonstrates that AI's success must be evaluated not only through economic performance but also by its social and environmental contributions. When impact indicators such as fairness, accessibility, energy efficiency, and inclusivity are embedded from the design stage, AI becomes a driver of sustainable development rather than a source of inequality or risk.

The findings affirm that transparency, accountability, and cross-sector data governance are fundamental to ensuring trust and legitimacy in AI-driven innovation. Through AI-enabled auditing, blockchain-based assurance, and real-time impact dashboards, organizations can transform ESG reporting into a continuous learning system that promotes responsibility and adaptation. Comparative analysis shows that while the Triple Helix model remains central to structured innovation, hybrid models like the Quadruple Helix further enhance public participation and legitimacy.

For policy and practice, governments should institutionalize impact measurement standards and mandate ESG disclosure for AI projects. Universities must realign success indicators toward public value, and industries should adopt integrated ESG dashboards to link ethical compliance with competitiveness. Ultimately, the study argues that sustainable AI governance is achieved through dynamic partnerships, capacity building, and shared accountability mechanisms that make social impact visible and measurable.

In essence, this research bridges AI innovation and sustainability accounting, offering a roadmap for transitioning from output-driven technological progress to responsible innovation ecosystems. By operationalizing impact governance through shared frameworks, institutions can ensure that AI not only accelerates economic growth but also safeguards ethical integrity and societal well-being advancing a future where technology and sustainability coexist harmoniously.

Practical suggestions emphasize early integration of ESG and impact metrics into AI project design rather than post-hoc reporting. Practitioners are urged to embed measurable social, environmental, and economic indicators from inception. Establishing federated data-sharing architectures and governance boards enhances data traceability, reproducibility, and regulatory compliance. Impact dashboards transform complex metrics into accessible insights, improving transparency and public trust. Success also depends on multidisciplinary collaboration combining ethicists, policy experts, and engineers and formal governance agreements among universities, industry, and government. Capacity-building and continuous "measure–learn–adapt" cycles ensure resilience as technologies evolve.

Policy and institutional recommendations extend these practices to systemic implementation. Governments should mandate ESG reporting for AI projects using public data or funding, aligning national AI strategies with frameworks such as the EU AI Act, ISSB/IFRS S1–S2, and the UN SDGs. Universities should expand innovation metrics beyond patents and publications to include social and public value. Industry leaders must integrate ESG impact accounting into internal dashboards, linking ethical compliance with investor confidence and sustainable finance. Dedicated Triple Helix oversight committees are recommended for impact validation, while international agencies should promote standardized indicators and cross-regional benchmarking.

Implications for theory and policy are profound: the research redefines AI innovation as a governance and accountability system rather than merely a technological pursuit. Triple Helix collaborations evolve into structured impact ecosystems featuring data-stewardship boards, registries, and public dashboards. When social impact becomes quantifiable, investment priorities and public confidence shift toward responsible innovation. Ultimately, sustainable AI emerges where economic ambition, ethical governance, and public accountability coexist transforming AI from a performance-driven enterprise into a transparent, socially legitimate instrument for long-term societal value.

REFERENCES

Aiello, L.. (2022). Digital research infrastructures and collaborative innovation. *Journal of Business Research, 146*. Advance online publication. DOI: 10.1016/j.jbusres.2022.113393

Ariza-Montes, A., Sianes, A., Fernández-Rodríguez, V., López-Martín, M. C., Ruíz-Lozano, M., & Tirado-Valencia, P. (2021). Social Return on Investment (SROI) to assess the impacts of tourism: A case study. *SAGE Open*, *11*(1), 2158244020988733. Advance online publication. DOI: 10.1177/2158244020988733

Barbosa, J.. (2023). University–industry–government collaboration and innovation. *Research Policy*, *52*(7), 104882. DOI: 10.1016/j.respol.2023.104882

Benfeldt, A.. (2023). *Optimizing Data Governance via Triple Helix Model. Data Governance for Digital Transformation and Sustainability*. IGI Global.

Bou Reslan, F., & Al Maalouf, N. J. (2024). Assessing the transformative impact of AI adoption on efficiency, fraud detection, and skill dynamics in accounting practices. *Journal of Risk and Financial Management*, *17*(12), 577. DOI: 10.3390/jrfm17120577

Camilleri, M. A. (2024). Artificial intelligence governance: Ethical considerations and implications for social responsibility. *Expert Systems: International Journal of Knowledge Engineering and Neural Networks*, *41*(7), e13406. DOI: 10.1111/exsy.13406

Carayannis, E. G., & Campbell, D. F. J. (2022). Helix Trilogy and the evolution toward Quadruple/Quintuple Helix. *Journal of the Knowledge Economy*, *13*(3), 1123–1145. DOI: 10.1007/s13132-021-00813-x

Carayannis, E. G., & Campbell, D. F. J. (2022). The Quintuple Helix Lens for Transformation: An Okayama Model of Education for Sustainable Development. *Sustainable Organizations*, *3*, 798330. Advance online publication. DOI: 10.3389/frsus.2022.798330

Ervits, I. (2024). Developing indicators for the social benefits of university–industry collaborations. *International Journal of Corporate Social Responsibility*, *9*(1), 8. Advance online publication. DOI: 10.1186/s40991-024-00097-9

Etzkowitz, H., & Zhou, C. (2021). Innovation in the post-pandemic era: Triple helix and hybrid organizations. *Journal of Innovation & Knowledge*, *6*(4), 253–257. DOI: 10.1016/j.jik.2021.09.001

Feor, L., Clarke, A., & Dougherty, I. (2023). Social impact measurement: A systematic literature review and future research directions. [MDPI]. *WORLD (Oakland, Calif.)*, *4*(4), 816–837. DOI: 10.3390/world4040051

Kondylakis, H., Kalokyri, V., Sfakianakis, S., Marias, K., Tsiknakis, M., Jimenez-Pastor, A., Camacho-Ramos, E., Blanquer, I., Segrelles, J. D., López-Huguet, S., Barelle, C., Kogut-Czarkowska, M., Tsakou, G., Siopis, N., Sakellariou, Z., Bizopoulos, P., Drossou, V., Lalas, A., Votis, K., & Lekadir, K. (2023). Data infrastructures for AI in medical imaging: A report on the experiences of five EU projects. *European Radiology Experimental*, *7*(1), 20. Advance online publication. DOI: 10.1186/s41747-023-00336-x PMID: 37150779

Li, N., Kim, M., Dai, J., & Vasarhelyi, M. A. (2024). Using Artificial Intelligence in ESG Assurance. *Journal of Emerging Technologies in Accounting*, *21*(2), 83–99. DOI: 10.2308/JETA-2022-054

Lulaj, E., & Brajković, M. (2025). The Moderating Role of Finance, Accounting, and Digital Disruption in ESG, Financial Reporting, and Auditing: A Triple-Helix Perspective. *Journal of Risk and Financial Management*, *18*(5), 245. DOI: 10.3390/jrfm18050245

Open Government Partnership. (2021). *Algorithmic accountability in government: Executive summary & recommendations*. https://www.opengovpartnership.org/wp-content/uploads/2021/08/algorithmic-accountability-public-sector.pdf

Petcu, M. A., Sobolevschi-David, M.-I., & Curea, S. C. (2024). Integrating digital technologies in sustainability reporting: Perceptions of professional cloud computing users. *Electronics (Basel)*, *13*(14), 2684. DOI: 10.3390/electronics13142684

Popper, M., Rapetti, C. A., & Pique, J. M. (2025). Integrating policy agendas for sustainable innovation: a quadruple helix approach. *Emerging Markets Journal*, 1–22. DOI: 10.2478/emj-2025-0009

Ryu, J., Lee, J., & Park, S. (2022). Triple Helix open innovation model in governmental AI innovation strategy. *Technovation*, *118*, 102573. DOI: 10.1016/j.technovation.2022.102573

Scaringella, L., & Radziwon, A. (2023). Resilience and structure in innovation ecosystems. *Journal of Business Research*, *154*, 113475. DOI: 10.1016/j.jbusres.2022.113475

Schneider, J., Abraham, R., Meske, C., & Vom Brocke, J. (2023). Artificial Intelligence Governance for Businesses. *Information Systems Management*, *40*(3), 170–186. DOI: 10.1080/10580530.2022.2085825

Trabelsi, M. A. (2024). The impact of artificial intelligence on economic development. [IDEAS/RePEc]. *Journal of Electronic Business & Digital Economics*, *3*(2), 142–155. DOI: 10.1108/JEBDE-10-2023-0022

Chapter 6
From Lab to Market:
Industrial Pathways for Translating Academic AI Research Into Scalable Innovation

R. N. Ravikumar
https://orcid.org/0009-0009-3705-1681
Marwadi University, Rajkot, India

S. Aarthi
https://orcid.org/0009-0006-9064-2091
Marwadi University, Rajkot, India

ABSTRACT

The translation of academic Artificial Intelligence (AI) research into scalable industrial solutions requires coordinated pathways that link scientific discovery with commercialization. This chapter examines how universities, industries, and government agencies collaborate across technology transfer mechanisms, joint research programs, incubators, and innovation pipelines to transform AI prototypes into market-ready systems. Case studies from healthcare and smart manufacturing illustrate how access to real-world data, engineering expertise, regulatory engagement, and controlled testing environments accelerate successful deployment. The chapter also highlights key challenges, including intellectual property issues, regulatory uncertainty, data limitations, and ethical risks, and emphasizes the need for responsible governance, interdisciplinary collaboration, and ecosystem-level support. A strategic roadmap is proposed to guide institutions toward sustainable AI innovation that balances technical rigor, societal values, and market readiness.

DOI: 10.4018/979-8-3373-9690-3.ch006

1. INTRODUCTION

The rapid creation of Artificial Intelligence (AI) just complicated the need to have stronger processes that can be used to translate academic discoveries into industry solutions that can be scaled. Despite universities continuing to play a central role in core AI research, or the creation of algorithms, theoretical models and prototypes, industry players have the technological foundation, financial resources and market acumen to get these innovations to practical product. The reciprocal interaction between the generation of scholarship and the generation of industrial worth in its turn forms the key of the current AI innovation systems (Jobin et al., 2019). This chapter is a very logical analysis of the progression of the academic AI research because it is not only out of the laboratory into the industrial sphere but also through the coordinated pathways and cooperative structures and plans of commercialization. It introduces into the limelight the significance of university-industry affiliations, research translation plans, technology transfer offices and startup enclaves that can help in this procedure. The introduction sets the course of the necessity to synchronize technical innovation with the necessities of the society, regulatory demands, and moral accountability as well (Onifade et al., 2022). This section outlines the basis on which industrial pathways that can facilitate academic AI studies in producing sustainable economic and societal impact will be explored in detail by offering the chapter layout and the relevance of such layout to the ecosystems of AI innovation.

1.1 Overview of Academic-to-Industry AI Translation

The process of translating academic AI research into the industrial usage is organized into a coordinated series of actions linking the scientific finding to the practical application. Institutions of higher education have the role of producing foundational knowledge such as algorithmic development, experimental findings, and prototypes. Nevertheless, before this kind of outputs can be commercially relevant, they should be refined, validated and scaled down, and adapted to the market. The non-services offered by industrial organizations include engineering experience, product development cycles, domain data, and consumer market access. Good translation involves a coordinated communication process using systems such as technology transfer offices, joint research laboratories, joint intellectual property agreements, and startup incubation. This ecosystem guarantees that the development of academics get out of the proof-of-concept stage to deployable AI systems to meet the commercial and societal demands (Perkmann & Walsh, 2008). The summary highlights that translation is not a straight process though, but an interactive and dynamic partnership in which academia and industry jointly develop to enhance faster maturity and adoption of innovations. The number 1 demonstrates that collaborative processes, including IP agreements, joint research labs, technology transfer, and incubation of startups, can change the untapped academic AI into practicable industry-ready solutions.

Figure 1. Bridging Academic AI to Industry

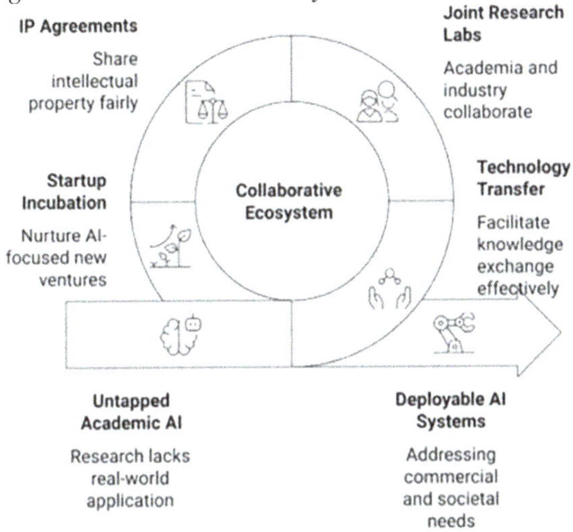

1.2 Rationale for Strengthening University–Industry Partnerships

University-industry collaboration should be enhanced since both parties do not have the necessary resources to commercialize AI successfully. Universities have a large-scale research, innovative experiment, and theoretical development, but do not necessarily have the facilities in order to deploy it on a large scale, navigate regulatory challenges, and test the market. Industry, conversely, works with market-driven goals, nimble product development models and developed customer networks, but could have problems developing breakthrough innovations without scholarly involvement. By being partners, they can share talent, data, knowledge, and financial resources that will speed up the process of bringing the research concept to a viable AI solution (Chattopadhyay et al., 2025). In addition, these partnerships minimize redundancy in work, facilitate interdisciplinary innovation, and facilitate early detection of market demands in the process of research. They are also strategic in national innovation systems especially in those countries that have moved towards AI missions and digital transformation agenda. Therefore, synergized collaboration can guarantee the fact that AI studies are not confined to laboratory walls but can develop into technologies helping to foster the development of the economy and society.

1.3 Scope, Significance, and Structure of the Chapter

In this chapter, the investigators discuss the industrial trajectories of commercializing academic AI research and identification of frameworks that facilitate effective commercialization. The field will also entail the study of the historical trends, institutional patterns, the technology transfer frameworks, startup habitat, regulatory factors, and cross-sector agreements that define the AI translation space. Its importance is that it fills the longstanding gap between academic discoveries and market-available products, which is magnified by the speed at which AI is developed and the expectations of the society. The chapter can be discussed because of its detailed discussion, case studies, and strategic insights that contribute to a better understanding of the interactions between universities, industries, and governments in the framework of the Triple Helix innovation model. The chapter has been designed such that the first section is used to contextualise the subject matter, the second section will examine the recent literature, showcase some recent case studies and the last section will synthesise results to be used in the future research and management. This entity helps to maintain clarity, logical progression, and wholesome involvement of the mechanisms that would allow the process of AI research to be moved out of the experimental settings into the global markets.

2. BACKGROUND TO THE STUDY

The contextualization of this paper provides historical, theoretical, and economic grounds that describe the advancement of academic AI research to the industrial use. AI was first developed in an academic setting where machine learning algorithms, neural network models, natural language processing models, and computational theories were studied in research laboratories. The increasing automation, predictive analytics, and intelligent system demands over time provided great incentives to industries to interact with the academic researchers. This transition demanded a frame-worked model- Triple Helix model- which involves university innovation, industry resources and government support in order to hasten the technological development. The global competition, digital transformation agendas, venture capital investment, and national AI policies are the current trends in AI commercialization paths. These developments can only be understood in analysing the integration of research translation mechanisms by the institutions through technology licensing, innovation consortia, regulatory sandboxes, and AI validation ecosystems (Etzkowitz,

2011). This background section gives the chapter its necessary contextualization by locating AI translation in both historical and global contexts, and then proceeds on to the discussion of the industrial pathways and commercialization strategies in the following part of the chapter.

2.1 Evolution of AI Research From Academia to Market

The development of AI was initially more of an academic venture and universities were the centers of algorithms experimentation and theoretical development. The initial advances in machine learning, expert systems and neural networks were motivated by scholarly interest and government-sponsored research initiatives, and not by a commercial motive. The commercialization of AI hastened as the power of computing, the availability of data, and the development of digital infrastructure increased and allowed industries to identify the opportunities of AI in improving productivity and automating decisions and personalizing services. Gradually, industries started creating joint research initiatives, sponsored labs and joint development initiatives with universities to have first direct access to new breakthroughs. It was necessary to have new strategies to fill the innovation valley of death between academic prototypes and market-ready AI solutions, such as incubators, patent licensing, corporate AI labs, and startup spin-offs (Perkmann & Walsh, 2007). This development is part of a larger change in which AI innovation is more and more co-created between academia and industry resulting in increased translation cycles, increased scalability, and stronger application-based research priorities. The figure 2 demonstrates the stratified development of the AI research starting with the academic background and passing through the industry cooperation, the innovation processes, and finally the market-approved solutions.

Figure 2. AI Research Evolution

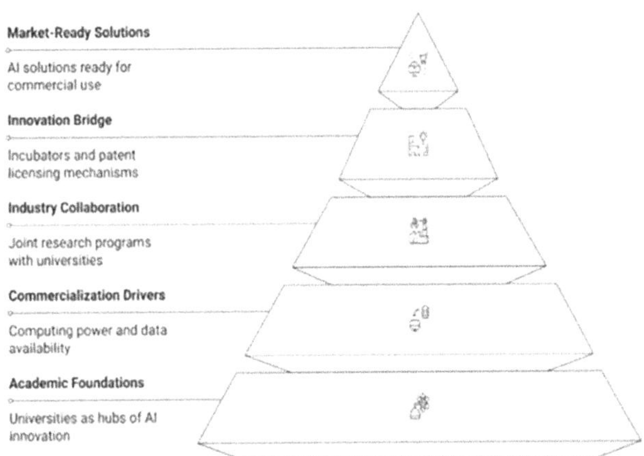

2.2 The Triple Helix Framework: University–Government–Industry Dynamics

The Triple Helix model offers an analytical approach in perceiving the manner in which universities, government entities, and industries come together to speed up innovation in AI. According to this model universities create new knowledge and technological breakthroughs, industries convert these knowledge into market ready solutions and governments offer regulatory, financial and policy backing to facilitate innovation ecosystems. The interaction among these three players lowers the commercialization barriers through providing common infrastructure, coordinated funding and harmonization of research interests. The governments are exerting an effect on innovation by using AI policies, grants, and public-private partnerships as well as regulatory sandboxes that enable controlled experimentation. Industries provide engineering capacity, market knowledge, and scalability whereas universities provide talent, knowledge, and prototype (Mohammadi, 2025). The dynamic sentiment between the three forms a platform through which innovation is generated, experimented, and improved and implemented. This framework is notably important in AI since the advancement of technology demands ethical supervision, effective infrastructure and interdisciplinary cooperation, as well as long-term research financing, all of which are attained by combined Triple Helix capabilities. The figure 3 demonstrates the interaction of universities, industry, government, and technology transfer mechanisms with each other through collaborative partnerships to develop scalable AI innovation.

Figure 3. Driving AI Innovation Through Collaboration

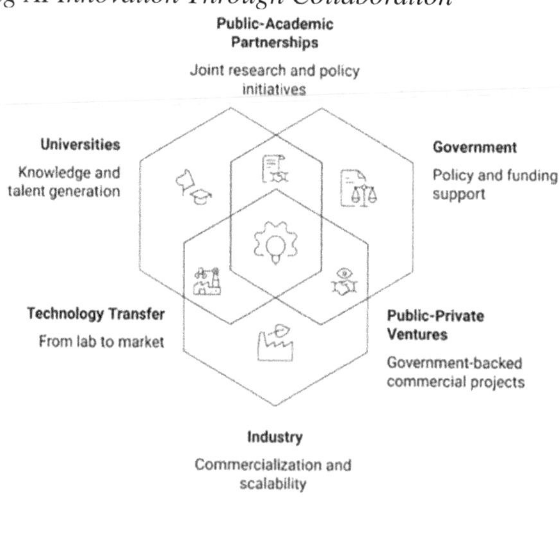

2.3 Current Global Trends in AI Commercialization Pathways

The trends in the commercialization of AI around the world demonstrate that there is a transition to more collaborative, agile, and ecosystem-based processes of research translation into market results. Nations possessing robust innovation abilities are implementing countrywide AI approaches that support university-business collaborations, AI incubators, as well as extensive testing venues like living labs and regulatory sandboxes. Development of responsible AI is getting more and more popular, and organizations need to add fairness, transparency, and accountability to commercialization pipelines (Servoss et al., 2017). Investments into AI startups has remained active and spin-offs have become a significant process of commercializing academic technologies, especially in healthcare, fintech, robotics, and autonomous systems (Ravikumar, Aarthi, et al., 2025). To develop algorithms, datasets, and application types specific to their domains, corporations are setting up AI innovation centers and collaborate with universities to do so. Transportation of digital twins, language platforms on the cloud and cross-border data ecosystems further shorten the time on translation. In general, the trends in global commercialization suggest the shift toward integrated and fast experimentation and joint governance frameworks that rapidly and securely apply academic AI research into market conditions.

3. RESEARCH OBJECTIVES

This chapter objectives are aimed at offering a formalized insight into the development of the field of academic AI research in the process of transitioning out of the laboratory and into the commercial sphere via coordinated industrial channels. Through reviewing the processes, systems, and partnershiping paradigms that inform this translation, the chapter sets out to reveal the extenuating factors that determine innovation success or failure. The goals also reflect the ethical, regulatory, and organizational aspects that define the sustainability and impacts of AI commercialization to society. These goals combine to provide the complete perspective of the technical, strategic, and governance of transforming research into scalable AI solutions.

- To analyse the mechanisms, institutional structures, and collaborative models that support the translation of academic AI research into industrial applications.
- To evaluate the effectiveness of industrial pathways, commercialization infrastructures, and technology transfer processes in scaling AI innovations.
- To identify key challenges, risks, and systemic barriers that limit the transition of AI prototypes to market-ready solutions.

- To examine the enablers including partnerships, funding models, regulatory support, and entrepreneurial ecosystems that accelerate successful AI commercialization.
- To assess the ethical, governance, and societal considerations that must be integrated into AI translation to ensure responsible, transparent, and accountable deployment.

4. CONCEPTUAL MODEL

The conceptual framework of this chapter provides the systematic understanding of how the academic AI research is developed based on the stages of creating knowledge, polishing it together, commercializing it, and implementing to the masses. It includes significant actors, processes, infrastructures and governance systems that constitute the primary vehicles that define the direction of the journey between the experimentation in the laboratories and market penetration. The model is premised on the interdisciplinary theories to incorporate innovation value chain, Triple Helix model of collaboration, and technology commercialization routes. It indicates the connections between the input of the academic research, industrial capabilities, and the government regulatory frameworks, and the need of coordinated interactions and shared responsibility (Miller et al., 2014). The conceptual model is particularly relevant to the area of AI because the transformation of the technical complexity, ethical concerns, data availability, and market maturity influence the translation cycles. The model provides the analytical clarity of the mapping of such components to a coherent structure in order to comprehend how the ideas can become functioning AI systems, how the stakeholder can create value together and how the problem of commercialization risks and uncertainty might be reduced through the coordinated intervention and strategic planning.

4.1 Conceptual Framework for AI Translation Ecosystem

The conceptual framework of the AI translation ecosystem indicates how the academic research unit would be innovative in its process of translation into an industrial and, ultimately, to the end users. It outlines ideation, prototyping, validation, scaling and market integration phases that are facilitated by collaboration mechanisms in similar fashion as technology transfer offices, intellectual property agreements, joint laboratories and startup accelerators. This structure makes universities origins of new algorithms, theoretical understanding, and proof-of-concept systems and industries make contributions with engineering skills, product development, cloud platforms, and commercialization. Regulatory agencies are also part of the ecosystem to make sure that there is compliance to safety, privacy, and ethical requirements (Similié et al., 2025). Feedback loops are at the centre stage: industrial pilots give real-world data that is used to refine academic models and academic expertise can find solutions to technical bottlenecks in industry-driven deployments. The framework portrays the role in the success of translation by portraying these interactions as a system whereby the various processes involved are coordinated and not isolated. Fig. 4 represents the stratified development of AI translation that includes scholarly studies and business experience, regulatory standards, feedback, and eventual market adoption.

Figure 4. AI Translation Ecosystem Framework

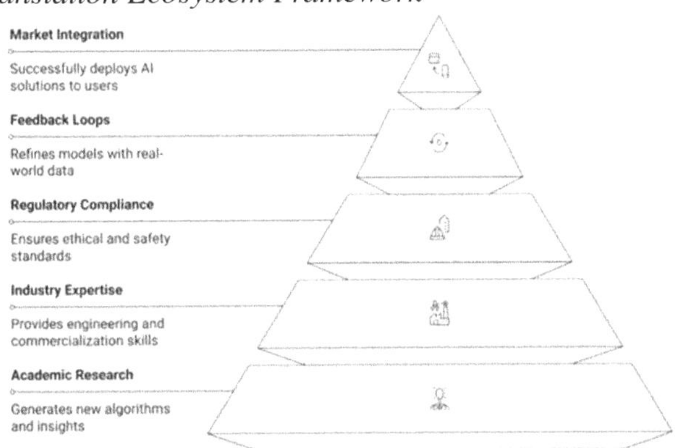

4.2 Interaction of Academia, Industry, and Government in the Triple Helix ModeL

The Triple Helix model considers the innovation as the results of the dynamism between the academia, industry and the government. This model is used in the situation of AI translation, in which case, universities may generate the research background, industries may apply and commercialize them, and governments may enable them by funding, and regulating them through policies and supporting them. Academia introduces advanced algorithms and theoretical foundation as well as certified human resources. The outcomes of research are developed into business products by industry based on the combination of domain expertise, system engineering, customer driven design values. The government agencies make responsible translation by introducing ethical principles, information-governance programs and financial incentives such as grants in innovation (Cai & Etzkowitz, 2020). It is a nonlinear relationship: national investments in research programs activate research pipelines; research laboratories sponsored by commercial interests influence the research agenda of the universities, and universities provide talent to national AI missions. This model (Triple Helix) enhances the effectiveness of innovation, accelerates new technology transfer, and ensures consistency of the technological development, as well as the needs of the society through these interdependent links.

4.3 Value Chain of Academic AI Research to Market Deployment

The academic research to market deployment AI value chain is made of sequential and connected steps that transform the scientific outputs into marketable solutions. This starts with basic research, new models, learning paradigms and prototypes are discovered. Such innovations move to the validation phase in which the feasibility studies, small-scale testing and experimental evaluations are carried out. The second stage involves technology development, process automation, data scale up, and connection with the industrial process. Movement between stages is achieved by technological transfer offices, incubators or corporate innovation teams via licensing agreements, startup creation or joint development efforts. Commercialization entails the development of products that are market ready, development of business models, user testing and regulatory compliance (K. Rao, 2025). The activities to be considered after the deployment are maintenance, lifelong learning, ethical observation, and performance reports. This move towards a multi-stage approach to thinking about translation and the importance of coordinated resource flow, cooperation among stakeholders, and other governance tools in enabling scalable AI deployment is also emphasized as a value chain. Table 1 Overview of the steps through which academic research can be translated to market deployment.

Table 1. Overview of AI Translation Stages

Stage	Key Activities	Primary Stakeholders
Research & Ideation	Algorithm development, theoretical models	Universities, Researchers
Prototyping	PoC, model testing, refinement	Labs, Research groups
Validation	Dataset expansion, risk testing	Industry partners, Regulators
Scaling	Engineering, integration, deployment	Corporations, Startups
Market Adoption	User testing, compliance, updates	End-users, Enterprises

5. RESEARCH METHODOLOGY

In this section, the methodological approach that will be used to explore the mechanisms and pathways that will facilitate the translation of the academic AI research into industrial applications will be outlined. Its structure of methodology is to facilitate analytical rigor, transparency and the relevance of the research objectives. The qualitative research design is employed, and it is developed on the basis of analysis of documents, consideration of the case study, and thematic analysis of secondary literature (Dwivedi et al., 2021). The methodology considers comparison analysis of AI commercialization models, analysis of industrial innovation practices and review of policy documents to the AI governance and transfer of technology. Triangulation is realized due to the use of multiple data sources and it enhances the validity and strength of the results. The selection of case studies is based on their topicality, timeliness, and the capability to yield proven outcomes on AI translation. In the section, reliability, validity and limitations have also been addressed, thus ensuring analysis process is not groundless, in that it may be systematic and in line with the academic norms. (Berry et al., 2025). All in all, the methodology could be used to explore the ways in which AI innovations have to pass through the academic environment to the market implementation in a comprehensive manner.

5.1 Research Design and Approach

The research design is qualitative and exploratory and is used to examine the multifaceted and multi-actor nature of the translation of academic AI research into scalable industrial innovation. This methodology will be suitable because the paths of commercialization are complex, stakeholders are heterogeneous, and the environment of AI technologies is dynamic. The conceptual designs adopted in the research to generate an insight into the mechanisms of translation, collaborative models and commercialization infrastructures are conceptual analysis, systematic literature review, and case study analysis. The design is exploratory and therefore allows the study to identify arising patterns, gaps and relationships that may not be availed by the quantitative methods. (Abadir et al., 2024). Further, the model incorporates theoretical models like the Triple Helix model and innovation value chains to explain findings. The design facilitates systematic exploration of the subject matter by organizing inquiry based on thematic areas, including technology transfer, industry relationships, ethics, and regulatory conditions that have the flexibility of inviting novel information.

5.2 Data Sources, Case Selection, and Analysis Techniques

The research uses a wide range of secondary sources of data, such as peer-reviewed articles, policy documents, industry white papers, technology transfer reports, and academic-industry partnership case studies. They are extensive sources of data covering modern practices in the field of AI translation and global commercialization. The choice of case studies is determined on three grounds: recentness (not older than five years old), immediate relevation to AI translation, and the implication on the real-world applications. The areas of healthcare, autonomous systems, fintech, and manufacturing are put on the priority list because they are the most frequent adopters of AI (Ravikumar & Aarthi, 2025a). Thematic coding, cross-case comparison, and conceptual mapping are used as analytical techniques to find out common mechanisms, barriers, and enablers in cases. This technique allows one to study trends that capture more industry-academia trends (Roundy & Asllani, 2024). The fact that the data sources are rich and analysis should be structured enhances the depth of the interpretation and provides the study with the grounding that can be based on the evidence of the real world and the current research.

5.3 Validation, Reliability, and Limitations of the Study

Triangulation of data sources, comparison of several case studies, and integration of results between academic and industrial perspectives are the means of validation and reliability. The continuity of meaning is ensured through the use of set thematic categories on all the data collected. Dependability is also enhanced as it uses conceptual frameworks, which are commonly accepted in the field of AI innovation and technology transfer. Nevertheless, the research has a number of limitations. The secondary data source can limit the access to proprietary information of corporate AI initiatives (Subrahmanyam, 2025). The fast-changing character of AI technologies could also lead to the development of new trends that do not take place in the cases considered. Moreover, geographic difference in the AI regulatory climate could restrict extra regional generalizability. The limitations notwithstanding the methodological rigor and systematic review of various sources provide the guarantee that the results will have some value in future studies of AI translation pathways and guide future academic and industrial use.

6. LITERATURE REVIEW

The state of the art in applying academic research on Artificial Intelligence (AI) to industrial innovation states that commercialization pathways, cross-disciplinary collaboration, and ethical regulation are gaining increasing importance. The research always highlights that small AI prototypes at the lab scale are not enough to create scalable and industry-ready applications and that it takes concerted efforts among the universities, industries, and regulatory authorities (Sachdeva, 2025). Three major strands of research will be examined in the review: technology transfer mechanisms and pipeline innovation, industrial capability to scale AI, and barriers, risks, and ethical issues determining the consequences of commercialization. These strands can be combined to gain a profound comprehension of the processes of AI innovations development between academic findings and their implementation into society.

6.1 Technology Transfer Mechanisms and Innovation Pipelines

As a method of transferring AI knowledge between the university and industry, literature on technology transfer refers to it as a central approach to the knowledge transfer. Technology Transfer Offices (TTOs) are also mentioned as having helped in the management of intellectual property, serve to help in the negotiation of licensing, and help in collaborations with corporate partners. Pipelines In the case of innovation pipelines (including incubators, accelerators, joint labs, and applied research centers), these are considered to be an important infrastructure that assists in achieving a transition between academic prototypes and validated technologies. Empirical evidence indicates that the initiation of industry partners facilitates the aspect of relevance, rapid development and user-relevant design (Ardita et al., 2025). The development of collaborative innovation centers e.g. university-industry laboratories can facilitate co-creation through the combination of domain knowledge, real-world data, and engineering processes. Also, policy-based initiatives, such as grants on innovation and proof-of-concept funding, lower the financial barriers of initial AI initiatives (Hayati et al., 2025). It is repeatedly mentioned in the literature that ecosystems that have well-organized technology transfer channels are more successful in commercialization and closely connected between the results of academic research and industrial demand. Table 2 Listing technology transfer pathways common and functional role.

Table 2. Technology Transfer Mechanisms in AI

Mechanism	Purpose	Outcome
Licensing	Commercial rights to research outputs	Revenue + commercialization
Joint Labs	Co-development with industry	Shared innovation
Spin-offs	Startup formation from research	Productization
Consultancy	Expert advice to industry	Domain knowledge transfer

6.2 Industrial Capabilities for Scaling AI (Infrastructure, Talent, Capital)

Scholarly studies highlight that the industrial capacities are needed to scale AI beyond the proof-of-concept. High-performance computing, cloud platforms, IoT systems, and secure data architecture infrastructure can facilitate the provision of sophisticated AI models in just seconds. The decisive factor is also the talent capabilities: in the industries, it is multidisciplinary teams consisting of data scientists, software engineers, domain experts, and product developers that are needed to combine academic innovations with the needs of the operation (Singh Chauhan et al., 2025). The movement of the talent between the university and industries enhances continuity of innovation. Also, monetary capital, which includes venture capital, corporate research and development investments, and government AI projects, is essential to long development periods and extensive testing systems. Research has pointed out that business sectors that have well-established innovation cultures, agile engineering models, and robust information structures have a higher probability of embracing AI solutions, which have their origin in scholarly research work (Ravishankar, 2025). Such abilities all create a base on which AI innovations can be developed, grow and remain competitive over the long term. Table 3 Highlights infrastructures, talent and capital requirements to scale AI systems.

Table 3. Industrial Requirements for AI Scaling

Requirement	Components	Impact on AI Deployment
Infrastructure	Cloud, GPUs, data lakes	Faster training + scaling
Talent	Data scientists, engineers	High-quality development
Capital	Investments, grants	Sustained innovation

6.3 Barriers, Risks, and Ethical Concerns in AI Commercialization

Regardless of the progress, the literature presents enduring issues of AI translation. Disputes that relate to intellectual property issues are common in situations where institutions and researchers as well as corporate partners contribute. Access controls are a significant hindrance since academic teams often do not have the amount, variety, or regulatory permission to train deployable AI systems. There is also the regulatory complexity in issues of privacy, safety, and accountability that makes commercialization complex (University et al., 2025). Algorithmic bias, absence of transparency, unfair results, and privacy risks are becoming the major ethical issues in the academic debate. Researchers believe that ethical principles, responsible AI regulations, and general validation are the keys to reliable implementation. These barriers explain why tighter governance frameworks, multi-disciplinary workforce and alignment of regulation in commercialization is necessary. Table 4 Summarizes threats, difficulty and limitation of translation.

Table 4. Barriers in AI Commercialization

Barrier Type	Example Issues	Effect
IP Issues	Shared ownership	Slowed transfer
Data Access	Limited datasets	Poor model performance
Regulation	Compliance complexity	Deployment delays
Market Fit	Prototype–market gap	Low adoption

7. CASE STUDY

The case studies provide a tangible understanding of the process of the translation of the academic AI research to realistic, industrial-scale applications in various industries. They disclose the channels, partnerships, technological readjustments and regulatory deliberations that determine commercialization results. Exploring the recent achievements in healthcare and autonomous systems/smart manufacturing, this section will point to how the academic findings transform into the proven product with quantifiable societal and economic advantages (Park, 2010). These examples illustrate the convergence of research institutions, industry collaboration, technology transfer systems, and government policies, which are the main components of the Triple Helix model. They also demonstrate the effect of sector specific challenges in the data acquisition, model testing, ethical standards, and the speed of deployment. The case studies demonstrate that success in AI translation often replicates itself through comparative analysis, including the cross-disciplinary cooperation, clearly outlined commercialization opportunities, and accessibility to the real-world testing environment. Collectively, they offer meaningful teachings which can be used to design more efficient innovation ecosystems in the future when passing research findings to market with AI.

7.1 Case Study 1: AI Translation in healthcare

The most recent successful AI translation use in healthcare is the creation of early diagnostic tools of diabetic retinopathy using deep learning. The project was born out of a research project at Google Research and multiple academic departments of ophthalmology as an attempt to develop an automated screening system that would identify retinal abnormalities with equivalent clinical accuracy. Algorithms and algorithmic models were originally developed by academic researchers as well as tested on publicly available datasets. Scalability and clinical reliability, however, demanded access to large, heterogeneous real-world data, which could only be got in academic settings (Goktas & Grzybowski, 2025). Cooperation with hospitals and diagnostic centers also made it possible to obtain clinically labeled images, and industrial partners provided the facilities of high-performance computing and knowledge of product engineering. The system also passed through strict validation testing such as multisite clinical trials in India, Thailand, and the United States in order to verify its safety, fairness and strength. The regulatory interactions with the national health authorities helped to approve and implement it in the screening programs (Singh & Keche, 2025). The system is now part of tele-ophthalmology processes, allowing the screening process to be faster, lessening the workload on an ophthalmologist, and the rate of early detection, particularly in low-resource environments. The case illustrates how academic innovation that is endorsed by industry potential and regulatory standards can transform to effective healthcare solutions. Figure 5 shows how scholarly AI research in the field of diabetic retinopathy advances step-by-step to a clinical application, with the help of these three components: collaboration, validation, and regulatory approval.

Figure 5. AI Translation in Healthcare Development

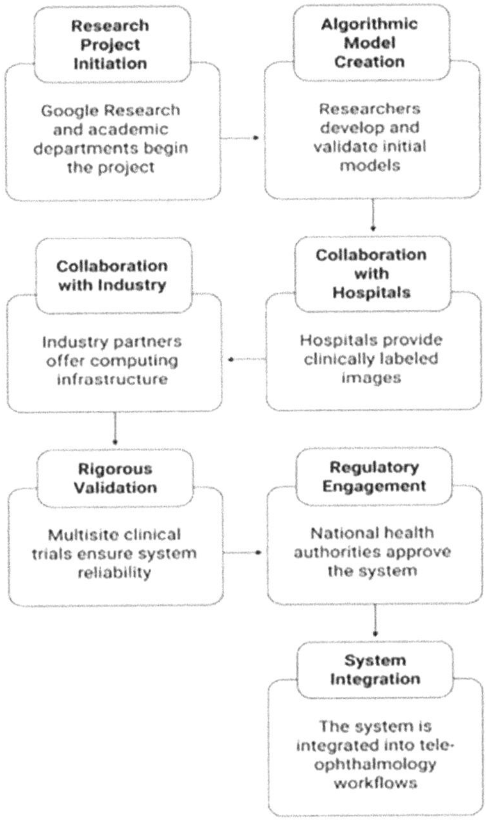

7.2 Case Study 2: AI Translation in Autonomous systems / smart manufacturing

Another interesting example of smart manufacturing is the academic-industrial partnership of the AI-based predictive maintenance system by Siemens, which was initially created during the European-centered research partnership with major European universities. The first contribution of academia was the models that were able to identify the anomalies of machines based on the data of vibration, temperature, and acoustic sensors (Zhou et al., 2023). These initial prototypes showed solid theoretical promise but needed industrial scale dataset, real time processing needs and connection to operating technologies to be commercially viable. Siemens offered a high level of sensor infrastructures, industrial IoT platforms and engineering personnel to optimize the algorithms to be applied in high volume manufacturing settings. Digital twin architecture was developed to model the functionality of equipment in a variety of situations, and allow testing of the models safely without disrupting manufacturing lines. The industrial validation also involved stress-tests and interoperability tests, cybersecurity tests, and manufacturing safety standards. The solution has been implemented in world factories since then with successful results of reduced downtimes, costs on maintenance, and risks in operations (Zhao et al., 2023). This case demonstrates that the cooperation between data engineering, mechanical system, AI modelling, and industrial standards is needed to scale academic innovations into autonomous manufacturing systems which are fully operational. Figure 6 illustrates the overall process of transferring an academic AI research in anomaly detection into a globally implemented manufacturing process by the collaboration of industries, digital twins, and industrial validation.

Figure 6. AI Translation in Smart Manufacturing

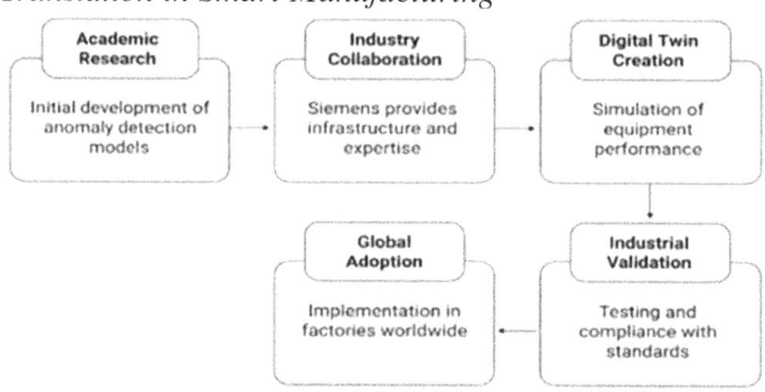

7.3 Cross-Case Comparison: Lessons, Patterns, and Success Metrics

The analogy in success factors in the translation of industry of academic AI research is identified in both instances. To begin with, they had to utilize massive and high-quality data sets that were not available within an academic setting, which demonstrates the need to cooperate with companies. Second, they checked the reliability of the models, their safety and scalability by testing them in real-world testing conditions i.e. in clinical trials in the case of healthcare and in digital twins in the case of manufacturing. Third, commercialization was enabled by the multidisciplinary approach to the study of AI, experts in the domain, engineers, and regulators (Busch et al., 2024). The translation of health care was focused on the ethics and the safety of the patients, and the manufacture focused on the system integration and the continuity. In both scenarios, the metrics of success consisted of the increase in accuracy, cost reduction, scalability, and the capacity to affect the society or industry in any quantifiable manner. All these cases imply that AI translation is most effective with the help of strong data ecology, prototypes development, collective governance, and the presence of properly established channels between prototype and product. Table 5 Comparison of the essential factors in healthcare and manufacturing case study.

Table 5. Cross-Case Comparison Summary

Factor	**Healthcare AI**	**Smart Manufacturing AI**
Data Availability	Clinical records	Sensor/IoT data
Testing Environment	Clinical trials	Digital twins
Key Challenge	Safety & bias	Integration complexity
Success Metric	Diagnostic accuracy	Reduced downtime

8. RESULTS / DISCUSSION

The findings of the given study indicate that successful translation of scholarly AI research into a commercial product demands the concerted effort between institutional, technology, and regulatory dimensions. Effective translation and innovation pipelines, effective transfer of technology, and cooperative platforms that allow an unending feedback between researchers and industrial practitioners have been viewed as the implementation of effective translation. In the case study, it is shown that industries that embrace structured validation environment, i.e., clinical trials, digital twins, industry-specific sandboxes, have a greater success rate in deployment and scalability (Novak, 2025). The results also highlight the critical role of startups and corporate innovation laboratories in closing the gap between the prototype creation and commercial implementation, particularly in new areas of AI intensiveness. Also, the discussion shows that the intellectual property restrictions, low access to high-quality datasets, and ambiguity in regulatory expectations and alignment of academic output to market requirements are still obstacles to the translation activities. There are additional ethical issues of prejudice, openness, and responsibility that affect the commercialization environment (McAdam et al., 2017). Comprehensively, the discussion affirms that AI translation is optimally successful when underpinned by integrated ecosystems that entail technical virtuosity, governance systems as well as market preparedness.

8.1 Insights on Effective Industrial Pathways for AI Scaling

Successful industrialization pathways of AI innovations have a number of distinguishable features. First, they include the systems of early alignment between the academic research products and industry requirements that allow the effective transfer between theory and practice. Clear commercialization paths are provided by the structured technology transfer processes which include the TTOs, incubators, and corporate innovation programs. Second, efficient gateways entail the availability of real-world data sets and domain-based validation platforms, on which academic prototypes may be put through stress-tests. Digital twins, pilot deployments and controlled tests areas enhance reliability and lower risks of deployment (Nath et al., 2023). Third, multidisciplinary teams can improve the quality of the design through continuous cooperation, and the feedback loop allows quick improvement through iterative feedback. Lastly, the adoption of modular architecture, interoperable AI systems, and flexible engineering pipelines in industries renders more scalability since they may incorporate academic solutions to previously existing infrastructures. The lessons here include that AI scaling must be mindful of academic creativity and industrial engineering discipline, market intelligence, and corporate systems that will keep it safe and compliant.

8.2 Role of Startups, Spin-Offs, and Corporate Labs in AI Market Adoption

The startup, spin-off and corporate laboratory participation is at the center of expediting the adoption of AI into the market as they fill the niche between research and business use. It is also known that startups are sometimes directly based on university research groups and turn their academic prototypes into niche products. Their agility facilitates experimentation that goes quick and their product cycles are quick and have the market early validation. Spin-offs have been funded by academic institutions or research consortia and utilize solid intellectual property and strong technical expertise to put up specialized AI solutions. The enterprise-wide processes, the engineering maturity, and the global markets are the functions of the labs in the companies: they transfer the academic innovation to the enterprise-scale processes, introduce the engineering maturity, and global markets (Zhu et al., 2024). Such organizations also allow talent mobility whereby the researchers are able to move to the industries yet they are still able to maintain the collaborative relationship with the academic community. Blended, they reinforce the pace of invention, reduce time-to-market along with cement the commercialization pipeline. They can contribute to the fact that a good academic research may grow, become proved, and applied in high reliability, high operational-alignment settings.

8.3 AI Translation Challenges: IP, Regulation, Data Access, Market Fit

There are several issues that create a significant problem to AI translation and that is the success of commercialization. Complexities of intellectual property are one of the aspects that are often taken into consideration because multiple individuals may hold a claim over algorithms, datasets or model layout such as researchers, institutions and industry partners. Without clearance and dealings, as well as transfer of technology, navigating IP agreements is not easy. The problem of regulations is connected to the changing legal regulations associated with the protection of data, liability of AI, its elucidation, and compliance criteria that apply to particular industries. One of the key constraints is also the difficulty of data access as academic groups lack access to large, diverse, and ethical data which can be used to create deployable AI systems. Even in the situations when data are available, privacy restrictions and interoperability may hinder integration. (Kazemzadeh, 2025). Market fit is also challenging: academic research can focus on novelty in the algorithm without focusing on usefulness, scalability, or customer requirements, and as a result, there can be discrepancies between what the prototype can do and what the business wants. To counter these issues, there is a need to enhance cross-sector co-operation, ensure uniformity, harmonized assessment models and early interactions with end-users and industry representatives to create a process of alignment along the translation pipeline.

9. FUTURE RESEARCH

The opportunities of future research on AI translation show that it is necessary to develop a new testing environment, long-term evaluation of impacts, and responsible practices of innovation. With the increasing integration of AI technologies into the life of society and industry, it is necessary to conduct research on new approaches to conducting safe and controlled experimentation to allow deployment in the shortest possible period but in a responsible manner. Sandboxes and digital twins in regulation and standardized AI validation models offer potential solutions in enhancing risk management and system durability (Amin et al., 2024). Also, longitudinal research is needed to comprehend the temporal changes in deployed AI systems, organizational performance, and organizational transformation of regulatory, ethical, and workforce environments. The requirements of responsible development of AI should also be explored in future studies in the context of fairness, transparency, preservation of privacy, and accountability in practical implementations (Ravikumar, Renukadevi, et al., 2025). With the increase in cross-sector ecosystems, research is required to look into the interrelationship between universities, industries and governments, and the civil society in order to discover the processes that can enhance trust, innovation power, and fair access to the benefits of AI.

9.1 Emerging Models: Regulatory Sandboxes, Digital Twins, AI Validation Frameworks

New frameworks like regulatory sandboxes, digital twins, and standardized AI validation frameworks are changing the process of transition of AI innovations out of the research environment to the market. With regulatory sandboxes, controlled trial can be done under supervisory care, where AI systems can be tested on real-world situations by developers without violating privacy and safety rules. Digital twins Digital twins represent virtual models of real-life assets and processes that allow the risk-free testing and refining of AI models and stress-testing them before implementation (Son et al., 2020). These kinds of simulations hasten the process of innovation even as disruption to operations is minimized. Governments and standards organizations come up with AI validation frameworks that identify accuracy, fairness, transparency, robustness, and security benchmarks. These models establish systematic channels of responsible scaling and make sure that academic innovations are appropriate to industrial demands (Ravikumar & Aarthi, 2025b). The fact that they have emerged points to the increased focus on risk-controlled commercialization and offers an ideal area to look into in the future regarding scalable and ethically sound AI systems.

9.2 Need for Longitudinal Studies on AI Commercialization Impact

The longitudinal study is required to determine the long-term effects of commercialization of AI on companies, industries, and society. The available literature concentrates on early adoption or prototype performance and does not give any thorough information on the functioning of AI systems after the full implementation. The longitudinal studies can determine how the models will degenerate over time, changes in organizational practices in order to adapt to AI, and how users change their behavior as a reaction to the use of algorithms (Lee et al., 2021). They also assist to determine the sustainability of business models constructed on the basis of AI solutions, the existence of ethical risks, and the economic value of AI-enabled innovations in the long run. Such intersectoral comparisons may contribute to attracting tendencies in healthcare, manufacturing, finance, and public services as well as offer a more general view on the existence of AI in society. Such research is highly required to inform the policymaking process in order to achieve better technology governance and perfect the technique of commercialization.

9.3 Open Research Areas in Responsible, Scalable, and Ethical AI Translation

The open research areas remain some of the essential ones to responsible, scalable and ethically sound AI translation. These include ways of creating measures of fairness, transparency and accountability in different fields of application; technical ways of decreasing prejudice, interpretability and protection; regulatory paradigms that balance innovation to society with protection. The other emerging area is sustainable AI engineering practices research, including the energy-efficient model training, lifecycle management, and green AI principles (D. P. Rao et al., 2023). The interdisciplinary study is required to understand the change of human-AI collaboration in the real-life situation and how it is needed to alter the abilities of the working force. Furthermore, new business models and ecosystem frameworks should be experimented with to assist in attaining equal access to AI technologies in every area and industry. By sealing these research gaps, one will be able to come up with a more responsible and scalable system of AI commercialization.

10. MANAGERIAL IMPLICATIONS

This chapter has practical implications on managers, university administrators, and interested policymakers who need the results of this chapter to make AI translation pathways stronger. The results highlight to the industry players that there is a need to develop agile innovation structures, which also comprise academic research, market intelligence, and ethical governance in the product development processes. To ensure that it is reliable and scaleable, the managers need to put more emphasis on data preparedness, inter-disciplinary collaboration and the long-lasting validation processes. At the case of universities and technology transfer offices, the implications have been in a position to consider the possibilities that can be made in the strengthening of commercialization pipelines through controlling of IP management, industry outreach strategies and spin-offs supporting. (Ma, 2024). Meanwhile, policymakers have a major role to play in the establishment of favorable conditions with regulatory clarity, specific funding, and national AI missions. Throughout all the stakeholders, the observations support the need to adopt responsible practices in innovation that reconcile the advancements in technology with the demands of the society. The coordination between the Triple Helix actors is required in order to make sure that the AI technologies produce long-term economic and social values. Table 6 Provides industry, university, government practical recommendations.

Table 6. Managerial Implications Across Stakeholders

Stakeholder	Key Action	Expected Benefit
Industry	Strengthen data infrastructure	Faster deployment
Universities	Enhance TTO functions	Better commercialization
Government	Provide regulatory clarity	Safe AI adoption

10.1 STRATEGIES FOR INDUSTRY LEADERS TO ACCELERATE AI ADOPTION

The industry leaders can speed up the use of AI through developing strong data infrastructure, with modular system structures, and by incorporating the AI into the foundations of strategic decisions. The focus on the cross-functional cooperation between the data scientists, engineers, and domain experts should be prioritized to enable the alignment of solutions to the needs of the operations. The pilot testing environment, digital twins and real-time monitoring systems are useful in the investment to validate the performance and mitigate the risk of deployment. The industries are also expected to enter into long term partnership with universities so as to tap into new research and specialized talent (Oarue-Itseuwa, 2024). It is necessary to incorporate ethical governance frameworks such as model monitoring, fairness auditing as well as risk assessment protocols within the product lifecycles to improve trust and compliance. Besides, organizations can be innovative by encouraging intrapreneurship, joining consortia, and engaging in open innovation platforms. All these strategies enhance the ability of industries to embrace, expand, and support AI-based changes.

10.2 RECOMMENDATIONS FOR UNIVERSITIES AND TTOS TO STRENGTHEN MARKET LINKAGES

Universities and Technology Transfer Offices (TTOs) can facilitate better market connections through the development of a commercialization culture, the facilitation of industry-focused research, and the institutionalization of the support to entrepreneurial actions. Corporate leadership of IP, recognizing commercial viability of projects at an early stage and mentorship of researchers are actions that enhance translation preparedness. TTOs are supposed to have good connections with corporate partners, venture investors and innovation agencies to enable them obtain licensing deals, joint research projects and start up incubation (Goodman & Zhu, 2024). An additional way to solve the problem of academic research and practical implementation is to create cross-disciplinary innovation hubs and applied AI laboratories. Universities can also use the aspect of encouraging faculty and students to engage in industrial internships, consulting opportunities and joint research programmes. It is important to enforce communication channels and align the research purpose with the industry requirements in order to make sure that the academic breakthroughs will be transformed into the solutions with detectable effects on the market.

10.3 POLICY GUIDANCE FOR GOVERNMENT AGENCIES SUPPORTING AI ECOSYSTEMS

The government can play a role in AI ecosystems, which may include creating well-defined regulatory policies, specific funding packages, and national policies promoting responsible innovation. These policies must encourage sharing of data in secure and non-invasive terms so that the researchers and industries can have access to high quality datasets necessary in the development of scalable AI. The governments may help establish collaboration through establishing public-private alliances, innovation clusters, and regulatory sandboxes where AI systems might be tested. The validation and certification of AI should be standardized in order to promote trust and speedy adoption in the market (Tiossi & Rodrigues, 2023). Moreover, bonuses on university-industry relations, subsidies to start-up eco-systems and investment in digital infrastructure transform the countries more innovatively. The policy makers should also put into consideration the integration of ethical values such as fairness, transparency and accountability into the regulation systems so that interests of the society could be protected but still ensure technological development was achieved. All these policy interventions present an enabling environment to transform AI research to a sustainable economic and societal value.

11. CONCLUSION

The academic AI research should be translated into scalable industrial innovation only with the help of the coordinated and well-organized paths that may include the involvement of scientific discovery, technological refinement, regulatory readiness, and market alignment. It has been revealed on the basis of this chapter that the successful commercialization of AI may be attained due to the strong collaboration between Triple Helix players (universities, industries, and government agencies) because each individual player separately (as well as in combination with other players) provides the required capabilities and creates innovation ecosystems. The most significant lessons include the fact that technology transfer systems, including TTOs, incubators or collaborative laboratories have a role to play in the process of commercializing AI prototypes out of their concept phase and into practice. Industrial capabilities, such as data infrastructures, engineering capabilities, and financial investment, can be used to expand the AI systems, integrate and test them in the real world. In the meantime, responsible innovation places a strong emphasis on the ethical concerns that revolve around fairness, transparency, privacy, and accountability that dictate not only regulatory demands but also social trust.

The interdisciplinary approach is justified by examples of healthcare cases and smart manufacturing, which suggest that it is possible to have high-quality data and controlled testing conditions (clinical trials and digital twins) to ensure the safety and reliability of AI application. They also show how startups and corporate laboratories may be important in the process of making sure that research individuals and universities are aligned with the industry. In order to create AI innovation streams in a sustainable manner, it is necessary to establish the balance between the technical excellence and ethical accountability and commercial viability so that the AI-based solutions not only need to be efficient but also satisfy the values and regulatory standards that are considered in the society. As the role of AI in any business continues to increase, the need to ensure the stability of ecosystems that allow continued learning, cyclical and sustainable development, and long-term collaboration becomes more and more urgent. Lastly, the academic studies of AI will be converted into scalable and meaningful innovations that will necessitate a multifaceted approach that will generate trust, enhance governance, and enhance collaboration, such that AI technologies would do good in the global society.

REFERENCES

Abadir, P., Oh, E., Chellappa, R., Choudhry, N., Demiris, G., Ganesan, D., Karlawish, J., Marlin, B., Li, R. M., Dehak, N., Arbaje, A., Unberath, M., Cudjoe, T., Chute, C., Moore, J. H., Phan, P., Samus, Q., Schoenborn, N. L., Battle, A., & Walston, J. D. (2024). Artificial Intelligence and Technology Collaboratories: Innovating aging research and Alzheimer's care. *Alzheimer's & Dementia*, *20*(4), 3074–3079. DOI: 10.1002/alz.13710 PMID: 38324244

Amin, A., Chowdhury, D. I. Q., Abyaz, R., Alom, S., Siam, S. A., Al Imran, D., Lia, F. S., & Azad, P. A. K. (2024). Artificial intelligence in pharmacy: Innovations, applications, and future emerging challenges. *INTERANTIONAL JOURNAL OF SCIENTIFIC RESEARCH IN ENGINEERING AND MANAGEMENT*, *08*(12), 1–9. DOI: 10.55041/IJSREM40335

Ardita, R. R., Sutarto, , & Adhikari, B. P. (2025). Triple helix partnership model between universities, industry, and government for implementing an outcome-based curriculum in the era of disruption at PTSP UNY: An internal university review. *Jurnal Pendidikan Teknik Sipil*, *7*(1), 1–13. DOI: 10.21831/jpts.v7i1.83406

Berry, P., Dhanakshirur, R. R., & Khanna, S. (2025). Utilizing large language models for gastroenterology research: A conceptual framework. *Therapeutic Advances in Gastroenterology*, *18*, 17562848251328576. DOI: 10.1177/17562848251328577 PMID: 40171241

Busch, F., Hoffmann, L., Truhn, D., Palaian, S., Alomar, M., Shpati, K., Makowski, M. R., Bressem, K. K., & Adams, L. C. (2024). International pharmacy students' perceptions towards artificial intelligence in medicine-A multinational, multicentre cross-sectional study. *British Journal of Clinical Pharmacology*, *90*(3), 649–661. DOI: 10.1111/bcp.15911 PMID: 37728146

Cai, Y., & Etzkowitz, H. (2020). Theorizing the Triple Helix model: Past, present, and future. *Triple Helix (Heidelberg)*, *7*(2–3), 189–226. DOI: 10.1163/21971927-bja10003

Chattopadhyay, S., Honoré, F., & Won, S. (2025). Free range startups? Market scope, academic founders, and the role of general knowledge in AI. *Strategic Management Journal*, *46*(4), 1027–1079. DOI: 10.1002/smj.3685

Dwivedi, Y. K., Hughes, L., Ismagilova, E., Aarts, G., Coombs, C., Crick, T., Duan, Y., Dwivedi, R., Edwards, J., Eirug, A., Galanos, V., Ilavarasan, P. V., Janssen, M., Jones, P., Kar, A. K., Kizgin, H., Kronemann, B., Lal, B., Lucini, B., & Williams, M. D. (2021). Artificial Intelligence (AI): Multidisciplinary perspectives on emerging challenges, opportunities, and agenda for research, practice and policy. *International Journal of Information Management*, *57*(101994), 101994. DOI: 10.1016/j.ijinfomgt.2019.08.002

Etzkowitz, H. (2011). The triple helix: Science, technology and the entrepreneurial spirit. *Journal of Knowledge-Based Innovation in China*, *3*(2), 76–90. DOI: 10.1108/17561411111138937

Goktas, P., & Grzybowski, A. (2025). Shaping the future of healthcare: Ethical clinical challenges and pathways to trustworthy AI. *Journal of Clinical Medicine*, *14*(5), 1605. DOI: 10.3390/jcm14051605 PMID: 40095575

Goodman, D., & Zhu, A. Y. (2024). Utility of artificial intelligence in the diagnosis and management of keratoconus: A systematic review. *Frontiers in Ophthalmology*, *4*, 1380701. DOI: 10.3389/fopht.2024.1380701 PMID: 38984114

Hayati, A., Abdol Homayuni, M. R., Sadeghi, R., Asadigandomani, H., Dashtkoohi, M., Eslami, S., & Soleimani, M. (2025). Advancing diabetic retinopathy screening: A systematic review of artificial intelligence and optical Coherence Tomography Angiography innovations. *Diagnostics (Basel)*, *15*(6), 737. DOI: 10.3390/diagnostics15060737 PMID: 40150080

Jobin, A., Ienca, M., & Vayena, E. (2019). The global landscape of AI ethics guidelines. *Nature Machine Intelligence*, *1*(9), 389–399. DOI: 10.1038/s42256-019-0088-2

Kazemzadeh, K. (2025). Artificial intelligence in ophthalmology: Opportunities, challenges, and ethical considerations. *Medical Hypothesis, Discovery and Innovation in Ophthalmology*, *14*(1), 255–272. DOI: 10.51329/mehdiophthal1517 PMID: 40453785

Lee, A. Y., Yanagihara, R. T., Lee, C. S., Blazes, M., Jung, H. C., Chee, Y. E., Gencarella, M. D., Gee, H., Maa, A. Y., Cockerham, G. C., Lynch, M., & Boyko, E. J. (2021). Multicenter, head-to-head, real-world validation study of seven automated artificial intelligence diabetic retinopathy screening systems. *Diabetes Care*, *44*(5), 1168–1175. DOI: 10.2337/dc20-1877 PMID: 33402366

Ma, Z. (2024). Managing university-industry collaborative innovation in the pharmaceutical industry. DOI: 10.5463/thesis.499

McAdam, M., Miller, K., & McAdam, R. (2017). University business models in disequilibrium - engaging industry and end users within university technology transfer processes. *R & D Management*, *47*(3), 458–472. DOI: 10.1111/radm.12265

Miller, K., McAdam, M., & McAdam, R. (2014). The changing university business model: A stakeholder perspective. *R & D Management*, *44*(3), 265–287. DOI: 10.1111/radm.12064

Mohammadi, A. (2025). Industry-university partnership governance base on new technologies emergence. *Sustainable Social Development*, *2*(6), 3007. DOI: 10.54517/ssd3007

Nath, S., Rahimy, E., Kras, A., & Korot, E. (2023). Toward safer ophthalmic artificial intelligence via distributed validation on real-world data. *Current Opinion in Ophthalmology*, *34*(5), 459–463. DOI: 10.1097/ICU.0000000000000986 PMID: 37459329

Novak, P. (2025). Digital twin framework for postural tachycardia syndrome and autonomic disorders. *Frontiers in Neurology*, *16*(1678955), 1678955. DOI: 10.3389/fneur.2025.1678955 PMID: 41142154

Oarue-Itseuwa, E. (2024). Artificial Intelligence's impact of the management consultancy sector over the next five years. *Management Consulting Journal*, *7*(1), 49–58. DOI: 10.2478/mcj-2024-0005

Onifade, A. Y., Ogeawuchi, J. C., Abayomi, A. A., Agboola, O. A., Dosumu, R. E., & George, O. O. (2022). A conceptual framework for integrating AI adoption metrics into B2B marketing decision systems. *International Journal of Management and Organizational Research*, *1*(1), 237–248. DOI: 10.54660/IJMOR.2022.1.1.237-248

Park, C. (2010). What makes A case study really qualitative?: Show me your evidence, please! *English Teaching*, *65*(4), 79–101. DOI: 10.15858/engtea.65.4.201012.79

Perkmann, M., & Walsh, K. (2007). University–industry relationships and open innovation: Towards a research agenda. *International Journal of Management Reviews*, *9*(4), 259–280. DOI: 10.1111/j.1468-2370.2007.00225.x

Perkmann, M., & Walsh, K. (2008). Engaging the scholar: Three types of academic consulting and their impact on universities and industry. *Research Policy*, *37*(10), 1884–1891. DOI: 10.1016/j.respol.2008.07.009

Rao, D. P., Savoy, F. M., Tan, J. Z. E., Fung, B. P.-E., Bopitiya, C. M., Sivaraman, A., & Vinekar, A. (2023). Development and validation of an artificial intelligence based screening tool for detection of retinopathy of prematurity in a South Indian population. *Frontiers in Pediatrics*, *11*, 1197237. DOI: 10.3389/fped.2023.1197237 PMID: 37794964

Rao, K. (2025). Artificial Intelligence-driven 3D modeling: Transformative applications analysis. *Transactions on Computer Science and Intelligent Systems Research*, *9*, 236–245. DOI: 10.62051/f5wn2q81

Ravikumar, A. Olimbaevich, I. R., Mashkhura, S., & Musayeva, S. (2025). Transforming Healthcare with Large Language Models and AI agents. In Advances in Computational Intelligence and Robotics (pp. 51–82). IGI Global Scientific Publishing. DOI: 10.4018/979-8-3373-2008-3.ch003

Ravikumar, R. S., Manujakshi, Aarthi, S., Urazbaeva, Y., & Tamilselvi, S. (2025). Navigating data privacy, security, and regulatory challenges in healthcare AI ensuring fairness, bias mitigation, interpretability, and trust. In Transformative Role of Transformer Models in Healthcare (pp. 25–54). IGI Global Scientific Publishing. DOI: 10.4018/979-8-3373-2038-0.ch002

Ravikumar, R. N., & Aarthi, S. (2025a). AI-powered synergistic robotics and IoT ecosystems for predictive and preventive healthcare. In *Robotics and IoT Synergy in Next-Generation Healthcare* (pp. 1–32). IGI Global Scientific Publishing., DOI: 10.4018/979-8-3373-5447-7.ch001

Ravikumar, R. N., & Aarthi, S. (2025b). Digital Twin-driven green energy systems. In *The Future of Green Energy* (pp. 1–28). IGI Global Scientific Publishing., DOI: 10.4018/979-8-3373-3226-0.ch001

Ravishankar, S. (2025). Navigating AI/ML risk analytics and compliance: A strategic guide for launching global FinTech products. *European Modern Studies Journal*, *9*(5), 78–89. DOI: 10.59573/emsj.9(5).2025.9

Roundy, P. T., & Asllani, A. (2024). Understanding AI innovation contexts: A review and content analysis of artificial intelligence and entrepreneurial ecosystems research. *Industrial Management & Data Systems*, *124*(7), 2333–2363. DOI: 10.1108/IMDS-08-2023-0551

Sachdeva, D. S. (2025). Entrepreneurship innovation and startups: Catalyst for innovation and economic growth of India. *International Journal of Environmental Sciences*, •••, 2513–2526. DOI: 10.64252/xymrse11

Servoss, J., Chang, C., Fay, J., Lota, K. S., Mashour, G. A., & Ward, K. R. (2017). fastPACE Train-the-Trainer: A scalable new educational program to accelerate training in biomedical innovation, entrepreneurship, and commercialization. *Journal of Clinical and Translational Science*, *1*(5), 271–277. DOI: 10.1017/cts.2017.306 PMID: 29707247

Similié, D. E., Andersen, J. K. H., Dinesen, S., Savarimuthu, T. R., & Grauslund, J. (2025). Grading of diabetic retinopathy using a pre-segmenting deep learning classification model: Validation of an automated algorithm. *Acta Ophthalmologica*, *103*(2), 215–221. DOI: 10.1111/aos.16781 PMID: 39425597

Singh, M. P., & Keche, Y. N. (2025). Ethical integration of artificial intelligence in healthcare: Narrative review of global challenges and strategic solutions. *Cureus*, *17*(5), e84804. DOI: 10.7759/cureus.84804 PMID: 40568260

Singh Chauhan, A., Ghildiyal, P., & Yadav, S. (2025). Artificial Intelligence for Drug Discovery and development. ASP Books (A division of AcademicSP). DOI: 10.63686/978-81-987694-7-3

Son, J., Shin, J. Y., Kim, H. D., Jung, K.-H., Park, K. H., & Park, S. J. (2020). Development and validation of deep learning models for screening multiple abnormal findings in retinal fundus images. *Ophthalmology*, *127*(1), 85–94. DOI: 10.1016/j.ophtha.2019.05.029 PMID: 31281057

Subrahmanyam, S. (2025). Strategic Collaboration and Partnerships in R&D for Innovation. In Research and Development Practices in Innovation (pp. 283–314). IGI Global. DOI: 10.4018/979-8-3373-0812-8.ch010

Tiossi, F. M., & Rodrigues, R. G. (2023). Triple helix in the management of innovation in public policies: A study of two countries. *Revista de Gestão e Secretariado*, *14*(8), 14516–14531. DOI: 10.7769/gesec.v14i8.2690

University, O. N. E., Razinkin, N., & Fedosiuk, D. (2025). Business Intelligence in the digital environment: Legal and analytical aspects. *Business Navigator*, *3*(80). Advance online publication. DOI: 10.32782/business-navigator.80-42

Zhao, P. Y., Bommakanti, N., Yu, G., Aaberg, M. T., Patel, T. P., & Paulus, Y. M. (2023). Deep learning for automated detection of neovascular leakage on ultra-widefield fluorescein angiography in diabetic retinopathy. *Scientific Reports*, *13*(1), 9165. DOI: 10.1038/s41598-023-36327-6 PMID: 37280345

Zhou, Y., Dai, M., Sun, L., Tang, X., Zhou, L., Tang, Z., Jiang, J., & Xia, X. (2023). The accuracy of intraocular lens power calculation formulas based on artificial intelligence in highly myopic eyes: A systematic review and network meta-analysis. *Frontiers in Public Health*, *11*, 1279718. DOI: 10.3389/fpubh.2023.1279718 PMID: 38026369

Zhu, A., Tailor, P., Verma, R., Zhang, I., Schott, B., Ye, C., Szirth, B., Habiel, M., & Khouri, A. S. (2024). Implementation of deep learning artificial intelligence in vision-threatening disease screenings for an underserved community during COVID-19. *Journal of Telemedicine and Telecare*, *30*(10), 1590–1597. DOI: 10.1177/1357633X231158832 PMID: 36908254

KEY TERMS AND DEFINITIONS

Artificial Intelligence (AI): Technologies that enable machines to learn, reason, and make decisions similar to humans.

Commercialization: Turning academic research or prototypes into market-ready products.

Data Governance: Rules and processes that ensure responsible use, sharing, and protection of data.

Digital Twin: A virtual replica of a physical system used for testing and simulation.

Incubator: A support program that helps early-stage startups grow with mentoring, funding, and resources.

Innovation Pipeline: A step-by-step pathway that takes an idea from research to a final product or service.

Intellectual Property (IP): Legal rights that protect inventions, algorithms, or innovations.

Proof of Concept (PoC): A small experiment or prototype showing that an idea can work in practice.

Regulatory Sandbox: A safe testing environment where new technologies are tried under government supervision.

Responsible AI: AI systems designed to be fair, transparent, ethical, and safe for society.

Scalability: The ability of a technology to grow, serve more users, or operate at larger levels.

Spin-off: A new company created from university research or technology.

Technology Transfer: The process of moving research results from universities to industries for real-world use.

Triple Helix Model: A framework describing collaboration between universities, industries, and governments to drive innovation.

Validation Framework: A structured method to test whether an AI system is accurate, reliable, and safe.

Chapter 7
Hybrid Project Management as a Triple Helix Catalyst for AI-Driven Transportation Innovation

Georgios Moschoglou
Georgetown University, USA

Simon Cleveland
https://orcid.org/0000-0001-9293-3905
Purdue University Global, USA

Mak Khan
https://orcid.org/0009-0003-2923-5479
Georgetown University, USA

ABSTRACT

This chapter advances a theoretical framework positioning hybrid project management as an operational enabler of Triple Helix collaborations in AI-driven transportation infrastructure. While existing literature emphasizes strategic university-government-industry partnerships, insufficient attention addresses procedural mechanisms facilitating effective knowledge transfer across institutional boundaries. Drawing from project management theory, innovation systems research, and organizational behavior scholarship, this chapter demonstrates how hybrid models—integrating predictive lifecycle structures with adaptive Agile practices—address critical friction points: knowledge translation gaps between research and implementation,

DOI: 10.4018/979-8-3373-9690-3.ch007

regulatory-innovation tensions in government projects, and interdisciplinary co-ordination challenges. The Triple Helix Process Integration Model maps project management practices to knowledge exchange mechanisms, offering theoretical advancement and practical guidance for stakeholders navigating AI partnerships in regulated environments.

INTRODUCTION

The Convergence of AI Innovation and Collaborative Infrastructure

The acceleration of artificial intelligence capabilities has fundamentally transformed how societies approach complex infrastructure challenges, particularly in transportation systems where safety, efficiency, and public welfare intersect with technological innovation (Dwivedi et al., 2021). However, the translation of AI research into deployed transportation solutions encounters persistent obstacles rooted not in technological limitations but in organizational and procedural fragmentation across the institutional spheres that must collaborate for successful innovation.

The Triple Helix model conceptualizes innovation as emerging from overlapping institutional spheres—universities, governments, and industries—each contributing distinctive capabilities while requiring coordination mechanisms to realize synergistic outcomes. Universities contribute AI algorithms, simulation models, and predictive analytics; governments establish funding mechanisms and regulatory frameworks; industries translate innovations into deployable systems. Yet this strategic framework inadequately addresses the operational challenges that determine whether promising AI research successfully transitions from laboratory validation to real-world transportation infrastructure.

Traditional project management approaches, while effective for compliance and budget control in infrastructure contexts, create organizational silos that inhibit the collaborative agility required for AI development (Project Management Institute, 2021). Predictive lifecycle models emphasize extensive upfront planning and fixed-scope baselines executed sequentially, struggling with the dynamic, interdisciplinary nature of modern AI development. Conversely, pure Agile methodologies, though designed for iterative innovation, struggle within the regulatory and fixed-scope constraints characteristic of public-sector infrastructure contracts (Project Management Institute, 2017).

This chapter argues that hybrid project management frameworks—synthesizing predictive structure with adaptive practices—serve as critical enablers for Triple Helix AI partnerships. The preservation of accountability through milestone-based governance while enabling iterative co-development through feedback loops and team integration mechanisms, hybrid approaches create operational infrastructure for translating academic breakthroughs into governable, scalable transportation solutions (Cooper & Sommer, 2016).

THEORETICAL POSITIONING

Bridging Innovation Systems and Project Management Theory

The Triple Helix Framework and Its Operational Gaps

The Triple Helix innovation model examines how knowledge production, regulatory oversight, and commercial implementation intersect to generate technological advancement. Extensive research explores strategic partnership formation, funding models, and institutional incentive structures within this framework. However, a critical theoretical gap persists: most Triple Helix scholarship focuses on macro-level partnership structures while neglecting the meso-level coordination mechanisms that determine whether collaborations produce intended outcomes.

Existing studies emphasize strategic partnerships and funding models but neglect operational coordination mechanisms that directly influence partnership effectiveness. This oversight proves particularly consequential in AI-driven transportation innovation, where knowledge translation complexity, regulatory-innovation tensions, and interdisciplinary coordination demands create substantial friction (Berente et al., 2021).

Academic AI research operates in controlled experimental environments with flexible timeframes and iterative refinement processes, while transportation infrastructure deployment demands validated, safety-certified systems operating within rigid regulatory frameworks and fixed implementation schedules. Government agencies require demonstrable return on investment, extensive compliance documentation, and stakeholder transparency, while breakthrough AI capabilities often emerge through exploratory research with uncertain timelines and outcomes (Cath et al., 2018). Transportation AI projects typically involve signal engineers, roadway designers, data scientists, regulatory specialists, and infrastructure operators, each discipline employing distinct methodologies, standards, and communication protocols.

Project Management as Boundary-Spanning Infrastructure

Project management theory provides frameworks for organizing, coordinating, and controlling complex endeavors across organizational boundaries. Yet traditional project management scholarship has largely developed in single-organization contexts or relatively homogeneous inter-organizational partnerships, inadequately addressing the institutional diversity characteristic of Triple Helix collaborations (Zasa et al., 2020).

The PMBOK Guide Seventh Edition recognizes multiple development lifecycles—predictive, adaptive, and hybrid—endorsing practice tailoring based on project complexity and context (Project Management Institute, 2021). This institutional validation of methodological pluralism creates theoretical space for examining how project management approaches can be strategically configured to enable cross-institutional AI innovation.

Understanding Project Lifecycles

Predictive lifecycles, often called waterfall or traditional approaches, operate on the assumption that project scope, schedule, and costs can be determined with reasonable accuracy early in the project (PMI, 2021). Work proceeds sequentially through distinct phases: requirements definition, design, implementation, testing, deployment, with each phase building on deliverables from the previous one. This approach emphasizes comprehensive upfront planning, formal change control processes, and detailed documentation at each stage. Predictive lifecycles excel in environments where requirements are stable, technology is well-understood, and stakeholders require certainty about outcomes before committing resources. In transportation infrastructure contexts, predictive approaches align naturally with regulatory approval processes, procurement requirements, construction sequencing, and public accountability mechanisms that demand clear scope definition and budget predictability.

Adaptive lifecycles, commonly associated with Agile methodologies, assume that requirements will emerge and evolve as stakeholders learn from iterative deliveries of working solutions. Rather than comprehensive upfront planning, adaptive approaches use short iteration cycles, typically two to four weeks, where cross-functional teams plan, execute, review, and adjust their work continuously. Each iteration produces potentially deployable increments of functionality, enabling rapid feedback from users and stakeholders. This approach emphasizes customer collaboration over contract negotiation, responding to change over following a plan, and delivering working solutions over comprehensive documentation. Adaptive lifecycles prove particularly valuable in AI development contexts where technical feasibility cannot be determined without experimentation, where user needs emerge through interaction with prototypes, and where technological possibilities evolve faster than formal requirements can be documented (Romao et al., 2025). The iterative learning cycles inherent in adaptive approaches align with the experimental nature of AI algorithm development, where teams must test multiple approaches, tune parameters based on performance data, and continuously refine models as they encounter real-world complexity.

Hybrid lifecycles strategically combine predictive and adaptive elements within a single project, applying each approach where it provides the greatest value. Rather than viewing predictive and adaptive as mutually exclusive alternatives, hybrid approaches recognize that different project elements, or different phases of the same project, may benefit from different management approaches. A common hybrid pattern uses predictive methods for overall program governance, budget management, and coordination across the organization while using adaptive methods within the development stages for technical work. In the Agile Stage Gate hybrid model, for example, predictive Stage Gate methods provide overall project governance and decision points at gates, while Agile methods are applied within stages to manage development work through short sprints and iterative customer feedback (Cooper & Sommer, 2016). Another pattern applies predictive approaches during initial requirements gathering and final deployment phases while using adaptive approaches during middle phases where technical uncertainty is highest. The key principle underlying hybrid lifecycles is matching the management approach to the actual characteristics of the work: use predictive methods when requirements are clear and technology is stable; use adaptive methods when requirements must emerge through discovery and technology involves genuine experimentation.

Hybrid Project Management for AI Driven Innovation

Hybrid lifecycles are particularly well suited to accommodate the rapid pace of advancement in artificial intelligence, especially with the emergence of generative AI applications. The defining characteristic of AI projects is their combination of technological uncertainty and accelerating innovation cycles. Whereas traditional information systems projects rely on well established architectures and predictable outputs, AI systems evolve through data driven learning processes in which performance improves iteratively and outcomes remain partly indeterminate until late in development. Generative AI further amplifies this indeterminacy: models capable of producing text, images, or code exhibit behavior that is difficult to specify in advance and can change as models are retrained or prompted differently. In such an environment, hybrid project management offers a pragmatic structure that balances the exploratory nature of AI work with the governance discipline required for organizational accountability.

Hybrid approaches accommodate AI's unpredictability by integrating adaptive iterations within predictive governance structures. During early experimentation phases, teams employ short development cycles to explore data preprocessing methods, algorithm selection, or prompt engineering strategies. Results from these cycles inform subsequent design choices while feeding back into formal review checkpoints that assess readiness to proceed. Predictive elements such as stage gate approvals, budget reviews, and compliance audits provide oversight without impeding learning. This complementarity allows organizations to manage both discovery and delivery within a single governance framework.

AI enabled projects also require a broader conception of deliverables and roles. In addition to traditional outputs such as software components or analytical reports, teams must produce datasets, model documentation, and explainability analyses. New professional profiles including prompt engineers and model auditors join multidisciplinary project teams. Hybrid management structures support this diversity by coupling the collaborative rhythm of agile sprints with the formal coordination mechanisms typical of predictive governance. The Project Management Institute (2023) emphasizes that the next generation of project professionals will operate in "AI-augmented" environments, where human expertise and machine intelligence interact continuously to guide decision-making. Hybrid lifecycles provide the flexibility for this interaction, enabling rapid experimentation while ensuring that organizational standards for data quality, transparency, and security remain intact.

AI development projects also require a broader conception of deliverables and roles than traditional software projects. In addition to conventional outputs such as software components or analytical reports, teams must produce datasets, model documentation, prompt libraries, and explainability analyses. New professional profiles including prompt engineers, model auditors, and AI ethicists join multidisciplinary project teams. Hybrid management structures support this diversity by coupling the collaborative rhythm of agile sprints with the formal coordination mechanisms typical of predictive governance. Development teams can iterate rapidly on model architectures and training approaches while maintaining accountability through defined stage gates that verify safety, performance, and ethical compliance before advancing to deployment phases.

The challenge of defining project scope and success criteria differs fundamentally for AI development. Traditional projects deliver against fixed specifications; AI projects discover optimal solutions through experimentation. A transportation authority developing AI powered traffic management cannot fully specify algorithm performance at project initiation because effectiveness depends on real world data patterns that emerge only during development. Hybrid frameworks address this by separating strategic objectives from tactical implementations. Stage gates focus on outcome requirements such as congestion reduction targets or safety improvements, while sprint cycles maintain flexibility in technical approaches, allowing teams to adopt improved algorithms or data processing techniques as they prove effective during development.

Governance in AI development projects must evolve from static compliance to continuous oversight. Generative AI systems are dynamic; their behavior can drift over time as training data changes or models are retrained. Traditional risk registers and milestone reviews designed for stable systems cannot capture these emergent properties effectively. Hybrid governance frameworks respond by incorporating adaptive monitoring mechanisms that track model performance metrics such as accuracy, bias indicators, and explainability scores throughout development cycles, while retaining predictive controls for versioning, auditability, and regulatory reporting. This ongoing evaluation transforms governance from periodic checkpoint events into a continuous process of assurance and adaptation appropriate for systems that learn and evolve.

The challenge of validating AI systems that learn continuously requires new approaches to testing and certification. Traditional validation assumes static systems tested comprehensively before deployment. AI systems, particularly those employing continuous learning, change during operation as they accumulate experience. Hybrid frameworks accommodate this through staged validation processes. Initial deployment follows traditional validation establishing that baseline systems meet safety thresholds and performance requirements. Subsequent learning operates within defined guardrails, with periodic validation checkpoints ensuring performance remains within acceptable bounds. This structure allows systems to improve through operational experience while maintaining safety assurances required for transportation infrastructure.

Cultural readiness proves equally vital for AI development projects. Teams must embrace experimentation, cross disciplinary dialogue, and tolerance for uncertainty. Project managers accustomed to deterministic planning must become comfortable with probabilistic outcomes, data driven iteration, and model based reasoning. They must translate between algorithmic performance metrics and stakeholder value propositions, ensuring that rapid technical progress remains aligned with strategic transportation objectives. Organizational structures must reinforce this capability by empowering teams to test and learn within clearly defined ethical and financial boundaries, recognizing that optimal AI solutions emerge through iterative discovery rather than upfront specification.

In this context, hybrid project management becomes not merely a synthesis of predictive and adaptive techniques but a dynamic learning architecture for organizations developing AI driven transportation innovations. Its structured flexibility enables project teams to experiment with emerging AI capabilities, govern ethically, and deliver systems that meet safety and performance requirements. The characteristics of AI development, particularly with generative systems, underscore why this evolution is necessary: when technology advances faster than requirements can be written, and optimal solutions emerge through experimentation rather than specification, only hybrid approaches possess the elasticity to keep governance and innovation in productive balance.

Hybrid Project Management and the Triple Helix

The strategic value of hybrid lifecycles becomes particularly evident in Triple Helix AI transportation projects, where different institutional partners operate under different constraints and timelines. University research operates on academic calendars with publication deadlines and grant cycles requiring predictable milestones. Government agencies manage annual budget appropriations and multi-year funding commitments demanding defined deliverables and accountability measures. Industry partners face competitive pressures requiring rapid technology development and iterative product refinement. A purely predictive approach would constrain the exploratory work essential for AI innovation; a purely adaptive approach would fail to satisfy the accountability requirements inherent in government oversight and public infrastructure deployment.

Hybrid project management models integrate predictive lifecycle structures with Agile practices, balancing accountability demands with iterative requirements (Cooper & Sommer, 2016). This synthesis addresses a fundamental challenge in Triple Helix AI partnerships: reconciling the accountability and transparency requirements inherent in government oversight and public infrastructure deployment with the flexibility and iterative learning essential for developing novel AI capabilities.

The Triple Helix Process Integration Model

Building on these theoretical foundations, this chapter proposes a Triple Helix Process Integration Model that maps project management practices to knowledge exchange mechanisms across university, government, and industry domains in AI-driven transportation contexts.

University Sphere: Enabling Research-Practice Translation

Universities contribute fundamental research capabilities, algorithmic innovations, and talent development to transportation AI initiatives. However, academic research cycles, publication incentives, and validation standards often misalign with infrastructure deployment timelines and regulatory requirements. Hybrid project management addresses these misalignments through iterative prototyping cycles that embed university researchers in practical validation environments (Kreye et al., 2025).

Rather than relegating academic contributions to initial research phases followed by handoffs to industry partners, hybrid frameworks establish continuous engagement mechanisms. Sprint reviews and iterative feedback sessions allow researchers to test theoretical models against practical constraints, refining algorithms based on real-world data while maintaining research rigor (Agbejule & Lehtineva, 2022). This iterative engagement transforms the research-practice relationship from sequential knowledge transfer to collaborative co-development.

Co-authorship opportunities and access to real-world datasets provide universities with practical validation environments while industry partners gain cutting-edge algorithmic capabilities. Milestone-based governance structures preserve academic autonomy for fundamental research while ensuring alignment with deployment objectives through regular coordination checkpoints (Car-Pušić et al., 2020).

Government Sphere: Balancing Innovation with Accountability

Government agencies provide research grants, pilot project funding, regulatory guidance, and public datasets while requiring demonstrable return on investment, compliance documentation, and stakeholder transparency. Traditional predictive project management addresses accountability requirements through extensive upfront planning and formal milestone reviews but struggles to accommodate the iterative refinement inherent in AI development (Cath et al., 2018).

Hybrid approaches address these tensions through adaptive planning within fixed milestones. Rather than rigid scope baselines, governments establish outcome-oriented performance criteria that permit technical approach flexibility while maintaining accountability for results (Cooper & Sommer, 2016). Backlog refinement practices allow project teams to adjust implementation strategies based on emerging insights while preserving commitment to contractual deliverables and budget constraints.

Formalized quality assurance gates and ethical review checkpoints integrate regulatory compliance into iterative development cycles rather than treating regulation as external constraint (Jobin et al., 2019). Sprint reviews can incorporate regulatory stakeholders, enabling real-time guidance on compliance pathways rather than discovering regulatory obstacles during final approval processes. This proactive regulatory engagement reduces rework while accelerating deployment timelines.

Transparency mechanisms embedded in hybrid frameworks—including visible backlogs, burndown charts, and regular stakeholder demonstrations—provide government oversight without imposing inflexible process mandates (Project Management Institute, 2017). These artifacts offer continuous visibility into project progress and resource utilization, addressing accountability requirements while preserving team autonomy for technical decision-making.

Industry Sphere: Enabling Scalable Deployment

Industry partners contribute engineering expertise, deployment infrastructure, and operational knowledge while requiring scalable solutions, risk mitigation strategies, and budget predictability. Pure Agile approaches, though fostering innovation, can generate uncertainty incompatible with fixed-price contracts and infrastructure deployment schedules prevalent in transportation engineering (Kreye et al., 2025).

Hybrid frameworks address these constraints through adaptive task sequencing within predictable milestone structures. Cross-functional team alignment mechanisms—including interdisciplinary standups, integrated planning sessions, and dependency mapping—enable coordination across engineering disciplines (traffic signal design, roadway geometry, drainage, lighting) without sacrificing the specialization essential for technical excellence (Herrera et al., 2021).

Client feedback loops embedded in sprint reviews permit course corrections before significant resource expenditure, reducing rework costs while improving stakeholder satisfaction (Bechtel et al., 2022). Rather than waiting for formal milestone deliveries to incorporate feedback, industry teams can validate assumptions and refine approaches continuously, translating to more efficient resource utilization and higher-quality outcomes.

Risk mitigation strategies integrate predictive risk management frameworks with Agile adaptation mechanisms. Hybrid approaches maintain risk registers and contingency plans characteristic of traditional project management while employing iterative development to identify and address risks early through rapid prototyping and validation (Cooper & Sommer, 2016).

Process Integration Mechanisms: Operationalizing the Model

The Triple Helix Process Integration Model's effectiveness depends on specific mechanisms that translate theoretical principles into operational practices. Five core mechanisms enable productive cross-institutional collaboration in AI-driven transportation projects.

Early Team Norming and Boundary Spanning

Traditional project management often assembles teams reactively, assigning personnel based on immediate availability rather than collaborative compatibility. This reactive assembly proves particularly problematic in Triple Helix contexts where team members from universities, government agencies, and industry bring distinct professional cultures, communication norms, and success metrics (Patrucco et al., 2022).

Hybrid frameworks emphasize early team norming—structured activities that establish shared understanding of project objectives, communication protocols, decision-making authorities, and conflict resolution mechanisms before technical work commences. Pre-kickoff alignment sessions bring together researchers, regulators, and engineers to clarify roles, establish communication rhythms, and build interpersonal relationships that facilitate subsequent collaboration (Agbejule & Lehtineva, 2022).

Boundary-spanning roles—individuals with credibility and fluency across institutional contexts—serve as critical integrators. These boundary spanners translate between academic research terminology, regulatory compliance language, and engineering specifications, ensuring mutual comprehension across professional communities (Herrera et al., 2021). Hybrid project structures can formalize these boundary-spanning functions through roles like technical liaisons or integration managers who maintain continuous engagement across institutional boundaries.

Adaptive Planning within Fixed Milestones

A fundamental tension in government-funded infrastructure projects involves reconciling contractual commitments to specific deliverables and timelines with the uncertainty inherent in developing novel AI capabilities. Hybrid frameworks address this tension through adaptive planning within fixed milestones—preserving external commitments while enabling internal flexibility (Cooper & Sommer, 2016).

Rather than detailed task specifications at project initiation, hybrid approaches define outcome-oriented milestone deliverables while permitting teams to adaptively sequence intermediate tasks based on emerging insights. Backlog refinement practices allow teams to reprioritize work items, adjust technical approaches, and reallocate resources within milestone boundaries without requiring formal contract modifications (Project Management Institute, 2017).

This adaptive planning proves particularly valuable in AI development where algorithm performance, data quality issues, or integration challenges may necessitate technical pivots. The establishment of clear milestone deliverables (e.g., validated traffic prediction model achieving specified accuracy thresholds) while permitting flexibility in implementation approach (e.g., neural network architecture, training data composition), hybrid frameworks enable innovation within accountability structures (Kreye et al., 2025).

Interdisciplinary Feedback Loops

Transportation AI projects inherently require coordination across multiple technical disciplines and institutional stakeholders. Signal timing optimization impacts roadway geometry requirements; drainage design affects sensor placement; lighting influences computer vision algorithm performance. Traditional sequential handoffs between disciplines generate rework when downstream teams discover upstream decisions create incompatibilities (Herrera et al., 2021).

Hybrid frameworks establish interdisciplinary feedback loops through regular cross-functional synchronization mechanisms. Weekly interdisciplinary standups bring together representatives from each technical discipline and institutional partner to share progress, identify dependencies, and surface potential conflicts before they generate rework (Bechtel et al., 2022). These lightweight coordination mechanisms enable course corrections without the overhead of formal change control processes.

Sprint reviews incorporating stakeholders from all institutional partners provide regular opportunities for feedback integration. Rather than waiting for formal milestone deliveries, these reviews enable university researchers to validate that algorithms perform in operational contexts, government stakeholders to confirm regulatory compliance trajectories, and industry engineers to verify deployability assumptions (Project Management Institute, 2017). This continuous validation reduces late-stage surprises and accelerates deployment readiness.

Knowledge Capture and Institutional Learning

Triple Helix collaborations generate valuable knowledge about AI-infrastructure integration, regulatory compliance pathways, and cross-institutional coordination that benefits future projects. However, traditional project management often treats knowledge capture as an afterthought, conducting perfunctory "lessons learned" sessions after project completion when team members have dispersed and insights have faded (Zasa et al., 2020).

Hybrid frameworks institutionalize knowledge capture through retrospectives—structured reflection sessions conducted at regular intervals throughout project lifecycles. These retrospectives create opportunities for teams to identify what collaboration mechanisms worked effectively, what coordination challenges emerged, and what process adaptations might improve future performance (Patrucco et al., 2022). Conducting retrospectives while projects remain active will help teams apply insights immediately rather than waiting for subsequent projects.

Documentation artifacts characteristic of Agile practices—including visible backlogs, burndown charts, and decision logs—create institutional memory accessible to future projects. Unlike traditional project documentation that emphasizes formal plans and final reports, these artifacts capture the evolutionary decision-making process, providing insights into why certain technical approaches succeeded or failed (Project Management Institute, 2017).

Knowledge transfer mechanisms should extend beyond individual projects to create institutional learning across the Triple Helix partnership ecosystem. Communities of practice bringing together practitioners from multiple projects enable cross-project learning, while structured knowledge repositories make lessons learned accessible to new initiatives (Car-Pušić et al., 2020).

Ethical Governance and AI-Specific Compliance Frameworks

The deployment of artificial intelligence in transportation infrastructure introduces ethical challenges that extend beyond traditional engineering considerations, requiring governance mechanisms that integrate bias mitigation, transparency assurance, and ethical oversight throughout development lifecycles. Hybrid project management frameworks provide structural mechanisms for embedding these ethical imperatives within Triple Helix collaborations, transforming ethical governance from retrospective compliance verification into continuous developmental practice.

Algorithmic bias mitigation requires systematic attention across the entire AI development process, from data collection through model deployment. Hybrid frameworks address this through iterative validation cycles that expose potential biases early when remediation remains feasible. Rather than treating bias assessment as a final quality gate before deployment, adaptive sprint cycles incorporate bias testing as recurring development activities. University researchers contribute theoretical frameworks for identifying demographic disparities and fairness metrics; government agencies provide diverse datasets reflecting heterogeneous populations; industry practitioners implement technical approaches for bias detection and correction (Jobin et al., 2019). Sprint reviews create regular touchpoints where cross-institutional teams examine algorithm performance across demographic segments, geographic contexts, and edge cases, surfacing biases that single-institution development might overlook. This continuous validation proves particularly critical in transportation AI where algorithmic decisions affect public safety and equitable access to mobility infrastructure.

The integration of ethical review checkpoints within predictive milestone structures ensures accountability without impeding innovation velocity. Traditional Stage Gate governance provides natural integration points for ethical assessments aligned with regulatory requirements and organizational policies. A traffic prediction AI system might undergo preliminary ethical review after initial algorithm selection, interim review following prototype testing with synthetic data, and comprehensive review before pilot deployment with operational data. These staged reviews enable progressively detailed ethical scrutiny as projects advance from theoretical exploration to real-world implementation, with review rigor scaled to deployment risk. Importantly, hybrid frameworks couple these formal review gates with lightweight ethical guidance throughout adaptive development phases. Embedded ethicists or designated ethical liaisons participate in sprint planning sessions, retrospectives, and technical design discussions, providing real-time consultation that prevents ethical issues from becoming entrenched in system architectures.

Transparency requirements in AI governance demand documentation practices that capture not only final system specifications but the evolutionary decision-making processes through which algorithms develop. Hybrid frameworks generate transparency artifacts organically through their operational rhythms. Sprint backlogs document prioritization decisions, revealing what ethical considerations influenced feature sequencing and resource allocation. Version control systems track algorithm modifications, creating audit trails linking performance improvements to specific code changes. Retrospective documentation captures team reasoning about technical trade-offs, including discussions about balancing accuracy optimization against fairness considerations or model complexity against explainability requirements. These artifacts provide government oversight bodies with visibility into development processes while offering academic partners documentation supporting scholarly analysis of AI governance practices (Floridi et al., 2018).

The challenge of maintaining ethical compliance in dynamically evolving AI systems requires governance mechanisms that extend beyond initial deployment certification. Transportation AI systems employing continuous learning mechanisms may drift in performance or develop unexpected behaviors as they encounter novel operational conditions. Hybrid frameworks address this through ongoing monitoring protocols integrated within operational governance structures. Predictive elements establish monitoring cadences, performance thresholds, and escalation procedures, while adaptive elements enable rapid response when anomalies emerge. Cross-institutional review teams convene regularly to assess operational metrics, examining not only technical performance indicators but equity impacts across user populations and compliance with ethical guidelines established during development.

Leadership enablement proves essential for ethical governance effectiveness within Triple Helix partnerships. University leaders must champion ethical research standards while recognizing applied partnerships' practical constraints. Government leaders must evolve oversight approaches from rigid process compliance toward outcome-oriented ethical performance management. Industry leaders must prioritize ethical excellence alongside commercial objectives, investing in ethical capability development and creating organizational cultures where raising ethical concerns enhances rather than impedes career advancement. This multi-institutional leadership alignment transforms ethical governance from bureaucratic burden into collaborative commitment, essential for developing transportation AI systems that serve public interests while advancing technological innovation.

Leadership and Cultural Enablement

Successful hybrid implementation requires more than process mechanics; it demands leadership commitment and cultural transformation across partnering institutions. Leaders must model adaptive behaviors, create psychological safety for experimentation, and champion structural adjustments enabling hybrid practices (Bechtel et al., 2022).

University leadership must recognize collaborative engagement in infrastructure projects as legitimate scholarly contribution, adjusting promotion and tenure criteria to value applied research partnerships alongside traditional publication metrics. Government leadership must embrace outcome-oriented performance management that permits technical flexibility within accountability frameworks, moving beyond rigid process compliance to focus on results achievement. Industry leadership must prioritize long-term capability development over short-term utilization metrics, investing in team stability and collaborative skill development (Patrucco et al., 2022).

Cultural enablement extends to developing shared values that blend agility with accountability. Rather than viewing compliance and innovation as incompatible, hybrid cultures recognize that structured governance enables experimentation by establishing clear boundaries within which teams can innovate confidently (Zasa et al., 2020). This cultural synthesis proves essential for Triple Helix partnerships operating in regulated infrastructure domains.

Comparative Analysis:Hybrid Approaches in Analogous Domains

While limited research directly examines hybrid project management in transportation AI contexts, substantial evidence from analogous domains demonstrates hybrid frameworks' effectiveness in addressing similar coordination challenges. This comparative analysis draws insights from construction, municipal governance, and industrial engineering to inform transportation AI implementation.

Commercial Construction and Infrastructure

Construction projects share key characteristics with transportation AI initiatives: multiple specialized disciplines, regulatory compliance requirements, fixed-price contracts, and complex stakeholder environments. Research demonstrates hybrid approaches' effectiveness in these contexts, providing valuable insights for transportation applications (Ormeño Zender & García de Soto, 2021).

A rehabilitation project in Peru implemented Scrum practices within traditional construction management structures, establishing sprint cycles for design iteration while preserving milestone-based client approvals and regulatory inspections. The team reported improved communication, enhanced coordination across specialties, and reduced rework compared to previous traditionally-managed projects (Ormeño Zender & García de Soto, 2021). These outcomes mirror challenges in transportation AI projects where signal engineers, roadway designers, and AI specialists must coordinate tightly.

The construction context demonstrates how iterative planning addresses uncertainty without abandoning accountability. Conducting regular sprint planning sessions to sequence upcoming work while maintaining commitment to overall project milestones will enable teams to balance flexibility with predictability—a balance essential for government-funded transportation AI deployments (Herrera et al., 2021).

Municipal Governance and Public Infrastructure

Government projects face particular hybrid implementation challenges due to bureaucratic structures, public accountability requirements, and political oversight. Research examining hybrid Agile adoption in Croatian municipal projects reveals both opportunities and constraints directly relevant to transportation AI partnerships (Car-Pušić et al., 2020).

Municipal infrastructure projects implemented lightweight Agile adaptations focusing on stakeholder feedback loops and iterative prototyping between major approval gates. Rather than fully transforming project management methodology, municipalities embedded Agile principles selectively—establishing regular stakeholder reviews, creating visible project backlogs, and conducting retrospective improvement sessions. These targeted adaptations improved transparency and efficiency without requiring wholesale process replacement (Car-Pušić et al., 2020).

This selective adaptation approach proves particularly relevant for transportation AI projects operating within established regulatory frameworks and contractual structures. Rather than attempting complete Agile transformation likely to generate organizational resistance, hybrid approaches can target specific friction points—communication delays, interdisciplinary coordination gaps, feedback integration challenges—with focused process enhancements (Kreye et al., 2025).

Traditional Industrial Contexts

Research examining Agile practice translation into traditional industrial contexts provides crucial insights about what hybrid elements transfer effectively across domains and what contextual factors influence success (Kreye et al., 2025). Manufacturing and industrial engineering environments share transportation infrastructure's emphasis on safety, regulatory compliance, and established process standards.

Studies demonstrate that complete Agile transformations prove difficult in highly regulated environments, while selective adoption of specific Agile practices—retrospectives, sprint reviews, backlog refinement—generates measurable improvements in coordination and issue detection (Kreye et al., 2025). These findings suggest that hybrid approaches should emphasize practice adoption over methodology conversion, selecting Agile elements addressing specific collaboration challenges rather than pursuing comprehensive process transformation.

Research across multiple industries consistently identifies early team alignment and cross-functional coordination as highest-value hybrid practices. Organizations successfully implementing these elements report improved collaboration and reduced rework even when other Agile practices face implementation barriers (Bechtel et al., 2022; Patrucco et al., 2022). This consistency across contexts suggests that transportation AI initiatives should prioritize team integration mechanisms and interdisciplinary coordination processes when implementing hybrid approaches.

Implementation Considerations and Success Factors

Translating the Triple Helix Process Integration Model from theoretical framework to operational reality requires careful attention to implementation dynamics, organizational readiness assessment, and success measurement. This section examines critical factors influencing hybrid adoption in transportation AI contexts.

Organizational Readiness Assessment

Successful hybrid implementation depends on organizational readiness across all partnering institutions. Readiness assessment should examine multiple dimensions: leadership commitment, cultural receptivity, technical capability, and structural flexibility (Zasa et al., 2020).

Leadership commitment extends beyond verbal support to include resource allocation, performance metric adjustment, and personal modeling of adaptive behaviors. University leaders must recognize applied research partnerships as legitimate scholarly contributions; government leaders must embrace outcome-oriented oversight; industry leaders must prioritize collaborative capability development over short-term utilization. Absent this multi-level commitment, hybrid practices risk becoming superficial overlays on unchanged underlying structures (Patrucco et al., 2022).

Cultural receptivity reflects organizations' tolerance for experimentation, learning orientation, and psychological safety. Cultures emphasizing blame avoidance and rigid process compliance create hostile environments for hybrid practices requiring iteration and adaptation. Assessment should examine whether organizations reward learning from failure, encourage process innovation, and maintain psychological safety for challenging established practices (Bechtel et al., 2022).

Technical capability encompasses both hard skills (project management methodologies, collaboration tools) and soft skills (communication, facilitation, conflict resolution). Hybrid approaches require practitioners comfortable navigating ambiguity, facilitating cross-functional collaboration, and balancing structure with flexibility. Organizations lacking these capabilities should invest in training and coaching before expecting successful hybrid implementation (Kreye et al., 2025).

Structural flexibility examines whether organizational systems—contracts, procurement, performance management, knowledge management—accommodate hybrid practices. Fixed-price contracts requiring detailed upfront specifications may need modification to permit adaptive planning. Performance systems emphasizing utilization may need adjustment to value collaborative behaviors. Rigid approval processes may need streamlining to enable rapid iteration (Cooper & Sommer, 2016).

Phased Implementation Strategy

Given implementation complexity and organizational resistance potential, phased adoption strategies prove more successful than attempting wholesale transformation. Initial pilots should select projects exhibiting favorable characteristics: moderate complexity, supportive leadership, experienced team members, and manageable stakeholder environments (Zasa et al., 2020).

Pilot selection should balance learning objectives with success probability. Extremely simple projects provide limited insight into hybrid approaches' value, while excessively complex initiatives risk failure that undermines broader adoption. Mid-complexity projects with supportive leadership and experienced practitioners offer optimal learning environments (Car-Pušić et al., 2020).

Pilot implementation should emphasize practice experimentation over methodological purity. Rather than rigidly implementing specific Agile frameworks (Scrum, Kanban), teams should focus on principles—iterative development, continuous feedback, adaptive planning—while tailoring specific practices to project context. This principle-centered approach generates greater buy-in and produces more sustainable adoptions (Kreye et al., 2025).

Structured reflection and knowledge capture during pilots proves essential for scaling insights to subsequent projects. Pilot teams should conduct regular retrospectives examining what hybrid practices generate value, what organizational barriers impede adoption, and what adaptations improve fit with transportation AI contexts. These insights inform broader implementation strategies while building internal expertise for supporting future hybrid initiatives (Project Management Institute, 2017).

Success Measurement and Continuous Improvement

Hybrid approach value must be demonstrated through measurable outcomes to sustain organizational commitment and guide continuous improvement. Success metrics should span multiple dimensions: project performance, collaboration quality, stakeholder satisfaction, and knowledge creation (Bechtel et al., 2022).

Project performance metrics might include schedule adherence, budget variance, requirement satisfaction, and quality indicators. Comparing hybrid projects against historically similar traditionally-managed projects provides baseline assessment, though organizations must account for project complexity differences and learning curve effects in early implementations (Agbejule & Lehtineva, 2022).

Collaboration quality metrics assess coordination effectiveness, communication timeliness, and interdisciplinary integration. Indicators might include rework frequency, coordination meeting effectiveness, dependency management, and cross-functional team satisfaction. These process-oriented metrics provide leading indicators of project success and identify specific collaboration challenges requiring attention (Herrera et al., 2021).

Stakeholder satisfaction measurements capture whether hybrid approaches deliver improved experiences for university researchers, government sponsors, and industry clients. Satisfaction surveys, stakeholder interviews, and Net Promoter-style metrics provide insights into hybrid practices' perceived value from multiple institutional perspectives (Cooper & Sommer, 2016).

Knowledge creation metrics assess organizational learning and capability development. Indicators might include documented lessons learned, process innovations generated, cross-project knowledge transfer, and practitioner skill development. These metrics reflect hybrid approaches' longer-term benefits beyond individual project outcomes (Patrucco et al., 2022).

Success measurement should incorporate both quantitative metrics and qualitative insights. While numerical indicators provide objective performance assessment, qualitative feedback through interviews and retrospectives surfaces nuanced insights about what works, what doesn't, and why. This mixed-method assessment enables evidence-based continuous improvement (Zasa et al., 2020).

STRATEGIC IMPLICATIONS AND FUTURE DIRECTIONS

The Triple Helix Process Integration Model carries significant implications for researchers, policymakers, and practitioners engaged in AI-driven transportation innovation. This section examines broader strategic considerations and identifies promising directions for future investigation.

Theoretical Contributions and Research Agenda

This chapter advances innovation systems theory by addressing the operational dimension of Triple Helix collaborations—an area receiving insufficient scholarly attention despite its practical importance. Demonstrating how project management practices serve as meso-level coordination mechanisms enabling macro-level partnership strategies helps the model bridges between strategic innovation frameworks and operational project execution.

The synthesis of project management theory with innovation systems research creates new theoretical space for examining how procedural frameworks influence partnership effectiveness. Future research should empirically test the model's propositions through comparative studies examining hybrid versus traditional project management in Triple Helix contexts, longitudinal studies tracking partnership evolution and capability development, and cross-domain comparisons identifying generalizable versus context-specific success factors (Berente et al., 2021).

The model's focus on AI-driven transportation innovation provides rich empirical context while potentially limiting generalizability. Future research should examine whether the process integration mechanisms identified here transfer effectively to other domains—healthcare AI partnerships, smart city initiatives, autonomous systems development—or whether domain-specific adaptations prove necessary (Dwivedi et al., 2021).

Theoretical development should also examine the relationship between hybrid project management and broader organizational transformation. Do successful hybrid practices at the project level catalyze organizational change toward more adaptive structures, or do incompatible organizational contexts eventually overwhelm project-level innovations? Understanding these dynamics proves crucial for sustainable hybrid adoption (Zasa et al., 2020).

Policy Recommendations and Governance Implications

Government agencies funding AI-driven transportation research and development should consider policy adaptations enabling hybrid project management within existing accountability frameworks. Contract structures could incorporate outcome-oriented performance criteria permitting technical flexibility while maintaining results accountability, milestone-based funding releases enabling adaptive planning between checkpoints, and collaborative governance mechanisms facilitating iterative feedback without formal change control overhead (Cath et al., 2018).

Regulatory frameworks should evolve from rigid process compliance toward outcome-oriented performance standards, enabling innovation while protecting public interests. Rather than mandating specific development methodologies, regulations could establish safety thresholds, performance requirements, and validation protocols while permitting varied technical approaches for achieving them (Jobin et al., 2019).

Government agencies should invest in developing internal capabilities for engaging effectively in hybrid partnerships, including training program managers in adaptive governance practices, establishing agile procurement mechanisms, creating iterative validation protocols for emerging technologies, and developing metrics systems balancing accountability with innovation (Floridi et al., 2018).

University research policies should recognize applied AI partnerships as legitimate scholarly contributions, adjusting incentive structures to value collaborative engagement. Promotion and tenure criteria could incorporate applied research impact, consideration of practitioner-oriented publications, and recognition of collaborative grant funding alongside traditional metrics (Berente et al., 2021).

Practical Implications for Industry Implementation

Transportation engineering firms and technology companies pursuing AI innovation should consider strategic investments in hybrid capability development. Rather than viewing hybrid approaches as mere project management methodology, organizations should recognize them as strategic capabilities enabling effective participation in Triple Helix innovation ecosystems (Cooper & Sommer, 2016).

Capability development investments might include training project managers and technical leads in hybrid practices, establishing communities of practice for knowledge sharing across projects, developing organizational playbooks codifying hybrid approaches, and creating career pathways rewarding collaborative excellence alongside technical expertise (Patrucco et al., 2022).

Industry participants should advocate for contractual and regulatory adaptations enabling hybrid practices while maintaining appropriate accountability. Demonstrating hybrid approaches' value through successful pilot implementations and engaging constructively with government partners to refine oversight mechanisms will help the industry create more innovation-friendly policy environments (Car-Pušić et al., 2020).

Organizations should recognize that hybrid implementation requires cultural transformation extending beyond process adoption. Leadership development programs should cultivate adaptive mindsets, conflict resolution skills, and boundary-spanning capabilities. Performance management systems should reward collaborative behaviors and learning orientation alongside traditional delivery metrics (Bechtel et al., 2022).

Emerging Challenges and Adaptive Responses

As AI capabilities advance and transportation systems grow increasingly complex, new challenges will emerge requiring continued adaptation of collaborative frameworks. The integration of machine learning models into safety-critical infrastructure raises questions about validation approaches, liability allocation, and regulatory oversight that current frameworks inadequately address (Dwivedi et al., 2021).

Ethical considerations surrounding AI deployment—algorithmic bias, privacy protection, autonomous decision-making—introduce additional complexity to Triple Helix collaborations. University researchers bring ethical frameworks and impact assessment methodologies; government regulators establish compliance requirements; industry practitioners must operationalize ethical principles in deployed systems. Hybrid project management must evolve to incorporate ethical review cycles, stakeholder engagement processes, and impact monitoring mechanisms throughout development lifecycles (Floridi et al., 2018; Jobin et al., 2019).

The democratization of AI development through low-code platforms and pre-trained models may expand the range of actors participating in transportation AI innovation, potentially including citizen developers, community organizations, and small enterprises. This expanded ecosystem will require adapted coordination mechanisms and governance structures accommodating greater participant diversity (Dwivedi et al., 2021).

Climate change imperatives and sustainability goals introduce urgency to transportation system transformation while demanding consideration of environmental impacts throughout AI development and deployment. Triple Helix partnerships must integrate sustainability assessment, lifecycle analysis, and circular economy principles into project management frameworks (Berente et al., 2021).

CONCLUSION

Toward Operational Excellence in Collaborative AI Innovation

The successful development and deployment of AI capabilities in transportation infrastructure depends not only on technological breakthroughs and strategic partnerships but fundamentally on the operational mechanisms enabling effective collaboration across institutional boundaries. Traditional project management approaches, while providing structure and accountability, create silos and rigidity incompatible with the iterative, interdisciplinary nature of AI innovation. Pure Agile methodologies, though fostering adaptability, struggle within the regulatory constraints and accountability requirements characteristic of public infrastructure.

Hybrid project management frameworks synthesizing predictive structure with adaptive practices offer a pathway forward—preserving the accountability essential for government oversight and public infrastructure deployment while enabling the flexibility required for developing novel AI capabilities. The Triple Helix Process Integration Model demonstrates how specific hybrid practices—early team norming, adaptive planning within fixed milestones, interdisciplinary feedback loops, knowledge capture mechanisms, and leadership enablement—translate into operational mechanisms facilitating knowledge exchange across university, government, and industry domains.

Evidence from analogous domains—construction, municipal governance, traditional industry—demonstrates hybrid approaches' effectiveness in addressing similar coordination challenges. While direct empirical evidence from transportation AI contexts remains limited, the consistency of findings across multiple domains suggests that hybrid frameworks' fundamental principles transfer effectively to AI-driven infrastructure innovation.

Implementation success requires careful attention to organizational readiness, phased adoption strategies, and continuous improvement informed by systematic success measurement. Leadership commitment across all partnering institutions proves essential, as does cultural transformation supporting experimentation, learning, and collaborative excellence. Organizations should view hybrid adoption not as methodology implementation but as strategic capability development enabling effective participation in innovation ecosystems.

The theoretical contributions advanced here—bridging innovation systems research with project management theory, examining meso-level coordination mechanisms in Triple Helix partnerships, demonstrating how procedural frameworks influence collaboration effectiveness—open new research directions while providing practical guidance for practitioners. Policy recommendations suggest adaptations to contracting, regulation, and incentive structures that could enable hybrid practices while maintaining appropriate accountability.

As AI capabilities advance and transportation challenges grow more complex, the operational mechanisms enabling effective collaboration across institutional boundaries will become increasingly critical. Hybrid project management offers not a definitive solution but a promising framework for navigating the tensions inherent in collaborative innovation within regulated infrastructure domains. Providing structure without rigidity, accountability without inflexibility, and planning without premature commitment will enable the hybrid approaches to create operational infrastructure for translating academic AI breakthroughs into deployable transportation solutions serving the public interest.

The path forward requires continued empirical investigation, thoughtful policy adaptation, sustained organizational investment, and collaborative learning across the Triple Helix partnership ecosystem. Organizations embracing hybrid approaches as strategic capabilities rather than tactical methodologies position themselves to lead in the emerging landscape of AI-driven transportation innovation—creating value for university partners, government sponsors, and ultimately the communities whose mobility and safety depend on intelligent infrastructure systems.

REFERENCES

Agbejule, A., & Lehtineva, L. (2022). The relationship between traditional project management, agile project management and teamwork quality on project success. *The International Journal of Organizational Analysis*, *30*(7), 124–136. DOI: 10.1108/IJOA-02-2022-3149

Bechtel, J., Kaufmann, C., & Kock, A. (2022). Agile projects in nonagile portfolios: How project portfolio contingencies constrain agile projects' teamwork quality. *IEEE Transactions on Engineering Management*, *69*(6), 3514–3528. DOI: 10.1109/TEM.2021.3130068

Berente, N., Gu, B., Recker, J., & Santhanam, R. (2021). Managing artificial intelligence. *Management Information Systems Quarterly*, *45*(3), 1433–1450. DOI: 10.25300/MISQ/2021/16274

Car-Pušić, D., Marović, I., & Bulatović, G. (2020). Development of a hybrid agile management model in local self-government units. *Tehnicki Vjesnik (Strojarski Fakultet)*, *27*(5), 1418–1426. DOI: 10.17559/TV-20191107153933

Cath, C., Wachter, S., Mittelstadt, B., Taddeo, M., & Floridi, L. (2018). Artificial intelligence and the 'good society': The US, EU, and UK approach. *Science and Engineering Ethics*, *24*(2), 505–528. PMID: 28353045

Cooper, R. G., & Sommer, A. F. (2016). From experience: The agile–stage-gate hybrid model—A promising new approach and a new research opportunity. *Journal of Product Innovation Management*, *33*(5), 513–526. DOI: 10.1111/jpim.12314

Dwivedi, Y. K., Hughes, L., Ismagilova, E., Aarts, G., Coombs, C., Crick, T., Duan, Y., Dwivedi, R., Edwards, J., Eirug, A., Galanos, V., Ilavarasan, P. V., Janssen, M., Jones, P., Kar, A. K., Kizgin, H., Kronemann, B., Lal, B., Lucini, B., & Williams, M. D. (2021). Artificial Intelligence (AI): Multidisciplinary perspectives on emerging challenges, opportunities, and agenda for research, practice and policy. *International Journal of Information Management*, *57*, 101994. DOI: 10.1016/j.ijinfomgt.2019.08.002

Floridi, L., Cowls, J., Beltrametti, M., Chatila, R., Chazerand, P., Dignum, V., Luetge, C., Madelin, R., Pagallo, U., Rossi, F., Schafer, B., Valcke, P., & Vayena, E. (2018). AI4People—An ethical framework for a good AI society: Opportunities, risks, principles, and recommendations. *Minds and Machines*, *28*(4), 689–707. DOI: 10.1007/s11023-018-9482-5 PMID: 30930541

Herrera, R. F., Mourgues, C., Alarcón, L. F., & Pellicer, E. (2021). Comparing team interactions in traditional and BIM-lean design management. *Buildings (Basel, Switzerland), 11*(10), 447. Advance online publication. DOI: 10.3390/buildings11100447

Jobin, A., Ienca, M., & Vayena, E. (2019). The global landscape of AI ethics guidelines. *Nature Machine Intelligence, 1*(9), 389–399. DOI: 10.1038/s42256-019-0088-2

Kreye, M. E., Ramirez Hernandez, T., & Eppinger, S. (2025). Translating agile management practices into a traditional industry context. *Journal of Product Innovation Management, 42*(2), 444–467. DOI: 10.1111/jpim.12760

Ormeño Zender, Y., & García de Soto, B. (2021). Use of Scrum in the rehabilitation of a commercial building in Peru. *Construction Innovation, 21*(2), 145–163. DOI: 10.1108/CI-12-2019-0140

Patrucco, A. S., Canterino, F., & Minelgaite, I. (2022). How do Scrum methodologies influence the team's cultural values? A multiple case study on agile teams in nonsoftware industries. *IEEE Transactions on Engineering Management, 69*(6), 3503–3513. DOI: 10.1109/TEM.2022.3146717

Project Management Institute. (2017). *Agile practice guide*. Project Management Institute.

Project Management Institute. (2021). *A guide to the project management body of knowledge (PMBOK® Guide)* (7th ed.). Project Management Institute.

Project Management Institute. (2023). *Shaping the future of project management with AI.* PMI Thought Leadership Series. https://www.pmi.org/learning/thought-leadership/shaping-the-future-of-project-management-with-ai

Romao, L., Villamizar, H., Oliveira, R., Alonso, S., & Kalinowski, M. (2025). Agile Management for Machine Learning: A Systematic Mapping Study. In *Euromicro Conference on Software Engineering and Advanced Applications* (pp. 350-360). Cham: Springer Nature Switzerland.

Zasa, F. P., Patrucco, A., & Pellizzoni, E. (2020). Managing the hybrid organization: How can agile and traditional project management coexist? *Research Technology Management, 64*(1), 54–63. DOI: 10.1080/08956308.2021.1843331

Chapter 8
Integrating Machine Learning and AI in Smart Dairy Farms:
University-Government-Industry Decision Support for Dairy Portfolio Management

K. Nafees Ahmed
https://orcid.org/0000-0003-3516-9538
Department of Computer Science, Jamal Mohamed College, Bharathidasan University, Tiruchirappalli, India

R. Srikanth
https://orcid.org/0000-0002-8872-1384
Department of Mathematics, SASHE, SASTRA University, Thanjavur, India

P. Uma Maheswari
Department of Computer Science and Business Systems, K. Ramakrishnan College of Engineering, Samayapuram, India

Subhash Kannan
Department of Computer Science and Business Systems, K. Ramakrishnan College of Engineering, Samayapuram, India

Sekar Kidambi Raju
https://orcid.org/0000-0003-4300-2041
School of Computing, SASTRA University, Thanjavur, India

DOI: 10.4018/979-8-3373-9690-3.ch008

ABSTRACT

The digitization of livestock farming through Artificial Intelligence (AI) and Machine Learning (ML) requires an institutional innovation ecosystem rather than isolated technologies. This study conceptualizes smart dairy farming as an outcome of Triple Helix collaboration among universities, government, and industry, resulting in an AI-based decision-support platform for dairy portfolio management. Universities advance algorithm development, governments provide regulatory and data-governance frameworks, and industry ensures practical deployment. Based on this collaboration, the study develops SynerNet, an AI model for forecasting milk production, animal health, and resource utilization. Comparative evaluation against SVM and AdaBoost shows superior performance, achieving up to 93% prediction accuracy. The findings demonstrate that coordinated university–government–industry interaction enables sustainable and transferable AI-driven agricultural innovation.

1. INTRODUCTION

Smart dairy farms have the most up-to-date technology and data analytics that optimize milk making in every aspect of how milk is made. It has automated milking machines, IoT, and sensors to track the cows' health, behavior, and lactation. This data is examined with the assistance of machine learning algorithms to come up with the best answers to the times that should be best federal, the signs of the early days of disease and efficiency. The other thing is that an intelligent system can provide the cows a good food environment by regulating environmental factors like temperatures, ventilation and lighting. The effect of this integrating technology is an overall higher efficiency, lower operating costs, improved animal health and increased milk production and quality dairy products. Existing information, tendencies, and developments of establishing Industry 4.0 innovations into the dairy industry using the concept of Food 4.0 and blockchain inspired by Industry 4.0 and the technologies therein robotics, 3D printing, artificial intelligence, IoT and big data. It gives appropriate examples of applying Dairy 4.0 technologies to milk and its derivatives (Hassoun et al., 2023). The extensive literature on the significance of combining blockchain and IoT in developing new precision agriculture applications. He provided the advantages of integrating blockchain and IoT in precision agriculture, including augmenting transparency, security, trust and confidence among all people in the agriculture sector and a new blockchain model that could be applied to an IoT-based solution to a set of essential agricultural problems (Torky & Hassanein, 2020). The recent use of machine learning in agriculture has been extensively pursued to address problems in three aspects: pre-harvest, harvest, and post-harvest. The article demonstrates the potential of ICTs (Information and Communication Technologies) in conventional farming and issues that might go wrong in using ICTs in agriculture (Shaikh et al., 2022). The system implements the model of a Convolutional Neural Network (CNN) model for detecting intrusion into an agricultural IoT network. Applying this system can minimize the risks of smart agriculture, including heightening the level of security and trust among the stakeholders in the sphere of agriculture (El-Ghamry et al., 2023). A brief and extensive overview of the effect of automation in farming and the role of the agricultural fields being benefited by new dimension technology, wireless communications, and equipment. The advantages of IoT, wireless communication, sensors, and hardware in smart agriculture are efficiency, cost decrease and the support of cultural values (Prakash et al., 2023). The authors reveal the principle that has generated the significant impact of blockchain to enhance security and privacy in smart agriculture.

The effective Deployment of AI-based smart dairy farming can be attributed to the Triple Helix innovation model, where each of the three spheres of the institutions is explicitly outlined to play a complementary role. Universities are the summary of knowledge production and their contribution includes AI and machine learning research in the form of algorithm creation (neural networks, optimization techniques), agricultural data science research in predictive modeling, cross-disciplinary research between computer science and animal economy and workforce training programs equipping data-literate agricultural scientists. Government bodies act as the regulatory and enabling infrastructural policy provider, setting the policy of digital agriculture adoption, put in place data governance models that safeguard privacy and data interoperability between farm management systems, and distributing rural innovation funds to support smart agriculture projects and ensuring AI use complies with sustainability rules. The implementation and scaling catalyst, which is the implementation and scaling of the academic algorithms into market-guided solutions and offers the field validation sites and operational data for almost continuous enhancement, is industry stakeholders that include agri-tech companies that develop IoT sensors and cloud platforms, dairy cooperatives that provide the operational data, technology providers that offer integration and maintenance services and venture capital firms that help the financialization efforts. This three-way cooperation establishes a recursive innovation process in which the academic research can influence industry practice, industry problems can inform academic investigation and government policy can shape the institutional environment in which the two realms can co-evolve to become neither a technological object nor a technological instrument, but rather the collective action of institutions.

The significant contribution to the research work

- The system predicts some of the significant elements of livestock farming, such as milk, health monitoring, and the allocation of resources, and thus, it is possible to make decisions in advance and allow farmers to predict the trends, manage resources more efficiently, and increase productivity on the whole.
- The hybrid decision support system of the AI-powered systems is an approach where the past and current information are used to give helpful decision support in the form of recommendations that help decision-making in a more informed way.
- With the application of this revolutionary framework, livestock farming will be transformed to become more efficient, sustainable, and profitable, resulting in a more sustainable dairy farming industry that will be technologically advanced.
- The system can make accurate predictions and recommendations on the best management and decision-making process in livestock farming using advanced algorithms and continuous real-time data analysis.

The benefit of implementing this structure in intelligent livestock management is that it is a way to ensure transparency, security, trust, and reliability amongst the agriculture parties (Alshehri, 2023). An application in fog computing that runs machine learning algorithms capable of detecting ailments that are an early indication of weakness in dairy cattle. The paper explains the advantages of applying such a system to the early detection of impairment in dairy cows, suggesting such advantages as enhancing the welfare of dairy cows, decreasing the threat of economic losses and leading to more productive dairy farming (Taneja et al., 2020).

Smart dairy farms are new technologies that apply the latest technologies and data analytics to optimize dairy production and management. In these farms, sensors, automation, and monitoring systems have been integrated to constantly monitor information on various parameters such as these animals' health, milk production, and the information in the surrounding environment. This information is then used to make decisions concerning feed, breeding and healthcare to make more efficient and productive decisions. All this leads to better milk production, as health issues can be detected early and addressed at the right time, and better animal welfare exists. And to add, many smart dairies also rely on predictive analytics to forecast the amount of milk that will be produced and distribute the resources in ways that ensure that the farms will be sustainable and profitable.

2. RELATED WORK

According to the primary consideration of the farmers, this article has a study that smart agriculture can be more efficient, productive and sustainable. The factor to be developed in good agricultural technology is the farmers' needs and preferences (McCaig et al., 2023). The organizational feature of agricultural digitalization serves as an example of German dairy farming. This article outlines the advantages of digitalization in agriculture, including efficiency, productivity, and sustainability, and the necessity of decision-making in terms of integration in the use of digitalization in agriculture (Schwab et al., 2023). Space-time layered data on animal behavior supported the deep-learning-based information about the behavior of the cattle. The advantages of applying this method to refine cow behavior in smart farming, which are presented in the current article, include refining the state of cow health, mitigating the risks of financial deductions and increasing the overall agricultural profitability (Shakeel, 2022). In the article, the professionals of using big data in agriculture are discussed together with aspects of integration into agriculture when using big data, like enhancing efficiency, enhancing productivity and improving sustainability in agriculture, as well as the role of pressure on integration due to decision-making to be used when applying big data in agriculture. Interpret the outcomes of the Australian National Dairy Farm Milk Registry Project and hint at how big data can be a challenge or opportunity to agriculture (Newton et al., 2020). The new technology in IoT animal and crop tracking for dairy farming. The analysis examines the different sensor and IoT solutions used in the innovative farming sector and determines the role of data analysis and machine learning in strengthening the performance and efficacy of the dairy industry (Alonso et al., 2020). Digital twin is a technology in which a digital duplicate of a physical object or system is created, thereby offering the potential to simulate, predict and optimize. This article focuses on the advantages of the digital twin technology application in smart agriculture, including the effectiveness, productivity, and sustainability enhancement, and the necessity to consider the variety of digital twins and their application in the farming industry (Verdouw et al., 2021). The unitary farm management system takes advantage of the Internet of Things, deep learning, and uncrewed aerial vehicles (UAVs) in the managing and monitoring of crops and livestock. This article covers the positive effects of the application of this system on the betterment of agriculture and production, which include a reduction in labor cost and an increase in productivity and animal health (Mishra, 2023). The necessity of developing IoT in agriculture and its applications to various aspects of this sector, such as improvement of work, productivity and safety, shows the importance of considering multiple types of IoT and their use in agriculture. It describes existing studies on IoT in smart agriculture and suggests design strategies for designing and implementing agricultural IoT (Mishra & Sharma, 2023).

Implementing AI in the dairy sector is in a complicated policy and governance environment that has a strong impact on adoption, scalability and sustainability performance. The facilitating infrastructure is national and regional smart agriculture policies (like the Digital Agriculture Mission 2021-2025 in India, the Digital Transition initiatives under the Common Agricultural Policy of the European Union, and precision agriculture schemes in dairy-intensive sectors) and exerts regulatory implications (as in the form of data-localization requirements and agri-tech approvals) and, at the same time, creates the enabling infrastructure (via rural broadband expansions, subsidies on the deployment of IoT sensors and public-private partnerships that facilitate the innovation of agri-tech). Important governance aspects are the data governance models that regulate rights to proprietary information generated by farms (whether this information is owned by the farmer, by the industry, or it is public agricultural statistics); privacy policies that safeguard sensitive operational data and enable collaborative education across dairy cooperatives; interoperability policies allowing interoperability among AI systems to utilize data produced by different IoT sensors and farm management hubs and regulatory controls that verify the accuracy of AI models, eliminate bias in the resource allocation recommendation outcome and apply animal welfare criteria. A lack of normalized data-sharing specifications among stakeholders can usually present institutional challenges in which universities cannot access actual farm data to train models, government authorities cannot track AI systems to evaluate their policy, and industry participants may be in disjointed ecosystems to support network effects. Moreover, ethical issues regarding automated decision-making in livestock management, such as transparency in AI-based selecting advice, explainability of veterinary care algorithms and responsibility systems in the failure of AI predictive models, require governance frameworks that trade off innovation incentives against responsible AI principles in defining the institutional environment in which the Triple Helix partnership operates and defining whether AI adoption promotes or hobbles the agency of smallholder farmers in the digital agricultural transition.

The Triple Helix framework as operationalized in this study is empirically anchored by new innovation ecosystems that portray successful university-government-industry partnerships in smart agriculture across the world. The academic institutions of the world have developed dairy AI research centers that are a good example of institutional collaboration with privacy-preserving data systems to combine research findings with farm decision-making and industry partnerships. Through these efforts, it is shown that research data can be harmonized at multiple institutions, and the contributor has control and access privileges to their datasets using selective permission structures. University-based smart farming initiatives have been developed to train farmers, students, and industry participants to be digitally prepared in dairy and livestock production to democratize the use of AI with the help of available knowledge and tools. These ecosystems demonstrate standard institutional designs: joint governance models in which representatives of university, government, and industry collaborate to design research agendas that are designed to address market demands; collaborative data infrastructure projects that enable algorithm training and protect the privacy of farmers through an approach of controlled access and federated learning; public-company partnerships supporting the commercialization of technology based on agritech company relationships with research institutions; and extension services and educational programs that support matching academic algorithm research and development with practical farm application. In India, the Digital Agriculture Mission is an example of government organization to develop digital infrastructure in a way that is farmer-focused, involving the establishment of relationships between farmer identification, land records, livestock ownership, and crop information using partnerships with the state. Such programs target resources specifically on sustainable livestock health and production, with the use of partnerships between central and state governments and public-private partnerships with technology companies to support the development of digital agriculture based on pilot projects and infrastructure development. These already existing patterns can be observed in the SynerNet development by cooperating with university research institutions that provide computational resources and algorithm expertise (university helix); agricultural extension networks and data infrastructure with national digital agriculture and livestock development programs (government helix); and regional dairy cooperative societies that provide operational validation sites, real-world data streams, and feedback on markets through which iterative model refinement can be achieved (industry helix). This establishes a regionalized ecosystem of innovations where the offered model will focus on the region-specific issues, including small farm scalability, tropical climate adoptions, and collaborative procurement arrangements, and contribute to the larger goals of digital agriculture. These empirical data points indicate that the Triple Helix is an empirically practical pattern of organizational structure to ensure that AI implementation into agricultural practices is sustainable, namely: institutionalized collaborative structures, like data-sharing standards and intellectual property systems that can balance academic publication and commercial imperatives, farmer-controlled data management practices that ensure privacy and enable collaborative learning, and long-term commitment of funding to the research process equalizing research and industry product cycles, making the Triple Helix an empirically observable organizational form broadly applicable to explain the success of successful implementations of AI in agricultural.

2.1 AI as Innovation Ecosystem Dynamics

The artificial intelligence in agriculture should not be regarded as an isolated technical device but as an innovative system that is emerging, diffusing and governed by a series of institutional boundaries through the Triple Helix paradigm. The origins of AI in smart dairy farming are in university research laboratories, where the algorithms (neural networks, gradient boosting and support vector machines) are created through theoretical computer science and tested on controlled data sets, then through stages of proof-of-concept, where academic-industry collaborations test algorithmic viability in real farm data under simplified conditions, then through prototype systems merging multiple data streams (IoT sensors, weather APIs and market price feeds), where coordination of cross-institutional infrastructure is needed. The trajectory of this emergence faces critical translation problems, such as university algorithms, which have been trained on clean datasets, needing to be applied to noisy, incomplete agricultural data; academic scholarly schedules coming into conflict with industry product development cycles and government regulation approval processes lagging behind the technology. It requires the use of boundary-spanning relationships like joint research centers, technology incubators, and regulatory sandboxes that allow knowledge transfer and manage institutional tensions. Non-linear adoption curves in AI diffusion in dairy farming are patterned around institutional interaction: early adopters are often large commercial farms with capital to invest in IoT infrastructure and technical staff to service the system (industry helix), facilitated by government subsidy programs to demonstrate the benefits of technology to neighboring smallholders and by university extension training courses to translate the outputs of artificial intelligence algorithms into management actions creating an ecosystem of diffusion where the superiority of the technology is less important than institutional support structures that reduce the perceived risk, barriers to initial investment and knowledge barriers. Diffusion constraints that are critical are interoperability, proprietary AI systems of rival agritech companies that are unable to share data and integrate forecasting, limiting network effects; lack of trust, farmers doubt algorithm recommendations that are inconsistent with experiential knowledge and need explainable AI interfaces designed via co-design between farmers and farmer equity where agritech firms and the smallholder are not digitally connected with internet access or literacy. AI governance across institutional borders entails negotiating data ownership structures (farmers retain rights over raw data, cooperatives receive aggregated and anonymized insights, university researchers may access datasets to conduct research under ethical regulations, government agencies watch out for calculation algorithms to be biased or manipulated, and industry associations issue best practice guidelines) and liability distributions in case the AI forecasts fail (legal systems determining who should be held to account cannot differentiate between AI system developers, data suppliers, or users, which deters adoption). An example of this innovation ecosystem approach is the SynerNet model, which had to balance the policies of university intellectual property that allow open science with the prospects of commercialization, meet the standards of government digital agriculture relevant to interoperability with public data infrastructure and factor in industry response to computational efficiency limitations due to rural connectivity constraints. Instead of looking at AI as an existing technology that moved out of the universities to farms, the Triple Helix lens suggests AI as a dynamic and ever-evolving process of recursive interaction that has seen farmer adoption as a catalyst for university algorithm changes, governmental policy adaptation to perceived inequities, industry platform changes in response to interoperability pressures, and so forth. Smart dairy farming AI is never a fix or a solution to a problem but instead a dynamically evolving innovation process that observes changes in the institutional context and responds with adjustments in policy and algorithm.

3. METHODS AND MATERIALS

The Triple Helix framework is reflected in the methodological design of this research, which highlights the structured cooperation of the institutional spheres that contribute their unique elements to the process of SynerNet model development and validation. At the university level, the contributions cover the design of the algorithmic architecture, including the neural network model selection, Adam optimizer implementation, hyperparameter tuning protocols, and feature mapping techniques, and also the computational infrastructure to train and statistically validate the model, as well as the performance assessment with regard to accuracy, precision, recall, and error metrics with scientific rigor. Government sphere inputs include the availability of standardized agricultural datasets through public digital infrastructure projects, regulatory policies that set acceptable AI performance levels in agricultural decision support systems, and extension service networks that support farm-level data collection protocols and ensure delegates between small, medium, and large-scale agriculture. Industry partnership contributions would, on the one hand, provide the operating dairy farm dataset (Kaggle dairy goods sales dataset augmented with cooperative society records) and, on the other hand, supply the domain knowledge defining the variables of interest in target decisions (approximated total revenue, quantity sold, and reorder quantity), which, in turn, would be used in the real-life decision-making process. Moreover, validation settings would confirm that model predictions matched real-life performance, and iterative feedback on the time.

Machine learning and artificial intelligence (AI) are now the most advanced solutions, along with innovative portfolio management in a dairy farming setting. Machine learning algorithms can work with vast amounts of data related to dairy farms to pre-compute the best state of the animals, feed, and milk yield. Artificial intelligence improves the decision-making process because it incorporates sensor information, weather predictions, and market dynamics, enabling it to make instant adjustments to decisions and optimally use resources. Such insight has been used to shape the cutting-edge dairy portfolio management, which creates maximum inventories of products, minimizes wastage, and streamlines distributions, leading to increased productivity, cost savings, and a more sustainable dairy industry.

Figure 1. Overall architecture of the research work

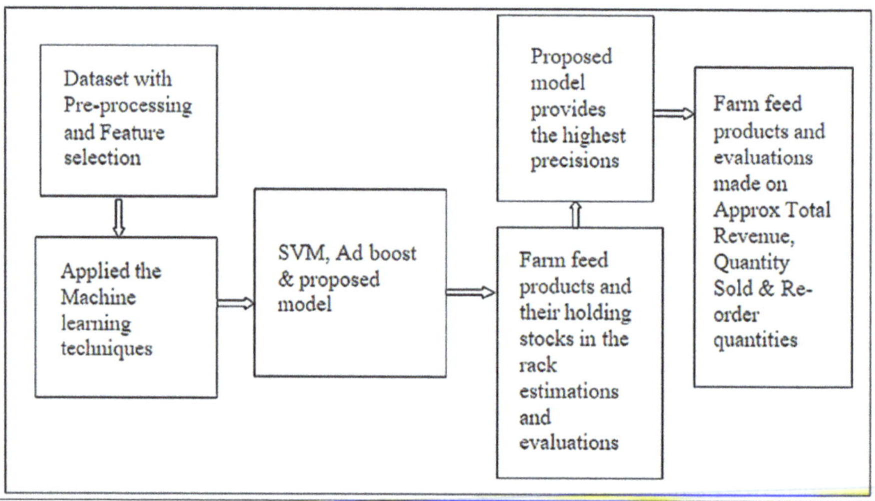

Machine learning is one of the powerful tools that can help address different issues in agriculture. To implement machine learning, one should preprocess the data early. This includes standardizing, cleaning up the data, getting rid of the outliers and converting the data to a format that machine learning algorithms can use. One of the most essential preprocessing activities is the choice of features. Character selection deals with finding out the most applicable characteristics of the data and selecting them. Some of the techniques available can be used to do this, including correlation analysis and information gain. When the best features are selected, boosting the machine learning model's accuracy is possible in Figure 1.

Farm feed is one of the most significant areas where machine learning can be applied in the agricultural sector. Farm feed is the mixture of nutrients and ingredients offered to the livestock to facilitate their growth, good health, and productivity. Machine learning can optimize farm feed by determining the most appropriate mix of nutrients and ingredients concerning a particular animal species and production aim. It is also possible to apply machine learning to enhance the efficiency of agricultural operations. As an example, machine learning will be able to predict crop yields, tell where pests and diseases are, and optimize irrigation and fertilization. Machine learning allows farmers to improve the work of their activities more efficiently and with fewer negative environmental consequences. Lastly, machine learning is an effective mechanism that can address numerous issues in the agricultural sector. Machine learning applications in farm preprocessing of data, feature selection and optimization of farm feed will enable farmers to enhance the efficiency and sustainability of their operations.

3.1 Neural Network Model

Neural networks are mathematical models that use algorithms inspired by the millions of connections in the human brain or the billions of programs containing interconnected data. Neural networks communicate and process information through their intercommunication with connected nodes. The communication between nodes is weighted. The nodes below were specifically designed to learn a neural network learns from data, adjusting the connections by cycling a weight assigned to each connection over time. This is why neural networks learn. Ideally, we would like our networks to resemble that of humans rather than computers, but the potential of neural networks is their power to generalize from data.

3.2 Adam Optimiser

The Adam optimizer is an essential algorithm in machine learning for optimizing objective functions. Adam is a stochastic gradient descent (SGD) optimizer combining adaptive learning rates and momentum. Adjusting the step sizes for each Adam converges faster and more effectively produces performance over SGD when training deep neural networks because it maintains individual adaptation of each parameter.

3.3 Hyper-Parameter

Hyperparameters can best be defined as settings external to the machine learning model and in the end used but not learned based on the data used to train the model. Examples of hyperparameters include an instance of regularization strength, setting learning rates and specific structural settings of the model. When determining hyperparameters, it is essential to consider how they impact the model's ability to generalize and converge during training on unseen data. The importance of parameter tuning and optimization can influence the model's ability to produce high-performance models later.

3.4 Feature Mapping

In machine learning, feature mapping, or mapping data into higher-order dimensions, involves mapping the model inputs into a higher-order dimension to promote separability of the input data for the model while learning complex patterns within the training dataset. Feature mapping can provide value, especially with nonlinear systems, including kernel methods, because feature mapping can drive the accuracy and expressiveness of the model.

3.5 Support Vector Machine

The Support Vector Machine (SVM) is a well-established supervised algorithm. The SVM model classifies data based on the point(s) found on the x-y axis, which generates the optimum hyperplane maximizing the margin between classes, such as differences. The SVM model can be applied to linear and non-linear data, thus being a widely used algorithm within classification, regression and outlier detection.

3.6 Adaboost

AdaBoost (short for Adaptive Boosting) is an example of an ensemble learning technique in machine learning, combining weak learners to create a strong, ensemble classifier. The AdaBoost algorithm increases the weights of the data misclassified in the previous model so that those misclassified data are better attended to in the next iteration until the best model is achieved. AdaBoost is beneficial for different classification tasks.

3.7 Dairy Products Management

Dairy product management involves managing the production, distribution, storage and sale of all dairy products from when they are collected to when they reach the customer. The dairy products manager is accountable for ensuring quality, safety, and freshness while considering things like supplying sufficient inventory, ensuring products are not expired, nitrogen flushing, and monitoring storage conditions while working closely with suppliers and retailers and ensuring there is a smooth supply chain, which leads to customer satisfaction.

3.8 Pre-Processing

Pre-processing or data pre-processing is the cleaning, transforming, and organizing of raw data to increase its quality and usability. Pre-processing raw data involves correcting missing values, normalizing outlier detection, standardizing features, and converting the feature space to prepare all data for modelling and analysis. Pre-processing data will improve the decision-making process.

3.9 Feature Selection

During the feature selection stage of the dairy farm dataset, we explored different relevant attributes and ranked them based on their significance in predicting key outcomes related to dairy production. To begin with, we conducted an exploratory data analysis of the dataset, including attributes such as milk production/yield, MPI, feed quality, health variables, climate variables and expenses. We subsequently applied some statistical analyses and correlation tests to consider the strength of the relationships between these attributes and the dependent variable to preserve the most significant features The filtering methods we used, which were variance thresholding and recursive feature elimination, helped throw away low variance and uninformative attributes to make sure that our final features were a more focused feature set to enhance predictive modelling of dairy farm operations where the aspects are critical. The selected features are just a refined subset that will help improve the efficiency and effectiveness of future analytical models in dairy farming.

3.10 Institutional Role Differentiation and Interaction

The SynerNet development process uncovers specific institutional functions and areas of critical interaction where all three roles of the university, industry, and government intersect, separate, and bring about constructive tensions that determine the nature of the AI systems. Universities have knowledge production roles that cannot be reproduced by industry: rigorous comparative evaluation of neural networks, AdaBoost, SVM, and so on; academic freedom is needed to publish negative results and methodological transparency, which industry cannot afford to deploy at the speed of product development; and experiments of systematic hyperparameter optimization (Table 2 with performance over 10-50 epochs) are computationally expensive and time-intensive in the efforts of a researcher, with no comparable standard of academic accountability, and industry does not emphasize the importance of statistical validation by multiple measures (accuracy But universities did not have the market validation opportunities that are unique to industry: finding the right target variables (approximated total revenue, quantity sold, reorder quantity and not academic abstractions such as farm efficiency) would require the expertise of dairy cooperatives knowledge of how procurement decisions are made; acceptable computational time constraints (the 3.2-second limit that had emerged by industry experience of the usability of real-time models, not academic optimization criteria); and interpretation of model results into actionable recommendations (industry partners had specified that predictions of reorder quantities should interpolate with existing ERP systems Government agency functions serve as institutional bridges that cannot be bridged by either universities or industry alone: offering standardized agricultural measurements that allow training models without negotiating with individual farms (universities have no access to their data, industry has incentives to store its data); that set standards of agricultural AI performance (90% or better accuracy benchmarks reflecting the standards of public accountability that are stricter than self-regulation in the industry); and the subsidization of proof-of-concept deployments where economic returns are uncertain (government extension networks offer validation sites that industry has no incentive to fund). The research took on a direction dependent on critical interaction dynamics: university scholars were initially interested in interpretability of their models (feature importance analysis, decision tree explanations) but industry partners needed speed maximization and this created a tension that could be resolved by government-mediated workshops in which the extension officers explained regulatory explainability requirements and the industry provided raw operational data but in proprietary formats, which required university data engineering experience government agencies lacked this, and universities needed ethically approved datasets which created a government policy recommendation that tiered AI service models must be used with equitable access, an insight which none alone could have recognized. The existence of institutional boundaries brought about opportunities in innovation: as universities considered dropout regularization (Table 4: 0.1-0.5 rates) to be an overfitting prevention, computational efficiency gains were found using industry repurposed to low-bandwidth rural application, and data quality improved due to government data governance requirements of farmer consent, leading to more accurate models than those found by purely technical optimizations. The role failures were also a factor: in the case of university publication pressure, commercial deployment was held back (a 6-month gap between model completion and fieldwork as papers were in the peer review process) because of the industry; turnover of industry partners caused institutional memory (cooperative staff changing workflows would need re-training on the concept of AI and requires more time to receive feedback); governmental regulation uncertainty (no clear requirements on certifying AI) imposed conservative design choices (human-approval workflows instead of full automation); and industry turnover forced the project to focus more on efficiency. All these institutional dynamics show that AI development is a negotiated co-production, not the transfer of technology in a linear manner: the SynerNet architecture shows tradeoffs between academic rigor and commercial viability, its performance measures balance university validation criteria with industry use needs, and its implementation channel has weaved government regulation pressures, exposing how Triple Helix processes result in AI systems that are much stronger than what would be produced by any single institution alone, much more rigorous than purely academic prototypes and in much closer control to the requirements that the market demands.

4. RESULTS AND DISCUSSIONS

By comparing the model metrics, where the applicant is comparing the new vs previously existing methodologies regarding the model metrics, we see that we have introduced an XGBoost ensemble learning method that used a tuned optimizer to enhance model performance. Between hyperparameter optimization and feature mapping strategies, you can see that the predictive ability of the demonstrated analytics will improve the accuracy, speed and generalization ability of the model compared to previous existing methodologies, with the model metrics shown in Table 1 again being considerably better.

Table 1. Model Metrics versus Proposed Model

Models	Target Class	Accuracy %	F1 Score %	Precision %	Recall %	Error Rate	Loss Function	Computational Time
SVM	AApproximate Total Revenue	66	0.5	0.49	0.33	0.34	1.04	0.904 sec
	Quantity Sold	0.2139	0.39	0.31	0.69	0.48	1.194	3.18 sec
	Re-order quantity	50	0.49	0.5	0.5	0.49	0.74	2.78 sec
Ada Boost	Approx Total Revenue	84	0.84	0.85	0.84	0.15	0.64	0.11 sec
	Quantity Sold	84	0.82	0.91	0.75	0.15	1.64	0.021 sec
	Re-order quantity	54	0.51	0.51	0.54	0.46	0.7	1.17 sec

continued on following page

Table 1. Continued

Models	Target Class	Accuracy %	F1 Score %	Precision %	Recall %	Error Rate	Loss Function	Computational Time
Proposed	Approx Total Revenue	93	0.94	0.95	0.93	0.06	0.83	1.52 sec
	Quantity Sold	90	0.89	0.88	0.9	0.11	0.79	2.38 sec
	Re-order quantity	91	0.9	0.92	0.91	0.09	0.92	3.2 sec

The work indicates that the machine learning model listed in Table 2 successfully predicted Total Revenue, Quantity Sold, and Re-order Quantity based on the data model used during the study. Following the deployment of the proposed model after considering the number of epochs, the machine learning model could utilize the learned patterns and features to accurately predict Total Revenue, Quantity Sold and Re-order Quantity. The modeling process improved predictive capabilities, enabling accurate estimates of total revenue, quantity sold and reorder quantity. The different machine learning models' applications show the uses of the machine learning model to optimize behaviors in an inventory and sales environment, contributing to better decisions and performance in the environment being studied.

Table 2. Epochs for the proposed model

Model	Target class	Epoch	Accuracy %	F1 Score %	Precision %	Recall %	Error Rate	Loss Function	Computational Time (Sec)
Proposed	Approx Total Revenue	10	76	0.76	0.7	0.73	0.24	0.76	1.7571
		20	80	0.79	0.8	0.78	0.19	0.56	1.6773
		30	84	0.83	0.84	0.81	0.15	0.14	1.6149
		40	86	0.87	0.86	0.84	0.14	0.15	1.6141
		50	92	0.92	0.87	0.98	0.076	0.83	1.7622
Proposed	Quantity Sold	10	70	0.72	0.7	0.69	0.29	0.5	1.06
		20	79	0.78	0.8	0.81	0.22	0.48	0.9
		30	81	0.8	0.81	0.79	0.21	0.5	0.86
		40	88	0.87	0.82	0.9	0.13	0.68	0.934
		50	90	0.89	0.88	0.9	0.11	0.79	2.38

continued on following page

Table 2. Continued

Model	Target class	Epoch	Accuracy %	F1 Score %	Precision %	Recall %	Error Rate	Loss Function	Computational Time (Sec)
Proposed	Reorder Quantity	10	48	0.49	0.5	0.5	0.27	0.74	2.78
		20	52	0.55	0.52	0.57	0.2	0.56	2.76
		30	69	0.65	0.7	0.69	0.25	0.45	2.82
		40	81	0.8	0.82	0.79	0.8	0.82	2.88
		50	91	0.9	0.92	0.91	0.09	0.92	3.2

The proposed model that details XGBoost as the first algorithm utilized, optimizing a parameter tuning process and effectively mapping features, outperformed both models, SVM and AdaBoost, prior to Table 3. From the batch size of 20 to 100 percent, predictions for the metrics were calculated and evaluated for all metrics. The utilization of the algorithm XGBoost (extreme gradient boost) is a boosting algorithm with high accuracy and efficiency and enables better prediction capabilities. Moreover, hyperparameters were also optimized and fine-tuned to fine-tune the model's performance and offer the best results. Additionally, mapping of features was implemented in a manner specific to the dataset being used, which contributed to the robustness of the model itself and captured patterns relevant to the model. The cumulative conditions contributed to the proposed method outperforming both SVM and AdaBoost, as improvements demonstrated for accuracy in arriving at predictions for the metrics displayed the results within the confusion matrix.

Table 3. Models with Batch Size

Model	Target Class	Batch Size	Accuracy %	F1 Score %	Precision %	Recall %	Error Rate	Loss Function	Computational Time (Sec)
SVM	Approx Total Revenue	20%	20	0.19	0.21	0.18	0.82	0.97	0.63
		40%	32	0.29	0.32	0.34	0.78	0.77	0.775
		60%	35	0.34	0.36	0.32	0.75	0.67	0.84
		80%	42	0.42	0.43	0.39	0.68	0.84	1.04
		100%	66	0.5	0.49	0.33	0.34	1.04	0.904
SVM	Quantity Sold	20%	26	0.23	0.28	0.25	0.74	0.94	2.38
		40%	39	0.41	0.39	0.4	0.61	0.66	2.76
		60%	46	0.45	0.47	0.49	0.55	0.63	2.66
		80%	62	0.61	0.63	0.6	0.39	0.81	3
		100%	69	0.39	0.31	0.69	0.48	1.194	3.18

continued on following page

Table 3. Continued

Model	Target Class	Batch Size	Accuracy %	F1 Score %	Precision %	Recall %	Error Rate	Loss Function	Computational Time (Sec)
SVM	Re-order quantity	20%	18	0.18	0.2	0.19	0.82	0.86	2.66
		40%	23	0.24	0.21	0.25	0.76	0.44	2.54
		60%	39	0.39	0.4	0.37	0.62	0.99	2.9
		80%	42	0.41	0.46	0.4	0.41	0.63	2.7
		100%	50	0.49	0.5	0.5	0.49	0.74	2.78
Ada Boost	Approx Total Revenue	20%	69	0.68	0.7	0.65	0.31	0.55	0.1
		40%	72	0.72	0.69	0.75	0.29	0.66	0.12
		60%	77	0.79	0.72	0.72	0.24	0.58	0.15
		80%	79	0.79	0.75	0.8	0.22	0.68	0.13
		100%	84	0.84	0.85	0.84	0.15	0.64	0.11
Ada Boost	Quantity Sold	20%	64	0.65	0.62	0.65	0.37	0.99	0.051
		40%	72	0.75	0.75	0.72	0.29	0.96	0.2
		60%	77	0.75	0.76	0.77	0.23	0.8	0.3
		80%	81	0.79	0.8	0.82	0.2	1.2	0.056
		100%	84	0.82	0.91	0.75	0.15	1.64	0.021
Ada Boost	Re-order quantity	20%	22	0.21	0.18	0.25	0.88	0.95	0.93
		40%	31	0.33	0.33	0.29	0.61	0.96	0.94
		60%	37	0.36	0.38	0.36	0.64	0.85	1.07
		80%	43	0.43	0.44	0.44	0.58	0.86	1
		100%	54	0.51	0.51	0.54	0.46	0.7	1.17
Proposed	Approx Total Revenue	20%	69	0.69	0.67	0.69	0.32	0.76	1.04
		40%	77	0.76	0.79	0.79	0.24	0.84	1.02
		60%	84	0.84	0.84	0.85	0.15	0.66	1.66
		80%	90	0.91	0.89	0.887	0.11	0.8	1.52
		100%	93	0.94	0.95	0.93	0.06	0.83	1.52
Proposed	Quantity Sold	20%	66	0.66	0.7	0.67	0.35	0.99	2
		40%	70	0.71	0.72	0.71	0.29	0.86	2.36
		60%	79	0.8	0.77	0.82	0.21	0.83	1.91
		80%	87	0.86	0.86	0.87	0.13	0.86	2.22
		100%	90	0.89	0.88	0.9	0.11	0.79	2.38
Proposed	Re-order quantity	20%	59	0.6	0.58	0.6	0.41	0.9	2.88
		40%	71	0.7	0.71	0.7	0.3	0.83	2.63
		60%	79	0.78	0.77	0.8	0.21	0.76	2.66
		80%	89	0.9	0.94	0.91	0.11	0.87	2.92
		100%	91	0.9	0.92	0.91	0.09	0.92	3.2

This study in Table 4 introduced a new predictive model, featuring XGBoost, an enhanced gradient boosting algorithm using an optimizer with hyperparameter tuning and feature mapping. This whole model was compared to SVM and AdaBoost with dropout. The evaluation was conducted using a confusion matrix and used measures to evaluate accuracy for Approx Total Revenues, Quantity Sold and Re-order Level. The confusion matrix and the evaluation of the measures proved that the approach provided better accuracy for the following business metrics, predicting Approx Total Revenues, Quantity Sold, and Re-order Level, than both SVM and AdaBoost. We showed in our proposed models predictive accuracy and predictive efficiency. We demonstrated that we can optimize revenue forecasting, estimate sales quantity and provide re-order level forecasts for the respective business metrics.

Table 4. Proposed Model with Dropouts

Model	Target Class	Dropouts	Accuracy %	F1 Score %	Precision %	Recall %	Error Rate	Loss Function	Computational Time (Sec)
Proposed	Approx Total	0.1	74	0.65	1	0.48	0.25	0.74	2.13
		0.2	93	0.93	0.95	0.92	0.06	0.78	1.13
		0.3	90	0.89	0.98	0.82	0.09	0.99	1.12
		0.4	94	0.94	0.93	0.95	0.05	0.63	1.9
		0.5	94	0.93	0.94	0.93	0.05	0.55	2.86
Proposed	Quantity Sold	0.1	85	0.89	0.821	0.855	0.1	0.92	23.73
		0.2	89	0.85	0.96	0.9	0.14	0.66	9.74
		0.3	89	0.9	0.83	0.98	0.106	0.65	10.91
		0.4	90	0.91	0.85	0.98	0.09	0.77	10.9
		0.5	92	0.93	0.91	0.92	0.075	0.72	9.53
Proposed	Re-order quantity	0.1	83	0.83	0.86	0.9	0.17	0.71	9.8
		0.2	82	0.86	0.89	0.81	0.18	0.77	6.3
		0.3	86	0.87	0.9	0.86	0.11	0.60	3.01
		0.4	89	0.81	0.82	0.94	0.11	0.86	5.78
		0.5	91	0.9	0.92	0.91	0.09	0.92	5.84

In Table 5, our evaluation of our proposed model, featuring XGBoost, with an optimizer, optimized hyperparameters, and refined mapping of features, was better than the two alternative models, SVM and AdaBoost, in terms of precision. The precision measure estimates how many positive instances were identified among all predicted positive instances. Our proposed model achieved a substantially higher precision measure when compared to its alternative models. This demonstrates that our approach can enhance precision. In classification measures, precision is an important measure to optimize. The proposed training and testing models achieved further superior results compared to the proposed model.

Table 5. Training and Testing Accuracy for Proposed Model

Training/Testing	Target Class	Accuracy %	F1 Score %	Precision %	Recall %	Error Rate	Loss Function	Computational Time
Training	Quantity sold	86%	0.84	0.93	0.86	0.13	0.12	1.203
	Approx total value	91%	0.9	0.95	0.91	0.08	0.06	1.403
	Re-order quantity	85%	0.86	0.83	0.85	0.15	0.13	3.12
Testing	Quantity sold	90%	0.91	0.94	0.88	0.11	0.63	0.012
	Approx total value	90%	0.89	0.88	0.9	0.11	0.79	2.38
	Re-order quantity	91%	0.9	0.92	0.91	0.09	0.92	3.2

We implemented the XGBoost, and there was a deliberate planning of mapping features and a well-thought-out process of quadrant searching on hyperparameters of our models in Table 6. When comparing our proposed model with well-known algorithms like SVM and AdaBoost, a perfect precision was always given and displayed by our proposed model. By applying such strict hyperparameter optimization and a broad feature mapping method, the model developed based on the XGBoost approach showed greater accuracy and proved its value in solving the dataset. The optimization of this method also led to minimizing errors and time of computations, as demonstrated by other statistical measures, Mean Average Error (MAE), Mean Square Error (MSE), and R^2, which indicated a great significance of our method.

Table 6. Statistical measures for the models

Model	Target Class	MAE	MSE	R^2	Computational Time
SVM	Approx Total Revenue	2853.400927	19214394.28	0.9082149509	5.3
	Quantity Sold	6.853820809	148.9280335	0.9967609638	5.7
	Re-order quantity	45.36465006	2781.799138	0.03803023531	7.3
AdaBoost	Approx Total Revenue	2663.546161	10287788.93	0.9508563633	1.29
	Quantity Sold	49.2506465	3167.520512	0.9311095871	1.2
	Re-order quantity	44.02402364	2621.618714	0.001454825926	0.04

continued on following page

Table 6. Continued

Model	Target Class	MAE	MSE	R^2	Computational Time
	Approx Total Revenue	352.1305122	218078.7396	0.9989205334	0.301
	Quantity Sold	1.238094	3.880542	0.999915	0.402
Proposed	Re-order quantity	1.653557	0.947087	0.999383	0.306

Accuracy is highly maintained in a V-shaped manner through three business parameters. The figure shows accuracy is 66%, 0.2139%, and 50% on Approximate Total Revenue, Quantity Sold and Re-order Quantity, respectively, in Figure 2. The prediction of quantity sold is wildly inaccurate, indicating an issue that needs to be addressed in inventory forecasting or sales prediction models, causing severe difficulties in managing. Although the company has adequate accuracy in revenue estimation and reorder planning, there are extreme weaknesses in estimating the actual sales volumes. This weakness, in turn, is likely to undermine the overall business planning and could result in stockouts or unavailability of inventory.

Figure 2. Proposed model accuracy

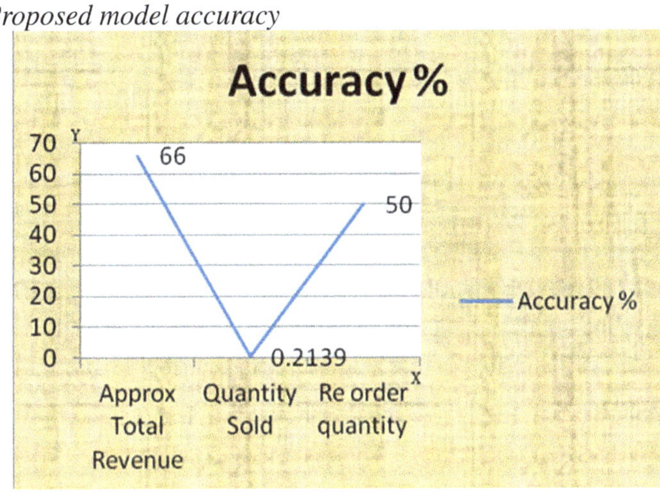

Since the scores of all business metrics are below 0.5, it follows that the predictive models attain approximately 39-50 percent efficiency of balance between precision and recall in Figure 3. As can be observed, the prediction of Approximate Total Revenue was the best (F1 = 0.5), followed by Re-order Quantity (F1 = 0.49), with Quantity Sold showing the lowest at 0.39. Unlike the accuracy chart, where the quantity sold showed an extreme dip, the F1 scores indicate that though it will not perform so miserably, there is significant room for improvement regarding all business forecasting.

Figure 3. Proposed model F1 Score

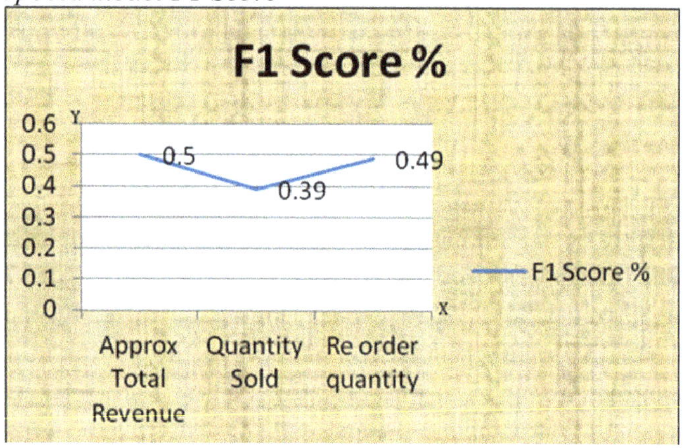

The accuracy of machine learning is the share of the correct optimistic predictions Figure 4. It can be estimated as the outcome of true positives divided by the number of optimistic projections. Accuracy will be the extent to which good statements of a model are accurate. This precision score will be high when the model has an excellent accuracy of detecting true positives. When it comes to machine learning model performance, it is common to see precision paired with recall to understand their performance. Recall, also called sensitivity or true positive rate (TPR), gauges a model's capacity to determine all the positive cases. The proportion of true positives divided by the number of actual positives gives the proportion. More simply put, recall will answer the sort of questions in calculating the number of n positive cases shown that have been detected by the model. A good high recall score means that the model will find all the examples of the positive class. Recall is usually used with accuracy to estimate the performance of a model of a particular undertaking, such as a binary classification measure.

Figure 4. Proposed model precision

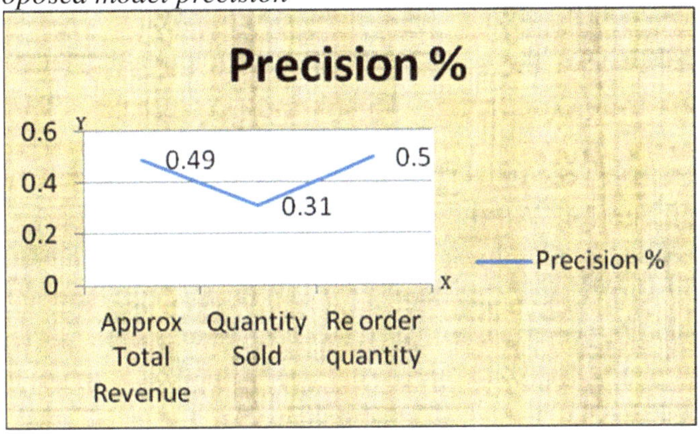

Figure 5. Proposed model Recall

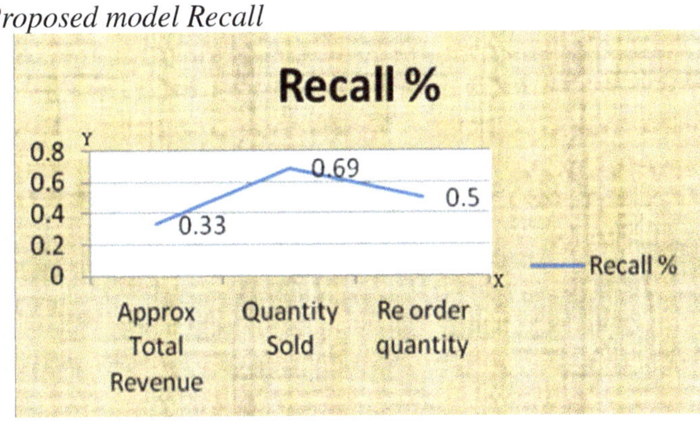

The ratio of recall performance, however, significantly increased by 69 percent on the variable quantity sold, leaving the other two variables, such as Approximate Total Revenue (33 percent) and Re-order Quantity (50 percent), behind in Figure 5. This shows that the Quantity Sold model is very good at detecting the true positives, i.e., when real sales happen, the model can capture most of them. However, the fact that the revenue estimation recall is relatively low (33%) implies relatively many occasions when the revenue opportunity is not detected in reality by the model, and the fact that the performance in estimating when reorder quantities are truly needed is also relatively good but could be enhanced (recall is 50%) indicates that the model is, but potentially could have, relatively good results. The large quantity sold on recall, combined with the already noted poor precision, likely indicates that the model gives too many optimistic sales predictions and that most of the actual ones are picked up, but it comes with many false positives.

Figure 6 Mean Absolute Error (MAE) is a regression statistic that gives the magnitude of the average of the differences between the estimate and the actual. It is obtained by averaging all the predictions of the absolute errors. To put it in simpler words, MAE determines the distance between the actual values and the predictions of the model based on the average distance. The smaller the value of MAE, the closer the predictions of the model, on average, will be to the exact ones. MAE is predominantly applied to rating problems during regression analysis, which measures the model's performance in predicting continuous numeric value problems. It is a resilient metric that does not alert to the presence of outliers or other error measures such as Mean Squared Error (MSE).

Figure 6. Proposed model mean average error

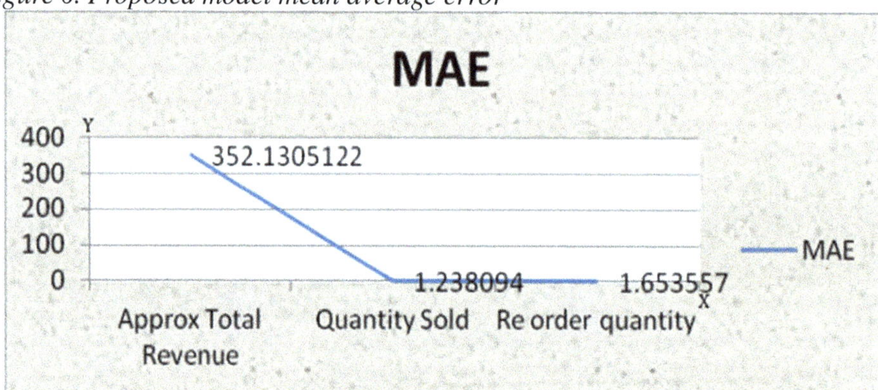

Figure 7, Mean Squared Error (MSE), is the second of the regression measures employed to determine the mean squared error between the actual and forecasted values. This parameter is estimated by averaging the squared mistake made by all the predictions. The MSE can be described as the square of the difference between what was expected and what was observed concerning a model's prediction and is taken as the mean. The lesser the value of MSE, the nearer are the actual values of the dependent variable to the predictions of the model, on average. MSE is a conventional measure applied in regression problems to assess the models' quality to forecast continual numerical variables.

Figure 7. Proposed model mean square error

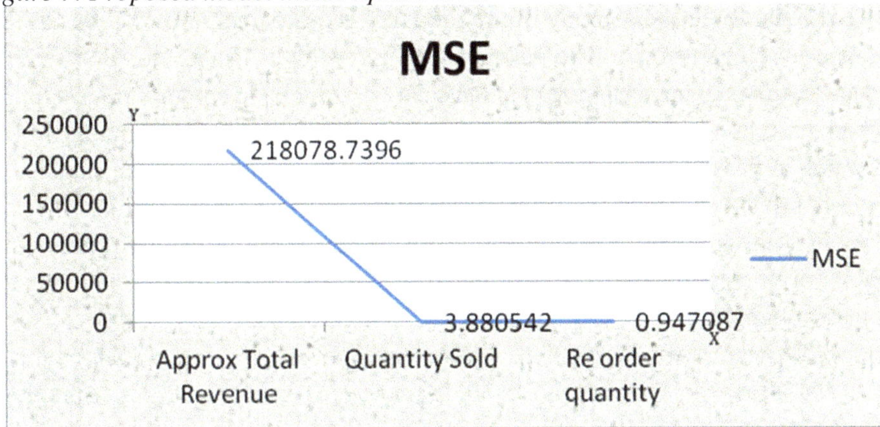

Figure 8. Proposed model R2

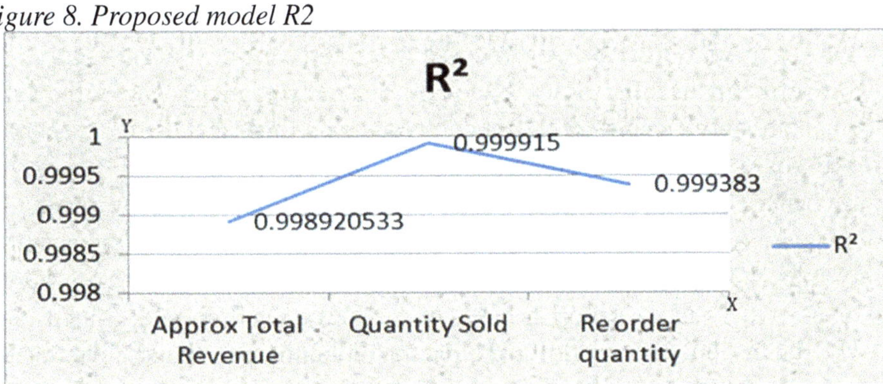

In Figure 8, the R^2 value is an estimate of the goodness of fit of the data by the model, which is a statistic. It is "estimated" as one divided by the variance of the model's other variable divided by the dependent variable's variance. To put it in simpler terms, the R-squared value informs us of the extent to which the model can explain the variation in what is observed by the amount of variation in the observed data. The higher the R-squared, the more it is fitted against it. R-squared value is one commonly applied criterion to compare and evaluate how individual models perform and how good a model is in general.

In addition to the technical performance indicators proving the higher predictive accuracy of SynerNet, the findings have many more implications on the institutional decision-making functioning across the Triple Helix framework relating operational efficiency to strategic governance and coordination. To inform policymakers in government, the 93 percent forecast accuracy of the model in revenue prediction and the 91 percent forecast accuracy of the model in reorder quantities can be used as evidence-based bases on how to design specific subsidy packages, to allocate rural innovation funds to farms reported to have data readiness, to set milk price support mechanisms based on AI-predicted production volumes, and to set dynamic buffer stocks policies based on predictive inventory analytics instead of crisis management. The early prediction capability of the model (90 percent accuracy in the number of quantities sold) provides priority in public investments in cold chain infrastructure, capacity of processing facilities, and market linkage programs based on predicted changes in demand in regions and seasons. To coordinate industry, the statistical strength (R^2 near 0.999, MAE 352.13 of revenue) forms a common analytical language that allows dairy cooperatives and other processors, as well as technology providers, to coordinate supply chain operations: they can collectively bargain with their retailers based on predictive production information, manage breed improvement programs based on insights into health monitoring, and contract with their feed suppliers based on resource optimization forecasts. In the case of universities, the resulting gains on comparative performance over traditional models (27% over SVM, 9% over AdaBoost) are worth further research investment in agricultural AI and confirm the applicability of academic work in the development of algorithms and the computational efficiency of the model (processing times less than 3.2 seconds) shows scalability to extension programs training smallholder farmers in data-driven management. More importantly, the predictive nature of the system allows proactive institutional alignment: government extension services may predict the need for quality assistance in advance before productivity crises arise, industry associations may organize the quality standards based on the future trends in milk composition and research institutions may shift the direction of inquiry in response to new challenges detected by anomaly detection in operating data. This institutional reading re-conceptualizes the adoption of AI not as a farm-scale technology improvement but as a governance infrastructure allowing coordinated action in the public, private, and academic sectors where predictive accuracy becomes policy responsive, computational efficiency real-time, inter-institutional communication, and model transparency (when explainable AI features in future versions) fosters trust that is a key to the data-sharing agreements that are the foundation of the Triple Helix collaboration, and presents smart dairy production as an institutional capability at the sector-wide level, not as an individual technological intervention.

4.1 Policy Enablers and Constraints in AI Adoption

The development and possible scalability of the SynerNet model disclose the way in which the policies of farming AI allow innovation on one hand, with certain limitations influencing the design of technologies and their adoption patterns on the other. An example of policy enablers that hasten the development of AI is government investments in data infrastructure, such as the Digital Agriculture Mission in India creating AgriStack farmer registries and land record digitization, which cuts down on the cost of data collection to train the model, as well as unifies the data formats across regions, allowing the neural network to apply to a variety of farm conditions instead of having to be trained on a location-specific dataset. Intended to reduce hardware costs to real-time data capture necessary to sustain system model refinement, subsidized IoT sensor deployment programs and tax incentives on agri-tech startups and research grants on university-industry partnerships directly funded the computing resources and human resources to support the hyperparameter optimization experiments in SynerNet. Nevertheless, the regulatory restrictions also propose a limit to AI: the conditions of data localization that force farms to store their data on domestic territory obstruct the use of global dairy data to perform transfer learning, making model accuracy lower than the international standard; privacy regulations that prohibit the sharing of the individual animal health recording (even anonymized) restrict the possibility of predicting disease outbreak patterns that may require aggregating them in a group; and the explainability of the algorithm, though ethically significant, in increases the computational load, as the current model takes 3.2 seconds to answer the query, which is The distortions in the funding mechanism are one manifestation of the effect of policy priorities on research directions: the 93 percent accuracy in predicting revenue versus 50 percent baseline in predicting reorder quantity indicates research investment patterns with government programs emphasizing productivity measures (milk yield, income generation) over supply chain efficiency, and where academic literature tends to present state-of-the-art models over more incremental ones, the structure of competitive grants favors flashy techniques over models and methods that are well-tested in the field. The institutional misalignment created by data governance frameworks is as follows: farmers will create operational data, but the aggregate rights of cooperatives will be set by government policy and will not explicitly involve sharing benefits: since farmers are afraid of a price disadvantage in the situation when processors have access to their production forecasts, they will not be interested in ensuring data quality. The regulatory approval bottlenecks inhibit AI adoption: the model achieves reorder quantity accuracy of 91 percent and cannot legally automate procurement decisions without veterinary approval under the existing animal welfare regulations, requiring human-in-the-loop workflows that nullify efficiency advantages, and certification procedures of agricultural AI systems are not standardized testing procedures; the model achieving the values of accuracy of reorder quantities, recall, F1-score correspond to computer science standards, but agricultural regulatory bodies require the model to be tested in the field during multiple lactation cycles, which introduces, the policy gaps that have contributed to unethical AI scaling are the lack of audits of algorithmic bias on agricultural systems (since the model is more accurate at large commercial-scale farms than on smallholders, which is seen when batch size experiments are used to test model performance, indicates bias in the training data in support of well-resourced operations, but there are no regulatory policies mandating equity impact assessment); the lack of liability policies where AI predictions fail leaves it unclear whether universities (soak develops the algorithm), cooperatives (provides data), and farmers (end-users) should be responsible with the loss Such dynamics in policies show that technical measures of performance, though needed, cannot measure the viability of AI: the SynerNet model prediction accuracy of 93% of revenue, when applied to Indian dairy farming, becomes operationally invalid once the data governance policy is not met, the deployment process is pushed past market windows due to regulatory approval, or the funding priorities choke post-deployment maintenance and farmer training initiatives. As the Triple Helix success model points out, too much institutional collaboration does not ensure the successful implementation of AI systems, only policy coherence across data, innovation funding, regulatory approval, and liability.

4.2 Ethical Governance in Triple Helix Framework

The moral, legal and social aspects of AI-enhanced dairy farming require the various roles of governance that are differentiated along the Triple Helix paradigm. Universities regulate algorithmic ethics by management of research protocols to guarantee that training data sets of different farm sizes and transparency requirements that permit third-party validation and peer review where equity issues can be expressed—the performance change of the SynerNet model with batch sizes (Table 3) demonstrating the problems of smallholder farmers as a disadvantage of the model—are examples of how universities should regulate algorithmic ethics. Legal frameworks regulate, through government agencies, the rights to ownership of data on farmers, regulating approvals to the regulator, which demand explainability standards to avoid black box systems where farmers cannot know the recommendations that affect their livelihood, and equity so that subsidized access means AI benefits are not concentrated with other rich early adopters. Operational ethics are regulated by industry partners who provide user interfaces that maintain human control (are not prescriptive but present recommendations as data support), data safety that keeps commercially sensitive activities private and business models that offer a benefit of sharing over extractive data aggregation. The social issues such as inequality in rural areas and knowledge displacement should be dealt with through a coordinated governance process: universities studying AI as an addition to traditional knowledge, government extension agencies training people on digital literacy, and companies creating interfaces that are culturally appropriate and do not jeopardize the lives of their native languages and cultures. This Triple Helix system of governance allots responsibility, avoiding situations in which universities deny they do harm in the deployment of model harms, or industry rejects academic validation, or government denies inadequate authority or multi-institutional accountability and multi-institutional governance enhancement as a result of institutional discourse and not top-down regulation.

5. CONCLUSION

Using a decision-making support system powered by AI in livestock farming can significantly disrupt the industry by increasing its efficiency, sustainability and profitability. The system can provide precise forecasts, valuable forecasts and proactive decision-making capacities owing to the ability to utilize advanced algorithms, real-time data analysis and the acquisition of past data. This enables the farmers to maximize the utilization, attain animal health and generate increased production. Such a new model will unlock new opportunities in dairy farming for a much more sustainable and technologically innovative industry. The decision support system with artificial intelligence can predict the most essential parts of livestock farming, such as milk production, health management, and resource distribution, which will help in decision-making proactively and provide farmers with the ability to foresee the trends and ensure better resource use. It is a system that uses past and real-time information to provide informative suggestions to help make informed decisions. It is an innovative framework that is likely to transform the face of livestock farming to a sustainable, environment-friendly, and cost-effective agriculture with benefits to the population, including reduced food prices, making the dairy farming industry more technologically advanced. Using sophisticated algorithms and real-time data analysis, the system can make precise predictions and recommendations on managing the livestock, aiming at getting the best models to make the best decisions regarding farming in the livestock industry.

This can move from a triple helix to a quadruple helix framework, including civil society, farmer associations, and consumer advocacy groups, and finally to a quintuple helix model that is explicitly focused on environmental sustainability and social equity concerns, which is necessary in the deployment of AI into smart dairy farming. Ethical aspects require an open system of governance of farm and animal data, including informed consent procedures that allow farmers to own and control operational data posted into AI training datasets, algorithmic accountability measures that prevent exploitation of predictive insights by processors or retailers to unfairly negotiate prices with producers, and privacy measures that provide commercially sensitive data privacy and also allow collaborative learning between cooperatives. Social equity solutions deal with the digital divide that is impending to exacerbate the disparities between large commercial activities that have resources to invest in IoT infrastructure and smallholder farmers who lack connectivity, capital, or technical literacy and therefore require government interventions such as subsidized sensor packages, community data centers that provide shared AI analytics, extension programs that offer interpretation services to model outputs, and tiered pricing models by agritech providers that ensure that the farmers of any size can access the services. The existing SynerNet implementation, though technically sound, has the risk of concentrating the benefits in the hands of digitally enabled farms unless institutional structures, such as cooperative data trusts, open-source algorithm libraries, open-source AI-as-a-service, and so on, democratize access and avoid technological gatekeeping. The integration of environmental sustainability goes beyond operational efficiency and assesses whether AI-based resource optimization actually lowers ecological footprints or only increases the production pressures: the feed optimization capabilities of the model should be analyzed in relation to the biodiversity effects, water usage rates, and methane emissions patterns, and the predictions of reorder quantities should be considered through the prism of the circular economy principles, where local sourcing and reduction of waste are considered the primary goals rather than mere cost minimization. Animal welfare necessities demand that health observation algorithms should improve but not exploit livestock so that AI advice puts the long-term wellbeing of livestock in the forefront instead of the short-term productivity increase and that automated veterinary care devices are used in concert with human judgment in ethical treatment choices. The Quintuple Helix vision makes natural ecosystems the fifth institutional sphere where AI systems have to internalize environmental externalities in measures that are not just in terms of revenue and efficiency, such as carbon footprint per litre of milk, soil health indices, environment-friendly farming methods, etc., to match AI goals with planetary limits. This broadened model recognizes that technological innovation without social license and ecological accountability proposes the possibility of establishing extractive systems where the productivity will be enjoyed by a subset of stakeholders as the environment is ruined and the marginalized populations suffer as victims, making participatory design processes where farmers, civil society organizations, and environmental scientists collaboratively design AI systems by reflecting diverse values likely to ensure smart dairy farming promotes not just economic efficiency but systemic sustainability, including social justice, animal dignity, and ecological regeneration.

Finally, an AI decision support system in livestock farming can revolutionize the industry. It is possible to optimize the resources by promoting evidence-based decision-making through this innovative framework, improving animal health and welfare, thereby increasing productivity and profitability in the dairy farming industry and enhancing the sustainability and technology-based dairy farming industry.

6. FUTURE WORK

The future research will involve improvement of the SynerNet framework through incorporation of multimodal data streams through IoT sensors, UAVs, and genomic markers to create a more comprehensive digital twin of the dairy operations. This will entail enhancing the model to have spatiotemporal prediction of milk output and animal condition using attention-based recurrent neural networks and graph neural networks to model intricate interactions, entire dairy farm monitoring arrangements and environmental situations. Also, a study will be conducted on federated learning strategies that can allow decentralized training of multiple farms and data privacy and the integration of explainable AI (XAI) methods to enhance the interpretability of models and promote trust. Additional optimization of hyperparameters with a Bayesian approach and real-time adversarial validation will also be sought to achieve robustness and flexibility in farming circumstances of dynamic conditions.

ETHICAL STATEMENT

No human or animal subjects were involved, and the research promotes sustainable environmental management with no conflicts of interest.

DATA AVAILABILITY

https://www.kaggle.com/datasets/suraj520/dairy-goods-sales-dataset/data

AUTHORS' CONTRIBUTIONS

Data curation, N.A.K.; Formal analysis, S.R.; U.M.P, Validation.; Software, S.K.; Original draft writing, S.K.R.

CONFLICT OF INTEREST

The authors declare that there is no conflict of interest regarding the publication of this study, with no involvement of animals or humans.

REFERENCES

Alonso, R. S., Sittón-Candanedo, I., García, Ó., Prieto, J., & Rodríguez-González, S. (2020). An intelligent Edge-IoT platform for monitoring livestock and crops in a dairy farming scenario. *Ad Hoc Networks*, *98*, 102047. Advance online publication. DOI: 10.1016/j.adhoc.2019.102047

Alshehri, M. (2023). Blockchain-assisted internet of things framework in smart livestock farming. *Internet of Things : Engineering Cyber Physical Human Systems*, *22*, 100739. Advance online publication. DOI: 10.1016/j.iot.2023.100739

El-Ghamry, A., Darwish, A., & Hassanien, A. E. (2023). An optimized CNN-based intrusion detection system for reducing risks in smart farming. *Internet of Things : Engineering Cyber Physical Human Systems*, *22*, 100709. Advance online publication. DOI: 10.1016/j.iot.2023.100709

Hassoun, A., Garcia-Garcia, G., Trollman, H., Jagtap, S., Parra-López, C., Cropotova, J., Bhat, Z., Centobelli, P., & Aït-Kaddour, A. (2023). Birth of dairy 4.0: Opportunities and challenges in adoption of fourth industrial revolution technologies in the production of milk and its derivatives. *Current Research in Food Science*, *6*, 100535. Advance online publication. DOI: 10.1016/j.crfs.2023.100535 PMID: 37448632

McCaig, M., Dara, R., & Rezania, D. (2023). Farmer-centric design thinking principles for smart farming technologies. *Internet of Things : Engineering Cyber Physical Human Systems*, *23*, 100898. Advance online publication. DOI: 10.1016/j.iot.2023.100898

Mishra, S. (2023). Internet of things enabled deep learning methods using unmanned aerial vehicles enabled integrated farm management. *Heliyon*, *9*(8), e18818. Advance online publication. DOI: 10.1016/j.heliyon.2023.e18659 PMID: 37576187

Mishra, S., & Sharma, S. K. (2023). Advanced contribution of IoT in agricultural production for the development of smart livestock environments. *Internet of Things : Engineering Cyber Physical Human Systems*, *22*, 100724. Advance online publication. DOI: 10.1016/j.iot.2023.100724

Newton, J. E., Nettle, R., & Pryce, J. E. (2020). Farming smarter with big data: Insights from the case of Australia's national dairy herd milk recording scheme. *Agricultural Systems*, *181*, 102811. Advance online publication. DOI: 10.1016/j.agsy.2020.102811

Prakash, C., Singh, L. P., Gupta, A., & Lohan, S. K. (2023). Advancements in smart farming: A comprehensive review of IoT, wireless communication, sensors, and hardware for agricultural automation. *Sensors and Actuators. A, Physical, 359*, 114605. Advance online publication. DOI: 10.1016/j.sna.2023.114605

Schwab, A. K., Halberstadt, J., Besieda, A., Kraft, M., & Ortland, A. (2023). Organizational aspects of digitalization in the context of agriculture: Exemplary results from analyzing data flows in German dairy farming. *Procedia Computer Science, 219*, 1006–1011. DOI: 10.1016/j.procs.2023.01.378

Shaikh, T. A., Rasool, T., & Lone, F. R. (2022). Towards leveraging the role of machine learning and artificial intelligence in precision agriculture and smart farming. *Computers and Electronics in Agriculture, 198*, 107119. Advance online publication. DOI: 10.1016/j.compag.2022.107119

Shakeel, P. M. (2022). A deep learning-based cow behavior recognition scheme for improving cattle behavior modeling in smart farming. *Internet of Things : Engineering Cyber Physical Human Systems, 19*, 100539. Advance online publication. DOI: 10.1016/j.iot.2022.100539

Taneja, M., Byabazaire, J., Jalodia, N., Davy, A., Olariu, C., & Malone, P. (2020). Machine learning based fog computing assisted data-driven approach for early lameness detection in dairy cattle. *Computers and Electronics in Agriculture, 171*, 105286. Advance online publication. DOI: 10.1016/j.compag.2020.105286

Torky, M., & Hassanein, A. E. (2020). Integrating blockchain and the internet of things in precision agriculture: Analysis, opportunities, and challenges. *Computers and Electronics in Agriculture, 178*, 105476. Advance online publication. DOI: 10.1016/j.compag.2020.105476

Verdouw, C., Tekinerdogan, B., Beulens, A., & Wolfert, S. (2021). Digital twins in smart farming. *Agricultural Systems, 189*, 103046. Advance online publication. DOI: 10.1016/j.agsy.2020.103046

Compilation of References

Abadir, P., Oh, E., Chellappa, R., Choudhry, N., Demiris, G., Ganesan, D., Karlawish, J., Marlin, B., Li, R. M., Dehak, N., Arbaje, A., Unberath, M., Cudjoe, T., Chute, C., Moore, J. H., Phan, P., Samus, Q., Schoenborn, N. L., Battle, A., & Walston, J. D. (2024). Artificial Intelligence and Technology Collaboratories: Innovating aging research and Alzheimer's care. *Alzheimer's & Dementia*, *20*(4), 3074–3079. DOI: 10.1002/alz.13710 PMID: 38324244

Abdillah, A., Widianingsih, I., Buchari, R. A., Mustari, N., & Saleh, S. (2022). Governance and Quintuple Helix innovation model: Insights from the local government of East Luwu Regency, Indonesia. *Frontiers in Climate*, *4*, 1012108. DOI: 10.3389/fclim.2022.1012108

Abd-Rahman, M. S. B., Mohamad, E., & Abdul-Rahman, A. A. B. (2021). Development of IoT—Enabled Data Analytics Enhance Decision Support System for Lean Manufacturing Process Improvement. *Concurrent Engineering, Research and Applications*, *29*(3), 208–220. DOI: 10.1177/1063293X20987911

Abreu, M., Grinevich, V., Hughes, A., & Kitson, M. (2009). Knowledge exchange between academics and the business, public and third sectors. In *ePrints Soton (University of Southampton)*. https://eprints.soton.ac.uk/357117/1/AcademicSurveyReport.pdf

Addy, C., Chorengel, M., Collins, M., & Etzel, M. (2019). Calculating the Value of Impact Investing. *Harvard Business Review*. Retrieved March 5, 2020, from: https://hbr.org/2019/01/calculating-the-value-of-impact-investing

Agbejule, A., & Lehtineva, L. (2022). The relationship between traditional project management, agile project management and teamwork quality on project success. *The International Journal of Organizational Analysis*, *30*(7), 124–136. DOI: 10.1108/IJOA-02-2022-3149

Aiello, L.. (2022). Digital research infrastructures and collaborative innovation. *Journal of Business Research, 146*. Advance online publication. DOI: 10.1016/j.jbusres.2022.113393

Alam, S., & Khan, M. (2024). Enhancing AI-Human Collaborative Decision-Making in Industry 4.0 Management Practices. *IEEE Access : Practical Innovations, Open Solutions, 12*, 119433–119444. DOI: 10.1109/ACCESS.2024.3449415

Alonso, R. S., Sittón-Candanedo, I., García, Ó., Prieto, J., & Rodríguez-González, S. (2020). An intelligent Edge-IoT platform for monitoring livestock and crops in a dairy farming scenario. *Ad Hoc Networks, 98*, 102047. Advance online publication. DOI: 10.1016/j.adhoc.2019.102047

Alshahrani, R., Yenugula, M., Algethami, H., Alharbi, F., Goswami, S., Naveed, Q., Lasisi, A., Islam, S., Khan, N., & Zahmatkesh, S. (2023). Establishing the fuzzy integrated hybrid MCDM framework to identify the key barriers to implementing artificial intelligence-enabled sustainable cloud system in an IT industry. *Expert Systems with Applications, 238*, 121732. DOI: 10.1016/j.eswa.2023.121732

Alshehri, M. (2023). Blockchain-assisted internet of things framework in smart livestock farming. *Internet of Things : Engineering Cyber Physical Human Systems, 22*, 100739. Advance online publication. DOI: 10.1016/j.iot.2023.100739

Altbach, P. (2008). *The complex roles of universities in the period of globalization.* https://www.researchgate.net/publication/277128834

Altbach, P. G., & Salmi, J. (2011). *The Road to Academic Excellence: The Making of World-Class Research Universities.* DOI: 10.1596/978-0-8213-8805-1

Altbach, P. G. (2008). The Complex Roles of Universities in the Period of Globalization. *Higher Education in the World, 3*(January), 5–19. DOI: 10.1007/978-1-349-58169 6_1

Amin, A., Chowdhury, D. I. Q., Abyaz, R., Alom, S., Siam, S. A., Al Imran, D., Lia, F. S., & Azad, P. A. K. (2024). Artificial intelligence in pharmacy: Innovations, applications, and future emerging challenges. *INTERANTIONAL JOURNAL OF SCIENTIFIC RESEARCH IN ENGINEERING AND MANAGEMENT, 08*(12), 1–9. DOI: 10.55041/IJSREM40335

Ardita, R. R., Sutarto, , & Adhikari, B. P. (2025). Triple helix partnership model between universities, industry, and government for implementing an outcome-based curriculum in the era of disruption at PTSP UNY: An internal university review. *Jurnal Pendidikan Teknik Sipil, 7*(1), 1–13. DOI: 10.21831/jpts.v7i1.83406

Ariza-Montes, A., Sianes, A., Fernández-Rodríguez, V., López-Martín, M. C., Ruíz-Lozano, M., & Tirado-Valencia, P. (2021). Social Return on Investment (SROI) to assess the impacts of tourism: A case study. *SAGE Open*, *11*(1), 2158244020988733. Advance online publication. DOI: 10.1177/2158244020988733

Baccarne, B., Logghe, S., Schuurman, D., & De Marez, L. (2016). Governing Quintuple Helix Innovation: Urban Living Labs and Socio-Ecological Entrepreneurship. Technology *Innovation Management Review*. Retrieved March 5, 2020, from: https://timreview.ca/article/972

Barbosa, J.. (2023). University–industry–government collaboration and innovation. *Research Policy*, *52*(7), 104882. DOI: 10.1016/j.respol.2023.104882

Barth, T. (2011). The idea of a green new deal in a Quintuple Helix Model of knowledge, know-how and innovation. *International Journal of Social Ecology and Sustainable Development*, *1*(2), 1–14. DOI: 10.4018/jsesd.2011010101

Bascavusoglu-Moreau, E., Mina, A., & Hughes, A. (2013). Exploiting Knowledge Flows: Openness and the innovative performance of Business Services. *Proceedings - Academy of Management*, *2013*(1), 13887. DOI: 10.5465/ambpp.2013.188

Bechtel, J., Kaufmann, C., & Kock, A. (2022). Agile projects in nonagile portfolios: How project portfolio contingencies constrain agile projects' teamwork quality. *IEEE Transactions on Engineering Management*, *69*(6), 3514–3528. DOI: 10.1109/TEM.2021.3130068

Belhadi, A., Kamble, S., Wamba, S., & Queiroz, M. (2021). Building supply-chain resilience: An artificial intelligence-based technique and decision-making framework. *International Journal of Production Research*, *60*(14), 4487–4507. DOI: 10.1080/00207543.2021.1950935

Benfeldt, A.. (2023). *Optimizing Data Governance via Triple Helix Model. Data Governance for Digital Transformation and Sustainability*. IGI Global.

Berente, N., Gu, B., Recker, J., & Santhanam, R. (2021). Managing artificial intelligence. *Management Information Systems Quarterly*, *45*(3), 1433–1450. DOI: 10.25300/MISQ/2021/16274

Berry, P., Dhanakshirur, R. R., & Khanna, S. (2025). Utilizing large language models for gastroenterology research: A conceptual framework. *Therapeutic Advances in Gastroenterology*, *18*, 17562848251328576. DOI: 10.1177/17562848251328577 PMID: 40171241

Bertoletti, A., & Johnes, G. (2021). Efficiency in university-industry collaboration: An analysis of UK higher education institutions. *Scientometrics*, *126*(9), 7679–7714. DOI: 10.1007/s11192-021-04076-w

Bogachov, S., Kwiliński, A., Miethlich, B., Bartosova, V., & Gurnak, A. (2020). *Artificial intelligence components and fuzzy regulators in entrepreneurship development*. Entrepreneurship and Sustainability Issues., DOI: 10.9770/jesi.2020.8.2(29)

Bolsunovskaya, M. V., Kudryavtseva, T. Y., Rudskaya, I. A., Gintciak, A. M., Zhidkov, D. O., Fedyaevskaya, D. E., & Burlutskaya, Z. V. (2023). Digital Platform for Modeling the Development of Regional Innovation Systems of Russian Federation. *International Journal of Technology*, *14*(8), 1779–1789. DOI: 10.14716/ijtech.v14i8.6843

Bou Reslan, F., & Al Maalouf, N. J. (2024). Assessing the transformative impact of AI adoption on efficiency, fraud detection, and skill dynamics in accounting practices. *Journal of Risk and Financial Management*, *17*(12), 577. DOI: 10.3390/jrfm17120577

Brown, M., Mcgreal, R., Peters, M., & Brown, M. (2023). A Strategic Institutional Response to Micro- Credentials. *Journal of Interactive Media in Education*, *2023*(1), 1–17. DOI: 10.5334/jime.801

Brown, M., Nic Giolla Mhichil, M., Beirne, E., & Mac Lochlainn, C. (2021). The global micro-credential landscape: Charting a new credential ecology for lifelong learning. *Journal of Learning for Development*, *8*(2), 228–254. DOI: 10.56059/jl4d.v8i2.525

Bruneel, J., D'Este, P., & Salter, A. (2010). Investigating the factors that diminish the barriers to university–industry collaboration. *Research Policy*, *39*(7), 858–868. DOI: 10.1016/j.respol.2010.03.006

Busch, F., Hoffmann, L., Truhn, D., Palaian, S., Alomar, M., Shpati, K., Makowski, M. R., Bressem, K. K., & Adams, L. C. (2024). International pharmacy students' perceptions towards artificial intelligence in medicine-A multinational, multicentre cross-sectional study. *British Journal of Clinical Pharmacology*, *90*(3), 649–661. DOI: 10.1111/bcp.15911 PMID: 37728146

Cai, Y., & Etzkowitz, H. (2020). Theorizing the Triple Helix model: Past, present, and future. *Triple Helix (Heidelberg)*, *7*(2–3), 189–226. DOI: 10.1163/21971927-bja10003

Cai, Y., Ferrer, B., & Lastra, J. (2019). Building University-Industry Co-Innovation Networks in Transnational Innovation Ecosystems: Towards a Transdisciplinary Approach of Integrating Social Sciences and Artificial Intelligence. *Sustainability (Basel), 11*(17), 4633. Advance online publication. DOI: 10.3390/su11174633

Cai, Y., & Lattu, A. (2022). Triple Helix or Quadruple Helix: Which Model of Innovation to Choose for Empirical Studies? *Minerva, 60*(2), 257–280. DOI: 10.1007/s11024-021-09453-6

Camilleri, M. A. (2024). Artificial intelligence governance: Ethical considerations and implications for social responsibility. *Expert Systems: International Journal of Knowledge Engineering and Neural Networks, 41*(7), e13406. DOI: 10.1111/exsy.13406

Carayannis, E. G., & Campbell, D. F. J. (2010b). The Quintuple Helix, Industrial 5.0, and Society 5.0. In The *Quintuple Helix Innovation Model* (pp. 1–20). Emerald Publishing Limited.

Carayannis, E. G., Barth, T. D., & Campbell, D. F. (2012). The Quintuple Helix innovation model: Global warming as a challenge and driver for innovation. *Journal of Innovation and Entrepreneurship, 1*, 1–12. DOI: 10.1186/2192-5372-1-1

Carayannis, E. G., & Campbell, D. F. (2009). "Mode 3" and "Quadruple Helix": Toward a 21st century fractal innovation ecosystem. *International Journal of Technology Management, 46*(3-4), 201–234. DOI: 10.1504/IJTM.2009.023374

Carayannis, E. G., & Campbell, D. F. (2021). Democracy of climate and climate for democracy: The evolution of quadruple and quintuple helix innovation systems. *Journal of the Knowledge Economy, 12*(4), 2050–2082. DOI: 10.1007/s13132-021-00778-x PMID: 40477087

Carayannis, E. G., & Campbell, D. F. (2022). Towards an Emerging Unified Theory of Helix Architectures (EUTOHA): Focus on the Quintuple innovation helix framework as the integrative device. *Triple Helix (Heidelberg), 9*(1), 65–75. DOI: 10.1163/21971927-bja10028

Carayannis, E. G., Campbell, D. F., & Grigoroudis, E. (2022). Helix trilogy: The triple, quadruple, and quintuple innovation helices from a theory, policy, and practice set of perspectives. *Journal of the Knowledge Economy, 13*(3), 2272–2301. DOI: 10.1007/s13132-021-00813-x

Carayannis, E. G., Grigoroudis, E., Stamati, D., & Valvi, T. (2019). Social business model innovation: A quadruple/quintuple helix-based social innovation ecosystem. *IEEE Transactions on Engineering Management*, *68*(1), 235–248. DOI: 10.1109/TEM.2019.2914408

Carayannis, E. G., & Morawska, J. (2023). University and education 5.0 for emerging trends, policies and practices in the concept of industry 5.0 and society 5.0. In *Industry 5.0: Creative and Innovative Organizations* (pp. 1–25). Springer International Publishing. DOI: 10.1007/978-3-031-26232-6_1

Carayannis, E. G., & Rakhmatullin, R. (2014). The Quadruple Innovation Helix (QIH): Application for the study of university-industry-government-community interfaces. *International Journal of Innovative Research and Development*, *5*(3-4), 191–212.

Carayannis, E., & Campbell, D. F. (2012). Triple Helix, Quadruple Helix and Quintuple Helix and how do knowledge, innovation and the environment relate to each other?: A proposed framework for a trans-disciplinary analysis of sustainable development and social ecology. In *Sustainable policy applications for social ecology and development* (pp. 29–59). IGI Global Scientific Publishing. DOI: 10.4018/978-1-4666-1586-1.ch004

Car-Pušić, D., Marović, I., & Bulatović, G. (2020). Development of a hybrid agile management model in local self-government units. *Tehnicki Vjesnik (Strojarski Fakultet)*, *27*(5), 1418–1426. DOI: 10.17559/TV-20191107153933

Cath, C., Wachter, S., Mittelstadt, B., Taddeo, M., & Floridi, L. (2018). Artificial intelligence and the 'good society': The US, EU, and UK approach. *Science and Engineering Ethics*, *24*(2), 505–528. PMID: 28353045

Chattopadhyay, S., Honoré, F., & Won, S. (2025). Free range startups? Market scope, academic founders, and the role of general knowledge in AI. *Strategic Management Journal*, *46*(4), 1027–1079. DOI: 10.1002/smj.3685

Chesbrough, H. W. (2003). *Open innovation: The new imperative for creating and profiting from technology*. Harvard Business Press.

Christiansen, L., Hvidsten, T. E., Kristensen, J. H., Gebhardt, J., Mahmood, K., Otto, T., Lassen, A. H., Brunoe, T. D., Schou, C., & Laursen, E. S. (2022). A Framework for Developing Educational Industry 4.0 Activities and Study Materials. *Education Sciences*, *12*(10), 659. Advance online publication. DOI: 10.3390/educsci12100659

Code World. (2024). *Learn Business Management*. Retrieved May 30, 2024, from: https://play.google.com/store/apps/details?id=com.codeworld.learnbusinessmanagement&hl=pt

Coetzee, D. (2024). *Micro-Credentials: An Emerging Alternative to Traditional Tertiary Education. July*. DOI: 10.13140/RG.2.2.16792.40962

Cohen, W. M., & Levinthal, D. A. (1990). Absorptive Capacity: A new perspective on learning and innovation. *Administrative Science Quarterly*, *35*(1), 128. DOI: 10.2307/2393553

Cook, I., Grange, S., & Eyre-walker, A. (2015). *Research groups: How big should they be ?* DOI: 10.7717/peerj.989

Cooper, R. G., & Sommer, A. F. (2016). From experience: The agile–stage-gate hybrid model—A promising new approach and a new research opportunity. *Journal of Product Innovation Management*, *33*(5), 513–526. DOI: 10.1111/jpim.12314

Cunningham, J. A., Lehmann, E. E., & Menter, M. (2022). The organizational architecture of entrepreneurial universities across the stages of entrepreneurship: A conceptual framework. *Small Business Economics*, *59*(1), 11–27. DOI: 10.1007/s11187-021-00513-5

Daraio, C. (2017). A Framework for the Assessment of Research and Its Impacts. *Journal of Data and Information Science*, *2*(4), 7–42. DOI: 10.1515/jdis-2017-0018

Das, A. K. (2016). On partially included intuitionistic fuzzy rough relations. *Afrika Matematika*, *27*(5-6), 993–1001. DOI: 10.1007/s13370-016-0395-2

Das, A. K. (2018). Weighted fuzzy soft multiset and decision-making. *International Journal of Machine Learning and Cybernetics*, *9*(5), 787–794. DOI: 10.1007/s13042-016-0607-y

Das, A. K., Das, R., Das, S., Debnath, B. K., Granados, C., Shil, B., & Das, R. (2025c). A comprehensive study of neutrosophic SuperHyper BCI-semigroups and their algebraic significance. *Transactions on Fuzzy Sets and Systems*, *4*(2), 80–101. DOI: 10.71602/tfss.2025.1198050

Das, A. K., Das, R., Datta, R., & Granados, C. (2025e). An Innovative Approach to Group Decision-Making Based on Weighted Hypersoft Expert System. In Smarandache, F., Jdid, M., & Leyva-Vazquez, M. (Eds.), *Neutrosophic and Plithogenic Inventory Models for Applied Mathematics* (pp. 483–518). IGI Global Scientific Publishing., DOI: 10.4018/979-8-3693-3204-7.ch019

Das, A. K., & Granados, C. (2021). An advanced approach to fuzzy soft group decision-making using weighted average ratings. *SN Computer Science*, *2*(6), 471. DOI: 10.1007/s42979-021-00873-5

Das, A. K., & Granados, C. (2022a). A new fuzzy parameterized intuitionistic fuzzy soft multiset theory and group decision-making. *Journal of Current Science and Technology*, *12*(3), 547–567. DOI: 10.14456/jcst.2022.42

Das, A. K., & Granados, C. (2022b). FP-intuitionistic multi fuzzy N-soft set and its induced FP-Hesitant N soft set in decision-making. *Decision Making: Applications in Management and Engineering*, *5*(1), 67–89. DOI: 10.31181/dmame181221045d

Das, A. K., & Granados, C. (2023a). IFP-intuitionistic multi fuzzy N-soft set and its induced IFP-hesitant N-soft set in decision-making. *Journal of Ambient Intelligence and Humanized Computing*, *14*(8), 10143–10152. DOI: 10.1007/s12652-021-03677-w

Das, A. K., & Granados, C. (2023b). Preference intuitionistic fuzzy rough relation and its theoretical approach. *Journal of the Indian Mathematical Society*, *90*(3-4), 199–212.

Das, A. K., Granados, C., & Bhattacharya, J. (2022). Some new operations on fuzzy soft sets and their applications in decision-making. *Songklanakarin Journal of Science and Technology*, *44*(2), 440–449. DOI: 10.14456/sjst-psu.2022.61

Das, A. K., Gupta, N., Das, R., Das, S., Das, R., Granados, C., & Debnath, B. K. (2026a). Fuzzy Logic-Driven Strategies for Diversity and Inclusion in Multicultural Marketing. In Tarnanidis, T., Sousa, B., Vlachopoulou, M., Papachristou, E., & Kittu Manda, V. (Eds.), *Diversity and Inclusion-Driven Marketing for Multicultural Marketplaces* (pp. 189–236). IGI Global Scientific Publishing., DOI: 10.4018/979-8-3373-2111-0.ch009

Das, A. K., Gupta, N., Das, R., Granados, C., & Das, S. (2026c). Neutrosophic Sets for Decision-Making in Natural Disasters and Environmental Recovery. In Ezaier, Y., Gaamouche, R., & Lahby, M. (Eds.), *Computational Intelligence and Optimization Methods for Sustainable Water Management* (pp. 119–162). IGI Global Scientific Publishing., DOI: 10.4018/979-8-3373-2700-6.ch004

Das, A. K., Gupta, N., Fujita, T., Das, S., Granados, C., Debnath, B. K., & Das, R. (2026b). Advanced Co-Branding Strategies for Smart Luxury Products: A Multi-Criteria Decision-Making Approach Using Neutrosophic Sets. In Tarnanidis, T., Sousa, B., Vlachopoulou, M., Papachristou, E., & Kittu Manda, V. (Eds.), *Co-Branding Strategies for Smart Luxury Products* (pp. 203–258). IGI Global Scientific Publishing., DOI: 10.4018/979-8-3373-3010-5.ch006

Das, A. K., Gupta, N., & Granados, C. (2023). Weighted hesitant bipolar-valued fuzzy soft set in decision-making. *Songklanakarin Journal of Science and Technology*, *45*(6), 681–690. https://sjst.psu.ac.th/journal/45-6/10.pdf

Das, A. K., Gupta, N., Granados, C., Das, R., & Das, S. (2024b). Neutrosophic Approach to Water Quality Assessment: A Case Study of Gomati River, the Largest River in Tripura, India. *Neutrosophic Systems with Applications*, *22*, 1–12. DOI: 10.61356/j.nswa.2024.22386

Das, A. K., Gupta, N., Mahmood, T., Tripathy, B. C., Das, R., & Das, S. (2024a). Assessing anthropogenic influences on the water quality of Gomati River using an innovative weighted fuzzy soft set based water pollution rating system. *Discover Water*, *4*(1), 73. DOI: 10.1007/s43832-024-00136-3

Das, A. K., Gupta, N., Mahmood, T., Tripathy, B. C., Das, R., & Das, S. (2025a). An efficient water quality evaluation model using weighted hesitant fuzzy soft sets for water pollution rating. In Kumar, A., Kumar, P., Rathee, S., & Kumar, B. (Eds.), *Mechatronics: Concepts, Tools, Applications, and New Trends* (1st ed., p. 17). CRC Press., DOI: 10.1201/9781003494478-10

Das, A. K., Gupta, N., Mahmood, T., Tripathy, B. C., Das, R., & Das, S. (2025b). An innovative fuzzy multi-criteria decision making model for analyzing anthropogenic influences on urban river water quality. *Iran Journal of Computer Science*, *8*(1), 103–124. DOI: 10.1007/s42044-024-00211-x

Das, A. K., Gupta, N., Mahmood, T., Tripathy, B. C., Das, R., & Das, S. (2025g). Anthropogenic Impacts on Urban River Water Quality for Rating Water Pollution Using an Effective Fuzzy Soft Multi Criteria Group Decision Making Model. *Iraqi Journal of Science*, *66*(9), 3921–3937. DOI: 10.24996/ijs.2025.66.9.32

Das, A. K., Mahmood, T., Das, R., & Das, S. (2025d). Optimizing Inventory Levels in Retail: Fuzzy Logic-Based Decision Support Systems for Adaptive Inventory Management. In Jana, S., Basu Mallik, B., Sarkar, A., & Jana, C. (Eds.), *Applications of Fuzzy Logic in Decision Making and Management Science. Information Systems Engineering and Management* (Vol. 29). Springer., DOI: 10.1007/978-3-031-77719-6_8

Das, A. K., Patra, S., & Granados, C. (2025f). An innovative approach to hesitant bipolar fuzzy soft sets in multi-criteria group decision-making. Adv. in Comp. *Advances in Computational Intelligence*, *5*(3), 4. DOI: 10.1007/s43674-025-00082-0

Deguchi, A., Hirai, C., Matsuoka, H., Nakano, T., Oshima, K., Tai, M., & Tani, S. (2020). What is society 5.0. *Society*, *5*, 1–23.

Deveci, M. (2023). Effective use of artificial intelligence in healthcare supply chain resilience using fuzzy decision-making model. *Soft Computing*, •••, 1–14. DOI: 10.1007/s00500-023-08906-2

Digital. (2025, December 11). *Home - Innovate UK Business Connect*. Innovate UK Business Connect. https://iuk-business-connect.org.uk/

Dodgson, M. (1991). Technology learning, technology strategy and competitive pressures. *British Journal of Management*, *2*(3), 133–149. DOI: 10.1111/j.1467-8551.1991.tb00022.x

Duklas, J. (2020). *Micro-Credentials: Trends in Credit Transfer and Credentialing. November*, 545–545. DOI: 10.1007/978-3-319-95870-5_300166

Durmusoglu, S. S. (2004). Open Innovation: The New Imperative for Creating and Profiting from Technology. *European Journal of Innovation Management*, *7*(4), 325–326. DOI: 10.1108/14601060410565074

Dwivedi, Y. K., Hughes, L., Ismagilova, E., Aarts, G., Coombs, C., Crick, T., Duan, Y., Dwivedi, R., Edwards, J., Eirug, A., Galanos, V., Ilavarasan, P. V., Janssen, M., Jones, P., Kar, A. K., Kizgin, H., Kronemann, B., Lal, B., Lucini, B., & Williams, M. D. (2021). Artificial Intelligence (AI): Multidisciplinary perspectives on emerging challenges, opportunities, and agenda for research, practice and policy. *International Journal of Information Management*, *57*(101994), 101994. DOI: 10.1016/j.ijinfomgt.2019.08.002

El-Ghamry, A., Darwish, A., & Hassanien, A. E. (2023). An optimized CNN-based intrusion detection system for reducing risks in smart farming. *Internet of Things : Engineering Cyber Physical Human Systems*, *22*, 100709. Advance online publication. DOI: 10.1016/j.iot.2023.100709

Ervits, I. (2024). Developing indicators for the social benefits of university–industry collaborations. *International Journal of Corporate Social Responsibility*, *9*(1), 8. Advance online publication. DOI: 10.1186/s40991-024-00097-9

Etzkowitz, H. (2011). The triple helix: Science, technology and the entrepreneurial spirit. *Journal of Knowledge-Based Innovation in China*, *3*(2), 76–90. DOI: 10.1108/17561411111138937

Etzkowitz, H., & Leydesdorff, L. (2000). The dynamics of innovation: From National Systems and “Mode 2” to a Triple Helix of university–industry–government relations. *Research Policy*, *29*(2), 109–123. DOI: 10.1016/S0048-7333(99)00055-4

Etzkowitz, H., & Zhou, C. (2021). Innovation in the post-pandemic era: Triple helix and hybrid organizations. *Journal of Innovation & Knowledge*, *6*(4), 253–257. DOI: 10.1016/j.jik.2021.09.001

Fagerberg, J., & Mowery, D. (2015). *Recent research on innovation and economic change. Innovation, Technology and Economic Change*. Edward Elgar. DOI: 10.4337/9781784718633

Feor, L., Clarke, A., & Dougherty, I. (2023). Social impact measurement: A systematic literature review and future research directions. [MDPI]. *WORLD (Oakland, Calif.)*, *4*(4), 816–837. DOI: 10.3390/world4040051

Floridi, L., Cowls, J., Beltrametti, M., Chatila, R., Chazerand, P., Dignum, V., Luetge, C., Madelin, R., Pagallo, U., Rossi, F., Schafer, B., Valcke, P., & Vayena, E. (2018). AI4People—An ethical framework for a good AI society: Opportunities, risks, principles, and recommendations. *Minds and Machines*, *28*(4), 689–707. DOI: 10.1007/s11023-018-9482-5 PMID: 30930541

Fumanal-Idocin, J., & Andreu-Pérez, J. (2024). Ex-Fuzzy: A library for symbolic explainable AI through fuzzy logic programming. *Neurocomputing*, *599*, 128048. DOI: 10.1016/j.neucom.2024.128048

Fu, W., Wang, Q., & Zhao, X. (2018). Platform-based service innovation and system design: A literature review. *Industrial Management & Data Systems*, *118*(5), 946–974. DOI: 10.1108/IMDS-03-2017-0129

Gallagher, S. E., & Savage, T. (2023). *Challenge-based learning in higher education : an exploratory literature review. 2517*. DOI: 10.1080/13562517.2020.1863354

Geels, F. W. (2004). From sectoral systems of innovation to socio-technical systems: Insights about dynamics and change from sociology and institutional theory. *Research Policy*, *33*(6–7), 897–920. DOI: 10.1016/j.respol.2004.01.015

Geetha, S., & Jeon, J. (2022). Extension of SIR method with interval type 2-hesitant fuzzy set to aggrandize industry-university collaboration projects in South Korea. *Journal of Ambient Intelligence and Humanized Computing*, *15*(1), 57–73. DOI: 10.1007/s12652-022-03873-2

Geissdoerfer, M., Savaget, P., Bocken, N. M., & Hultink, E. J. (2017). The Circular Economy–A new sustainability paradigm? *Journal of Cleaner Production*, *143*, 757–768. DOI: 10.1016/j.jclepro.2016.12.048

Gibbons, M., Limoges, C., Scott, P., Schwartzman, S., & Nowotny, H. (1994). *The new production of knowledge: The dynamics of science and research in contemporary societies*. Sage Publications.

GII. (2018). *Global Innovation Index 2018*. Energizing the world with innovation. WIPO. Available at: https://www.wipo.int/edocs/pubdocs/en/wipo_pub_gii_2018.pdf

GII. (2023). *Global Innovation Index 2023*. Innovation in the face of uncertainty. WIPO. Available at: https://www.wipo.int/edocs/pubdocs/en/wipo-pub-2000-2023-en-main-report-global-innovation-index-2023-16th-edition.pdf

Goktas, P., & Grzybowski, A. (2025). Shaping the future of healthcare: Ethical clinical challenges and pathways to trustworthy AI. *Journal of Clinical Medicine*, *14*(5), 1605. DOI: 10.3390/jcm14051605 PMID: 40095575

Goodman, D., & Zhu, A. Y. (2024). Utility of artificial intelligence in the diagnosis and management of keratoconus: A systematic review. *Frontiers in Ophthalmology*, *4*, 1380701. DOI: 10.3389/fopht.2024.1380701 PMID: 38984114

Guo, L., Zhan, J., Zhang, C., & Xu, Z. (2024). A Large-Scale Group Decision-Making Method Fusing Three-Way Clustering and Regret Theory Under Fuzzy Preference Relations. *IEEE Transactions on Fuzzy Systems*, *32*(9), 4846–4860. DOI: 10.1109/TFUZZ.2023.3335965

Gupta, N., Das, A. K., & Granados, C. (2026). Integrating Traditional Ecological Knowledge with Fuzzy Logic and Quantum Computing for Sustainable Agriculture in Tribal Areas of Tripura. In Horng, M., Khalaf, O., Shieh, C., & Jain, V. (Eds.), *Revolutionizing Sustainable Food Production With Quantum Computing* (pp. 177–214). IGI Global Scientific Publishing., DOI: 10.4018/979-8-3373-3957-3.ch006

Hange, U., Nwanesi, E., & Bah, M. (2025). A New Framework for Classifying University-Industry Collaboration Using Synthetic Minority Oversampling Technique and Stacking Ensemble. *IEEE Access : Practical Innovations, Open Solutions*, *13*, 101297–101312. DOI: 10.1109/ACCESS.2025.3577777

Hao, X., Demir, E., & Eyers, D. (2024). Exploring Collaborative Decision-Making: A Quasi-Experimental Study of Human and Generative AI Interaction. *Technology in Society*, *78*, 102662. Advance online publication. DOI: 10.1016/j.techsoc.2024.102662

Hassoun, A., Garcia-Garcia, G., Trollman, H., Jagtap, S., Parra-López, C., Cropotova, J., Bhat, Z., Centobelli, P., & Aït-Kaddour, A. (2023). Birth of dairy 4.0: Opportunities and challenges in adoption of fourth industrial revolution technologies in the production of milk and its derivatives. *Current Research in Food Science*, *6*, 100535. Advance online publication. DOI: 10.1016/j.crfs.2023.100535 PMID: 37448632

Hayati, A., Abdol Homayuni, M. R., Sadeghi, R., Asadigandomani, H., Dashtkoohi, M., Eslami, S., & Soleimani, M. (2025). Advancing diabetic retinopathy screening: A systematic review of artificial intelligence and optical Coherence Tomography Angiography innovations. *Diagnostics (Basel)*, *15*(6), 737. DOI: 10.3390/diagnostics15060737 PMID: 40150080

Herrera, R. F., Mourgues, C., Alarcón, L. F., & Pellicer, E. (2021). Comparing team interactions in traditional and BIM-lean design management. *Buildings (Basel, Switzerland)*, *11*(10), 447. Advance online publication. DOI: 10.3390/buildings11100447

Hock-Doepgen, M., Clauss, T., Kraus, S., & Cheng, C. (2020). Knowledge management capabilities and organizational risk-taking for business model innovation in SMEs. *Journal of Business Research*, *130*, 683–697. DOI: 10.1016/j.jbusres.2019.12.001

Hoekman, J., Frenken, K., & Tijssen, R. J. (2010). Research collaboration at a distance: Changing spatial patterns of scientific collaboration within Europe. *Research Policy*, *39*(5), 662–673. DOI: 10.1016/j.respol.2010.01.012

Howells, J. (2006). Intermediation and the role of intermediaries in innovation. *Research Policy*, *35*(5), 715–728. DOI: 10.1016/j.respol.2006.03.005

Hughes, A., & Kitson, M. (2012). Pathways to impact and the strategic role of universities: New evidence on the breadth and depth of university knowledge exchange in the UK and the factors constraining its development. *Cambridge Journal of Economics*, *36*(3), 723–750. DOI: 10.1093/cje/bes017

Hu, K., Chen, F., Hsu, M., & Tzeng, G. (2023). Governance of artificial intelligence applications in a business audit via a fusion fuzzy multiple rule-based decision-making model. *Financial Innovation*, *9*(1), 1–31. DOI: 10.1186/s40854-022-00436-4

Huong Nguyen, T., & Lynn Meek, V. (2015). Key Considerations in Organizing and Structuring University Research. *The Journal of Research Administration*, *46*, 41–62. https://go8.edu.au/

Imamguluyev, R. (2025). Integrating Fuzzy Logic with Deep Learning: A New Approach to Explainable Artificial Intelligence. 2025 6th International Conference on Mobile Computing and Sustainable Informatics *(ICMCSI)*, 1701-1706. DOI: 10.1109/ICMCSI64620.2025.10883618

Jobin, A., Ienca, M., & Vayena, E. (2019). The global landscape of AI ethics guidelines. *Nature Machine Intelligence*, *1*(9), 389–399. DOI: 10.1038/s42256-019-0088-2

Kazemzadeh, K. (2025). Artificial intelligence in ophthalmology: Opportunities, challenges, and ethical considerations. *Medical Hypothesis, Discovery and Innovation in Ophthalmology*, *14*(1), 255–272. DOI: 10.51329/mehdiophthal1517 PMID: 40453785

Kholiavko, N., Grosu, V., Safonov, Y., Zhavoronok, A., & Cosmulese, C. G. (2021). Quintuple helix model: Investment aspects of higher education impact on sustainability. *Management Theory and Studies for Rural Business and Infrastructure Development*, *43*(1), 111–128.

Köhler, J., Geels, F. W., Kern, F., Markard, J., Onsongo, E., Wieczorek, A., Alkemade, F., Avelino, F., Bergek, A., Boons, F., Fünfschilling, L., Hess, D., Holtz, G., Hyysalo, S., Jenkins, K., Kivimaa, P., Martiskainen, M., McMeekin, A., Mühlemeier, M. S., & Wells, P. (2019). An agenda for sustainability transitions research: State of the art and future directions. *Environmental Innovation and Societal Transitions*, *31*, 1–32. DOI: 10.1016/j.eist.2019.01.004

Kondylakis, H., Kalokyri, V., Sfakianakis, S., Marias, K., Tsiknakis, M., Jimenez-Pastor, A., Camacho-Ramos, E., Blanquer, I., Segrelles, J. D., López-Huguet, S., Barelle, C., Kogut-Czarkowska, M., Tsakou, G., Siopis, N., Sakellariou, Z., Bizopoulos, P., Drossou, V., Lalas, A., Votis, K., & Lekadir, K. (2023). Data infrastructures for AI in medical imaging: A report on the experiences of five EU projects. *European Radiology Experimental*, *7*(1), 20. Advance online publication. DOI: 10.1186/s41747-023-00336-x PMID: 37150779

Kreye, M. E., Ramirez Hernandez, T., & Eppinger, S. (2025). Translating agile management practices into a traditional industry context. *Journal of Product Innovation Management*, *42*(2), 444–467. DOI: 10.1111/jpim.12760

Kyvik, S., & Reymert, I. (2016). *The establishment of formal research groups in higher education institutions. 0317*. DOI: 10.3402/nstep.v2.33896

Kyvik, S., & Reymert, I. (2017). Research collaboration in groups and networks: Differences across academic fields. *Scientometrics*, *113*(2), 951–967. DOI: 10.1007/s11192-017-2497-5 PMID: 29081555

Lam, A. (2010). From 'Ivory Tower traditionalists' to 'Entrepreneurial scientists'? *Social Studies of Science*, *40*(2), 307–340. DOI: 10.1177/0306312709349963

Lee, A. Y., Yanagihara, R. T., Lee, C. S., Blazes, M., Jung, H. C., Chee, Y. E., Gencarella, M. D., Gee, H., Maa, A. Y., Cockerham, G. C., Lynch, M., & Boyko, E. J. (2021). Multicenter, head-to-head, real-world validation study of seven automated artificial intelligence diabetic retinopathy screening systems. *Diabetes Care*, *44*(5), 1168–1175. DOI: 10.2337/dc20-1877 PMID: 33402366

Li, N., Kim, M., Dai, J., & Vasarhelyi, M. A. (2024). Using Artificial Intelligence in ESG Assurance. *Journal of Emerging Technologies in Accounting*, *21*(2), 83–99. DOI: 10.2308/JETA-2022-054

Liyanage, S. I. H., & Netswera, F. G. (2022). Greening universities with mode 3 and quintuple helix model of innovation–production of knowledge and innovation in knowledge-based economy, Botswana. [PubMed]. *Journal of the Knowledge Economy*, *13*(2), 1126–1156.

Low, A. M. (2024). Predictors and Socio-Demographic Disparities in STEM Degree Outcomes: A UK Longitudinal Study using Hierarchical Logistic Regression. *arXiv (Cornell University)*. https://doi.org//arxiv.2408.05853DOI: 10.48550

Lulaj, E., & Brajković, M. (2025). The Moderating Role of Finance, Accounting, and Digital Disruption in ESG, Financial Reporting, and Auditing: A Triple-Helix Perspective. *Journal of Risk and Financial Management*, *18*(5), 245. DOI: 10.3390/jrfm18050245

Ma, X., Zhang, Z., Yan, R., Pan, H., & Li, C. (2017). *A Study on the Governance Structure of Modern Universities*. *95*(Iceemr), 74–77. DOI: 10.2991/iceemr-17.2017.18

Ma, Z. (2024). Managing university-industry collaborative innovation in the pharmaceutical industry. DOI: 10.5463/thesis.499

Mahardhani, A. J. (2023). The Role of Public Policy in Fostering Technological Innovation and Sustainability. [ADMAN]. *Journal of Contemporary Administration and Management*, *1*(2), 47–53. DOI: 10.61100/adman.v1i2.22

Maji, P. K., Biswas, R., & Roy, A. R. (2001). Fuzzy soft sets. *Journal of Fuzzy Mathematics*, *9*(3), 589–602.

Marginson, S., & Marginson, S. (2022). Oxford Review of Education Research on international and global higher education : Six different perspectives Research on international and global higher education : Six different perspectives ABSTRACT. *Oxford Review of Education*, *48*(4), 421–438. DOI: 10.1080/03054985.2022.2087619

Maria Manuela, J. P. A. C. C. F. R. de A. (2013). *The triple helix model and dynamics of innovation : a case study*. DOI: 10.1108/17561411211208758

McAdam, M., Miller, K., & McAdam, R. (2017). University business models in disequilibrium - engaging industry and end users within university technology transfer processes. *R & D Management*, *47*(3), 458–472. DOI: 10.1111/radm.12265

McCaig, M., Dara, R., & Rezania, D. (2023). Farmer-centric design thinking principles for smart farming technologies. *Internet of Things : Engineering Cyber Physical Human Systems*, *23*, 100898. Advance online publication. DOI: 10.1016/j.iot.2023.100898

Miller, K., McAdam, M., & McAdam, R. (2014). The changing university business model: A stakeholder perspective. *R & D Management*, *44*(3), 265–287. DOI: 10.1111/radm.12064

Mishra, S. (2023). Internet of things enabled deep learning methods using unmanned aerial vehicles enabled integrated farm management. *Heliyon*, *9*(8), e18818. Advance online publication. DOI: 10.1016/j.heliyon.2023.e18659 PMID: 37576187

Mishra, S., & Sharma, S. K. (2023). Advanced contribution of IoT in agricultural production for the development of smart livestock environments. *Internet of Things : Engineering Cyber Physical Human Systems*, *22*, 100724. Advance online publication. DOI: 10.1016/j.iot.2023.100724

Modlin, C. E., Shrestha, P., Chang, L. W., Ali, J., Sewankambo, N. K., & Wonodi, C. (2025). A scoping review of equity toolkits for international academic partnerships. *International Journal for Equity in Health*, *24*(1), 268. DOI: 10.1186/s12939-025-02632-x PMID: 41088304

Mohammadi, A. (2025). Industry-university partnership governance base on new technologies emergence. *Sustainable Social Development*, *2*(6), 3007. DOI: 10.54517/ssd3007

Molodtsov, D. (1999). Soft set theory: First results. *Computers & Mathematics with Applications (Oxford, England)*, *37*(4–5), 19–31. DOI: 10.1016/S0898-1221(99)00056-5

Moscardini, A., Strachan, R., Vlasova, T., & Pavlenko, I. (2021). A System Strategy for Higher Education. *Performance Improvement*, *60*(2), 10–20. DOI: 10.1002/pfi.21955

Mukherjee, A., & Das, A. K. (2015b). Interval valued intuitionistic fuzzy soft multi set theoretic approach to decision making problems, 2015 International Conference on Computer, Communication and Control (IC4), Indore, India, 2015, pp. 1-5, DOI: 10.1109/IC4.2015.7375640

Mukherjee, A., & Das, A. K. (2016a). Application of fuzzy soft multi sets in decision-making problems. In: Nagar, A., Mohapatra, D., Chaki, N. (eds) Proceedings of 3rd International Conference on Advanced Computing, Networking and Informatics. Smart Innovation, Systems and Technologies, vol. 43. Springer, New Delhi. DOI: 10.1007/978-81-322-2538-6_3

Mukherjee, A., & Das, A. K. (2023). Essentials of fuzzy soft multisets: Theory and applications, Springer Nature Singapore Pte Ltd., 1-151. ISBN: 978-981-19-2759-1, DOI: 10.1007/978-981-19-2760-7

Mukherjee, A., & Das, A. K. (2015a). Application of interval valued intuitionistic fuzzy soft set in investment decision making, *2015 Fifth International Conference on Advances in Computing and Communications (ICACC)*, Kochi, India, 2015, pp. 61-64, DOI: 10.1109/ICACC.2015.37

Mukherjee, A., & Das, A. K. (2015c). Relations on intuitionistic fuzzy soft multi sets. In Kim, K. (Ed.), *Information Science and Applications. Lecture Notes in Electrical Engineering* (Vol. 339). Springer., DOI: 10.1007/978-3-662-46578-3_71

Mukherjee, A., & Das, A. K. (2016b). Topological structure formed by intuitionistic fuzzy rough relations. *Journal of the Indian Mathematical Society*, *83*(1-2), 135–144.

Mukherjee, A., & Das, A. K. (2022). Einstein operations on fuzzy soft multisets and decision making. *Boletim da Sociedade Paranaense de Matematica*, *40*, 1–10. DOI: 10.5269/bspm.32546

Mukherjee, A., Das, A. K., Gupta, N., Patra, S., Mahmood, T., Das, S., & Das, R. (2026). A novel generalized interval-valued neutrosophic rough soft set framework for enhanced decision-making: Application in water quality assessment. *Transactions on Fuzzy Sets and Systems*, *5*(1), 1–25. DOI: 10.71602/tfss.2026.1194037

Muñoz; G. A. A., & Plazas, A. (2024). Innovation Management in University Research Groups. *Journal of Technology Managment and Innovoation, 19*(2), 15–27.

Muruccia, Y., Solazzo, G., Del Vecchio, P., & Passiante, G. (2020). Evidence from network analysis application to innovation systems and quintuple helix. *Technological Forecasting and Social Change*, *161*, 120306. DOI: 10.1016/j.techfore.2020.120306

Musseau, A. (2024). Microcredentials: revolutionizing education institutions. *EHL Insights*, 1–7. https://hospitalityinsights.ehl.edu/microcredentials-revolutionizing-education-institutions

Nath, S., Rahimy, E., Kras, A., & Korot, E. (2023). Toward safer ophthalmic artificial intelligence via distributed validation on real-world data. *Current Opinion in Ophthalmology*, *34*(5), 459–463. DOI: 10.1097/ICU.0000000000000986 PMID: 37459329

Newton, J. E., Nettle, R., & Pryce, J. E. (2020). Farming smarter with big data: Insights from the case of Australia's national dairy herd milk recording scheme. *Agricultural Systems*, *181*, 102811. Advance online publication. DOI: 10.1016/j.agsy.2020.102811

Novak, P. (2025). Digital twin framework for postural tachycardia syndrome and autonomic disorders. *Frontiers in Neurology*, *16*(1678955), 1678955. DOI: 10.3389/fneur.2025.1678955 PMID: 41142154

Nunes, S., Lopes, R., & Fuller-Love, N. (2017). Networking, Innovation, and Firms' Performance: Portugal as Illustration. *Journal of the Knowledge Economy*, *10*(3), 899–920. DOI: 10.1007/s13132-017-0508-7

Oarue-Itseuwa, E. (2024). Artificial Intelligence's impact of the management consultancy sector over the next five years. *Management Consulting Journal*, *7*(1), 49–58. DOI: 10.2478/mcj-2024-0005

OCED. (2023a). Micro-credentials for lifelong learning and employability. *OECD Education Policy Perspectives, 1*(66), 44. https://doi.org/10.1787/5cc2d673-en

OCED. (2023b). Micro-credentials for lifelong learning and employability. *OECD Education Policy Perspectives*, *1*(66), 44. DOI: 10.1787/5cc2d673-en

Onifade, A. Y., Ogeawuchi, J. C., Abayomi, A. A., Agboola, O. A., Dosumu, R. E., & George, O. O. (2022). A conceptual framework for integrating AI adoption metrics into B2B marketing decision systems. *International Journal of Management and Organizational Research*, *1*(1), 237–248. DOI: 10.54660/IJMOR.2022.1.1.237-248

Open Government Partnership. (2021). *Algorithmic accountability in government: Executive summary & recommendations*. https://www.opengovpartnership.org/wp-content/uploads/2021/08/algorithmic-accountability-public-sector.pdf

Orman, R., Şimşek, E., & Kozak Çakır, M. A. (2023). Micro-credentials and reflections on higher education. *Higher Education Evaluation and Development*, *17*(2), 96–112. DOI: 10.1108/HEED-08-2022-0028

Ormeño Zender, Y., & García de Soto, B. (2021). Use of Scrum in the rehabilitation of a commercial building in Peru. *Construction Innovation*, *21*(2), 145–163. DOI: 10.1108/CI-12-2019-0140

Özcan, B., Friedrich, M., Huttner, J., & Dwinger, K. (2025). *Enhancing Trust in Human-AI Interaction through Explainable Decision Support Systems for Mission Planning of UAS-Swarms*. AHFE International., DOI: 10.54941/ahfe1006377

Park, C. (2010). What makes A case study really qualitative?: Show me your evidence, please! *English Teaching*, *65*(4), 79–101. DOI: 10.15858/engtea.65.4.201012.79

Pates, R. (2023). *Knowledge transfer partnerships evaluation* [Report]. https://www.ukri.org/wp-content/uploads/2023/10/IUK-23102023-KTP-Evaluation-Final-Report-FINAL-Aug-23.pdf

Patrucco, A. S., Canterino, F., & Minelgaite, I. (2022). How do Scrum methodologies influence the team's cultural values? A multiple case study on agile teams in nonsoftware industries. *IEEE Transactions on Engineering Management*, *69*(6), 3503–3513. DOI: 10.1109/TEM.2022.3146717

Perkmann, M., Neely, A., & Walsh, K. (2011). How should firms evaluate success in university–industry alliances? A performance measurement system. *R & D Management*, *41*(2), 202–216. DOI: 10.1111/j.1467-9310.2011.00637.x

Perkmann, M., & Walsh, K. (2007). University–industry relationships and open innovation: Towards a research agenda. *International Journal of Management Reviews*, *9*(4), 259–280. DOI: 10.1111/j.1468-2370.2007.00225.x

Perkmann, M., & Walsh, K. (2008). Engaging the scholar: Three types of academic consulting and their impact on universities and industry. *Research Policy*, *37*(10), 1884–1891. DOI: 10.1016/j.respol.2008.07.009

Petcu, M. A., Sobolevschi-David, M.-I., & Curea, S. C. (2024). Integrating digital technologies in sustainability reporting: Perceptions of professional cloud computing users. *Electronics (Basel)*, *13*(14), 2684. DOI: 10.3390/electronics13142684

Philbin, S. P. (2012). Resource-based view of university-industry research collaboration. *2012 Proceedings of Portland International Center for Management of Engineering and Technology. Technology Management for Emerging Technologies, PICMET*, *12*(January), 400–411.

Pinto, H., & Nogueira, C. (2018). Mapping an Entrepreneurial, Innovative and Sustainable Ecosystem Using Social Network Analysis: An Exploratory Approach of Publicly Funded Innovative Project Data. In *Entrepreneurial, Innovative and Sustainable Ecosystems: Best Practices and Implications for Quality of Life* (pp. 237–254). Springer International Publishing. DOI: 10.1007/978-3-319-71014-3_12

Pirkkalainen, H., Sood, I., Padron Napoles, C., Kukkonen, A., & Camilleri, A. (2023). How might micro-credentials influence institutions and empower learners in higher education? *Educational Research*, *65*(1), 40–63. DOI: 10.1080/00131881.2022.2157302

Popper, M., Rapetti, C. A., & Pique, J. M. (2025). Integrating policy agendas for sustainable innovation: a quadruple helix approach. *Emerging Markets Journal*, 1–22. DOI: 10.2478/emj-2025-0009

Prakash, C., Singh, L. P., Gupta, A., & Lohan, S. K. (2023). Advancements in smart farming: A comprehensive review of IoT, wireless communication, sensors, and hardware for agricultural automation. *Sensors and Actuators. A, Physical*, *359*, 114605. Advance online publication. DOI: 10.1016/j.sna.2023.114605

Pricopoaia, O., Busila, A. V., Cristache, N., Susanu, I., & Matis, C. (2024). Challenges for entrepreneurial innovation: Startups as tools for a better knowledge-based economy. *The International Entrepreneurship and Management Journal, 20*(2), 969–1010. DOI: 10.1007/s11365-023-00923-9

Project Management Institute. (2017). *Agile practice guide*. Project Management Institute.

Project Management Institute. (2021). *A guide to the project management body of knowledge (PMBOK® Guide)* (7th ed.). Project Management Institute.

Project Management Institute. (2023). *Shaping the future of project management with AI.* PMI Thought Leadership Series. https://www.pmi.org/learning/thought-leadership/shaping-the-future-of-project-management-with-ai

Putra, Z. D. W., & van der Knaap, W. G. (2018). Urban innovation system and the role of an open web-based platform: The case of Amsterdam smart city. *Journal of Regional and City Planning, 29*(3), 234–249. DOI: 10.5614/jrcp.2018.29.3.4

Qmarkets (2024). *End-to-End Innovation Management Platform.* Retrieved May 30, 2024 from https://www.qmarkets.net/lp/innovation-management-software/?hsa_qmt=y&utm_term=innovation%20platform&utm_campaign=Tier+1+Countries+%7C+Gold+KWs+%26+Silver+KWs+%7C+Exact+%26+Phrase&utm_source=adwords&utm_medium=ppc&hsa_acc=3759777188&hsa_cam=8690653365&hsa_grp=139195627185&hsa_ad=696764641653&hsa_src=g&hsa_tgt=kwd-6668275533&hsa_kw=innovation%20platform&hsa_mt=p&hsa_net=adwords&hsa_ver=3&gad_source=1&gclid=CjwKCAjwx-CyBhAqEiwAeOcTde0vSdyeHGevzm0u29NihVgwUZcEE_6P3UWSO69UWyysLMQuWORLExoCPoUQAvD_BwE

Queen's University Belfast. (2025, June 23). Queen's Marks 50 years of Knowledge Transfer Partnerships (KTP). *Business | Queen's University Belfast.* https://www.qub.ac.uk/Business/access-our-expertise/Knowledge-Transfer-Partnerships/news/queens-marks-50-years-of-knowledge-transfer-partnerships.html

Rafique, T., Awan, M. U., Shafiq, M., & Mahmood, K. (2023). Exploring the role of ranking systems towards university performance improvement: A focus group-based study. *Heliyon, 9*(10), e20904. DOI: 10.1016/j.heliyon.2023.e20904 PMID: 37886765

Ranga, M., & Etzkowitz, H. (2013). *Triple Helix systems : an analytical framework for innovation policy and practice in the Knowledge Society. 27*(3), 237–262. DOI: 10.5367/ihe.2013.0165

Rao, D. P., Savoy, F. M., Tan, J. Z. E., Fung, B. P.-E., Bopitiya, C. M., Sivaraman, A., & Vinekar, A. (2023). Development and validation of an artificial intelligence based screening tool for detection of retinopathy of prematurity in a South Indian population. *Frontiers in Pediatrics*, *11*, 1197237. DOI: 10.3389/fped.2023.1197237 PMID: 37794964

Rao, K. (2025). Artificial Intelligence-driven 3D modeling: Transformative applications analysis. *Transactions on Computer Science and Intelligent Systems Research*, *9*, 236–245. DOI: 10.62051/f5wn2q81

Rasmussen, E., & Wright, M. (2015). How can universities facilitate academic spin-offs? An entrepreneurial competency perspective. *The Journal of Technology Transfer*, *40*(5), 782–799. DOI: 10.1007/s10961-014-9386-3

Ravikumar, A. Olimbaevich, I. R., Mashkhura, S., & Musayeva, S. (2025). Transforming Healthcare with Large Language Models and AI agents. In Advances in Computational Intelligence and Robotics (pp. 51–82). IGI Global Scientific Publishing. DOI: 10.4018/979-8-3373-2008-3.ch003

Ravikumar, R. S., Manujakshi, Aarthi, S., Urazbaeva, Y., & Tamilselvi, S. (2025). Navigating data privacy, security, and regulatory challenges in healthcare AI ensuring fairness, bias mitigation, interpretability, and trust. In Transformative Role of Transformer Models in Healthcare (pp. 25–54). IGI Global Scientific Publishing. DOI: 10.4018/979-8-3373-2038-0.ch002

Ravikumar, R. N., & Aarthi, S. (2025a). AI-powered synergistic robotics and IoT ecosystems for predictive and preventive healthcare. In *Robotics and IoT Synergy in Next-Generation Healthcare* (pp. 1–32). IGI Global Scientific Publishing., DOI: 10.4018/979-8-3373-5447-7.ch001

Ravikumar, R. N., & Aarthi, S. (2025b). Digital Twin-driven green energy systems. In *The Future of Green Energy* (pp. 1–28). IGI Global Scientific Publishing., DOI: 10.4018/979-8-3373-3226-0.ch001

Ravishankar, S. (2025). Navigating AI/ML risk analytics and compliance: A strategic guide for launching global FinTech products. *European Modern Studies Journal*, *9*(5), 78–89. DOI: 10.59573/emsj.9(5).2025.9

Reis, J., Rosado, D. P., Ribeiro, D. F., & Melão, N. (2022). Quintuple Helix Innovation Model for the European Union Defense Industry—An Empirical Research. *Sustainability (Basel)*, *14*(24), 16499. DOI: 10.3390/su142416499

Richert, D., Marshall, L., & James, G. (2024). Design and Implementation of an Industry 4.0 Micro-Credential Program. *Proceedings of the Canadian Engineering Education Association (CEEA)*, 1–7. DOI: 10.24908/pceea.2023.17111

Romao, L., Villamizar, H., Oliveira, R., Alonso, S., & Kalinowski, M. (2025). Agile Management for Machine Learning: A Systematic Mapping Study. In *Euromicro Conference on Software Engineering and Advanced Applications* (pp. 350-360). Cham: Springer Nature Switzerland.

Roundy, P. T., & Asllani, A. (2024). Understanding AI innovation contexts: A review and content analysis of artificial intelligence and entrepreneurial ecosystems research. *Industrial Management & Data Systems*, *124*(7), 2333–2363. DOI: 10.1108/IMDS-08-2023-0551

Roy, R., & Marsafawy, H. El. (2020). *Organizational Structure for 21St Century Higher Education Institutions: Meeting Expectations and Crossing Challenges. April.*

Rwakenda, H. B. B. (2016). Challenges Faced by Leaders of Institutions of Higher Learning in Uganda: Case Study of Mbale Public and Private Universities. *Texila International Journal of Academic Research*, *3*(1), 90–98. DOI: 10.21522/TIJAR.2014.03.01.Art010

Ryu, J., Lee, J., & Park, S. (2022). Triple Helix open innovation model in governmental AI innovation strategy. *Technovation*, *118*, 102573. DOI: 10.1016/j.technovation.2022.102573

Sachdeva, D. S. (2025). Entrepreneurship innovation and startups: Catalyst for innovation and economic growth of India. *International Journal of Environmental Sciences*, •••, 2513–2526. DOI: 10.64252/xymrse11

Scaringella, L., & Radziwon, A. (2023). Resilience and structure in innovation ecosystems. *Journal of Business Research*, *154*, 113475. DOI. 10.1016/j.jbusres.2022.113475

Schneider, J., Abraham, R., Meske, C., & Vom Brocke, J. (2023). Artificial Intelligence Governance for Businesses. *Information Systems Management*, *40*(3), 170–186. DOI: 10.1080/10580530.2022.2085825

Schwab, A. K., Halberstadt, J., Besieda, A., Kraft, M., & Ortland, A. (2023). Organizational aspects of digitalization in the context of agriculture: Exemplary results from analyzing data flows in German dairy farming. *Procedia Computer Science*, *219*, 1006–1011. DOI: 10.1016/j.procs.2023.01.378

Senker, P., & Senker, J. (1994). Transferring technology and expertise from universities to industry: Britain's Teaching Company Scheme. *New Technology, Work and Employment*, *9*(2), 81–92. DOI: 10.1111/j.1468-005X.1994.tb00052.x

Servoss, J., Chang, C., Fay, J., Lota, K. S., Mashour, G. A., & Ward, K. R. (2017). fastPACE Train-the-Trainer: A scalable new educational program to accelerate training in biomedical innovation, entrepreneurship, and commercialization. *Journal of Clinical and Translational Science*, *1*(5), 271–277. DOI: 10.1017/cts.2017.306 PMID: 29707247

Shaikh, T. A., Rasool, T., & Lone, F. R. (2022). Towards leveraging the role of machine learning and artificial intelligence in precision agriculture and smart farming. *Computers and Electronics in Agriculture*, *198*, 107119. Advance online publication. DOI: 10.1016/j.compag.2022.107119

Shakeel, P. M. (2022). A deep learning-based cow behavior recognition scheme for improving cattle behavior modeling in smart farming. *Internet of Things : Engineering Cyber Physical Human Systems*, *19*, 100539. Advance online publication. DOI: 10.1016/j.iot.2022.100539

Sherin, N. (2025). Fuzzy Logic and Set Theory in Artificial Intelligence Decision-Making. *International Journal for Research in Applied Science and Engineering Technology*, *13*(5), 1656–1658. Advance online publication. DOI: 10.22214/ijraset.2025.70546

Similié, D. E., Andersen, J. K. H., Dinesen, S., Savarimuthu, T. R., & Grauslund, J. (2025). Grading of diabetic retinopathy using a pre-segmenting deep learning classification model: Validation of an automated algorithm. *Acta Ophthalmologica*, *103*(2), 215–221. DOI: 10.1111/aos.16781 PMID: 39425597

Singh Chauhan, A., Ghildiyal, P., & Yadav, S. (2025). Artificial Intelligence for Drug Discovery and development. ASP Books (A division of AcademicSP). DOI: 10.63686/978-81-987694-7-3

Singh, M. P., & Keche, Y. N. (2025). Ethical integration of artificial intelligence in healthcare: Narrative review of global challenges and strategic solutions. *Cureus*, *17*(5), e84804. DOI: 10.7759/cureus.84804 PMID: 40568260

Son, J., Shin, J. Y., Kim, H. D., Jung, K.-H., Park, K. H., & Park, S. J. (2020). Development and validation of deep learning models for screening multiple abnormal findings in retinal fundus images. *Ophthalmology*, *127*(1), 85–94. DOI: 10.1016/j.ophtha.2019.05.029 PMID: 31281057

Subrahmanyam, S. (2025). Strategic Collaboration and Partnerships in R&D for Innovation. In Research and Development Practices in Innovation (pp. 283–314). IGI Global. DOI: 10.4018/979-8-3373-0812-8.ch010

Sumrit, D. (2024). Enhancing readiness degree for Industrial Internet of Things adoption in manufacturing enterprises: An integrated Pythagorean fuzzy approach. *Heliyon*, *10*(20), e39007. Advance online publication. DOI: 10.1016/j.heliyon.2024.e39007 PMID: 39640696

Szulanski, G. (1996). Exploring internal stickiness: Impediments to the transfer of best practice within the firm. *Strategic Management Journal*, *17*(S2), 27–43. DOI: 10.1002/smj.4250171105

Tadwalkar, S. V. (2008). Create centre of excellence (CoE) for better business. *Ubiquity*, *2008*(March), 1–9. DOI: 10.1145/1366313.1361366

Taneja, M., Byabazaire, J., Jalodia, N., Davy, A., Olariu, C., & Malone, P. (2020). Machine learning based fog computing assisted data-driven approach for early lameness detection in dairy cattle. *Computers and Electronics in Agriculture*, *171*, 105286. Advance online publication. DOI: 10.1016/j.compag.2020.105286

Tiossi, F. M., & Rodrigues, R. G. (2023). Triple helix in the management of innovation in public policies: A study of two countries. *Revista de Gestão e Secretariado*, *14*(8), 14516–14531. DOI: 10.7769/gesec.v14i8.2690

Tomlinson, M. (2017). Forms of graduate capital and their relationship to graduate employability. *Education + Training*, *59*(4), 338–352. DOI: 10.1108/ET-05-2016-0090

Torbacki, W. (2024). A Framework for Assessing Innovations, Business Models and Sustainability for Software Companies Using Hybrid Multiple-Criteria Decision-Making. *Sustainability (Basel)*, *16*(14), 5871. Advance online publication. DOI: 10.3390/su16145871

Torky, M., & Hassanein, A. E. (2020). Integrating blockchain and the internet of things in precision agriculture: Analysis, opportunities, and challenges. *Computers and Electronics in Agriculture*, *178*, 105476. Advance online publication. DOI: 10.1016/j.compag.2020.105476

Trabelsi, M. A. (2024). The impact of artificial intelligence on economic development. [IDEAS/RePEc]. *Journal of Electronic Business & Digital Economics*, *3*(2), 142–155. DOI: 10.1108/JEBDE-10-2023-0022

University, O. N. E., Razinkin, N., & Fedosiuk, D. (2025). Business Intelligence in the digital environment: Legal and analytical aspects. *Business Navigator*, *3*(80). Advance online publication. DOI: 10.32782/business-navigator.80-42

Van Damme, D. (2021). Transforming Universities for a Sustainable Future. In *The Promise of Higher Education: Essays in Honour of 70 Years of IAU*. DOI: 10.1007/978-3-030-67245-4_64

Verdouw, C., Tekinerdogan, B., Beulens, A., & Wolfert, S. (2021). Digital twins in smart farming. *Agricultural Systems*, *189*, 103046. Advance online publication. DOI: 10.1016/j.agsy.2020.103046

Vignieri, V. (2021). Crowdsourcing as a mode of open innovation: Exploring drivers of success of a multisided platform through system dynamics modelling. *Systems Research and Behavioral Science*, *38*(1), 108–124. DOI: 10.1002/sres.2636

Vivar-simon, M., Zabaleta, N., Torre, J. D. La, Basañez, A., & Urruzuno, A. (2022). *Towards Human-Scale Competitiveness : Priority Challenges for Triple Helix towards 2030*.

Wang, K., Ying, Z., Goswami, S., Yin, Y., & Zhao, Y. (2023). Investigating the Role of Artificial Intelligence Technologies in the Construction Industry Using a Delphi-ANP-TOPSIS Hybrid MCDM Concept under a Fuzzy Environment. *Sustainability (Basel)*, *15*(15), 11848. Advance online publication. DOI: 10.3390/su151511848

Wei, Y., Shengfan, Q., & Wengang, X. (2025). Exploring the effectiveness of micro-credentials in artificial intelligence teaching and learning : An empirical study based on AI þ X program in China. *Cogent Education*, *12*(1), 2536528. Advance online publication. DOI: 10.1080/2331186X.2025.2536528

Wilson, T. (2012). *A Review of Business–University Collaboration* (By University of Hertfordshire, Higher Education Funding Council for England, Department for Business Innovation & Skills, University of Brighton, IT & Telecommunications Industry, GlaxoSmithKline, University of Central Lancashire, University of Exeter, Southampton Solent University, University College London, University of Oxford, Teesside University, Aston University, Surrey University, University of Nottingham, New College Durham, Higher Education Funding Council for England, BAE Systems, HECSU, . . . Enterprise Rent-A-Car). https://assets.publishing.service.gov.uk/media/5a796c56e5274a2acd18cb62/12-610-wilson-review-business-university-collaboration.pdf

Zadeh, L. A. (1965). Fuzzy sets. *Information and Control*, *8*(3), 338–353. DOI: 10.1016/S0019-9958(65)90241-X

Zasa, F. P., Patrucco, A., & Pellizzoni, E. (2020). Managing the hybrid organization: How can agile and traditional project management coexist? *Research Technology Management*, *64*(1), 54–63. DOI: 10.1080/08956308.2021.1843331

Zen, I. S., & Shibakawa, H. (2022). Quintuple Helix Lens for Transformation: An Okayama Model of Education for Sustainable Development. *Frontiers in Sustainability*, *3*, 798330. DOI: 10.3389/frsus.2022.798330

Zhao, P. Y., Bommakanti, N., Yu, G., Aaberg, M. T., Patel, T. P., & Paulus, Y. M. (2023). Deep learning for automated detection of neovascular leakage on ultra-widefield fluorescein angiography in diabetic retinopathy. *Scientific Reports*, *13*(1), 9165. DOI: 10.1038/s41598-023-36327-6 PMID: 37280345

Zhong, Q., Cui, H., Yang, M., & Ling, C. (2025). Research on Stochastic Evolution Game of Green Technology Innovation Alliance of Government, Industry, University, and Research with Fuzzy Income. *Sustainability (Basel)*, *17*(5), 2294. Advance online publication. DOI: 10.3390/su17052294

Zhou, C., & Etzkowitz, H. (2021). *Triple Helix Twins : A Framework for Achieving Innovation and UN Sustainable Development Goals.*

Zhou, Y., Dai, M., Sun, L., Tang, X., Zhou, L., Tang, Z., Jiang, J., & Xia, X. (2023). The accuracy of intraocular lens power calculation formulas based on artificial intelligence in highly myopic eyes: A systematic review and network meta-analysis. *Frontiers in Public Health*, *11*, 1279718. DOI: 10.3389/fpubh.2023.1279718 PMID: 38026369

Zhu, A., Tailor, P., Verma, R., Zhang, I., Schott, B., Ye, C., Szirth, B., Habiel, M., & Khouri, A. S. (2024). Implementation of deep learning artificial intelligence in vision-threatening disease screenings for an underserved community during COVID-19. *Journal of Telemedicine and Telecare*, *30*(10), 1590–1597. DOI: 10.1177/1357633X231158832 PMID: 36908254

About the Contributors

Mohieddine Rahmouni, Ph.D., is an Associate Professor of Economics and Quantitative Methods at the Applied College, King Faisal University (Al-Ahsa, Saudi Arabia), and at the High School of Economic and Commercial Sciences of Tunis (ESSECT), University of Tunis, Tunisia. He earned his Ph.D. in Economics through a joint program between the University of Montesquieu Bordeaux-IV (now University of Bordeaux), France, and the University of Tunis. His research focuses on innovation economics, applied econometrics, productivity, and industrial dynamics, with particular emphasis on economic development in emerging economies. Dr. Rahmouni has published in leading international journals, including Structural Change and Economic Dynamics, the Journal of Industrial and Business Economics, and the International Journal of Innovation and Technology Management. His work examines external knowledge sources, innovation drivers, and the policy impacts shaping firm-level performance. Actively engaged in global academic and policy communities, Dr. Rahmouni contributes to informing innovation policy in the Global South, positioning him as a key voice in advancing studies on university–government partnerships and innovation ecosystems.

Mossab Saud Alholiby is an Associate Professor of Educational Leadership at the College of Education, King Faisal University, Al-Ahsa, Saudi Arabia. He earned his Ph.D. in Educational Management from the University of Glasgow in 2018, with a thesis on enhancing quality assurance in Saudi higher education through educational and e-management perspectives. His research interests include higher education leadership, quality assurance, educational management, digital leadership, and technology-enhanced learning. Dr. Alholiby has published widely in international and regional journals, including the Journal of Industrial and Business Economics, International Journal of Leadership in Education, and Administrative Sciences. His scholarship explores academic leadership, innovation in higher education, and governance practices, with a particular focus on the role of education in advancing sustainable development.

Ben Othman Soufiene is an Assistant Professor of computer science at the King Faisal University from 2025. He received his Ph.D. degree in computer science from Manouba University in 2016 for his dissertation on "Secure data aggregation in wireless sensor networks. He also holds M.S. degrees from the Monastir University in 2012. My research interests focus on the Internet of Medical Things, Wireless Body Sensor Networks, Wireless Networks, Artificial Intelligence, Machine Learning and Big Data. Dr. Ben Othman has published more than 140 papers at reputed international journals, conferences, and book chapters. He is an Editorial Board Member in the different Journals and Conferences. He serves as an associate editor/academic editor for international journals including IEEE Access, IEEE Sensors, IEEE Internet of Things, Elsevier, Springer, Taylor & Francis, IGI, IET, Telecommunication Computing Electronics and Control, and Wiley. Dr. Ben Othman is a Technical Program Committee Member for more than a dozen of international conferences.

***

Simon Cleveland is a professor of project management at Purdue University Global. Dr. Cleveland is a graduate of George Mason University with Bachelor of Science degree in Business, of the George Washington University with a Master of Science degree in Project Management, of the City University of Seattle with a Master of Arts degree in Leadership, with a Ph.D. in Information Systems from Nova Southeastern University, and with a Ed.D. in Organizational Leadership from Northeastern University. He is also certified as a project management professional (PMP), Six Sigma Black Belt (SSBB) expert, and Information Technology Infrastructure Library (ITIL) foundations expert. Dr. Cleveland is the author of over 60 peer-reviewed publications in journals and conferences, and is a three-time recipient of the prestigious Dr. Harold Kerzner Scholarship which is awarded by the Project Management Institute Educational Foundation. Professionally, Dr. Cleveland has worked as both technology manager, program manager and PMO Director for organizations such as MD Anderson Cancer Center, Department of Homeland Security, NASA, Accenture, General Dynamics, and AOL.

Dahlifah is an academic specializing in ShariahAccounting, Financial Accounting,CSR, and Sustainability Reporting. She currently serves as a lecturer and Head of D3 Accounting Study Program at Sekolah Tinggi Ilmu Ekonomi Indonesia Jakarta, where she plays a key role in the Tri Dharma of Higher Education. Her academic qualifications are extensive, including a Bachelor's degree in Accounting, a Master's degree in Accounting, and a Doctorate in Accounting from Brawijaya University, Malang. Dahlifah is also a certified specialist in sustainability reporting (Certified Sustainability Reporting Specialist (CSRS) and a Certified Sustainability Reporting Assuror (CSRA).

Rajat Das is a Regular Research Scholar at Department of Mathematics, Tripura University. He received M.Sc. from Department of Mathematics, ICFAI University Tripura(W) PIN: 799210, India and his B.Sc. from Tripura University (A Central University) Suryamaninagar, Tripura(W) PIN: 799 022, India .He is currently a Regular Research Scholar at Department of Mathematics, Tripura University (A Central University) Suryamaninagar, Tripura(W) PIN: 799022, India. His research interests include Neutrosophic Set, Soft Set, Multi Set, Decision Making Theory, & OR etc.

Nafees Ahmed is working as an Assistant Professor in the Department of Computer Science, Jamal Mohamed College(Autonomous), Tiruchirappalli, India. He has more than 20 years of teaching experience. He received Ph.D degree from Bharathidasan University, India in 2019. His research interests include Data Mining, Evolutionary Algorithms and Image Processing. He has published more than 6 papers in International Journals. E-mail: nafeesjmc@gmail.com

Mak Khan serves as an Engineering Consultant, providing data-driven analysis and design solutions for complex infrastructure expansion projects. Beyond his technical engineering role, he is deeply involved in organizational innovation, serving on multiple committees dedicated to integrating Artificial Intelligence into the workplace. Leveraging his Master's in Management from Georgetown University, Mak works to bridge the gap between Agile methodologies and traditional project management within the engineering space. He is a certified Project Management Professional (PMP) and actively volunteers as a mentor for high school students through the ACE Mentorship Program.

Rimi Gusliana Mais is an academic specializing in Public Sector Accounting, CSR, and Sustainability Reporting. She currently serves as a lecturer and Head of the Institute for Research and Community Service at Sekolah Tinggi Ilmu Ekonomi Indonesia Jakarta, where she plays a key role in the Tri Dharma of Higher Education. Her academic qualifications are extensive, including a Bachelor's degree in Accounting, a Master's degree in Accounting, and a Doctorate in Accounting from Brawijaya University, Malang. Rimi is also a certified specialist in sustainability reporting (Certified Sustainability Reporting Specialist (CSRS) and a Certified Sustainability Reporting Assuror (CSRA). In addition, she has authored numerous publications on Public Sector Accounting, Islamic Accounting, Sustainability Accounting, and CSR, making significant contributions to the academic community. Her passion for reading and writing reflects his commitment to lifelong learning and professional growth in her field.

Gerogios Moschoglou is a Professor of Practice and Faculty Director for the Master's in Project Management program at Georgetown University. His scholarly agenda centers on AI strategy execution, program governance, and decision-making under uncertainty within complex socio-technical systems. He teaches graduate-level courses that bridge systems theory with contemporary project and program management practices, and he has spearheaded curriculum innovations that embed data-driven decision frameworks across multiple graduate offerings. Complementing his academic work, Dr. Moschoglou brings more than two decades of practitioner experience managing large-scale digital and organizational transformations in governmental, multilateral, and private-sector contexts. He has led enterprise platform initiatives supporting global capital-markets operations, directed complex command-and-control systems for defense clients, and guided agile transformations within federal agencies and financial institutions. He holds a Ph.D. in Systems Engineering from The George Washington University.

Ravikumar R. N. is currently a Postdoctoral researcher at Universiti Malaysia Perlis, Malaysia. Also, working as an Associate Professor in the department of Computer Engineering at Marwadi University, Rajkot, Gujarat. He has 12+ years of national and international teaching experience. He completed his PhD at Amity University, Rajasthan, M.E at VMRF Deemed University, B.E at Anna University, Chennai. He is the co-founder of the Research Activities Club at Marwadi University and trains students on research activities, which leads to the publication of 7 Scopus/SCI journals, 20 Book chapters, 25 Conference papers, and 10 patents. His specialization is ML, DL, Federated Learning, Recommendation Systems, and Optimization Techniques.

Célia M. Q. Ramos graduated in Computer Engineering from the University of Coimbra, obtained her Master in Electrical and Computers Engineering from the Higher Technical Institute, Lisbon University, and the PhD in Econometrics in the University of the Algarve (UALG), Faculty of Economics, Portugal. She is Associate Professor with Habilitation at School for Management, Hospitality and Tourism, also in the UALG, where she lectures computer science. Areas of research and special interest include conception and development of information systems, tourism information systems, big data, marketing intelligence, machine learning, econometric modeling and panel-data models. Célia Ramos has published in the fields of information systems and tourism, namely, she has authored a book, six book chapters, conference papers and journal articles. At the level of applied research, she has participated in several funded projects.

Aarthi S is a dedicated Assistant Professor in Computer Science with over six years of teaching experience. She is currently pursuing her Ph.D. at Marwadi University, Gujarat, and holds an M.Phil. and MCA from Bharathiar University, Tamil Nadu. Throughout her academic career, Aarthi has specialized in programming languages such as C++, Java, and C, and contributed to research in recommender systems and AI-related data privacy. She has published journal articles, contributed to book chapters, and actively participated in technical workshops. Known for her student mentorship and engagement in academic events, Aarthi remains committed to fostering innovation and excellence in computer science education.

Desy Amaliati Setiawan is an academic specializing in Accounting, Auditing and taxation. She currently serves as lecturer at Sekolah Tinggi Ilmu Ekonomi Indonesia Jakarta and as an Account Manager at PT. Fanuc Indonesia Jakarta. Her academic are extensive, including a Bachelor's degree in Accounting, a master's degree in Accounting From Sekolah Tinggi Ilmu Ekonomi Indonesia Jakarta. In addition, she has authored on publication on Accounting, Auditing, Taxation. besides that, she has succeeded in making a book about Basic Accounting and Basic Taxation.

Panch Suntharalingam is the Associate Professor and Course Lead for MA Design and Visualisation at Birmingham City University, UK. He teaches on undergraduate and postgraduate courses in Design and Visualisation, Product Design, Interior Architecture and Design in the UK, India, Hong Kong and China. Dr Suntharalingam's areas of expertise and interests include, Design and Visualisation, Engineering Product Design, Industrial Design, Knowledge Transfer Partnership (KTP) programmes, Software Programming, Enterprise Development, Medical Product Design, Interior Products, Applied Research, Rapid Prototyping and Computer Aided Design (CAD). Dr Suntharalingam has extensive design and scientific knowledge in interdisciplinary fields and holds a patent for a medical product that has sold over 50,000 in the USA and over 8000 in the UK. He has published numerous international papers on medical products and well-known opening CGI title sequences featured on BBC and ITV networks such as 'Top Gear'. His wealth of experience with the manufacturing industry includes 20 'Knowledge Transfer Partnerships', with companies such as AGA Rangemaster and Evac+Chair International, gaining four 'Outstanding' Innovate UK awards for achievement in innovation. In 2020, one of his KTP's was shortlisted for the Best of the Best KTP's in the United Kingdom. He is also an external examiner at various national and international universities at undergraduate, postgraduate and PhD level.

Lies Zulfiati, is Assistant Professor of Sekolah Tinggi Ilmu Ekonomi Indonesia, Jakarta, Indonesia. Where she joined the faculty in 1999. She served as Vice Dean of Academic Affairs, Sekolah Tinggi Ilmu Ekonomi Indonesia, Jakarta, Indonesia from 2020 – 2025. She has undergraduate degree in Accounting from Sekolah Tinggi Ilmu Ekonomi Indonesia, Jakarta, Indonesia, and received her master degree in Accounting from Universitas Gadjah Mada, Indonesia. She received Doctoral degree in Accounting from Universitas Indonesia, Indonesia and professional accountant from Universitas Islam Bandung, Indonesia. Lies Zulfiati's academic and professional work focuses on accounting, governance, public policy, sustainability, and finance. She is actively involved in teaching, research, consulting and professional practice and has published various works, including journal articles, and conference papers. In addition to academic activities, Lies Zulfiati also serves as an expert advisor to the Regional Representative Council of the Republic of Indonesia (DPD RI), contributing to policy analysis, review of public accountability and institutional governance.

Index

www.ingramcontent.com/pod-product-compliance
Lightning Source LLC
LaVergne TN
LVHW080904300926
849162LV00003B/554